Test Bank

Sociology
A Global Perspective

SEVENTH EDITION

Joan Ferrante
Northern Kentucky State University

Prepared by

Joan Ferrante
Northern Kentucky State University

THOMSON
WADSWORTH

Australia • Brazil • Canada • Mexico • Singapore • Spain • United Kingdom • United States

© 2008 Thomson Wadsworth, a part of The Thomson Corporation. Thomson, the Star logo, and Wadsworth are trademarks used herein under license.

ALL RIGHTS RESERVED. No part of this work covered by the copyright hereon may be reproduced or used in any form or by any means—graphic, electronic, or mechanical, including photocopying, recording, taping, Web distribution, information storage and retrieval systems, or in any other manner—except as may be permitted by the license terms herein.

Printed in the United States of America

1 2 3 4 5 6 7 11 10 09 08 07

ISBN-13: 978-0-495-50694-2
ISBN-10: 0-495-50694-X

Thomson Higher Education
10 Davis Drive
Belmont, CA 94002-3098
USA

For more information about our products, contact us at:
Thomson Learning Academic Resource Center
1-800-423-0563

For permission to use material from this text or product, submit a request online at
http://www.thomsonrights.com.
Any additional questions about permissions can be submitted by email to **thomsonrights@thomson.com.**

Contents

	Preface	
1	**The Sociological Imagination**	1
2	**Theoretical Perspectives and Methods of Social Research**	34
3	**Culture**	83
4	**Socialization**	116
5	**Social Interaction**	158
6	**Formal Organizations**	195
7	**Deviance, Conformity, and Social Control**	231
8	**Social Stratification**	273
9	**Race and Ethnicity**	307
10	**Gender**	345
11	**Economics and Politics**	379
12	**Family and Aging**	417
13	**Education**	447
14	**Religion**	477
15	**Population and Urbanization**	510
16	**Social Change**	537
	References	578

Preface

In creating the test bank for the seventh edition of *Sociology: A Global Perspective*, I have worked hard to write meaningful questions. Most questions in this test bank are geared toward measuring students' understanding of concepts and their ability to apply concepts to real situations. My multiple-choice questions have four clear choices—I do not give "none of the above," "all the above," or "a and c" as possible responses. I believe including such choices invite uninspiring questions. Furthermore, I do not offer picky questions that test small facts and details. While I have included some questions that do test factual knowledge, the facts tested are critical to understanding a point made in the book. For example, it is important to know that the United States is 4.6 percent of the world's population yet it consumes more than 20 percent of oil produced in the world each year.

This test bank includes more than 2000 multiple choice and true-false questions. At least 500 questions are completely new to this edition. The questions retained from previous editions have been examined and edited to improve on wording and on their general overall quality. I have included an alternative to the standard true-false and multiple-choice questions known as "concept applications." For these questions students read a scenario and then decide which concept or concepts covered in that chapter best apply to the scenario. The concept applications also appear in the study guide. Finally I have included approximately 20 short-answer questions and two-to-five comprehensive essay questions for each chapter.

Chapter 1

The Sociological Imagination

Multiple-Choice Questions

1. The quotation "It can be said that the first wisdom of sociology is this—things are not what they seem" can be attributed to
    a. Peter Berger.
    b. Emile Durkheim.
    c. C. Wright Mills.
    d. W.E.B. DuBois.

    ANS: A   PG: 2   TYP: knowledge

2. Sociology is the study of human behavior as it is affected by
    a. genetic disposition.
    b. social interactions.
    c. mental processes.
    d. personality.

    ANS: B   PG: 4   TYP: comprehension   SOURCE: new

3. The behaviors sociologists study include a parent serving a child a glass of apple juice and a soldier responding to an enemy's rocket fire. These behaviors are
    a. social interactions.
    b. globalization.
    c. instrumental action.
    d. solidarity.

    ANS: A   PG: 4   TYP: application   SOURCE: new

Chapter 1

4. Sociologists maintain that there is a system to interaction. "System" means that
   a. interaction is chaotic.
   b. established rules (often unspoken) guide interaction.
   c. interaction is unpredictable.
   d. people make up the rules as they interact.

   ANS: B   PG: 4   TYP: comprehension   SOURCE : new; study guide

5. Which one of the following does *not* represent social interaction?
   a. a couple planning their wedding
   b. soldiers fighting wars
   c. restaurant employees serving customers
   d. two friends who, when passing, do not notice one another

   ANS: D   PG: 4   TYP: application

6. There is a system to social interaction when the interaction
   a. is chaotic.
   b. is guided by rules (often unspoken) about how to interpret the situation and how to behave.
   c. involves playing a game, such as baseball.
   d. involves people who refuse to play by the rules.

   ANS: B   PG: 4   TYP: comprehension

7. When sociologists study social interaction, they focus on all *but* which one of the following?
   a. the ways in which people who do *not* know each other manage to interact
   b. the system guiding social interaction
   c. the personalities of those involved
   d. the spoken and unspoken rules guiding that interaction

   ANS: C   PG: 5   TYP: comprehension   SOURCE: study guide

8. Emile Durkheim defined social facts as
   a. census statistics.
   b. having the remarkable property of existing outside the individual.
   c. fundamentally psychological.
   d. things we know to be true.

   ANS: B   PG: 6   TYP: knowledge

9. Only when people _____ do they come to know the power of social facts.
   a. grow older
   b. cooperate
   c. comply
   d. rebel against established ways of doing things

   ANS: D   PG: 6   TYP: comprehension   SOURCE: new

10. Durkheim wrote that he was not forced to speak French or to use the legal currency, but it was impossible for him to do otherwise. Durkheim was writing about
    a. mechanical solidarity.
    b. social relativity.
    c. social facts.
    d. social interaction.

    ANS: C   PG: 5   TYP: application   SOURCE: new

11. Durkheim wrote, "Even when, in fact, I can struggle free from these rules and successfully break them, it is never without being forced to fight against them." This statement is a reference to
    a. mechanical solidarity.
    b. social relativity.
    c. social facts.
    d. social interaction.

    ANS: C   PG: 5   TYP: application   SOURCE: new

12. A woman writes, "I can't be anything but what my skin color tells people I am. I am black because I look black. It does not matter that my family has a complicated biological heritage." She is writing about the power of
    a. social facts.
    b. troubles.
    c. the sociological imagination.
    d. rationalization.

    ANS: A   PG: 6   TYP: application   SOURCE: study guide

Chapter 1

13. An American traveling to Ghana, Africa, on business notices that the "men, including the men I was with, hold hands. One day one of the men I was with took my hand as we walked. In order not to offend him, I took his hand in mine." The American is responding to a(n)
    a. trouble.
    b. issue.
    c. social fact.
    d. traditional action.

    ANS: C   PG: 6   TYP: application   SOURCE: new

14. Sociologists argue that people fall in love
    a. when they experience a violent, irresistible attraction to another person.
    b. only once in the course of a lifetime.
    c. when certain conditions are met.
    d. with people like themselves.

    ANS: C   PG: 6   TYP: comprehension

15. In the United States, approximately _____ percent of people have been married at least once by age 75.
    a. 95
    b. 75
    c. 50
    d. 33

    ANS: A   PG: 6   TYP: knowledge   SOURCE: study guide

16. Peter L. Berger equates the sociologist with
    a. a curious observer who, walking down the neighborhood streets of a large city, is fascinated with what he or she cannot see taking place behind the building walls.
    b. an Internal Revenue Service auditor.
    c. a judge giving instructions to a jury.
    d. a talk show host interviewing guests.

    ANS: A   PG: 5   TYP: knowledge

17. Peter Berger argues that the logic of sociology presupposes a measure of suspicion about the way in which human events are officially interpreted by authorities. This suspicion speaks to _____, which defines the sociological consciousness.
    a. solidarity
    b. the debunking motif
    c. rationalization
    d. false consciousness

    ANS: B   PG: 7   TYP: comprehension

18. A sociologist views a photo of an American soldier and an Iraqi child bumping fists. The image prompts the sociologist to ask:
    a. What does it mean for the U.S. to occupy/liberate a country where 40 percent of the population is 14 and under?
    b. Does the American soldier have a child of his own?
    c. Is the soldier an occupier or a liberator?
    d. How many American soldiers are stationed in Iraq?

    ANS: A   PG: 8   TYP: comprehension   SOURCE: study guide

19. A sociologist observes a duck sitting on a nest made, in part, from discarded plastic bags. This image prompts sociologists to ask:
    a. What percentage of the 500 billion to 1 trillion plastic bags end up in creeks, streams, rivers, lakes, and oceans?
    b. Why do people litter when there are trash cans around?
    c. Why do ducks use plastic bags to make nests?
    d. How would ducks make nests if there were no discarded plastic bags?

    ANS: A   PG: 8   TYP: comprehension   SOURCE: new

20. A trouble is
    a. an issue.
    b. deeply and significantly social.
    c. caused by character flaws.
    d. outside an individual's control.

    ANS: C   PG: 7   TYP: knowledge

Chapter 1

21. Unemployment is a(n) _____ when it results from corporate downsizing.
    a. issue
    b. trouble
    c. private matter
    d. social fact

    ANS: A   PG: 10   TYP: application

22. Which of the following explanations would someone use to explain an issue?
    a. "She had the opportunity but didn't take it."
    b. "He is lazy."
    c. "There is a flaw or breakdown in an institutional arrangement."
    d. "She didn't try very hard in school."

    ANS: C   PG: 11   TYP: application   SOURCE: study guide

23. When in a nation of 50 million employees, 15 million are unemployed, that is
    a. an issue.
    b. a trouble.
    c. a series of private troubles.
    d. a result of basic character flaws.

    ANS: A   PG: 10   TYP: application

24. The high school dropout rate in the United States is greater than 25 percent. C. Wright Mills would classify this situation as
    a. a trouble.
    b. an issue.
    c. value-rational action.
    d. a social fact.

    ANS: B   PG: 10   TYP: application   SOURCE: study guide

25. The resolution of an issue involves changing
    a. institutions.
    b. individual character.
    c. motivation level.
    d. human nature.

    ANS: A   PG: 11   TYP: comprehension

26. The sociologist _____ is associated with the concepts "troubles" and "issues."
    a. Karl Marx
    b. Robert K. Merton
    c. C. Wright Mills
    d. Emile Durkheim

    ANS: C   PG: 7   TYP: knowledge

27. A(n) _____ is a relatively stable and predictable arrangement among people that has emerged over time with the purpose of coordinating human interaction and behavior in ways that meet some social need.
    a. manifesto
    b. institution
    c. issue
    d. trouble

    ANS: B   PG: 10   TYP: knowledge

28. Sociologists do not define the cause of unemployment simply in terms of individual shortcomings because
    a. profit-generating strategies include laying off employees.
    b. people may decide to quit their jobs.
    c. employees have the power to stay if they really want to.
    d. most people are good workers.

    ANS: A   PG: 10   TYP: comprehension

29. Sociologist C. Wright Mills believed that people, in order to gain some sense of control over their lives, need
    a. to keep up with the news.
    b. regular breaks from their hectic schedule.
    c. a quality of mind to help them grasp the interplay between their biographies and institutional arrangements.
    d. to take personal responsibility for their actions.

    ANS: C   PG: 11   TYP: knowledge

Chapter 1

30. A young woman is troubled that the hair growth on her face and body makes her appear masculine.
    a. Her troubles can be traced to male hormones.
    b. a capitalist system that commercializes gender ideals and uses insecurity to sell its products.
    c. a lack of support from her family.
    d. the woman's psychological insecurities.

    ANS: B   PG: 10   TYP: application

31. The sociological imagination is the ability to
    a. see the connection between self and immediate relationships.
    b. distinguish between mechanical and organic solidarity.
    c. see that problems can be solved by changing the character of the individual.
    d. make a distinction between troubles and issues.

    ANS: D   PG: 11   TYP: comprehension   SOURCE: study guide

32. The quality of mind that enables us to connect seemingly impersonal and remote historical forces to the most basic incidents of an individual's life is
    a. the sociological imagination.
    b. the structure of opportunities.
    c. independent thinking.
    d. common sense.

    ANS: A   PG: 11   TYP: knowledge

33. The payoff for those who possess _____ is that they can understand their inner life in terms of institutional arrangements and larger historical forces.
    a. the sociological imagination
    b. common sense
    c. independent thinking
    d. a sense of self

    ANS: A   PG: 11   TYP: knowledge   SOURCE: new

8

34. The addition of external sources of power from burning coals and oil to hand tools and modes of transportation is
    a. standardization.
    b. affective action.
    c. modernization.
    d. mechanization.

    ANS: D   PG: 12   TYP: knowledge

35. The _____ refers to a time of the most rapid colonial expansion in history.
    a. Age of Reason
    b. Age of Imperialism
    c. Middle Ages
    d. European century

    ANS: B   PG: 12   TYP: knowledge

36. The period in history known as the Age of Imperialism (1880-1914)
    a. was one of the most peaceful periods in modern history.
    b. represents the most rapid colonial expansion in history.
    c. preceded the period in history known as the Industrial Revolution.
    d. corresponds with the Cold War between the United States and the former Soviet Union.

    ANS: B   PG: 12   TYP: knowledge

37. One fundamental feature of the Industrial Revolution is
    a. craftsmanship.
    b. solidarity.
    c. manual labor.
    d. mechanization.

    ANS: D   PG: 12   TYP: comprehension

38. The Industrial Revolution transformed the nature of work in which one of the following ways?
    a. Machine production was replaced by hand production.
    b. People now could say, "I made this; this is a unique product of my labor."
    c. Products became standardized, and workers performed specific tasks in the production process.
    d. The workers' power over the production process increased dramatically.

    ANS: C   PG: 12   TYP: comprehension   SOURCE: study guide

39. "Within a few decades, a social order that had existed for centuries vanished, and a new one, familiar in its outline to us in the twentieth century, appeared." This assessment applies to which historical event?
    a. European colonization
    b. the Industrial Revolution
    c. the Cold War
    d. the emergence of sociology

    ANS: B   PG: 12   TYP: comprehension

40. The early sociologists spent most of their professional life attempting to understand the consequences of which one of the following events?
    a. World War I
    b. World War II
    c. the Industrial Revolution
    d. the Enlightenment

    ANS: C   PG: 13   TYP: knowledge   SOURCE: new

41. The name *sociology* and the corresponding academic discipline was born during the
    a. American Revolution.
    b. Civil War.
    c. Vietnam era.
    d. Industrial Revolution.

    ANS: D   PG: 13   TYP: knowledge   SOURCE: new; study guide

42. Which one of the following invented the term *sociology*?
    a. Auguste Comte
    b. Emile Durkheim
    c. Max Weber
    d. Karl Marx

    ANS: A   PG: 13   TYP: knowledge   SOURCE: new

43. In addition to the Industrial Revolution, which one of the following helps to explain the emergence of sociology as a discipline?
    a. mechanization
    b. the widespread acceptance of the scientific method
    c. the Age of Imperialism
    d. rationalization

    ANS: B   PG: 13   TYP: comprehension   SOURCE: new

44. Auguste Comte defined sociology as the scientific study of the collective and cumulative results of the human intellect. The words *collective* and *cumulative* suggest that sociology involves the study of
    a. people and history.
    b. social and psychological forces.
    c. social interactions across cultures and throughout time.
    d. the mind and body.

    ANS: C   PG: 13   TYP: comprehension   SOURCE: new

45. _____ died "beloved, revered, and mourned by millions of revolutionary fellow workers—from the mines of Siberia to California."
    a. W.E.B. DuBois
    b. Harriet Martineau
    c. Karl Marx
    d. Max Weber

    ANS: C   PG: 13   TYP: comprehension

Chapter 1

46. *The Communist Manifesto* and *Das Kapital* are associated with
    a. W.E.B. DuBois.
    b. Karl Marx.
    c. Emile Durkheim.
    d. Max Weber.

    ANS: B   PG: 13   TYP: knowledge

47. Marx's legacy has been obscured by
    a. his inability to accurately describe capitalism.
    b. a personality disorder.
    c. the failure of Communism.
    d. the fact that he published in German (not English).

    ANS: C   PG: 13   TYP: knowledge   SOURCE: study guide

48. *The Communist Manifesto* begins with the line
    a. "A specter is haunting Europe—the specter of Communism."
    b. "Workers of all countries, unite."
    c. "I am not a Marxist."
    d. "The global economy is restless, anxious, and competitive."

    ANS: A   PG: 13   TYP: knowledge

49. Karl Marx described capitalism in all <u>but</u> which one of the following ways?
    a. a boundless thirst
    b. a werewolf-like hunger
    c. socially conscious
    d. blood-sucking

    ANS: C   PG: 14   TYP: comprehension

50. With mechanization, the rise of two distinct classes emerged. The one that owns the means of production is called
    a. a proletariat.
    b. the bourgeoisie.
    c. a socialist.
    d. a communist.

    ANS: B   PG: 14   TYP: knowledge

51. According to Karl Marx, the character of class conflict is shaped directly and profoundly by
    a. social facts.
    b. solidarity.
    c. the means of production.
    d. sociological imagination.

    ANS: C   PG: 14   TYP: comprehension

52. Land, tools, equipment, factories, modes of transportation, and labor are
    a. owned by the proletariat.
    b. part of the means of production.
    c. essential for providing services.
    d. owned by the intellectual classes.

    ANS: B   PG: 14   TYP: application   SOURCE: study guide

53. In his writings, Karl Marx expressed profound moral outrage over the plight of the
    a. bourgeoisie.
    b. middle class.
    c. proletariat.
    d. intellectual class.

    ANS: C   PG: 14   TYP: comprehension

54. Marx believed that _____ was the first economic system that could maximize the immense productive potential of human labor and ingenuity.
    a. capitalism
    b. socialism
    c. communism
    d. democracy

    ANS: A   PG: 14   TYP: knowledge   SOURCE: new

55. Durkheim believed that the sociologist's task was to analyze and explain
    a. the means of production.
    b. solidarity.
    c. troubles.
    d. issues.

    ANS: B   PG: 14   TYP: comprehension   SOURCE: new

Chapter 1

56. Durkheim observed that as a society industrialized,
    a. class conflict increased.
    b. value-rational action guided behavior.
    c. the means of production shaped life chances.
    d. ties that bound individuals to one another changed in profound ways.

    ANS: D   PG: 15   TYP: knowledge

57. _____ is the author of *Suicide*.
    a. Emile Durkheim
    b. Karl Marx
    c. W.E.B. DuBois
    d. Max Weber

    ANS: A   PG: 15   TYP: knowledge

58. From a sociological perspective, suicide is
    a. an act of intentionally killing oneself.
    b. the result of personal disappointment and sorrow.
    c. self-hatred actualized.
    d. the severing of relationships.

    ANS: D   PG: 15   TYP: knowledge   SOURCE: study guide

59. The term _____ describes a state in which ties attaching individuals to others in the society are weak.
    a. egoistic
    b. altruistic
    c. anomic
    d. fatalistic

    ANS: A   PG: 15   TYP: application

60. _____ suicide occurs when people kill themselves because they have been cast into a lower status.
   a. Egoistic
   b. Altruistic
   c. Anomic
   d. Fatalistic

   ANS: C   PG: 16   TYP: application

61. _____ suicide occurs when individuals kill themselves because they see their futures as hopelessly blocked.
   a. Egoistic
   b. Altruistic
   c. Anomic
   d. Fatalistic

   ANS: D   PG: 17   TYP: application

62. _____ countries are among those with the highest suicide rates.
   a. South American
   b. Middle Eastern
   c. Eastern European
   d. Asian

   ANS: C   PG: 16   TYP: knowledge   SOURCE: new

63. _____ countries are among those with the lowest suicide rates.
   a. Former Soviet
   b. Middle Eastern
   c. Eastern European
   d. Asian

   ANS: B   PG: 16   TYP: knowledge   SOURCE: new

Chapter 1

64. When people commit _____ suicide, it is on behalf of the group they love more than themselves.
    a. egoistic
    b. altruistic
    c. anomic
    d. fatalistic

    ANS: B   PG: 15   TYP: application   SOURCE: new; study guide

65. When people are cast into a lower status, they must reduce their requirements, restrain their needs, and practice self-control. This situation describes a(n) _____ situation.
    a. egoistic
    b. altruistic
    c. anomic
    d. fatalistic

    ANS: C   PG: 16   TYP: application   SOURCE: new

66. A quilt maker may work years creating a one-of-a-kind object from fabrics saved or purchased and then give it to a special person. Weber would classify the quilt maker's actions as driven by
    a. rationalization.
    b. specialization.
    c. an emotion, such as love, loyalty, or revenge.
    d. value-rational motives.

    ANS: C   PG: 17   TYP: application

67. Max Weber focused on the Industrial Revolution and its effect on
    a. the means of production.
    b. social actions.
    c. ties that bind individuals to one another.
    d. the color line.

    ANS: B   PG: 17   TYP: knowledge

68. Weber maintained that with industrialization, behavior was less likely to be guided by _____ and more likely to be value-rational.
    a. efficiency or expediency
    b. subjective meaning
    c. tradition or emotion
    d. rational thought

    ANS: C   PG: 17   TYP: comprehension

69. Max Weber maintained that the sociologist's task was to focus on
    a. social facts.
    b. social action.
    c. the broad reasons people pursue goals.
    d. debunking "reality."

    ANS: B   PG: 17   TYP: knowledge

70. If an individual pursues a college degree because everyone in his or her family going back five generations is college-educated, the action can be classified as
    a. traditional.
    b. affectional.
    c. value-rational.
    d. instrumental.

    ANS: A   PG: 18   TYP: application   SOURCE: study guide

71. If an individual pursues college for the love and pleasure of learning, the action is
    a. traditional.
    b. affectional.
    c. value-rational.
    d. instrumental.

    ANS: B   PG: 18   TYP: application

Chapter 1

72. If an individual pursues a college degree because potential employers value and demand a diploma, the action is classified as
    a. traditional.
    b. affectional.
    c. value-rational.
    d. instrumental.

    ANS: C   PG: 18   TYP: application   SOURCE: new

73. A well thought out, careful approach to defining and achieving goals applies to _____ action.
    a. traditional
    b. affectional
    c. value-rational
    d. instrumental

    ANS: D   PG: 18   TYP: comprehension   SOURCE: new

74. Harriet Martineau maintained that it is important to
    a. analyze and explain the ties that connect individuals to one another.
    b. study forces that give rise to conflict.
    c. see a country in all its diversity.
    d. understand the power of social facts.

    ANS: C   PG: 18   TYP: knowledge

75. _____ translated from French into English Auguste Comte's six volume work *The Positive Philosophy*.
    a. Harriet Martineau
    b. Karl Marx
    c. Max Weber
    d. W.E.B. Dubois

    ANS: A   PG: 18   TYP: knowledge   SOURCE: new

76. W.E.B. DuBois coined the phrase
    a. the ties that bind people to one another.
    b. the "strange meaning of being black."
    c. the means of production.
    d. the course and consequences of social action.

    ANS: B   PG: 18   TYP: knowledge   SOURCE: study guide

77. W.E.B. DuBois described the American Negro as "two souls, two thoughts, two unreconciled strivings; two warring ideals in one dark body, whose dogged strength alone keep its from being torn asunder." DuBois was describing
    a. the sociological imagination.
    b. a trouble.
    c. an issue.
    d. double consciousness.

    ANS: D   PG: 18   TYP: application   SOURCE: new

78. W.E.B. Dubois traced the _____ to the scramble for Africa's resources, beginning with the slave trade.
    a. color line
    b. double consciousness
    c. troubles
    d. disenchantment

    ANS: A   PG: 19   TYP: knowledge   SOURCE: new

79. DuBois wrote that the world was able "to endure this horrible tragedy by deliberately stopping its ears and changing the subject in conversation." The tragedy was
    a. the scramble for Africa's resources, including the slave trade.
    b. double consciousness.
    c. the mechanization, which left people without jobs.
    d. the carnage of World War I and World War II.

    ANS: A   PG: 19   TYP: comprehension   SOURCE: new

Chapter 1

80. If scientists discover how to control the aging mechanisms and human life expectancy increases to 150 years, the category of people best able to give insights about the consequence of this change would be
    a. the early sociologists.
    b. those born after this discovery is made.
    c. those who live both before and after the discovery.
    d. those born a century or more after the discovery.

    ANS: C   PG: 13   TYP: comprehension

For the following questions, use one of these responses to identify the thinker associated with each statement.

    a. Karl Marx
    b. Emile Durkheim
    c. Max Weber
    d. Harriet Martineau
    e. W.E.B. DuBois

81. The sociologist's task is to study social facts.

    ANS: B   PG: 5   SOURCE: study guide

82. Every historical period is characterized by a system of production that gives rise to specific types of confrontation between an exploiting and an exploited class.

    ANS: A   PG: 14

83. In conducting social research, it is important to see a country in all its diversity.

    ANS: D   PG: 18   SOURCE: study guide

84. The sociologist's task is to analyze and explain the course and the consequences of social action.

    ANS: C   PG: 17

85. "The problem of the twentieth century is the problem of the color line."

ANS: E   PG: 18

86. "The workers have nothing to lose but their chains; they have a whole world to gain. Workers of all countries unite."

ANS: A   PG: 13

87. Capitalism has unleashed "wonders far surpassing Egyptian pyramids, Roman aqueducts, and Gothic cathedrals."

ANS: A   PG: 13   SOURCE: study guide

88. It is important to hear "the casual conversation of all kinds of people."

ANS: D   PG: 18

89. Which one of the following assumptions corresponds to a global perspective?
    a. Social interaction stops at national borders.
    b. Globalization is a relatively new phenomenon.
    c. Local events shape the individual biography.
    d. Globally established social arrangements that we never see deliver products and services.

ANS: D   PG: 20   TYP: comprehension   SOURCE: new

90. _____ is the largest exporter of goods and services.
    a. The United States
    b. The People's Republic of China
    c. Japan
    d. Canada

ANS: A   PG: 21   TYP: comprehension   SOURCE: new

Chapter 1

91. Which one of the following statements would be most likely to convince an employer of the worth of a sociology degree?
    a. "I like people, and sociology is about people."
    b. "I want to work with people. That is why I majored in sociology."
    c. "I didn't have to take a statistics course."
    d. "Among other things, a degree in sociology helps me to identify and project population trends."

    ANS: D   PG: 22   TYP: application   SOURCE: study guide

92. Six of the founding members of the American Sociological Society helped to organize which one of the following organizations?
    a. National Association for the Advancement of Colored People
    b. National Rifle Association
    c. Americans for Communism
    d. American Medical Association

    ANS: A   PG: 22   TYP: knowledge   SOURCE: new

Multiple Choice Questions on the Web

1. The distinctiveness of the sociological perspective lies with its focus on
    a. suicide.
    b. the individual.
    c. social interaction.
    d. troubles.

    ANS: C   PG: 4   TYP: comprehension

2. "Because I refuse to shave under my arms, I have to pay a price. On a personal level, this price was my mother's hostility. On a public level, the price is dealing with the stares of strangers." This statement illustrates
    a. mechanical solidarity.
    b. social relativity.
    c. the power of social facts.
    d. the idea of double consciousness.

    ANS: C   PG: 6   TYP: application

3. With regard to the systematic character of interaction, sociologists are interested in which one of the following questions?
   a. By what means is it all held together?
   b. Why can't we all just get along?
   c. How do people who know one another interact smoothly?
   d. Who determines morality?

   ANS: A   PG: 5   TYP: comprehension   SOURCE: new

4. "The fascination of sociology lies in the fact that its perspective makes us see in a new light the very world in which we have lived all our lives." This vision of sociology can be attributed to
   a. Peter Berger.
   b. Emile Durkheim.
   c. C. Wright Mills.
   d. W.E.B. DuBois.

   ANS: A   PG: 7   TYP: knowledge

5. While reading a newspaper, a sociologist sees a photograph of President George W. Bush holding hands with a Saudi prince. This photograph would prompt the sociologists to ask:
   a. Is President Bush gay?
   b. Is Saudi Arabia more tolerant of gays than the United States?
   c. Why is hand-holding between same-sex adults prohibited in the U.S. and not in other countries?
   d. Is President Bush betraying American culture?

   ANS: C   PG: 8   TYP: comprehension   SOURCE: new

6. Which one of the following is not a characteristic of an issue?
   a. An issue is a public matter.
   b. An issue is caused by flaws in institutional structures.
   c. The cause of an issue can be traced to personal weaknesses.
   d. Issues transcend the life of any one individual.

   ANS: C   PG: 11   TYP: comprehension

Chapter 1

7. Sociology emerged as a discipline in reaction to which one of the following events?
   a. World War I
   b. World War II
   c. the Agricultural Revolution
   d. the Industrial Revolution

   ANS: D   PG: 13   TYP: knowledge

8. Which one of the following sociologists said the thirst for profit "chases the bourgeoisie over the whole surface of the globe"?
   a. Karl Marx
   b. Emile Durkheim
   c. Max Weber
   d. Harriet Martineau

   ANS: A   PG: 13   TYP: comprehension

9. During World War II, Japanese pilots committed suicide by flying small planes into targets. This suicide would qualify as
   a. egoistic.
   b. altruistic.
   c. anomic.
   d. fatalistic.

   ANS: B   PG: 15   TYP: application   SOURCE: new

10. _____ is this sense of always looking at one's self through the eyes of others and of measuring one's soul by the tape of a world that looks on in amused contempt and pity.
    a. The sociological imagination
    b. A trouble
    c. An issue
    d. Double consciousness

    ANS: D   PG: 18   TYP: comprehension

True/False Questions

1. Dole apple juice is made from concentrate that comes from two places: the United States and Mexico.

    ANS: False   PG: 3   SOURCE: new

2. The interactions sociologists study can involve two people or thousands of people.

    ANS: True   PG: 2   SOURCE: study guide

3. Sociologists focus on the role personality plays in driving social interactions.

    ANS: False   PG: 5   SOURCE: new; study guide

4. Sociologists focus on how social interaction is guided by established rules.

    ANS: True   PG: 4   SOURCE: new

5. For the most part, social interactions are chaotic.

    ANS: False   PG: 4

6. The rules governing social interaction are analogous to the rules governing games, such as baseball or Monopoly.

    ANS: True   PG: 4

7. Sociologists argue that people have to know someone in order to interact with him or her.

    ANS: False   PG: 5   SOURCE: new

8. Sociologists maintain that love is a violent, irresistible emotion that strikes someone at random.

    ANS: False   PG: 6   SOURCE: study guide

Chapter 1

9. Sociologists view the emotion of love as irrelevant in explaining why people marry.

   ANS: False   PG: 6

10. Nineteen of 20 people get married at least once in their lifetime.

    ANS: True   PG: 6   SOURCE: new; study guide

11. Sociologists' temperaments are such that they are driven to debunk the social systems they study.

    ANS: False   PG: 7   SOURCE: new

12. From a sociological perspective, high unemployment can be solved by changing the negative attitudes of the unemployed.

    ANS: False   PG: 11

13. Sociologist C. Wright Mills argues that most people cannot or do not want to see how their successes connect to others' failures.

    ANS: True   PG: 10   SOURCE: new; study guide

14. By 1914, almost all of Africa had been divided into European colonies.

    ANS: True   PG: 12

15. The most fundamental feature of industrialization was mechanization.

    ANS: True   PG: 12   SOURCE: new

16. The changes triggered by the Industrial Revolution are incalculable.

    ANS: True   PG: 12   SOURCE: study guide

17. Sociology emerged in an effort to understand the immeasurable effects of the Industrial Revolution on human life across the globe.

    ANS: True   PG: 12   SOURCE: new

18. Emile Durkheim invented the term *sociology*.

    ANS: False   PG: 13   SOURCE: new

19. Karl Marx's writings described how a communist society should operate.

    ANS: False   PG: 13   SOURCE: new

20. Karl Marx should be judged as a student of capitalism.

    ANS: True   PG: 13

21. In a capitalist system, the search for profit drives global expansion.

    ANS: True   PG: 13

22. For Marx, conflict prevents social change.

    ANS: False   PG: 14

23. In analyzing suicide rates, Durkheim emphasized the personal situation of the victim.

    ANS: False   PG: 15   SOURCE: study guide

24. Durkheim was able to describe a central emotional quality common to all suicides.

    ANS: False   PG: 14   SOURCE: new

25. Max Weber was preoccupied with the "strange meaning of being black" in America.

    ANS: False   PG: 17

26. Max Weber maintained that the sociologist's task was to study social action.

    ANS: True   PG: 17

27. DuBois believed that the problem of the twentieth century was the problem of the color line.

    ANS: True   PG: 18   SOURCE: study guide

28. Of the four types of social action, the most complex type is traditional.

    ANS: False   PG: 18   SOURCE: new

29. DuBois' preoccupation with the "strange meaning of being black" was no doubt affected by the fact that he was of French, African, and Dutch descent.

    ANS: True   PG: 19   SOURCE: new

30. Globalization is a relatively new phenomenon, which can be traced to the 1990s.

    ANS: False   PG: 20   SOURCE: new; study guide

31. Multinational and global corporations are key forces in structuring social relationships that transcend national boundaries.

    ANS: True   PG: 20   SOURCE: new

32. A degree in sociology leads to very few career tracks.

    ANS: False   PG: 20   SOURCE: study guide

33. The American Sociological Society was formed in 1905.

    ANS: True   PG: 22   SOURCE: new

34. The recognized founder of American sociology is Lester F. Ward.

    ANS: True   PG: 22   SOURCE: new

Concept Application (also in study guide)

Consider the concepts listed below. Match one or more of the concepts with each scenario. Explain your choices.

  a. Anomic
  b. Double consciousness
  c. Global interdependence
  d. Means of production
  e. Troubles/Issues

Scenario 1 new
Excerpts from a suicide letter suggest that Kevin Morrissey, a 51-year-old Berkeley man, killed his family in a murder-suicide this week because he was at a "financial breaking point" as the family skin-care business failed and because he found other work opportunities "unattractive" (Rayburn and Hill 2007).

    ANS: A

Scenario 2
"The world's trade in bananas is dominated by just three huge food multinationals: United Brands (with a 34 percent market share in 1974), Standard Fruit (with a 23 percent market share), and Del Monte (with a 10 percent market share). As with many other commodities, the companies control the transport, packaging, shipment, storage, and marketing of the fruit. As a result, the profits from bananas go largely into western pockets, while the producer countries get only a pittance" (Harrison 1987:348).

    ANS: D

Chapter 1

Scenario 3

"*Black Soldiers in Jim Crow Texas* introduces readers to African American soldiers who were assigned to one of four black regiments (9th and 10th Cavalries and 24th and 25th Infantries). Not only did these men bear arms and fight gallantly in the Spanish-American War, but at times, they used their military weapons in struggles for racial equality in the United States as well. More than three decades after the Emancipation Proclamation, black soldiers grew intolerant of 'racial slurs, refusal of service at some businesses, and harassment.' Texas's 'lower-status Hispanics, the bulk of the population…shared southern white prejudice against blacks. The war with Spain in 1898,' Christian asserts, 'acted as a catalyst that converted impatience into retaliation. The United States bestowed six Medals of Honor and twenty-six Certificates of Merit on their members, and all four regiments inspired laudatory press coverage.' Yet these men faced the indignities of racism when serving at military installations in the United States" (Moore 1996:478).

ANS: B

Scenario 4 (new)

On the progressive care unit where she works, nurses regularly have five or more patients. Over the years, hospital procedures with which nurses assist have become more complicated, and patients are sicker. Brandon said there are not always enough nurses to go around. "You get your running shoes on, take off, and go," Brandon said. "The current nursing shortage is just beginning in Wyoming," said Julie Cann-Taylor, registered nurse and director of critical care at the hospital. "There had been a nursing vacancy rate of 3 to 4 percent at the hospital for years, but it jumped to 7 percent last fall," she said. Matt Kaiser, director of human resources at the hospital, said there are about 40 registered nurse positions available, creating a vacancy rate of about 11 percent (Rupp 2007).

ANS: E

Scenario 5

Five foreign-born players appeared in the National Basketball Association All-Star game last month, and another five played in the Rookie Challenge game. Of the 348 active players in the NBA, 49 are from abroad…Lenny Wilken, coach of the Toronto Rapters, has said, "I wouldn't be surprised if there is double the number of players in the next five years or so." (Shield's 2002:56)

ANS: C

Short Essay Questions

1. What is sociology? What do sociologists study?

2. What is social interaction?

3. Durkheim maintains that the sociologist's task is to study social facts. What are social facts?

4. When do people experience the power of social facts?

5. In the classic book *Invitation to Sociology*, Peter L. Berger presents sociology as a form of consciousness. Explain.

6. In studying patterns of courtship and marriage, what would sociologists emphasize?

7. Peter Berger maintains that a "debunking motif" defines the sociological consciousness. Explain.

8. Give two examples of the kinds of questions sociologists ask.

9. Distinguish between troubles and issues.

10. Explain the connection between troubles and institutional crisis.

11. What is the sociological imagination?

12. What major historical event shaped the discipline of sociology? Why?

13. How did the Industrial Revolution affect the nature of work and social interaction?

14. Who was Auguste Comte? How did he define sociology? Does his definition speak to the importance of social interaction?

15. For which writings is Marx most famous?

16. Define Karl Marx's vision of the sociologist's task. What concepts and assumptions drive his analysis of society?

17. Who are the bourgeoisie and the proletariat? How are they connected to the means of production?

18. How did Durkheim define suicide?

19. Distinguish between egoistic, altruistic, anomic, and fatalistic suicide.

20. What is social action? What are the four types? Give an example of each.

21. Who is Harriet Martineau? What contributions did she make to sociology?

22. Explain the phrase "strange meaning of being black." What life experience may have influenced DuBois' preoccupation with this phrase?

23. According to DuBois, how did the color line come into being?

24. What is double consciousness?

25. Describe three assumptions that underlie the global perspective.

26. Imagine that you majored in sociology. How would you explain the usefulness of the sociological perspective? What skills would you bring to the workplace?

Comprehensive Essay Questions

1. Think about a problem or challenge you are facing or have faced or one that someone close to you is facing or has faced. Describe that problem or challenge: (1) as if it were an issue and (2) as if it were a trouble.

2. Durkheim defines social facts as ideas, feelings, and ways of behaving that possess the remarkable property of existing outside the consciousness of the individual. Explain. Give two examples of social facts.

3. Why is the Industrial Revolution considered pivotal to the development of sociology as a discipline?

Chapter 2

Theoretical Perspectives and Methods of Social Research

Multiple-Choice Questions

1. Which one of the following is a false statement regarding the relationship between theory and research?
    a. Theory inspires research.
    b. Research inspires theory creation.
    c. Theory is used to interpret research findings.
    d. Theory comes before research.

    ANS: D   PG: 26   TYP: comprehension   SOURCE: new

2. Sociologists view theory and research as
    a. interdependent.
    b. independent.
    c. separate but equal.
    d. unrelated.

    ANS: A   PG: 26   TYP: comprehension   SOURCE: new

3. The United States shares a _____-mile long border with Mexico.
    a. 200
    b. 800
    c. 2,000
    d. 5,000

    ANS: C   PG: 27   TYP: knowledge   SOURCE: study guide

4. In Mexico, the border fences are referred to as
    a. Operation Gatekeeper.
    b. the Wall of Shame.
    c. Operation Safeguard.
    d. Hold-the-Line.

    ANS: B PG: 27 TYP: knowledge SOURCE: new

5. A _____ is a set of core assumptions and concepts broadly describing how societies operate and how people in them relate to one another.
    a. fact
    b. sociological theory
    c. concept
    d. method of research

    ANS: B PG: 28 TYP: knowledge SOURCE: new

6. Functionalists are most inspired by which one of the following thinkers?
    a. Karl Marx
    b. Emile Durkheim
    c. Max Weber
    d. Erving Goffman

    ANS: B PG: 28 TYP: knowledge SOURCE: new

7. A _____ is the contribution a part makes to order and stability within the society.
    a. dysfunction
    b. façade of legitimacy
    c. symbol
    d. function

    ANS: D PG: 28 TYP: comprehension SOURCE: new

8. _____ use biological analogies to explain how society operates.
    a. Conflict theorists
    b. Symbolic interactionists
    c. Functionalists
    d. Action theorists

    ANS: A PG: 28 TYP: comprehension

Chapter 2

9. From a purely functionalist perspective, sports teams
    a. divide the community and benefit team owners.
    b. foster a sense of belonging to a school, city, or country associated with them.
    c. direct fans' attention away from the real issues a city faces.
    d. are ultimately a drain on the economy.

    ANS: B   PG: 29   TYP: comprehension

10. Early functionalists were criticized for
    a. their condescending manner toward conflict and symbolic interactionist perspectives.
    b. defending existing social arrangements.
    c. linking poverty to personal character.
    d. using biological analogies..

    ANS: B   PG: 28   TYP: comprehension   SOURCE: new

11. According to functionalists, poverty exists because
    a. the poor lack skills to do better.
    b. it contributes in some way to the stability of the overall society.
    c. the poor lack the drive to do better.
    d. somebody has to be on the bottom.

    ANS: B   PG: 29   TYP: comprehension   SOURCE: study guide

12. _____ means anticipated or intended.
    a. Latent
    b. Manifest
    c. Function
    d. Dysfunction

    ANS: B   PG: 29   TYP: comprehension   SOURCE: new

13. _____ means unanticipated or unintended.
    a. Latent
    b. Manifest
    c. Function
    d. Dysfunction

    ANS: A   PG: 29   TYP: comprehension   SOURCE: new

14. A community celebration provides an occasion to plan activities with family and friends. This represents a
    a. manifest function.
    b. latent function.
    c. manifest dysfunction.
    d. latent dysfunction.

    ANS: A   PG: 29   TYP: application

15. Community-wide celebrations have the unintended consequence of breaking down barriers across neighborhoods. Such a consequence is known as a
    a. manifest function.
    b. latent function.
    c. manifest dysfunction.
    d. latent dysfunction.

    ANS: B   PG: 29   TYP: application   SOURCE: new

16. _____ are consequences disruptive to the system or to some segment of society.
    a. Functions
    b. Dysfunctions
    c. Facades of legitimacy
    d. Symbols

    ANS: B   PG: 29   TYP: comprehension

17. Which one of the following is a latent or unexpected function of community-wide celebrations (as discussed in the textbook)?
    a. The celebration functions as a marketing and public relations event for the corporate sponsors.
    b. The celebration provides an occasion to plan activities with friends.
    c. Community celebrations give a visible role to public transportation systems.
    d. The celebration unifies the community through a shared experience.

    ANS: C   PG: 29   TYP: application

Chapter 2

18. Sometimes police departments choose to negotiate contracts with the host city just before a community-wide celebration, thereby using the event as a bargaining tool to secure a good contract. From the *city's perspective*, this represents a _____ of the community-wide celebration.
    a. latent dysfunction
    b. latent function
    c. manifest function
    d. facade of legitimacy

    ANS: A   PG: 30   TYP: application   SOURCE: study guide

19. Traffic jams, closed streets, piles of garbage, and shortages of clean public toilets are some of the anticipated disruptions to order and stability that accompany community-wide celebrations. These kinds of disruptions are known as
    a. manifest dysfunctions.
    b. latent functions.
    c. manifest functions.
    d. latent dysfunctions.

    ANS: A   PG: 29   TYP: application   SOURCE: new

For questions 20-23, refer to cells in this chart.

	Function	Dysfunction
Manifest	Cell #1	Cell #2
Latent	Cell #3	Cell #4

20. Cell one represents
    a. anticipated order and stability consequences.
    b. unanticipated disruptive consequences.
    c. anticipated disruptive consequences.
    d. unanticipated order and stability consequences.

    ANS: A   PG: 29   TYP: application   SOURCE: new

21. Cell two represents
    a. anticipated order and stability consequences.
    b. unanticipated disruptive consequences.
    c. anticipated disruptive consequences.
    d. unanticipated order and stability consequences.

    ANS: C   PG: 29   TYP: application

22. Cell three represents
    a. anticipated order and stability consequences.
    b. unanticipated disruptive consequences.
    c. anticipated disruptive consequences.
    d. unanticipated order and stability consequences.

    ANS: D   PG: 29   TYP: application

23. Cell four represents
    a. anticipated order and stability consequences.
    b. unanticipated disruptive consequences.
    c. anticipated disruptive consequences.
    d. unanticipated order and stability consequences.

    ANS: D   PG: 29   TYP: application

24. _____ authorized 700 miles of additional fencing and security along the U.S.-Mexican border.
    a. Operation Jump Start
    b. The Secure Fence Act of 2006
    c. Operation Hold-the-Line
    d. The Stop the Flow Act of 2006

    ANS: B   PG: 30   TYP: knowledge

Chapter 2

Think about the anticipated and unanticipated consequences of the border fence along the U.S.-Mexican border. For questions 25-28, fill in the cells using the following responses.

   a. Overall drop in the crime rate along the border
   b. Fatalities along the border as the undocumented seek to enter the U.S. through inhospitable terrain
   c. Ranchers, farmers, and sport fishers denied access to the Rio Grande River
   d. A border fence that doubles as a volleyball net

	Function	**Dysfunction**
Manifest	Cell #1	Cell #2
Latent	Cell #3	Cell #4

25. Cell one contains which one of the four responses?

    ANS: A   PG: 31   TYP: application   SOURCE: new

26. Cell two contains which one of the four responses?

    ANS: B   PG: 31   TYP: application   SOURCE: new

27. Cell three contains which one of the four responses?

    ANS: D   PG: 31   TYP: application   SOURCE: new

28. Cell four contains which one of the four responses?

    ANS: D   PG: 31   TYP: application   SOURCE: new

29. An *unexpected outcome* of the border fence is the emergence of humanitarian groups that save the lives of many illegal immigrants but, in doing so, help people circumvent the law. This outcome is an example of a
    a. manifest function.
    b. manifest dysfunction.
    c. latent function.
    d. latent dysfunction.

    ANS: D   PG: 31   TYP: application   SOURCE: new; study guide

30. An *unexpected outcome* of the border fence construction is longer, and perhaps permanent, stays in the United States by migrant laborers who do not return home for fear that will be unable to get back into the United States. This outcome is an example of a
    a. manifest function.
    b. latent function.
    c. manifest dysfunction.
    d. latent dysfunction.

    ANS: D   PG: 31   TYP: application   SOURCE: new

31. An *anticipated outcome* of the border fence construction is success at forcing illegal entries away from now-fenced urban areas to less populated areas and through rough terrain and climates to give border patrol agents a strategic advantage. This outcome is an example of a
    a. manifest function.
    b. latent function.
    c. manifest dysfunction.
    d. latent dysfunction.

    ANS: A   PG: 31   TYP: application   SOURCE: new

32. The border fence construction redirected the flow of illegal immigrants to areas unaccustomed to such movement, fueling a perception that illegal immigration was out of control. The unanticipated disruption is an example of a
    a. manifest function.
    b. latent function.
    c. manifest dysfunction.
    d. latent dysfunction.

    ANS: D   PG: 31   TYP: application   SOURCE: new

Chapter 2

33. Conflict theorists are inspired by
    a. Max Weber.
    b. Emile Durkheim.
    c. Karl Marx.
    d. C. Wright Mills.

    ANS: C   PG: 32   TYP: knowledge   SOURCE: study guide

34. Which one of the questions listed below is a conflict theorist *most* likely to ask?
    a. How is social order possible?
    b. How do meanings change over time?
    c. How does a part contribute to societal stability?
    d. Who benefits from a particular pattern or social arrangement, and at whose expense?

    ANS: D   PG: 32   TYP: comprehension

35. Conflict theorists focus on
    a. the political system.
    b. the legal system.
    c. competition over scarce and valued resources.
    d. family dynamics.

    ANS: C   PG: 32   TYP: comprehension

36. The question "Who benefits from a particular pattern or social arrangement?" is of most interest to a(n)
    a. functionalist.
    b. conflict theorist.
    c. symbolic interactionist.
    d. action theorist.

    ANS: B   PG: 32   TYP: comprehension

37. Marx defined the proletariat as being all <u>but</u> which one of the following?
    a. the most powerful class
    b. unionized
    c. own nothing of the production process
    d. profit-seeking

    ANS: B   PG: 32   TYP: comprehension

42

Theoretical Perspectives and Methods of Social Research

38. According to Marx, the proletariat
    a. have considerable leverage over employers because they can always threaten to strike.
    b. own nothing of the production process except their labor.
    c. are in a position to negotiate a decent wage.
    d. search for ways to expand markets for their products.

    ANS: B   PG: 32   TYP: comprehension   SOURCE: new

39. Which one of the following key words is associated with the conflict perspective?
    a. symbol
    b. façade of legitimacy
    c. order
    d. stability

    ANS: B   PG: 32   TYP: comprehension

40. A woman argues that the low salary she pays someone from Mexico to watch her children is fair because "she got paid more than she would have gotten paid in Mexico." Conflict theorists call this line of reasoning
    a. cultural relativity.
    b. the facade of legitimacy.
    c. a latent function.
    d. class consciousness.

    ANS: B   PG: 33   TYP: application

41. Which one of the following concepts applies to the façade of legitimacy?
    a. complete analysis
    b. well-documented and supported assertions
    c. misleading arguments
    d. strong premises

    ANS: C   PG: 32   TYP: comprehension   SOURCE: new

42. "The Capitalist, if he cannot agree with the Labourer, can afford to wait and live upon his capital." This line, written in 1881, applies to the situation of the
    a. proletariat.
    b. bourgeoisie.
    c. means of production.
    d. subordinate group.

    ANS: B   PG: 33   TYP: application

43. The worker "has but wages to live upon, and must therefore take work when, where, and at what terms he can get it." This line, written in 1881, applies to the situation of the
    a. proletariat.
    b. bourgeoisie.
    c. means of production.
    d. capitalist.

    ANS: A   PG: 33   TYP: application   SOURCE: study guide

44. Conflict theorists maintain that exploitation is disguised by the
    a. proletariat.
    b. means of production.
    c. façade of legitimacy.
    d. bourgeoisie.

    ANS: C   PG: 32   TYP: comprehension   SOURCE: new

45. Many illegal immigrants risk life and limb to escape an economy in which they are being paid approximately _____ per day to enter one that pays approximately _____ per day.
    a. $4; $60-$80
    b. $1; $25-$30
    c. $10; $40-$50
    d. $12; $150.

    ANS: A   PG: 33   TYP: knowledge   SOURCE: new

Theoretical Perspectives and Methods of Social Research

46. Conflict theorists argue that _____ benefit least from the fence construction and stepped-up border security.
    a. undocumented workers
    b. American consumers
    c. American employers
    d. private contractors

    ANS: A   PG: 34   TYP: comprehension   SOURCE: new

47. _____ coined the term *symbolic interactionism*.
    a. Emile Durkheim
    b. Herbert Blumer
    c. Karl Marx
    d. Peter Berger

    ANS: B   PG: 36   TYP: knowledge   SOURCE: new

48. Which perspective focuses on social interaction?
    a. functionalism
    b. conflict theory
    c. symbolic interaction
    d. action theory

    ANS: C   PG: 36   TYP: comprehension   SOURCE: new

49. Which one of the theorists is most likely to ask "How do involved parties experience, interpret, influence, and respond to what they and others are doing while interacting?"
    a. functionalists
    b. conflict theorists
    c. symbolic interactionists
    d. classic theorists

    ANS: C   PG: 36   TYP: application   SOURCE: new

Chapter 2

50. _____ consist(s) of situations in which two people communicate, interpret, and respond to each other's words and actions.
    a. Symbols
    b. Social interaction
    c. The façade of legitimacy
    d. Functions

    ANS: B   PG: 36   TYP: comprehension

51. A(n) _____ is any kind of physical phenomenon—a word, object, color, or sound—to which people assign a name, meaning, or value.
    a. value
    b. preconception
    c. symbol
    d. observation

    ANS: C   PG: 37   TYP: comprehension   SOURCE: new

52. _____ maintain that people must share a symbol system if they are to communicate with one another.
    a. Functionalists
    b. Conflict theorists
    c. Symbolic interactionists
    d. Social action theorists

    ANS: C   PG: 37   TYP: comprehension

53. "Meaning is not evident from the physical phenomenon alone." This statement suggests that
    a. people assign meaning to that phenomenon.
    b. meaning is fixed and universal.
    c. people can tell what something "means" just by looking at it.
    d. seeing is believing.

    ANS: A   PG: 37   TYP: comprehension   SOURCE: study guide

Theoretical Perspectives and Methods of Social Research

54. Self-awareness takes place through
    a. symbols.
    b. reflexive thinking.
    c. the negotiated order.
    d. collective consciousness.

    ANS: B   PG: 37   TYP: knowledge   SOURCE: new

55. A sociologist observing border crossings notes that the primary inspectors have 45 seconds to clear a car for entry or subject it to further inspection. That sociologist is likely to be a
    a. functionalist.
    b. conflict theorist.
    c. symbolic interactionist.
    d. social action theorist.

    ANS: C   PG: 37   TYP: comprehension   SOURCE: new

56. Which one of the following topics would be of greatest interest to a symbolic interactionist?
    a. unintended disruptions to order and stability associated with the construction of border fences
    b. expected disruptions to order and stability associated with the construction of border fences
    c. the ways in which American consumers and employees benefit from low wage labor of illegal immigrants
    d. strategies illegal immigrants use to escape detection when passing through official border crossings

    ANS: D   PG: 37   TYP: application

For the following statements (#57-#62), identify the theoretical perspective associated with each.

    a. Functionalism
    b. Conflict Theory
    c. Symbolic interaction
    d. Social action theory

Chapter 2

57. The construction of barriers along the border had the unanticipated effect of creating a Border Patrol Search, Trauma, and Rescue Team that responds to all incidents involving people in distress.

    ANS: A   PG: 31   TYP: application   SOURCE: new

58. Without some shared meanings, encounters with others would be very confusing.

    ANS: C   PG: 37   TYP: application   SOURCE: new

59. The construction of border fences is associated with an overall drop in crime rate.

    ANS: A   PG: 31   TYP: application   SOURCE: new

60. Many unauthorized immigrants manage to blend in with the crowds passing through official ports of entry.

    ANS: C   PG: 36   TYP: application   SOURCE: new

61. The border fences have been constructed to stop or, at least, control the free movement of labor from the low-wage to the high-wage side of the border.

    ANS: B   PG: 32   TYP: application   SOURCE: new

62. The United States has relied on low-wage labor from Mexico since at least
    a. 1880.
    b. 1945.
    c. 1966.
    d. 1990.

    ANS: A   PG: 33   TYP: knowledge   SOURCE: new

63. Which one of the following statements represents a criticism of the functionalist perspective?
    a. It is too liberal.
    b. It focuses on the "small stuff."
    c. It offers no technique for determining the "overall net effect."
    d. It focuses on the "have nots."

    ANS: C   PG: 39   TYP: comprehension   SOURCE: study guide

64. A major criticism of the conflict theory is that it
    a. overemphasizes the stability and order that exist in a society.
    b. offers a simplistic view of the employer-employee relationship.
    c. focuses too strongly on consumer groups, citizen groups, and the worker's ability to promote change.
    d. understates the tensions and divisions that exist in society.

    ANS: B   PG: 39   TYP: comprehension   SOURCE: new

65. A weakness of the _____ theory is that it tends to present a simplistic view of the relationship between dominant and subordinate groups.
    a. functionalist
    b. conflict
    c. symbolic interaction
    d. sociological

    ANS: B   PG: 39   TYP: comprehension   SOURCE: new

66. One strength of the _____ perspective is that it offers a balanced view that includes intended and unintended consequences related to order and disorder.
    a. functionalist
    b. conflict
    c. symbolic interaction
    d. sociological

    ANS: A   PG: 39   TYP: comprehension   SOURCE: new

Chapter 2

67. One strength of the _____ perspective is that it forces us to look beyond popular justifications and explore questions about whose interests are being protected and promoted and at whose expense.
    a. functionalist
    b. conflict
    c. symbolic interaction
    d. sociological

    ANS: B   PG: 39   TYP: comprehension   SOURCE: new

68. One weakness of the _____ perspective is that specific observations are difficult to generalize.
    a. functionalist
    b. conflict
    c. symbolic interaction
    d. sociological

    ANS: C   PG: 39   TYP: comprehension   SOURCE: new

69. One strength of the _____ perspective is that it encourages first-hand, extensive observation of an issue.
    a. functionalist
    b. conflict
    c. symbolic interaction
    d. sociological

    ANS: C   PG: 39   TYP: comprehension   SOURCE: new

70. Which one of the following statements best describes how the three perspectives should be viewed?
    a. A single perspective can give us a complete picture of a process or an event.
    b. Most sociologists maintain that one perspective only should be adopted when analyzing an issue.
    c. The three perspectives should be viewed as opposing viewpoints.
    d. We can gain greater understanding of a process or an event if we examine it from the point of view of more than one perspective.

    ANS: D   PG: 39   TYP: application

71. Which one of the following questions about illegal immigration from Mexico to the U.S. would be of most interest to a conflict theorist?
    a. How does illegal immigration contribute to order and stability in Mexico and the U.S.?
    b. Who benefits from the existence of illegal immigration, and at whose expense?
    c. Does everyone in the U.S. and Mexico see illegal immigration in the same way?
    d. Why doesn't the U.S close its borders to foreign workers?

    ANS: B   PG: 39   TYP: application   SOURCE: study guide

72. Which one of the following questions about illegal immigration from Mexico to the U.S. would be of most interest to a functionalist?
    a. How does illegal immigration contribute to order and stability in Mexico and the U.S.?
    b. Who benefits from the existence of illegal immigration, and at whose expense?
    c. Does everyone in the U.S. and Mexico see illegal immigration in the same way?
    d. Why doesn't the U.S close its borders to foreign workers?

    ANS: A   PG: 39   TYP: application

73. Which one of the following questions about illegal immigration from Mexico to the U.S. would be of most interest to a symbolic interactionist?
    a. How does illegal immigration contribute to order and stability in Mexico and the U.S.?
    b. Who benefits from the existence of illegal immigration, and at whose expense?
    c. How do illegal immigrants come to interact with potential employers?
    d. Why doesn't the U.S close its borders to foreign workers?

    ANS: C   PG: 39   TYP: application

74. A functionalist reads the headline "U.S. strengthens patrols along Mexican border." He or she would begin to think about
    a. how the presence of border guards contributes to order and stability in both societies.
    b. interactions between border guards and illegal Mexican immigrants.
    c. who benefits from the existence of border guards, and at whose expense.
    d. identifying policies to stop the flow.

    ANS: A   PG: 39   TYP: application

Chapter 2

75. _____ is a fact-gathering and fact-explaining enterprise governed by strict rules.
    a. Research
    b. Theory
    c. Sociological theory
    d. A perspective

    ANS: A   PG: 40   TYP: comprehension   SOURCE: new

76. Sociologists adhere to the scientific method, which means that they acquire data through
    a. testing.
    b. surveys.
    c. observation.
    d. personal interviews.

    ANS: C   PG: 40   TYP: comprehension   SOURCE: new

77. Which one of the following assumptions applies to the scientific method?
    a. Knowledge is always subjective.
    b. Research findings can be manipulated to advance a good cause.
    c. Truth is confirmed through faith.
    d. Knowledge is acquired through observation.

    ANS: D   PG: 40   TYP: comprehension   SOURCE: study guide

78. Which of the following is a <u>false</u> statement about the characteristics of high-quality sociological research?
    a. Once a sociological study is completed, findings and conclusions are considered final.
    b. Sociologists collect data that is observable to others.
    c. Sociological findings endure as long as they can be duplicated and as long as they can withstand reexamination.
    d. Sociologists do not let personal and subjective views about the topic influence the outcome of the research.

    ANS: A   PG: 40   TYP: comprehension

79. Sociological research is guided by
    a. methods unique to the discipline.
    b. a passion to change society.
    c. emotion and personal interest.
    d. the scientific method.

    ANS: D   PG: 40   TYP: comprehension   SOURCE: study guide

80. "Duplication is the heart of good research." This means that
    a. no findings can be taken seriously unless others can repeat the process and obtain the same results.
    b. the researcher does the study twice under different conditions.
    c. the research is published at least twice.
    d. two sets of reviewers reach the same evaluation of the research.

    ANS: A   PG: 40   TYP: comprehension

81. Researchers should maintain *objectivity*. This means they should
    a. stay away from topics in which they have a personal interest.
    b. not accept funding.
    c. clearly define the objects of their investigation.
    d. not let personal and subjective views about the topic influence the observations or outcome.

    ANS: D   PG: 40   TYP: comprehension

82. In theory, the first step in undertaking a sociological research project is
    a. consulting existing research.
    b. collecting data.
    c. choosing a topic for investigation.
    d. analyzing the data.

    ANS: C   PG: 41   TYP: comprehension   SOURCE: study guide

Chapter 2

83. Perhaps one of the most significant and most often understated reasons a researcher chooses to study a specific topic is
    a. that funding is available.
    b. sociological appeal.
    c. personal interest.
    d. to understand how society works.

    ANS: C   PG: 41   TYP: comprehension

84. Sociologists Audrey Singer and Douglas S. Massey studied the social process of undocumented border crossings among Mexican migrants. The two researchers chose this topic because
    a. it is a issue that is of little interest to people in the United States.
    b. knowing the extent of undocumented entries helps us to judge whether fences and other barriers are effective.
    c. there is an overwhelming amount of research describing how migrants evade borders guarded by agents.
    d. illegal entries into the United States is a relatively new phenomenon.

    ANS: C   PG: 41   TYP: comprehension   SOURCE: new

85. For their research on undocumented border crossing, sociologists Audrey Singer and Douglas S. Massey focus on the undocumented immigrants' social ties to others who have crossed successfully without authorization. This focus suggests that Singer and Massy are using the _____ perspective to frame their research.
    a. functionalist
    b. conflict
    c. symbolic interaction
    d. sociological

    ANS: C   PG: 41   TYP: application   SOURCE: new

54

86. Sociologists Audrey Singer and Douglas S. Massey maintain that "constructing fences and implementing other border control strategies sits well with the public as the government appears to be defending the United States against alien invaders while not antagonizing U.S. business interests." This statement suggests the two sociologists are taking a _____ perspective to frame their research.
   a. functionalist
   b. conflict
   c. symbolic interaction
   d. sociological

   ANS: B   PG: 41   TYP: application   SOURCE: new; study guide

87. _____ are powerful thinking tools and communication tools that enable researchers to efficiently give and receive complex information.
   a. Concepts
   b. Theories
   c. Methods
   d. Facts

   ANS: A   PG: 42   TYP: comprehension   SOURCE: new

88. Core sociological concepts give focus to researchers' observations. For example, the concept "interpersonal ties" as it relates to undocumented entry into the United States focuses a researcher's attention on
   a. those who own nothing of the production process but their labor.
   b. the owners of the means of production.
   c. the functions of poverty.
   d. connections to those who can help a migrant remain undetected.

   ANS: D   PG: 42   TYP: comprehension   SOURCE: new

89. The plan for gathering data on the topic a researcher has chosen is known as the
   a. scientific method.
   b. hypothesis.
   c. research design.
   d. hidden curriculum.

   ANS: C   PG: 42   TYP: comprehension

Chapter 2

90. The most common "thing" sociologists study is
    a. documents.
    b. individuals.
    c. small groups.
    d. households.

    ANS: B   PG: 43   TYP: knowledge

91. _____ are materials or other evidence that yields information about human activity, including items that people throw away or the number of lights left on in homes at a particular time.
    a. Traces
    b. Documents
    c. Territories
    d. Households

    ANS: A   PG: 42   TYP: comprehension   SOURCE: new; study guide

92. Which one of the following examples shows what sociologists study when they focus on traces?
    a. household income
    b. interaction between border patrol agents and bus passengers
    c. doctor-patient relationships
    d. the number of lights turned on in homes at a particular time of day

    ANS: D   PG: 42   TYP: application   SOURCE: new

93. A sampling frame is
    a. a complete list of every case in a population.
    b. a portion of cases from a particular population.
    c. the plan for gathering data to test hypotheses.
    d. a sample with the same distribution of characteristics as the population from which it is drawn.

    ANS: A   PG: 42   TYP: knowledge

Theoretical Perspectives and Methods of Social Research

94. Researchers who study litter that undocumented immigrants leave behind on the paths used to enter the United States are studying
    a. traces.
    b. documents.
    c. territories.
    d. households.

    ANS: A   PG: 42   TYP: comprehension   SOURCE: new

95. Researchers that study letters undocumented workers have sent home to family members are studying
    a. traces.
    b. documents.
    c. territories.
    d. households.

    ANS: B   PG: 43   TYP: application   SOURCE: new

96. Sociologists observing social activity at a specific border crossing have chosen to study
    a. traces.
    b. documents.
    c. territories.
    d. households.

    ANS: C   PG: 43   TYP: comprehension   SOURCE: new

97. For his book *Patrolling Chaos*, sociologist Robert Maril accompanied 12 border patrol agents on 60 ten-hour shifts along the border. Maril had chosen to study
    a. small groups.
    b. documents.
    c. territories.
    d. households.

    ANS: A   PG: 44   TYP: comprehension   SOURCE: new; study guide

Chapter 2

98. When there is as likely a chance that any one member of the population will be selected for a sample, the sample is said to be
    a. controlled.
    b. biased.
    c. random.
    d. nonrandom.

    ANS: C PG: 43 TYP: comprehension

99. Which of the following would be the best option to obtain a representative sample of students at your college?
    a. Ask students eating in the cafeteria at lunchtime to participate in an important study.
    b. At random, draw a list of students from the most recent college registrar's list.
    c. Stop people as they are walking to their cars in the parking lot and ask them to participate.
    d. Go to all the sociology classes and recruit students to participate in a project.

    ANS: B PG: 43 TYP: application

100. Researchers choose to study nonrepresentative samples for all but which one of the following reasons.
    a. They are easy to study.
    b. When little is known about the members who make up the sample
    c. When those in the sample have special or unique characteristics
    d. When the experiences of those in the sample help to clarify important social issues

    ANS: A PG: 43 TYP: comprehension SOURCE: new

101. For his book *Patrolling Chaos*, sociologist Robert Maril accompanied 12 border patrol agents on 60 ten-hour shift along the border. Maril was studying a _____ sample.
    a. controlled
    b. biased
    c. random
    d. nonrandom

    ANS: D PG: 44 TYP: application SOURCE: new

102. The U.S. census form, which is mailed out to every household every 10 years, is an example of
    a. an experiment.
    b. an observation.
    c. a self-administered questionnaire.
    d. secondary research.

    ANS: C   PG: 44   TYP: application

103. This data-gathering method does not include the possibility that the researcher's facial expression or body language will influence respondents to answer in a particular way. This method is
    a. structured interviews.
    b. unstructured interviews.
    c. participant observation.
    d. self-administered questionnaires.

    ANS: D   PG: 44   TYP: application   SOURCE: new

104. In a structured interview, the question-answer sequence
    a. is largely spontaneous.
    b. resembles a conversation.
    c. is set in advance.
    d. can be altered.

    ANS: C   PG: 44   TYP: comprehension

105. In an unstructured interview, the question-answer sequence is
    a. forced-choice.
    b. set in advance.
    c. rigid and cannot be altered.
    d. flexible and open-ended.

    ANS: D   PG: 45   TYP: comprehension   SOURCE: new

106. For his book *Patrolling Chaos*, sociologist Robert Maril rode with border agents during their 10-hour shifts and talked with them "under the scorching sun and in the dead of night…about what they knew, what they had seen, and what they thought." Maril used which one of the following methods?
    a. structured interviews
    b. unstructured interviews
    c. nonparticipant observation
    d. self-administered questionnaires

    ANS: B PG: 45 TYP: application SOURCE: new

107. _____ is especially useful for studying behavior as it occurs.
    a. A self-administered questionnaire
    b. Secondary data analysis
    c. An interview
    d. Observation

    ANS: D PG: 45 TYP: comprehension SOURCE: study guide

108. When engaged in _____, researchers must be especially careful not to misinterpret or misrepresent what is happening.
    a. structured interviews
    b. unstructured interviews
    c. observation research
    d. survey research

    ANS: C PG: 46 TYP: application SOURCE: new

109. For his book *Coyotes: A Journey through the Secret World of America's Illegal Aliens*, Ted Conover used _____ by choosing to live with his subjects.
    a. structured interviews
    b. self-administered questionnaires
    c. observation research
    d. survey research

    ANS: C PG: 46 TYP: application SOURCE: new

110. An unintended effect resulting from the attention one receives from being the subject of the research is the
    a. Hawthorne effect.
    b. latent effect.
    c. special subject effect.
    d. experimental effect.

    ANS: A   PG: 47   TYP: application

111. One of the primary reasons researchers engaged in participant observation conceal their identity is to eliminate
    a. legal problems.
    b. the need for confidentiality.
    c. the Hawthorne effect.
    d. ethical considerations.

    ANS: C   PG: 47   TYP: comprehension   SOURCE: study guide

112. For the *Gender Concepts of Swedish and American Youth* study, researchers distributed surveys to Swedish and American teens. The instructions asked them to list attributes they thought "characterized most women, most men, most boys, most girls, and themselves; to write 'change-sex stories' about what their lives would be like if they found they had become the other sex." The researchers used which one of the following methods?
    a. self-administered questionnaire
    b. nonparticipant observation
    c. participant observation
    d. secondary sources

    ANS: A   PG: 44   TYP: application

113. The research for the book *Unbound Feet* drew upon "45 years of a Chinese language newspaper and numerous organizational archives, such as the Presbyterian Mission Homes, the Chinese YWCA, the Square and Circles Club, and the Chinese Ladies Garment Workers Union." The researchers used which one of the following methods?
    a. self-administered questionnaire
    b. nonparticipant observation
    c. participant observation
    d. secondary sources

    ANS: D   PG: 47   TYP: application

Chapter 2

114. Researcher Kandi Stinson spent two years as a weight loss group member, "studying how women spoke about and understood losing weight." Stinson used which one of the following methods?
    a. self-administered questionnaire
    b. nonparticipant observation
    c. participant observation
    d. secondary sources

    ANS: C   PG: 46   TYP: application

115. The variable that helps to explain and predict the behavior of interest is known as the _____ variable.
    a. independent
    b. dependent
    c. control
    d. spurious

    ANS: A   PG: 47   TYP: comprehension

116. In research, the variable to be explained or predicted is known as
    a. the dependent variable.
    b. the independent variable.
    c. the hypothesis.
    d. the control variable.

    ANS: A   PG: 47   TYP: comprehension   SOURCE: study guide

117. A dependent variable is
    a. the variable of cause.
    b. a trial idea.
    c. the variable to be explained.
    d. the core concept.

    ANS: C   PG: 47   TYP: comprehension

118. The *independent* variable in the hypothesis "Retired populations have a higher suicide rate than employed populations" is
    a. employment status.
    b. suicide rate.
    c. retired populations.
    d. employed populations.

    ANS: A   PG: 47   TYP: application

119. The *dependent* variable in the hypothesis "Retired populations have a higher suicide rate than employed populations" is
    a. employment status.
    b. suicide rate.
    c. retired populations.
    d. employed populations.

    ANS: B   PG: 47   TYP: application   SOURCE: new

120. The *independent* variable in the hypothesis "the longer a U.S. line worker has been employed at a U.S.-based assembly plant, the more difficult it is for that worker to find new employment when the assembly plant moves to Mexico" is
    a. employment at U.S. based assembly plant.
    b. assembly plants in Mexico.
    c. the length of time employed at line work in U.S. assembly plant.
    d. the length of time to find new employment.

    ANS: C   PG: 47   TYP: application

121. The *dependent* variable in the hypothesis "the longer a U.S. line worker has been employed at a U.S.-based assembly plant, the more time it takes for that worker to find new employment when the assembly plant moves to Mexico" is
    a. employment at U.S. based assembly plant.
    b. assembly plants in Mexico.
    c. the length of time employed at line work in U.S. assembly plant.
    d. the length of time to find new employment.

    ANS: D   PG: 47   TYP: application   SOURCE: study guide

Chapter 2

122. The *independent* variable in the hypothesis "the more proficient in English undocumented immigrants are, the less likely they are to be apprehended by Border Patrol" is
    a. likelihood of apprehension.
    b. English language proficiency.
    c. undocumented immigrants.
    d. Border Patrol agents.

    ANS: B   PG: 47   TYP: application   SOURCE : new

123. A trial explanation predicting a relationship between independent and dependent variables is a(n)
    a. hypothesis.
    b. theory.
    c. fact.
    d. observation.

    ANS: A   PG: 47   TYP: comprehension

124. An analogy can be drawn between an operational definition and
    a. a control variable.
    b. a bank statement.
    c. a recipe.
    d. the human body.

    ANS: C   PG: 48   TYP: comprehension

125. _____ are concrete and specific criteria for observing and measuring independent and dependent variables.
    a. Operational definitions
    b. Hypotheses
    c. Units of analysis
    d. Traces

    ANS: A   PG: 48   TYP: comprehension

126. The question "Is this operational definition really measuring what it claims to measure?" addresses
   a. concerns surrounding
   b. sampling.
   c. validity.
   d. reliability.
   e. correlations.

   ANS: B   PG: 48   TYP: comprehension

127. A researcher studying handwashing uses guidelines set by the American Society of Microbiology to determine if handwashing has taken place: use warm or hot running water and soap while washing for 10 to 15 seconds all surfaces, including wrists, palms, backs of hands, and under fingernails. This guideline is considered
   a. an operational definition.
   b. the Hawthorne effect.
   c. a correlation.
   d. a test.

   ANS: A   PG: 48   TYP: application   SOURCE: new

128. If one respondent gives different answers to the same question at two different points in time, the researcher should be concerned about
   a. reliability.
   b. validity.
   c. representativeness.
   d. the Hawthorne effect.

   ANS: A   PG: 48   TYP: application

129. A professor tells a class that exams will cover information from class lectures, class discussion, and reading assignments. However, the exam includes questions related to only reading assignments. Students complain because the exam is
   a. not reliable.
   b. not valid.
   c. not reliable or valid.
   d. objective.

   ANS: B   PG: 48   TYP: application   SOURCE: study guide

Chapter 2

130. When assessing _____, always ask if the operational definition measures what it claims to measure.
    a. reliability
    b. validity
    c. methods of data gathering
    d. hypotheses

    ANS: B   PG: 48   TYP: comprehension   SOURCE: new

131. Asking if the number of apprehensions is a good measure of the effectiveness of border fences relates to assessing
    a. reliability.
    b. validity.
    c. methods of data gathering.
    d. hypotheses.

    ANS: B   PG: 48   TYP: comprehension   SOURCE: new

132. For each of the 254 counties in the state of Texas, Derrick finds the percentage of people living at or below the poverty level. In one county, 5 percent of the population lives at or below poverty. No other county has such a low percentage. Derrick has found the
    a. range.
    b. minimum.
    c. maximum.
    d. standard deviation.

    ANS: B   PG: 49   TYP: application

133. For each of the 254 counties in the state of Texas, Erin finds the percentage of people in each county that are classified as Hispanic. She finds that 14.5 percent was the number in which 50 percent of the counties fell below and 50 percent fell above. Erin has found the
    a. mode.
    b. median.
    c. mean.
    d. standard deviation.

    ANS: B   PG: 49   TYP: application

134. Of the 254 counties in Texas, the percentage of the population who live at or below poverty level falls between 0 and 60 percent. The range is
    a. 6
    b. 20
    c. 30
    d. 60

    ANS: D   PG: 49   TYP: application   SOURCE: study guide

135. Shelby reviews statistics on the number of unauthorized immigrants apprehended for each of the past 12 years and finds the lowest number to be 910,000 in 2003. Shelby has identified the
    a. range.
    b. minimum.
    c. maximum.
    d. standard deviation.

    ANS: B   PG: 49   TYP: application   SOURCE: new

136. Sam reviews statistics on the number of unauthorized immigrants apprehended for each of the past 12 years and finds the highest number to be 1.64 million in 2005. Sam has identified the
    a. range.
    b. minimum.
    c. maximum.
    d. standard deviation.

    ANS: C   PG: 49   TYP: application   SOURCE: new

137. School officials announce that 90 percent of the student body support starting a football team. The sample consisted of 200 students who returned a survey that appeared in the campus newspaper. On the basis of this information, one could question the study with regard to
    a. reliability.
    b. generalizability.
    c. validity.
    d. the unit of analysis.

    ANS: B   PG: 51   TYP: application

138. The findings from research by Robert Maril (*Patroling Chaos*) and Audrey Singer and Douglas S. Massey (undocumented works and personal ties) suggest that highly visible border control strategies, such as fences are
    a. highly effective.
    b. a grand pretense.
    c. somewhat effective.
    d. pork barrel projects.

    ANS: B   PG: 51   TYP: comprehension   SOURCE: new

139. When a sample is randomly selected and almost everyone agrees to participate, the findings are considered
    a. reliable because the sample is representative.
    b. valid because the sample is not one of convenience.
    c. generalizable to the population from which the sample was drawn.
    d. operational because the research is basing findings in a representative sample.

    ANS: C   PG: 51   TYP: comprehension

140. An independent variable explains a dependent variable when
    a. the dependent variable precedes the independent variable in time.
    b. the independent variable and the dependent variable remain uncorrelated.
    c. there is no evidence of a spurious correlation between the independent and dependent variables.
    d. the correlation coefficient between the independent and dependent variables is 0.05.

    ANS: C   PG: 51   TYP: knowledge

141. The correlation between the variables "percentage of population living at or below poverty level" and "percentage of population classified as Hispanic" is +0.60. This means that the _____ the percentage of the population living at or above the poverty level, the _____ the percentage of the population classified as Hispanic.
    a. greater; greater
    b. greater; lower
    c. lower; greater
    d. fewer; higher

    ANS: A   PG: 51   TYP: application

142. A researcher finds a strong correlation between hair length and test scores. When the researcher takes sex into account, that correlation disappears. In this situation, sex is
   a. a dependent variable.
   b. a control variable.
   c. an independent variable.
   d. the standard deviation.

   ANS: B   PG: 52   TYP: application

143. Under which one of the following conditions are findings from a sample not generalizable to a larger population?
   a. The sample is a series of interesting case studies.
   b. The response rate is high.
   c. Almost all the subjects agree to participate.
   d. The sample is random.

   ANS: A   PG: 51   TYP: comprehension

144. The correlation coefficient between two variables is a negative number when the value of one variable
   a. increases while the other increases.
   b. decreases while the other decreases.
   c. remains constant while the other increases.
   d. increases while the other decreases.

   ANS: D   PG: 51   TYP: application

145. A spurious correlation is one that is
   a. planned.
   b. coincidental or accidental.
   c. causal.
   d. spontaneous.

   ANS: B   PG: 51   TYP: comprehension

Chapter 2

Multiple Choice Questions on the Web

1. In Chapter 2, the three major sociological theories and methods of social research are used to assess the causes and consequences of
   a. U.S. dependence on Mexico's oil.
   b. illegal drugs entering into the United States from Mexico.
   c. the proposed and existing fence along the U.S.-Mexican border.
   d. NAFTA.

   ANS: C   PG: 27   TYP: comprehension

2. The early functionalists used _____ to illustrate society as a system of interrelated parts.
   a. the changing seasons
   b. a cloth-weaving analogy
   c. the metaphor of a machine
   d. the human body

   ANS: D   PG: 28   TYP: comprehension

3. A functionalist would ask which one of the following questions about *the border fences*?
   a. Why do border fences exist on the border, and what anticipated and unanticipated consequences do they have for American and Mexican societies?
   b. Who benefits from the border fences, and at whose expense?
   c. Does everyone in the U.S. and Mexico see the border fence in the same way?
   d. Do taxpayers want border fences?

   ANS: A   PG: 30   TYP: application   SOURCE: new

4. "The real purpose of the fence construction is to prevent the free movement of labor from a low wage economy into a high wage one." This statement is most likely to be made by a
   a. functionalist.
   b. conflict theorist.
   c. symbolic interactionist.
   d. social action theorist.

   ANS: B   PG: 33   TYP: application   SOURCE: new

5. Symbolic interactionists believe that during interaction, the parties involved
    a. respond directly to their surroundings and to each other's actions.
    b. first interpret each other's actions, words, and gestures and then respond based on that interpretation.
    c. communicate effectively even when they do not share the same symbol system.
    d. do not have to share a symbol system.

    ANS: B   PG: 36   TYP: comprehension   SOURCE: new

6. Which theorists are most likely to study interactions between border control agents and those people crossing legally and illegally?
    a. functionalists
    b. conflict theorists
    c. symbolic interactionists
    d. social action theorists

    ANS: C   PG: 37   TYP: comprehension   SOURCE: new

7. A researcher who chooses to study the items people throw away is studying
    a. traces.
    b. documents.
    c. individuals.
    d. households.

    ANS: A   PG: 43   TYP: application

8. If researchers directly interact and become involved with the people they are researching, the method they are using is
    a. participant observation.
    b. nonparticipant observation.
    c. a case study.
    d. secondary analysis.

    ANS: A   PG: 46   TYP: comprehension

9. The *dependent* variable in the hypothesis "the more proficient in English undocumented immigrants are, the less likely they are to be apprehended by Border Patrol" is
    a. likelihood of apprehension.
    b. English language proficiency.
    c. undocumented immigrants.
    d. Border Patrol agents.

    ANS: A   PG: 47   TYP: application   SOURCE: new

10. For each of the 265 counties in the state of Texas, Erin finds the percentage of people in each county that are classified as Hispanic. She finds that, on average, each county has a Hispanic population of 23.6 percent. Erin has found the
    a. mode.
    b. median.
    c. mean.
    d. standard deviation.

    ANS: C   PG: 49   TYP: application

True/False Questions

1. In the United States, about 97 percent of all apprehensions of illegal immigrants occur on the U.S.- Mexican border.

    ANS: True   PG: 28   SOURCE: new

2. Functionalists focus on conflict over scarce and valued resources.

    ANS: False   PG: 32   SOURCE: new

3. From a functionalist viewpoint, poverty contributes to the stability of the overall society.

    ANS: True   PG: 29   SOURCE: study guide

4. Functionalists argue that sports teams have no real purpose in society.

    ANS: False   PG: 29

5. "Latent" means intended, anticipated, or expected.

   ANS: False   PG: 29   SOURCE: study guide

6. In the mid-1990s, three major border cities in the United States constructed eighty miles of fence.

   ANS: True   PG: 30   SOURCE: new

7. A latent function of the border fences was the creation of a highly trained Border Patrol Search, Trauma, and Rescue Team, which rescues anyone in need of emergency assistance.

   ANS: True   PG: 31   SOURCE: new

8. The functionalist approach gives us no techniques for assessing the overall impact of *maquiladoras* on Mexican and American society.

   ANS: True   PG: 39   SOURCE: new

9. The border fences have forced illegal immigrants to enter the United States through desert and other inhospitable terrain.

   ANS: True   PG: 39   SOURCE: new; study guide

10. Conflict theorists emphasize order and stability.

    ANS: False   PG: 32   SOURCE: new

11. The façade of legitimacy is an explanation that members of dominant groups give to justify exploitive actions.

    ANS: True   PG: 32   SOURCE: new; study guide

12. In the United States, the construction industry is the largest employer of undocumented workers.

    ANS: True   PG: 33

Chapter 2

13. Legal and illegal migration of labor from Mexico to the United States has been ongoing since at least 1880.

    ANS: True   PG: 33   SOURCE: new

14. Many households in Mexico have come to rely on remittance income.

    ANS: True   PG: 35   SOURCE: new; study guide

15. Conflict theorists give special attention to the factors pushing immigrants from Mexico to the United States.

    ANS: False   PG: 34   SOURCE: new

16. All evidence suggests that most illegal immigrants "sneak" across the Southwest border into the United States.

    ANS: False   PG: 35   SOURCE: new

17. A symbolic interactionist focuses on social interaction.

    ANS: True   PG: 35   SOURCE: new; study guide

18. Interaction depends on shared symbols.

    ANS: True   PG: 36   SOURCE: new

19. The border region extends 60 miles into the United States and 60 miles into Mexico.

    ANS: True   PG: 38   SOURCE: new

20. One strength of the symbolic interactionist perspective is that it gives a balanced overview of intended and unintended consequences.

    ANS: False   PG: 39   SOURCE: new; study guide

21. Personal interest should not be a factor in choosing a topic.

    ANS: False   PG: 40

22. Researchers do not always follow in order the steps of scientific method.

    ANS: True   PG: 41   SOURCE: study guide

23. Researchers can manipulate data if the deception supports well-intentioned personal, economic, and political agendas.

    ANS: False   PG: 40

24. It is impossible to compile a list of topics that sociologists study.

    ANS: True   PG: 41

25. Sociology is distinguished from other disciplines not by the topics it studies but by the perspective it uses to study any topic.

    ANS: True   PG: 41   SOURCE: new

26. All good researchers place their research in the context of existing research.

    ANS: True   PG: 41

27. Structured interviews are flexible and open-ended in style.

    ANS: False   PG: 45   SOURCE: new; study guide

28. Researchers should never hide their identity and purpose from those they are observing.

    ANS: False   PG: 46   SOURCE: new

Chapter 2

29. Validity is the extent to which an operational definition gives consistent results.

    ANS: False   PG: 48

30. A correlation of -1.0 suggests that there is no relationship between two variables.

    ANS: False   PG: 51   SOURCE: study guide

Concept Application (also in study guide)

Consider the concepts listed below. Match one or more of the concepts with each scenario. Explain your choices.

   a. Function
   b. Dysfunction
   c. Symbol
   d. Territories
   e. Participant observation
   f. Spurious correlation
   g. Proletariat

Scenario 1
   "The influx of Korean-owned firms conferred obvious economic benefits on Los Angeles. (1) Korean firms tended to service low income, nonwhite neighborhoods generally ignored and underserved by big corporations….(2) The Korean influx restored the [deteriorating and underutilized] neighborhoods in which Koreans settled….(3) Their residential and commercial interests compelled Koreans to combat street crime….(4) Koreans valued public education and improved it. Indeed, many Korean families had emigrated to the United States because of this country's superior educational opportunities" (Light and Bonacich 1988:6-7).

    ANS: A

Scenario 2
   "Dr. Louise Keating became 'Trash Czar' for a few days. Dr. Keating, director of Red Cross Blood Services in Cleveland, found her center almost engulfed by mounds of debris—dressings, needles, plastic tubes—most of it the usual detritus of any organization, but some of it splashed with the blood of donors. Her center was not generating any more trash than usual. But suddenly, no one was willing to cart it away. AIDS could be transmitted through blood, we had now learned. Last year's innocuous garbage had become this year's plague vector. Or so it seemed to Cleveland's carters. And the refuse piles grew."

"Dr. Keating did solve her problem. Now, all waste that has any blood on it is sterilized in an autoclave until nothing, not even a virus, survives. But AIDS has created many other problems in the nation's blood supply: for those, like Dr. Keating and her colleagues, who must find donors and ensure that the blood obtained is safe; for those who give blood; and for those who receive it" (Murray 1990:205).

ANS: B

Scenario 3

Some Americans venturing into Mexico probably hear the word [gringo] and wonder if somebody is picking a fight. The answer seems to depend on who says it and how. "It's all in the tone; usually the eyes will tell you something as well," said Tony Garza, the U.S. ambassador to Mexico, who grew up in Brownsville. "It can mean everything from 'I am going to try and kick your butt,' to 'friend, let's have a drink,'" Garza added. "Let's jus say it is very situation-specific." When gringo is used in Mexico, it tends to be applied to anyone born in the United States, regardless of race or background (Schiller 2004).

ANS: C   SOURCE: new

Scenario 4

"I gained access to the enterprise through a friend who was a manager in a local bank from which the enterprise borrowed commercial loans. Management and workers in both factories knew I was a graduate student writing a dissertation. I was a full-time assembly worker in the Hong Kong plant, visited workers' homes, and participated in their weekend activities. In Shenzhen, I observed and talked with workers and managers on the shop floor and the office, but management allowed me to work on the line only occasionally. I lived in factory dormitories together with other Hong Kong managerial staff, but I visited and interviewed workers in workers' dormitories. I also participated in both workers' and managers' gatherings after work" (Lee 1995:380).

ANS: E

Chapter 2

Scenario 5
For the class, the suburban mall became the microsocial setting for investigating macrotheoretical issues. Students examined specific features of their selected malls, such as the surrounding physical environment (entrance, parking, sidewalks), financial condition (unoccupied spaces, needed repairs, open-air merchants), design of interior space (escalators, lighting, plants), types of stores (prestige, anchors, discounters, specialties), clientele (social class, gender, race, ethnicity), nationality as well as race and ethnicity and gender of merchants (especially subcontractors within stores) and employees, pricing structure (including types of credit cards accepted or interest-free purchase options), mall names and distinctive linguistic terms, treatment of shoppers by employees, safety and security issues, and the presence of "mall zombies" as a crude indicator of the dehumanizing effects associated with "irrationality of rationality" (Manning, Price, and Rich 1997:18).

ANS: D

Scenario 6
There is a positive correlation between ice cream sales and deaths due to drowning: the more ice cream sold, the more drownings and vice versa. The third variable at work here is *season* or *temperature*. Most drowning deaths occur during the warm days of summer—and that's the peak period for ice cream sales. There is no direct link between ice cream and drowning (Babbie 1995:70).

ANS: F

Scenario 7
In April, KenSa started production in a rented, temporary facility in San Pedro Sula while a new factory was being built. It hired 150 workers to make Chrysler minivan door wire harnesses at the Honduran minimum wage of about 55 cents an hour. It turned hundreds of people away…But the jobs provide no economic miracle. Factory work barely provides enough to live…Most workers at foreign-owned factories in Honduras make $4.44 a day. That's less than the $5 a day Henry Ford paid his Highland Park workers 90 years ago in 1914. Ford's pay (the equivalent of $11 an hour today) more than doubled the minimum wage at the time and helped give birth to America's blue-collar middle class…U.S. companies have no such incentive in countries such as Honduras. Products are built for export back to America. Raising worker salaries in San Pedro Sula won't sell even one more SUV in Detroit (French 2004).

ANS: G   SOURCE: new

Short Essay Questions

1. Why is Mexico (in particular, the border fence) the focus of Chapter 2?

2. What are the names of the three theoretical perspectives? How do the three theoretical perspectives help us to think about any social event or issue?

3. What is a function? Give an example.

4. According to the functionalist perspective, why has poverty not been eliminated?

5. What concepts did Robert K. Merton introduce to counter criticisms of the functionalist perspective? Briefly define each concept, and explain how they strengthen the perspective. What criticism is not addressed by Merton's concepts?

6. Use the following chart to summarize a functionalist analysis of community-wide celebrations.

	Function	Dysfunction
Manifest		
Latent		

7. For what reasons did the United States construct fences (and plan to construct more fences) along the U.S.-Mexico border?

8. List one example of a manifest function, manifest dysfunction, latent function, and latent dysfunction associated with the construction of border fences.

9. What question guides conflict theorists is their analysis of any social issue? In answering that question, what do conflict theorists emphasize?

10. How does a conflict theorist explain the purpose of the fences along the U.S.-Mexico border?

11. What are international remittances? Explain their importance.

12. What central concepts and questions guide the symbolic interactionist perspective?

13. How would a symbolic interactionist study border crossings?

14. What are the strengths and weaknesses of each theoretical perspective?

15. Define research methods.

16. What assumptions underlie the scientific method? Under what circumstances do research findings endure? Contrast the ideal of the research process with reality.

17. Why is it important for researchers to explain their reasons for choosing to investigate a particular topic? Why did Singer and Massey study undocumented border crossings?

18. Why should researchers review the literature before beginning to investigate a topic?

19. What are concepts, and how do they relate to the research process?

20. What kinds of "things" do sociologists study? Give examples.

21. Why do sociologists study random samples? Why are random samples difficult to secure? Under what conditions are nonrandom samples acceptable?

22. Give a brief description of each method of data collection.

    Self-Administered Questionnaires

    Structured Interviews

    Unstructured Interviews

    Participant Observation

    Secondary Sources

23. What is the Hawthorne effect?

24. What is a hypothesis? Give an example of a hypothesis. Identify the independent and dependent variables.

25. What is an operational definition? Give an example.

26. Distinguish between reliability and validity.

27. How do basic statistics help to describe apprehensions involving illegal immigrants over the past 12 years?

28. What is generalizability? Under what conditions are findings considered generalizable?

29. What three conditions must be met before a researcher can claim that an independent variable contributes significantly to explaining a dependent variable?

Chapter 2

Comprehensive Essay Questions

1. Compare and contrast the conflict and functionalist perspectives. In answering the question, be sure to consider the central questions, key terms, visions of society, and the focus.

2. Think of an event that has been the center of recent media attention. How would the three perspectives help give focus to that event?

3. Explain the following statement: The quality of the research findings and conclusions depends on the operational definition.

4. Describe an operational definition that affects your life (Hint: Any "formula" that is used to evaluate performance at work or at school qualifies). Comment on the operational definition's reliability and validity.

5. Use the research of Maril (*Patrolling Chaos*) and Singer and Massey (on undocumented entries) to illustrate four concepts related to social research.

Chapter 3

Culture

Multiple-Choice Questions

1. U.S. military involvement in Korea dates back to
    a. the end of WWII (1945).
    b. the Korean War (1952).
    c. the Vietnam War.
    d. the early 1980s.

    ANS: A   PG: 59   TYP: knowledge

2. Which one of the following events has affected the life of every North and South Korean resident who lived through the event and who has since been born?
    a. the dropping of an atomic bomb on Hiroshima and Nagasaki
    b. the division of North and South Korea
    c. the presidency of Kim Il Sung
    d. the presidency of Kim Il Jong

    ANS: B   PG: 59   TYP: knowledge   SOURCE: new

3. Currently there are about _____ U.S. military personnel stationed in South Korea.
    a. 10,000
    b. 30,000
    c. 83,000
    d. 100,000

    ANS: B   PG: 59   TYP: knowledge   SOURCE: study guide

Chapter 3

4. Which one of the following descriptions applies to South Korea?
   a. communist-style government
   b. isolated
   c. centrally-planned economy
   d. top 20 economy

   ANS: D   PG: 59   TYP: knowledge   SOURCE: study guide

5. Which one of the following descriptions applies to North Korea?
   a. democratically elected governments
   b. integrated into the global economy
   c. isolated
   d. top 20 economy

   ANS: C   PG: 59   TYP: knowledge

6. Our everyday use of the word "culture" suggests that we use the word in ways that emphasize
   a. tolerance.
   b. understanding.
   c. differences.
   d. overlap.

   ANS: C   PG: 60   TYP: comprehension

7. A _____ is a group of interacting people who share, perpetuate, and create culture.
   a. culture
   b. society
   c. counter culture
   d. subculture

   ANS: B   PG: 60   TYP: comprehension   SOURCE: new

8. Sociologists face a number of challenges in studying culture. Those challenges include all but which one of the following?
    a. describing culture
    b. determining who belongs to a culture
    c. identifying the distinguishing characteristics that set one culture apart from another
    d. identifying overlap among cultures

    ANS: D   PG: 60   TYP: comprehension   SOURCE: study guide

9. The Island of Gorée, a slave-trading center from the 15th to 19th centuries, qualifies as
    a. nonmaterial culture.
    b. material culture.
    c. values.
    d. beliefs.

    ANS: B   PG: 62   TYP: application   SOURCE: new

10. The idea of establishing a system for protecting cultural and natural wonders around the world gained momentum after
    a. the U.S. government dropped nuclear bombs on two Japanese cities.
    b. the Japanese government destroyed Korean culture.
    c. the Egyptian government decided to construct the Aswan High Dam to control the Nile River.
    d. the Iraqi government invaded Kuwait.

    ANS: C   PG: 62   TYP: knowledge

11. Which one of the following represents the best example of material culture?
    a. physical objects people have invented, such as a diamond ring
    b. conceptions of what is right and good, such as "true friendship"
    c. rules for behavior, such as "stop for pedestrians in crosswalk"
    d. the belief that athletic talent is inherited

    ANS: A   PG: 61   TYP: comprehension

Chapter 3

12. "It is acceptable for young children of both sexes to bathe with their mothers and other women in public." This statement is an example of a
    a. belief.
    b. value.
    c. norm.
    d. folkway.

    ANS: A   PG: 63   TYP: application   SOURCE: new

13. American sociologists studying Korean bathhouses would be struck by the
    a. private nature of the bath.
    b. tense atmosphere.
    c. lack of self-consciousness regarding the body.
    d. casual relationships between adult men and women.

    ANS: C   PG: 63   TYP: knowledge   SOURCE: new; study guide

14. Plants, trees, and other natural resources people use for a purpose are examples of
    a. nonmaterial culture.
    b. material culture.
    c. institutional completeness.
    d. a folkway.

    ANS: B   PG: 61   TYP: application

15. The microwave falls under the category
    a. nonmaterial culture.
    b. beliefs.
    c. norms.
    d. material culture.

    ANS: D   PG: 61   TYP: comprehension

16. Beliefs, values, and norms are part of
    a. nonmaterial culture.
    b. material culture.
    c. cultural diffusion.
    d. reentry shock.

    ANS: A   PG: 63   TYP: comprehension

17. Material culture includes
    a. norms.
    b. values.
    c. beliefs.
    d. inventions.

    ANS: D   PG: 61   TYP: comprehension   SOURCE: new

18. In analyzing material culture, sociologists focus on
    a. the most obvious and practical uses.
    b. the inventor.
    c. the country of origin.
    d. the meanings assigned to it by the people who use it.

    ANS: D   PG: 61   TYP: comprehension

19. Which one of the following is an example of material culture?
    a. a saying (i.e., "a stitch in time saves nine")
    b. a belief in an afterlife
    c. democracy
    d. a radio

    ANS: D   PG: 61   TYP: application

20. "Continuous conversation, rather than silence, validates a relationship." This statement is an example of a
    a. belief.
    b. value.
    c. norm.
    d. folkway.

    ANS: A   PG: 64   TYP: application

21. _____ are socially shared ideas about what is good, right, and desirable.
    a. Values
    b. Norms
    c. Beliefs
    d. Expressive symbols

    ANS: A   PG: 63   TYP: comprehension

Chapter 3

22. _____ are ideas that people accept as true about how the world operates and about the place of the individual in it.
   a. Values
   b. Norms
   c. Beliefs
   d. Symbols

   ANS: C   PG: 63   TYP: comprehension

23. Signs that read "No Smoking," "Honk Horn to Open," and "Emergency Exit Only" specify
   a. values.
   b. norms.
   c. beliefs.
   d. mores.

   ANS: B   PG: 64   TYP: application

24. Sociologist William Graham Sumner wrote that "_____ give us discipline and support of routine and habit"; if we were forced constantly to make decisions about these details, "the burden would be unbearable"
   a. mores
   b. folkways
   c. beliefs
   d. values

   ANS: B   PG: 64   TYP: comprehension   SOURCE: study guide

25. South Korea's top ice climber proclaimed, "I am not so special. Anyone can do it." This statement reflects the Korean emphasis on
   a. innate talent.
   b. a desire to win.
   c. disciplined practice habits.
   d. individual achievement.

   ANS: C   PG: 64   TYP: application

Culture

26. In the United States, many diners pass items around the table and use special serving utensils to take food from bowls and plates. These behaviors represent
    a. values.
    b. norms.
    c. beliefs.
    d. expressive symbols.

    ANS: B   PG: 64   TYP: application

27. _____ give us discipline and support of routine and habit.
    a. Folkways
    b. Mores
    c. Beliefs
    d. Feeling rules

    ANS: A   PG: 64   TYP: comprehension

28. A folkway is
    a. a fable parents read to their children.
    b. a norm that applies to routine and everyday matters.
    c. a norm that applies to serious matters.
    d. a myth about how a culture came to be.

    ANS: B   PG: 64   TYP: comprehension

29. An international guide to business recommends that executives traveling to South Korea wait for the eldest person at the table to begin eating before everyone begins. This advice represents a(n)
    a. more.
    b. folkway.
    c. idiom.
    d. belief.

    ANS: B   PG: 64   TYP: application

Chapter 3

30. An international business guide recommends that executives who do business in South Korea should not pour their own drinks. This recommendation qualifies as a(n)
    a. more.
    b. folkway.
    c. idiom.
    d. belief.

    ANS: B   PG: 64   TYP: application   SOURCE: new

31. Most Americans have strong _____ against public nudity, especially when adults are in the presence of children.
    a. mores
    b. folkways
    c. idioms
    d. beliefs

    ANS: A   PG: 64   TYP: application   SOURCE: new

32. Mores are defined as
    a. norms that apply to routine matters.
    b. rules that govern the use of resources in a society.
    c. norms that people define as essential to a group's well-being.
    d. norms that are enforced through informal sanctions.

    ANS: C   PG: 64   TYP: comprehension

33. A sociologist seeking to *explain* why Koreans work harder to save energy than Americans work explores the role of
    a. genes.
    b. norms.
    c. values.
    d. geographic and historical factors.

    ANS: D   PG: 66   TYP: comprehension   SOURCE: new; study guide

34. _____ are physical and conceptual phenomena to which people assign a name and a meaning or value.
   a. Beliefs
   b. Values
   c. Norms
   d. Symbols

   ANS: D   PG: 65   TYP: comprehension   SOURCE: new

35. For North Koreans, the Year 97 represents the number of years since Kim Il Sung founded their country. From a sociological perspective, 97 is a
   a. belief.
   b. symbol.
   c. norm.
   d. historical factor.

   ANS: B   PG: 65   TYP: application   SOURCE: new

36. In time, American women who visit Korean bathhouses report that they
   a. simply cannot adjust to social nudity.
   b. are emotionally drained from the experience.
   c. come to see being naked with other women and children as unremarkable.
   d. see social nakedness as morally wrong, especially with children.

   ANS: C   PG: 65   TYP: comprehension   SOURCE: new

37. Language is a predictable social arrangement among people that has emerged over time to facilitate human interaction and communication. In this sense, language is a
   a. social institution.
   b. value.
   c. norm.
   d. belief system.

   ANS: A   PG: 65   TYP: comprehension   SOURCE: new

38. North Korea must import _____ percent of its oil needs.
    a. 20
    b. 40
    c. 100
    d. 80

    ANS: C   PG: 68   TYP: knowledge

39. South Korea must import _____ percent of its oil needs.
    a. 100
    b. 80
    c. 50
    d. 30

    ANS: A   PG: 68   TYP: knowledge

40. One important historical event that has shaped the way Americans think about and use energy is the
    a. Gold Rush of 1849.
    b. discovery of Spindletop (a Texas oil gusher) in 1901.
    c. invention of the car.
    d. Iran-Iraq War in the 1980s.

    ANS: B   PG: 67   TYP: knowledge   SOURCE: new

41. Consumption- and conservation-oriented behaviors seem to be related to
    a. genetic qualities.
    b. culture.
    c. resource abundance and scarcity.
    d. population size.

    ANS: C   PG: 68   TYP: comprehension

42. Part of the reason Koreans and Americans open refrigerators differently has to do with
    a. innate differences.
    b. the conservative nature of Koreans.
    c. the amount of natural resources in each country.
    d. the fact that Americans are simply wasteful.

    ANS: C   PG: 67   TYP: comprehension   SOURCE: new

43. Which one of the following countries spends 33.9 percent of its Gross Domestic Product on its military?
    a. South Korea
    b. North Korea
    c. The United States
    d. Mexico

    ANS: B   PG: 66   TYP: knowledge

44. The value underlying Korean use of "our" versus "my" is
    a. survival of the fittest.
    b. the self-made person.
    c. the importance of the group.
    d. individual achievement.

    ANS: C   PG: 63   TYP: application   SOURCE: study guide

45. The use of the word "my" (e.g., my mother) as opposed to "our" (e.g., our mother) reflects a preoccupation with
    a. the needs of the group.
    b. the needs of the individual.
    c. parenthood.
    d. the maternal instinct.

    ANS: B   PG: 69   TYP: comprehension

46. In the United States, singular possessive pronouns (e.g., "my") are used to refer to things over which we do not have exclusive control. This reflects the American preoccupation with
    a. the group.
    b. the individual.
    c. competitiveness.
    d. resources.

    ANS: B   PG: 69   TYP: application

Chapter 3

47. Which one of the following statements speaks to the role of age in the Korean language?
    a. It is impossible to carry on a conversation without taking age into consideration.
    b. Korean language has very few references to age.
    c. Korean forms of address require the speaker to refer to elder brothers and sisters by their first names.
    d. Koreans must use a special name to address a younger sibling.

    ANS: A   PG: 69   TYP: application   SOURCE: new

48. North Korean president Kim Il-Sung was raised a Christian and even played the church organ. After taking power, Kim completely wiped out Christianity from his country. This example supports the view that
    a. people are cultural replicas of one another.
    b. people have the power to reject, manipulate, and create culture.
    c. there are cultural formulas for passing on cultural experiences.
    d. people are passive agents who absorb one version of culture.

    ANS: B   PG: 70   TYP: comprehension   SOURCE: study guide

49. "No two languages are ever sufficiently similar to be considered as representing the same social reality." This sentence applies to
    a. ethnocentrism.
    b. culture shock.
    c. the linguistic relativity hypothesis.
    d. cultural diffusion.

    ANS: C   PG: 69   TYP: comprehension   SOURCE: new

50. "The sounds coming from a bird leads a speaker of English to think that the bird is singing, while it leads a speaker of Korean to think that the bird is weeping." This difference supports the
    a. reentry shock concept.
    b. linguistic relativity hypothesis.
    c. idea of institutional completeness.
    d. existence of counter cultures.

    ANS: B   PG: 69   TYP: concept application   SOURCE: new

51. A U.S. service woman stationed in South Korea spends the weekends meeting with the Korean people who live away from the military base. In the process, she picks up enough of the Korean language to communicate basic information. From a sociological point of view, this woman is
    a. adding to her menu of cultural options.
    b. ethnocentric.
    c. institutionally complete.
    d. no longer American (in a cultural sense).

    ANS: A   PG: 70   TYP: concept application   SOURCE: new

52. One indicator of culture's influence on satisfying hunger is that
    a. only a portion of the potential food available is defined as edible.
    b. people everywhere eat three meals a day.
    c. fast food appeals to people everywhere.
    d. if people are hungry enough, they will eat just about anything.

    ANS: A   PG: 71   TYP: comprehension   SOURCE: study guide

53. _____ is a staple of the Korean diet.
    a. Rice
    b. Fish
    c. Tea
    d. Fruit

    ANS: A   PG: 71   TYP: knowledge

54. _____ is a staple of the American diet.
    a. Hamburgers
    b. Hot dogs
    c. Rice
    d. Corn

    ANS: D   PG: 71   TYP: knowledge   SOURCE: study guide

Chapter 3

55. _____ is a staple of the North Korean diet.
    a. Rice
    b. Wheat
    c. Corn
    d. Sugar cane

    ANS: C   PG: 71   TYP: knowledge   SOURCE: new

56. _____ are internal bodily sensations that we experience in relationships with other people.
    a. Social emotions
    b. Feeling rules
    c. Emotional states
    d. Expressive norms

    ANS: A   PG: 71   TYP: comprehension   SOURCE: study guide

57. Feeling rules are
    a. the same in all cultures.
    b. norms that specify appropriate ways to express physical sensations. .
    c. innate, not learned.
    d. unique to each individual.

    ANS: B   PG: 71   TYP: comprehension   SOURCE: new

58. Which one of the following practices helps to explain how Kim Il-Sung and his son Kim Jong-Il have come to dominate North Korean emotional life?
    a. Images of Kim Il-Sung and Kim Jong-Il are rarely seen.
    b. Objects that the two leaders touch are destroyed.
    c. Five percent of book titles in North Korea are about the two Kims.
    d. North Korean students at all levels take hundreds of hours of coursework that focus on the lives and accomplishments of the two Kims.

    ANS: D   PG: 72   TYP: knowledge

Culture

59. Molly walks in on her father, Carl, while he is comforting and holding his friend, Ep, whose wife has just died. For some reason, this bothered Molly, and she decided to keep it to herself. Molly's decision is influenced by
    a. material culture.
    b. feeling rules.
    c. reverse ethnocentrism.
    d. idioms.

    ANS: B   PG: 71   TYP: application

60. The U.S. Army publishes a list of "Must Know Items" about South Korea for American soldiers who are stationed there. One item says, "Don't be surprised if you see two Korean women or men walking arm in arm. They are just good friends, and there is nothing sexual implied." The Army is alerting soldiers to
    a. material culture.
    b. feeling rules.
    c. reverse ethnocentrism.
    d. idioms.

    ANS: B   PG: 71   TYP: application   SOURCE: study guide

61. Gregory is five years old and has lived in Japan all his life. When asked what his favorite Japanese food is, he replies, "McDonald's." This answer illustrates that most people
    a. see McDonald's as a global corporation.
    b. tend to think that the material culture that surrounds them is "homegrown."
    c. see an interconnection between material and nonmaterial culture.
    d. do not distinguish between Japanese and American food.

    ANS: B   PG: 72   TYP: application

62. "I once asked my five-year-old son, who had grown up largely in Tokyo, about his favorite Japanese food. He thought about it for a moment before saying "rice-balls and McDonald's." This example supports the idea that
    a. language shapes thinking.
    b. the U.S. borrowed the McDonald's concept from Japan.
    c. folkways and mores have to be taught.
    d. most people tend to think that the material items that surround them originated in their society.

    ANS: D   PG: 72   TYP: comprehension

Chapter 3

63. The 86,000 South Korean Jehovah's Witnesses trace the roots of their religion to _____, the home of the *Watchtower* publication.
    a. Pittsburgh, Pennsylvania
    b. New York, New York
    c. Chicago, Illinois
    d. Mexico City

    ANS: A   PG: 72   TYP: knowledge   SOURCE: new; study guide

64. Which one of the following newspaper headlines suggests that cultural diffusion is at work?
    a. "Global Goliath: Coke Conquers the World"
    b. "Korea Has Few Oil Reserves"
    c. "Korea Goes It Alone"
    d. "Few Americans Study Abroad"

    ANS: A   PG: 72   TYP: application

65. People of one society borrow ideas, materials, or inventions from another culture
    a. indiscriminately.
    b. selectively.
    c. regardless of the usefulness of what is borrowed.
    d. even though it is always a troublesome process.

    ANS: B   PG: 73   TYP: comprehension

66. An American-born boy visits South Korea and learns that South Koreans use two snow balls instead of three snowballs to make a snowperson. When he returns home to the United States, he uses two snowballs to make his snowperson. Sociologists consider this an example of
    a. Reverse ethnocentrsim.
    b. cultural shock.
    c. cultural diffusion.
    d. reentry shock.

    ANS: C   PG: 73   TYP: application   SOURCE: new

67. The practice of male circumcision in South Korea can be traced to
    a. contact with the U.S. military during the Korean War.
    b. Korean students studying in the United States.
    c. Jehovah's Witness missionaries working in Korea.
    d. a Confucian tradition.

    ANS: A   PG: 73   TYP: knowledge

68. Most male circumcisions in South Korea take place at which one of the following points in life?
    a. at birth
    b. between the ages of one and five
    c. during elementary and middle school years
    d. around 21 years of age

    ANS: C   PG: 73   TYP: knowledge

69. The North Korean government restricts cultural diffusion. However, some North Koreans are finding ways to acquire illicit radios, mobile phones, CD players, and so on. Those North Koreans live
    a. close to the border with China.
    b. near the DMZ.
    c. near the South Korean border.
    d. in the capital city.

    ANS: A   PG: 74   TYP: comprehension   SOURCE: new

70. The North Korean government prohibits its 23 million people from receiving mail or telephone calls from outside the country. By doing this, the North Korean government is
    a. creating a society lacking in culture.
    b. severely limiting opportunities for cultural diffusion.
    c. supporting cultural relativism.
    d. introducing culture shock.

    ANS: B   PG: 73   TYP: application   SOURCE: new; study guide

Chapter 3

71. _____ culture is any component of society's culture that is embraced by the masses within and outside that society.
    a. Material
    b. Nonmaterial
    c. Popular
    d. Relative

    ANS: C   PG: 75   TYP: comprehension   SOURCE: new

72. The Oprah Winfrey Show is viewed by people in 122 countries. Sociologists would label the Oprah Show as which one of the following types of culture?
    a. material
    b. nonmaterial
    c. popular
    d. relative

    ANS: C   PG: 75   TYP: application   SOURCE: new

73. _____ is the strain that people from one culture experience when they must orient themselves to the ways of a new culture.
    a. Culture shock
    b. Ethnocentrism
    c. Diffusion
    d. Reverse ethnocentrism

    ANS: A   PG: 74   TYP: comprehension   SOURCE: study guide

74. The intensity of culture shock depends on all <u>but</u> which one of the following?
    a. the extent to which home and foreign cultures are different
    b. the level of preparation or knowledge about the new culture
    c. the circumstances surrounding the encounter with the new culture
    d. the mode of transportation one employs to enter a foreign country

    ANS: D   PG: 74   TYP: comprehension

75. Upon returning home to the U.S. after a long stay overseas, Michael and Renée felt like they were going "crazy." They hated American television "telling" them to buy products in order to be liked. They were experiencing
    a. institutional completeness.
    b. cultural relativity.
    c. reentry shock.
    d. cultural transmission.

    ANS: C   PG: 74   TYP: application

76. A U.S. soldier returning to the U.S. after a tour of duty in Iraq stated that he was "less tolerant of stupid people...stupid people doing stupid things" and that he was particularly irritated by the question, "Did you kill anyone?" The soldier is experiencing
    a. institutional completeness.
    b. cultural relativity.
    c. reentry shock.
    d. cultural diffusion.

    ANS: C   PG: 74   TYP: application

77. The tendency to hold your own culture as a standard against which other cultures are judged is
    a. cultural relativity.
    b. cultural awareness.
    c. ethnocentrism.
    d. multicultural relativism.

    ANS: C   PG: 75   TYP: comprehension   SOURCE: study guide

78. The most extreme and most destructive form of ethnocentrism is
    a. reverse ethnocentrism.
    b. defining foreign ways as peculiar.
    c. cultural genocide.
    d. self-determination.

    ANS: C   PG: 76   TYP: application

Chapter 3

79. Reentry shock is _____ in reverse; it is experienced upon returning home after living in another culture.
    a. material culture
    b. culture shock
    c. ethnocentrism
    d. cultural relativity

    ANS: B   PG: 74   TYP: application   SOURCE: new; study guide

80. In the July and August before the Seoul Olympics, foreign correspondents wrote so many stories about canine cuisine that, from abroad, it appeared that all Koreans ate dog. In addition, few media correspondents sought to understand this practice. The media correspondents took
    a. an ethnocentric perspective.
    b. a position of cultural relativity.
    c. a position of reverse ethnocentrism.
    d. an institutional completeness approach.

    ANS: A   PG: 76   TYP: application

81. According to sociologist Everett Hughes, "One can think so exclusively in terms of his or her own social world that he or she has no set of concepts for comparing one social world to the next." Hughes is describing
    a. cultural genocide.
    b. a kind of ethnocentrism.
    c. institutional completeness.
    d. a state of cultural relativity.

    ANS: B   PG: 77   TYP: comprehension

82. From a(n) _____ viewpoint, one's group is the center and all others are scaled and rated with reference to it.
    a. cultural relative
    b. reentry shock
    c. sociological
    d. ethnocentric

    ANS: D   PG: 75   TYP: comprehension

83. Under Japanese rule, Korean students were taught by Japanese teachers, Korean names were changed to Japanese names, and practically everything Korean was abandoned. The Japanese were guilty of
    a. cultural relativity.
    b. institutional completeness.
    c. reverse ethnocentrism.
    d. cultural genocide.

    ANS: D   PG: 76   TYP: application   SOURCE: study guide

84. Reverse ethnocentrism is best reflected in which of the following statements?
    a. America—Love it or leave it!
    b. We have to become more like the Koreans.
    c. Buy American.
    d. Korea is the next Japan.

    ANS: B   PG: 77   TYP: application

85. The view that any aspect of culture must be assessed in the context of the society in which it is found is called
    a. ethnocentrism.
    b. cultural relativity.
    c. cultural genocide.
    d. cultural borrowing.

    ANS: B   PG: 77   TYP: comprehension

86. A visiting professor teaching at a South Korean university noted that the students were preoccupied with the United States. They viewed America as a paradise; "They really believed everyone was rich and lived in big houses." These students were expressing
    a. reverse ethnocentrism.
    b. ethnocentrism.
    c. cultural relativism.
    d. culture shock.

    ANS: A   PG: 77   TYP: application   SOURCE: new

Chapter 3

87. An individual who adopts cultural relativism aims to _____ a cultural practice.
    a. understand
    b. condone
    c. discredit
    d. accept uncritically

    ANS: A   PG: 78   TYP: comprehension   SOURCE: study guide

88. Which one of the following statements is not a type of ethnocentrism?
    a. A foreign culture is perceived as the standard for judging the worth of a home culture.
    b. Outsiders deem a culture so offensive that they believe it must be destroyed.
    c. People believe so deeply in their culture's ways that they have no framework for thinking about other cultures.
    d. A cultural practice is considered in light of its own cultural context.

    ANS: D   PG: 77   TYP: comprehension

89. Subcultures are _____ when their members do not have to interact with anyone outside their group to shop for food, attend schools, receive medical care, or find companionship.
    a. countercultures
    b. culturally complete
    c. subversive
    d. institutionally complete

    ANS: D   PG: 78   TYP: comprehension

90. The 29,600 American men and women stationed in South Korea spend most of their time at one of 46 military bases. This suggests that the military in South Korea is
    a. institutionally complete.
    b. promoting cultural diffusion.
    c. encouraging cultural immersion.
    d. advocating reverse ethnocentrism.

    ANS: A   PG: 79   TYP: application   SOURCE: study guide

Culture

91. _____ are groups that share in some parts of the dominant culture but have their own distinctive values, norms, beliefs, symbols, language, and material culture.
    a. Countercultures
    b. Subcultures
    c. Institutions
    d. Cultural replicas

    ANS: B   PG: 78   TYP: comprehension   SOURCE: new

92. Which one of the following groups represents an example of a counterculture?
    a. a sorority
    b. a fraternity
    c. a retirement community
    d. Buddhist monks

    ANS: D   PG: 79   TYP: application   SOURCE: new: study guide

93. Which one of the following core concepts is correctly stated?
    a. Culture is an innate characteristic.
    b. People from the same culture are essentially replicas of one another.
    c. In every society, some groups possess distinctive traits that set them apart from the main culture.
    d. For the most part, people reject material and nonmaterial culture from other cultures.

    ANS: C   PG: 82   TYP: comprehension   SOURCE: new

Multiple-Choice Questions on the Web

1. _____ has one of the world's most centrally planned and isolated economies.
    a. South Korea
    b. The United States
    c. North Korea
    d. Mexico

    ANS: C   PG: 59   TYP: knowledge

105

Chapter 3

2. The Great Wall of China, the Statue of Liberty, and the Rock Drawing of Alta qualify as
   a. nonmaterial culture.
   b. material culture.
   c. beliefs.
   d. values.

   ANS: B   PG: 62   TYP: application   SOURCE: new

3. Which of the following represents the best example of a belief?
   a. physical objects people have invented, such as the radio
   b. conceptions of what is right and good, such as "true friendship"
   c. rules for behavior, such as "stop for pedestrians in crosswalk"
   d. the idea that "children should live with their parents until they get married"

   ANS: D   PG: 63   TYP: comprehension

4. In Korea, diners reach and stretch across one another and use their chopsticks to take food from serving bowls. These behaviors are
   a. values.
   b. norms.
   c. beliefs.
   d. expressive symbols.

   ANS: B   PG: 64   TYP: application

5. A sociologist seeking to *explain* why Koreans work harder to save energy than Americans work explores the role of
   a. genes.
   b. norms.
   c. values.
   d. geographic and historical factors.

   ANS: D   PG: 66   TYP: comprehension

6. "Few Americans realized that their country was different or particularly fortunate . . . They soon began to take their subterranean wealth for granted . . . People in other industrialized nations were more aware of America's blessing. Being less sure of their sources of energy, they were warier about its dispensation." This description describes the beginning of U.S. dependence on
    a. water.
    b. oil.
    c. coal.
    d. the automobile.

    ANS: B   PG: 67   TYP: comprehension

7. Korean-American youths who participate in cultural immersion programs that involve study in Korea often observe that "they never felt so American as when they are slurping noodles in Korea. Even their slurps have American accents." This example suggests that
    a. our genes endow us with our cultural characteristics.
    b. there is connection between physical appearance and culture.
    c. people learn the ways of the culture into which they are born and raised.
    d. humans are born with cultural characteristics.

    ANS: C   PG: 68   TYP: application

8. One indicator of culture's influence on satisfying hunger is that
    a. only a portion of the potential food available is defined as edible.
    b. people everywhere eat three meals a day.
    c. fast food appeals to people everywhere.
    d. if people are hungry enough, they will eat just about anything.

    ANS: A   PG: 70   TYP: comprehension

9. The newspaper headline "World's Top Donut Chains Roll into South Korea" suggests that _____ is at work.
    a. cultural diffusion
    b. ethnocentrism
    c. a folkway
    d. subversive forces

    ANS: A   PG: 72   TYP: application   SOURCE: new

Chapter 3

10. Most people take an ethnocentric view toward foreign cultures; that is, they
    a. use their home culture as the standard for judging the worth of another culture.
    b. use a foreign culture as the standard to judge all other cultures.
    c. seek to understand a culture.
    d. seek to destroy the foreign culture.

    ANS: A   PG: 75   TYP: comprehension

True/False Questions

1. People from the same culture are essentially cultural replicas of one another.

    ANS: False   PG: 60   SOURCE: new

2. U.S. service men and women have fought, died, and otherwise served in Korea to unite the North and South.

    ANS: False   PG: 59   SOURCE: new; study guide

3. The DMZ separates North and South Korea.

    ANS: True   PG: 59   SOURCE: new

4. South Korea possesses one of the top 20 economies in the world.

    ANS: True   PG: 59   SOURCE: study guide

5. Sociologists classify the Great Wall of China and Rock Drawings of Alta as material culture.

    ANS: True   PG: 62   SOURCE: new

6. For the most part, North and South Korea share the same culture.

    ANS: False   PG: 60   SOURCE: new

7. Much of the Korean identity is intricately linked with the idea of being "not Japanese."

    ANS: True   PG: 60   SOURCE: study guide

8. Mores are more important norms than folkways.

    ANS: True   PG: 64

9. Mores are norms that people define as critical to the well-being of a group.

    ANS: True   PG: 64

10. The Korean language is such that it is virtually impossible to carry on a conversation without referring to age.

    ANS: True   PG: 69

11. The discovery of Spindletop in 1901 made the U.S. the largest producer of oil in the world at that time.

    ANS: True   PG: 67   SOURCE: new

12. Babies are destined to learn a culture that corresponds with their physical appearance.

    ANS: False   PG: 68   SOURCE: new

13. In North Korea, the year 97 is a symbol for years since the birth of Kim Il Sung.

    ANS: True   PG: 65   SOURCE: new

14. For the most part, people are passive agents who absorb culture.

    ANS: False   PG: 69

Chapter 3

15. Rice is a staple of the South Korean diet.

    ANS: True   PG: 71   SOURCE: new

16. Corn is a staple of the American diet.

    ANS: True   PG: 71   SOURCE: new

17. The opportunity for cultural diffusion occurs whenever people from different cultures make contact.

    ANS: True   PG: 72   SOURCE: new; study guide

18. Some South Koreans have "borrowed" the religion of the Jehovah's Witnesses, which originated in the United States.

    ANS: True   PG: 72   SOURCE: new

19. The North Korean government encourages cultural diffusion.

    ANS: False   PG: 73   SOURCE: new; study guide

20. Travelers are more likely to prepare for the experience of culture shock than to prepare for reentry shock.

    ANS: True   PG: 74   SOURCE: study guide

21. After Japan annexed Korea in 1910, Japanese became the official language in Korea.

    ANS: True   PG: 76

22. For the most part, the 23 million people of North Korea are not permitted to travel beyond their country's borders.

    ANS: True   PG: 73   SOURCE: study guide

23. Reentry shock is the glorification of a home country.

    ANS: False   PG: 74   SOURCE: new; study guide

24. People who engage in reverse ethnocentrism idealize another culture as perfect.

    ANS: True   PG: 77

25. The statement "whatever they do is fine" reflects a perspective of cultural relativism.

    ANS: False   PG: 78   SOURCE: study guide

26. Retirement communities are an example of a subculture.

    ANS: True   PG: 78   SOURCE: new

27. Buddhist monks who reject the trappings of capitalistic society and devote themselves to simple living constitute a counterculture.

    ANS: True   PG: 79   SOURCE: new

Concept Application (also in study guide)

Consider the concepts listed below. Match one or more of the concepts with each scenario. Explain your choices.

   a. Diffusion
   b. Feeling rules
   c. Norms
   d. Reentry shock
   e. Reverse ethnocentrism
   f. Subculture

Chapter 3

Scenario 1
"Overseas, the home country environment becomes irrationally glorified. All difficulties and problems are forgotten, and only the good things back home are remembered. Upon returning to the United States, people may be surprised to find that they not only miss their host country and its people, culture, and customs but also the people with whom they shared the experience. They realize how well they actually got along under a different set of living conditions and how much happened and changed back home in their absence. As one woman said to me, 'Three years is a long time to be immersed in another way of life, and I felt numb and kind of left out or not in on things happening in the United States. It was a very unhappy time for me because I had expected to be ecstatic to get home'" (Koehler 1986:90).

ANS: E; D

Scenario 2
"Yesterday, my four-year-old stopped crying. He fell off his bike, held his breath, and gritted his teeth. 'I'm not gonna cry, Mom,' he said. 'I'm really not.' Where did this pint-size stoicism come from? Batman videos? Preschool name-callers? Maybe the neighbors who tell their kid, 'Crying will get you nowhere.' You hear it everywhere. You'd better not pout, you'd better not cry. Big boys don't cry. Grin and bear it, hide it, stifle it, but whatever you do, don't cry. Please don't cry. I'll give you a cookie if you stop" (Hogan 1994:E1).

ANS: B

Scenario 3
Teens who embrace Goth "celebrate the darker side of humanity, with most young people wearing black clothing, pale makeup with dark accents, and jet-black hair styled in an unusual manner, though it's much more than appearance… American Goths wear piercings and tattoos across their faces and bodies. Goths sometimes pierce their lips, foreheads, and eyebrows, as well as their ear lobes" (Brooks 2007).

ANS: F

Scenario 4
"Some of the world's top donut chains have come rolling into China, Taiwan, South Korea and Japan, and elsewhere in the region as Asians embrace the Western fast food fad. Chains like Krispy Kreme, Dunkin' Donuts, and Mister Donut are setting up shop in a region not known for its sweet tooth, reflecting a growing openness to foreign foods and rising living standards according to the chains and consumers who sometimes wait in line for hours for the treats" (Young 2007).

ANS: A

Scenario 5

"Japanese frequently bow to one another—for instance, when greeting someone—as a gesture of respect and sincerity. The type of bow depends on the formality of the situation, the type of personal relationship (e.g., close or distant), and the differences in social status of the individuals involved. The bow might be no more than a simple nod of the head or, on more formal occasions, a deeper bow from the waist. The most formal bow involves kneeling, placing one's hands out in front on the floor, and lowering the head slowly so that it almost touches the floor. Bowing is not always required, however. Family members and close friends do not usually bow to each other, but a child might bow to his or her mother when apologizing for mischievous behavior" (Japan Information Center 1988:61).

ANS: C

Short Essay Questions

1. Why were North and South Korea chosen to illustrate the concept of culture?

2. How is the word "culture" typically used among English speakers?

3. What three conceptual challenges do sociologists face in defining culture?

4. Distinguish between nonmaterial and material culture.

5. Distinguish between beliefs and values. Give an example of each.

6. What are norms? Distinguish between folkways and mores.

7. What are symbols? Is language a symbol? Explain.

8. How do geographical and historical forces shape culture?

9. Explain: "Regardless of their physical traits, babies are destined to learn the ways of the culture into which they are born and raised."

10. In what ways does language channel thinking?

11. What is the linguistic relativity hypothesis?

12. How are people products of cultural experiences, yet not cultural replicas of one another?

13. Explain: "All cultures have developed formulas to help their members respond to biological inevitabilities."

14. What makes an emotion social? What is the connection between feeling rules and social emotions?

15. What is diffusion? Give two examples of the diffusion process. Why is diffusion a selective process?

16. Give two examples of opportunities for cultural diffusion between Americans and South Koreans.

17. What is culture shock? How is it related to ethnocentrism?

18. What are the various types of ethnocentrism? Give examples of each. (Don't forget reverse ethnocentrism.)

19. Explain reentry shock.

20. What viewpoint should one take when studying other cultures?

21. Is cultural relativism equivalent to moral relativism? Explain.

22. What are subcultures? When are subcultures institutionally complete?

Comprehensive Essay Questions

1. Imagine that you have been asked to present a seminar to a group of people planning to visit another culture. What 5 concepts or points in the culture chapter would you emphasize in your presentation?

2. If you were a high school language teacher, what would you say to your class on the first day to impress upon them that learning a language is also learning a culture?

3. Imagine you are a consultant to the author of *Sociology: A Global Perspective*. Recommend a country to replace the focus country of Chapter 3. Write the "Why Focus on" segment to make your case.

Chapter 4

Socialization

Multiple-Choice Questions

1. The conflict between Israelis and Palestinians has lasted _____ years.
   a. 100
   b. 50
   c. 25
   d. 5

   ANS: A   PG: 85   TYP: knowledge

2. In Israel and the Palestinian Territories, Sesame Street airs as Sesame Stories because
   a. the featured scenes in the program involve Palestinians and Israelis reading stories to one another.
   b. the idea that a "street" exists where Palestinians and Israelis might gather together is not a possibility.
   c. there is no word for street in Hebrew or in the Arabic languages.
   d. Sesame Street formed a partnership with the corporation Sesame Stories.

   ANS: A   PG: 85   TYP: knowledge

3. Most children are biologically ready to show concern for what adults regard as the rules of life when they are
   a. born.
   b. about two years old.
   c. about six years old.
   d. about 16 years old.

   ANS: B   PG: 86   TYP: knowledge

4. Socialization takes hold through a process known as
   a. internalization.
   b. nature.
   c. nurture.
   d. social contact.

   ANS: D   PG: 86   TYP: comprehension

5. The process by which people take as their own and accept as binding the norms, values, beliefs, and language needed to participate in the larger community is termed
   a. adaptation.
   b. internalization.
   c. assimilation.
   d. acculturation.

   ANS: B   PG: 85   TYP: comprehension   SOURCE: study guide

6. _____ in the West Bank, Gaza, and East Jerusalem represent one of the most difficult issues of the peace process.
   a. Israeli settlements
   b. The high death rates
   c. The rapidly increasing elderly populations
   d. The electrified fences

   ANS: A   PG: 88   TYP: knowledge   SOURCE: new

7. Both Israelis and Palestinians claim _____ as their capital.
   a. Jericho
   b. Bethlehem
   c. the West Bank
   d. Jerusalem

   ANS: D   PG: 88   TYP: knowledge

Chapter 4

8. _____ represents one of the most difficult issues of the Palestinian-Israeli peace process.
   a. Solving ethnic and cultural differences
   b. Religious misunderstanding
   c. The status of Jerusalem
   d. The difference in language

   ANS: C   PG: 88   TYP: knowledge

9. In studying the Israeli-Palestinian conflict, sociologists ask all but which one of the following questions?
   a. How do members learn about and come to terms with the environment they have inherited?
   b. How is conflict passed down from one generation to another?
   c. What roles do nature and nurture play in creating a "Palestinian" and an "Israeli" identity?
   d. Why can't we all just get along?

   ANS: D   PG: 85   TYP: comprehension   SOURCE : study guide

10. The West Bank Barrier is
    a. a term used to describe the Palestinian resistance to the peace process.
    b. the electrified razor wires, trenches, and concrete walls that wind and snake through the West Bank.
    c. a psychological barrier that keeps Palestinians from feeling sympathy for Israelis.
    d. a psychological barrier that keeps Israelis from feeling sympathy for Palestinians.

    ANS: B   PG: 88   TYP: knowledge

11. Jerusalem is located
    a. in Gaza.
    b. on the border of Gaza and Israel proper.
    c. in the West Bank.
    d. on the border of the West Bank and Israel proper.

    ANS: D   PG: 88   TYP: knowledge

12. _____ refers to the environment or the interaction experiences that make up every individual's life.
    a. Nature
    b. Nurture
    c. Engram
    d. Internalization

    ANS: B   PG: 86   TYP: knowledge

13. _____ is the term for human genetic makeup or biological inheritance.
    a. Nature
    b. Nurture
    c. Internalization
    d. Socialization

    ANS: A   PG: 86   TYP: comprehension   SOURCE: study guide

14. Nature refers to _____, and nurture refers to _____.
    a. learned traits; inborn traits
    b. genetic factors; environmental factors
    c. interaction factors; biological factors
    d. social capacities; biological potential

    ANS: B   PG: 86   TYP: comprehension

15. The part of the human brain that allows us to organize, remember, communicate, understand, and create is
    a. the cerebral cortex.
    b. the central processing unit.
    c. the stem.
    d. grey matter.

    ANS: A   PG: 86   TYP: knowledge

Chapter 4

16. Babies are able to babble the sounds needed to speak all languages
    a. at birth.
    b. in the first months of life.
    c. at age one.
    d. at age two.

    ANS: B   PG: 86   TYP: knowledge

17. The _____ allows us to organize, remember, communicate, understand, and create.
    a. cortex
    b. cerebral cortex
    c. left side of the brain
    d. right side of the brain

    ANS: B   PG: 86   TYP: knowledge   SOURCE: study guide

18. Tiffany's parents introduced her to soccer as soon as she was able to walk. This strategy corresponds to
    a. nurture.
    b. nature.
    c. social contact.
    d. engrams.

    ANS: A   PG: 86   TYP: application

19. Anna was described as having "no glimmering of speech, absolutely no ability to walk, no sense of gesture, nor the least capacity to feed herself even when food was put in front of her, and no comprehension of cleanliness." Anna's desperate state can be traced to a lack of
    a. collective memory.
    b. nature.
    c. social contact.
    d. engrams.

    ANS: C   PG: 86   TYP: application   SOURCE : new

20. The cases of Anna and Isabelle were used to illustrate
    a. the importance of social contact for normal development.
    b. the fact that humans are born with a great learning capacity.
    c. that people are born with preconceived notions about standards of appearance and behavior.
    d. that two-year-olds are bothered when rules are violated.

    ANS: A   PG: 87   TYP: knowledge   SOURCE: study guide

21. _____ are Jewish populated communities in the Palestinian Territories.
    a. Settlements
    b. Kibbutzes
    c. Engrams
    d. Expatriates

    ANS: A   PG: 89   TYP: knowledge   SOURCE: new

22. _____ is classified as a terrorist organization by Israel, United States, and the European Union.
    a. Fatah
    b. Kibbutz
    c. Hamas
    d. The Palestinian Party

    ANS: C   PG: 89   TYP: knowledge   SOURCE: new

23. _____ control(s) the West Bank, and _____ control(s) the Gaza Strip.
    a. Fatah; Hamas
    b. Kibbutz; Engrams
    c. Hamas; Fatah
    d. Palestinians; Israelis

    ANS: A   PG: 89   TYP: knowledge   SOURCE: study guide

Chapter 4

24. Palestinians registered as refugees with the UN seek
    a. to become citizens of Israel.
    b. the right to return to the land within Israel from which they fled or were evicted.
    c. to swap Gaza for Israel proper.
    d. the right to live in various locations around the world.

    ANS: B   PG: 89   TYP: knowledge   SOURCE: new

25. Rene Spitz studied 91 physically and emotionally normal infants who were placed in orphanages because of unfortunate circumstances. A significant number of these children died because
    a. their basic physical needs were not met.
    b. they were malnourished.
    c. they suffered emotional starvation due to lack of physical contact.
    d. they contracted measles from one another due to crowded conditions.

    ANS: C   PG: 88   TYP: knowledge

26. A bond of mutual expectation is established between caregiver and baby when
    a. a caregiver knows the baby well enough to understand its needs and feelings.
    b. the baby is put on a strict feeding and sleeping schedule.
    c. the baby learns to talk to the caregiver.
    d. the caregiver can leave the baby alone in a room without the baby crying.

    ANS: A   PG: 90   TYP: comprehension

27. Which one of the following scenarios indicates that a bond of mutual expectation has developed between a baby and his or her caretaker?
    a. A baby learns to comfort itself when it feels distress.
    b. A baby cannot tell how its mother will react to its cries.
    c. A baby sleeps through the night.
    d. A baby comes to expect that if it cries, a caretaker will offer comfort.

    ANS: D   PG: 90   TYP: application   SOURCE: study guide

28. Memory is stored in
    a. neurons.
    b. glial cells.
    c. engrams.
    d. nerve cells.

    ANS: C   PG: 91   TYP: knowledge

29. _____ is the sociological term for experiences shared and recalled by significant numbers of people.
    a. Group memory
    b. Community memory
    c. Historical memory
    d. Collective memory

    ANS: D   PG: 91   TYP: comprehension

30. In Israel, there are 900 memorials to the war dead. Memorials are a vehicle for preserving and recalling shared experiences also known as
    a. reflexive thinking.
    b. active adaptation.
    c. collective memory.
    d. internalization.

    ANS: C   PG: 91   TYP: application

31. Displaced Palestinians pass on memories of their homeland by showing their children keys and deeds to the houses in which they once lived. This sharing preserves and passes on
    a. reflexive thinking.
    b. active adaptation.
    c. collective memory.
    d. internalization.

    ANS: C   PG: 91   TYP: application

Chapter 4

32. A cultural center located in the West Bank has established a memorial honoring the lives of Palestinians killed in the second *intifada*. The memorial serves as a vehicle for instilling
    a. active adaptation.
    b. reflective thinking.
    c. engrams.
    d. collective memory.

    ANS: D   PG: 91   TYP: application   SOURCE: study guide

33. From a sociological viewpoint, memory of past experiences is important to society because it
    a. shapes individuals' unique character.
    b. allows individuals to participate in society and shape their environment.
    c. allows people to store experiences unique to their lives.
    d. sheds light on the biological quality of memory.

    ANS: B   PG: 91   TYP: comprehension

34. When author David Grossman asked a group of Palestinian children in a West Bank refugee camp to tell him their birthplace, each replied with the name
    a. Palestine.
    b. Israel.
    c. of a former Arab town.
    d. Jerusalem.

    ANS: C   PG: 91   TYP: knowledge

35. The Holocaust claimed the lives of more than 6 million Jews. That figure represents approximately _____ of European Jews.
    a. one-half
    b. 90 percent
    c. one-third
    d. 10 percent

    ANS: C   PG: 92   TYP: knowledge

36. The _____ increased the flow of Jewish refugees to Palestine during World War II.
    a. Six Day War
    b. dropping of the atomic bomb
    c. Nazi Holocaust
    d. *Intifada*

    ANS: C   PG: 92   TYP: knowledge

37. The state of Palestine ceased to exist, and Israel came into being in _____ after the Jews defeated the Arab armies.
    a. 1898
    b. 1987
    c. 1948
    d. 1540

    ANS: C   PG: 92   TYP: knowledge

38. The _____ voted in 1947 to partition Palestine into two independent states: one Jewish and the other Palestinian.
    a. Arab States
    b. World Bank
    c. G-8
    d. United Nations

    ANS: D   PG: 92   TYP: knowledge

39. The Miami Beach Holocaust Memorial is a copper green hand reaching toward the heavens with human figures climbing up the forearm. The design calls out to those that visit it to remember the Nazi's mass slaughtering of Jews and other groups during World War II. The monument relates to a process known as
    a. nurture.
    b. nature.
    c. collective memory.
    d. resocialization.

    ANS: C   PG: 93   TYP: application   SOURCE: new

Chapter 4

40. According to George Herbert Mead, the "me" is the part of the self that
    a. is spontaneous and creative.
    b. acts in unconventional ways.
    c. develops through imitation, play, and games.
    d. is capable of rejecting expectations.

    ANS: C   PG: 94   TYP: comprehension   SOURCE: study guide

41. According to George Herbert Mead, the _____ takes chances and violates expectations.
    a. "me"
    b. "I"
    c. "we"
    d. "self"

    ANS: B   PG: 94   TYP: application

42. George Herbert Mead maintained that children acquire a sense of self when they "become objects to themselves." This means that
    a. children are able to mimic and imitate others in their environment.
    b. the spontaneous, creative self must exist.
    c. children must be able to imagine the effect of their words and actions on other people.
    d. the children have developed a strong tie with a caring adult.

    ANS: C   PG: 94   TYP: comprehension

43. A student expressed her shock over a test grade by exclaiming to the class and professor, "A 50! I skipped two classes to study for this stupid test!" George Herbert Mead would argue that this remark is a product of the student's
    a. "I."
    b. "me."
    c. reflexive thinking.
    d. looking-glass self.

    ANS: A   PG: 94   TYP: concept application

44. George Herbert Mead wrote, "It is impossible to conceive of a self arising outside of social experience." This statement emphasizes the importance of
    a. nature.
    b. nurture.
    c. internalization.
    d. engrams.

    ANS: B   PG: 94   TYP: comprehension

45. Language, facial expressions, tone of voice, and posture are all examples of
    a. socialization.
    b. significant symbols.
    c. reflexive thinking.
    d. role taking.

    ANS: B   PG: 93   TYP: comprehension   SOURCE: study guide

46. From the sociological point of view, Mead viewed play and games as important to children's social development because they
    a. give them practice in agility.
    b. increase motor skills.
    c. help develop mental toughness.
    d. allow children to learn and practice taking the role of the other.

    ANS: D   PG: 94   TYP: comprehension

47. The stage at which children are unable to take the role of the other is the
    a. preparatory stage.
    b. play stage.
    c. game stage.
    d. looking-glass self stage.

    ANS: A   PG: 94   TYP: comprehension

Chapter 4

48. In this stage, children have <u>not</u> yet developed the mental capabilities that allow them to role-take. This stage is the
    a. play stage.
    b. preparatory stage.
    c. game stage.
    d. presocialization stage.

    ANS: B   PG: 94   TYP: comprehension

49. Tyler sits at the computer, mimicking the behavior of her mother. Tyler's family encourages this by telling her how cute she is. Tyler is in the
    a. preparatory stage.
    b. play stage.
    c. game stage.
    d. looking-glass self stage.

    ANS: A   PG: 94   TYP: application   SOURCE: study guide

50. Palestinian children that pretend to be Israeli soldiers arresting and beating stone throwers are in the _____ stage.
    a. preparatory
    b. play
    c. game
    d. looking-glass self

    ANS: B   PG: 96   TYP: comprehension

51. The three stages of role-taking (in the correct sequence) are
    a. play–preparatory–game.
    b. game–play–imitation.
    c. preparatory–play–game.
    d. reflexive thinking–internalization–socialization.

    ANS: C   PG: 96   TYP: knowledge

52. The preparatory, play, and game stages allow children to practice
    a. internalization.
    b. collective memory.
    c. imitation.
    d. role-taking.

    ANS: D   PG: 94   TYP: comprehension

53. When children are in the game stage, they
    a. engage in voluntary, spontaneous activity with few or no formal rules.
    b. practice fitting their behavior into an established behavior system.
    c. pretend to be significant others.
    d. have not yet developed the mental capabilities that allow them to role-take.

    ANS: B   PG: 96   TYP: comprehension

54. During the game stage, children learn
    a. to make up rules as they go.
    b. to mimic and imitate people in their environment.
    c. to pretend to be people significant in their lives.
    d. to see how their position fits relative to all other positions.

    ANS: D   PG: 96   TYP: comprehension   SOURCE: study guide

55. In this stage, children practice fitting their behavior into an already established behavior system that governs a game, such as baseball. This stage is the
    a. play stage.
    b. preparatory stage.
    c. game stage.
    d. post-socialization stage.

    ANS: C   PG: 96   TYP: application

Chapter 4

56. Which one of the following is a characteristic of games?
    a. spontaneous
    b. rules can change
    c. established rules and roles
    d. few or no formal rules

    ANS: C   PG: 96   TYP: comprehension

57. Palestinian and Israeli children, like children everywhere, learn to sing patriotic songs and say prayers before they can understand the words. This occurs when children are in the _____ stage.
    a. preparatory
    b. role-taking
    c. play
    d. game

    ANS: A   PG: 95   TYP: application   SOURCE: new

58. Which of the following is a characteristic of play?
    a. spontaneous
    b. established rules
    c. set roles
    d. formal rules

    ANS: A   PG: 96   TYP: comprehension   SOURCE: new

59. Charles Horton Cooley and George Herbert Mead would agree that
    a. the self is a product of social experiences.
    b. personality is primarily a product of biological drives.
    c. interaction has little or no impact on personality.
    d. nature is more important than nurture.

    ANS: A   PG: 97   TYP: knowledge

60. An Israeli soldier observes that some Palestinian girls are frightened to death when he is standing in their path. The soldier is engaging in
    a. socialization.
    b. internalization.
    c. role-taking.
    d. collective memory.

    ANS: C   PG: 97   TYP: application   SOURCE: study guide

61. Charles Horton Cooley, who wrote about the looking-glass self, goes so far as to argue that the solid facts of social life are the facts of
    a. memory.
    b. cognition.
    c. biology.
    d. the imagination.

    ANS: D   PG: 97   TYP: knowledge

62. Which one of the following statements is <u>false</u> in regard to Charles Horton Cooley's conception of the looking-glass self?
    a. We see ourselves reflected in others' reactions to our appearance and behaviors.
    b. We acquire a sense of self by being sensitive to the appraisals of us that we perceive others to have.
    c. The imagining or interpreting of others' reactions is critical to self-awareness.
    d. People respond to others' *actual* reactions to them.

    ANS: D   PG: 97   TYP: comprehension

63. _____ coined the term "looking-glass self."
    a. Charles Horton Cooley
    b. George Herbert Mead
    c. Renee Spitz
    d. Jean Piaget

    ANS: A   PG: 97   TYP: knowledge

Chapter 4

64. Piaget's ideas about how children develop were inspired by his study of
    a. water snails.
    b. monkeys.
    c. pigeons.
    d. zoo babies.

    ANS: A   PG: 98   TYP: knowledge

65. Which one of the following statements is a characteristic of Piaget's model of cognitive development?
    a. Cognitive development involves three broad stages.
    b. A child can proceed from one stage to another, even if reasoning challenges of an earlier stage are not mastered.
    c. A more sophisticated level of cognitive understanding will not show itself until the brain is ready.
    d. The theme of ingroup-outgroup runs through all stages.

    ANS: C   PG: 98   TYP: knowledge

66. Which one of the following thinkers is associated with the concept of "active adaptation"?
    a. Erving Goffman
    b. Charles Horton Cooley
    c. George H. Mead
    d. Jean Piaget

    ANS: D   PG: 98   TYP: knowledge   SOURCE: study guide

67. Piaget's model of cognitive development includes four broad stages. Those stages, in correct order, are
    a. sensorimotor—preoperational—concrete operational—formal operational.
    b. formal operational—sensorimotor—preoperational—concrete operational.
    c. concrete operational—preoperational—formal operational—sensorimotor.
    d. preoperational—sensorimotor—formal operational—concrete operational.

    ANS: A   PG: 98   TYP: comprehension

68. Piaget maintained that learning and reasoning are rooted in
    a. reflexive thinking.
    b. role-playing.
    c. active adaptation.
    d. the looking-glass self.

    ANS: C   PG: 98   TYP: comprehension

69. During the _____ stage of cognitive development, children believe that objects removed from sight no longer exist.
    a. sensorimotor
    b. preoperational
    c. concrete operational
    d. formal operational

    ANS: A   PG: 98   TYP: comprehension

70. A very young child acts as if an object does not exist when she can no longer see it. She is in the _____ stage.
    a. sensorimotor
    b. preoperational
    c. concrete operational
    d. formal operational

    ANS: A   PG: 98   TYP: application

71. A six-year-old believes that a nail sinks to the bottom of the glass because it is tired. That child is in the _____ stage.
    a. sensorimotor
    b. preoperational
    c. concrete operational
    d. formal operational

    ANS: B   PG: 99   TYP: application

72. Desmond has trouble envisioning a life without him in it. He notes, "I am the beginning and the end; the world begins and ends with me." This thinking is characteristic of the _____ stage.
    a. sensorimotor
    b. preoperational
    c. concrete operational
    d. formal operational

    ANS: C   PG: 99   TYP: application

73. _____ shape(s) our sense of self and teach(es) us about the groups to which we do and do not belong.
    a. Scapegoats
    b. The looking-glass self
    c. Symbolic gestures
    d. Agents of socialization

    ANS: D   PG: 100   TYP: comprehension   SOURCE: new

74. Significant others, primary groups, ingroups and outgroups, and institutions, such as mass media, are known as
    a. scapegoats.
    b. the looking-glass self.
    c. significant symbols.
    d. agents of socialization.

    ANS: D   PG: 100   TYP: application   SOURCE: study guide

75. When Israeli and Palestinian children dream about meeting one another, the other appears in their dreams as
    a. a friend.
    b. a classmate.
    c. a terrorist or an oppressor.
    d. a relative.

    ANS: C   PG: 102   TYP: knowledge   SOURCE: new

76. The family is an important _____ group.
    a. primary
    b. intimate
    c. secondary
    d. out-

    ANS: A   PG: 100   TYP: concept application

77. Researchers Ben-David and Lavee studied Israeli families to learn how members behaved toward one another during a missile attack. The researchers studied
    a. an outgroup.
    b. significant symbols.
    c. a primary group.
    d. collective memory.

    ANS: C   PG: 100   TYP: concept application

78. From a sociological point of view, a group consists of _____ or more persons who share an identity, feel a sense of belonging, and interact with one another.
    a. two
    b. six
    c. ten
    d. fifteen

    ANS: A   PG: 100   TYP: knowledge

79. Which of the following is not a primary group?
    a. military unit
    b. family
    c. McDonald's
    d. basketball team

    ANS: C   PG: 100   TYP: comprehension

Chapter 4

80. Sociologists Amith Ben-David and Yoah Lavee's study in which they describe how Israeli family members interacted with one another during the SCUD missile attack shows that the family
    a. can serve to buffer its members against the effects of negative circumstances or can exacerbate those effects.
    b. is a supportive and positive influence during a crisis.
    c. increases the stress of a crisis.
    d. becomes divided and tense during a crisis.

    ANS: A   PG: 100   TYP: comprehension

81. Which one of the following is not one of the strategies the military would use to make recruits feel inseparable from their unit?
    a. have recruits wear uniforms
    b. have recruits sleep and eat together
    c. have recruits march in unison
    d. reward recruits for individual achievements

    ANS: D   PG: 101   TYP: concept application

82. Those groups with which people identify and to which they feel closely attached, particularly when that attachment is founded on hatred of another group, are
    a. essential groups.
    b. respected groups.
    c. outgroups.
    d. ingroups.

    ANS: D   PG: 101   TYP: comprehension   SOURCE: study guide

83. Which of the following best describes ingroup-outgroup dynamics?
    a. Ingroup members identify with the personal struggles of outgroup members.
    b. The existence of an outgroup can unify ingroup members.
    c. The presence of an outgroup can unify an ingroup even when the ingroup members are very different from one another.
    d. Because they hate each other, members of an ingroup and outgroup usually know a lot about one another.

    ANS: C   PG: 101   TYP: comprehension

84. Almost every Israeli can claim membership in which one of the following primary groups?
    a. a sports team
    b. a college sorority
    c. the Jewish faith
    d. a military unit

    ANS: D   PG: 101   TYP: knowledge   SOURCE: study guide

85. Carmen writes, "When I was in high school, there were different groups such as 'preps,' 'hoods,' and 'nerds.' It was easy to tell who belonged to each group simply by looking at their dress and general physical appearance. People who belonged to one group didn't have much to do with those in the other two groups." Carmen is describing
    a. collective memory.
    b. ingroup-outgroup.
    c. primary-secondary group.
    d. internalization.

    ANS: B   PG: 101   TYP: application

86. The presence of an outgroup
    a. weakens the bond between ingroup members.
    b. undermines the loyalty ingroup members feel for one another.
    c. magnifies the characteristics that distinguish an ingroup from an outgroup.
    d. takes away an ingroup's sense of purpose.

    ANS: C   PG: 101   TYP: comprehension

87. Dr. Yorum Bilu analyzed the contents of over 300 dreams and found that when Palestinians and Jews dream about one another,
    a. the characters in the dream have names that are familiar to the dreamer.
    b. the majority of interactions deal with trying to establish friendships.
    c. the characters in the dream are described as "the terrorists" or "the oppressors."
    d. they dream of solving their differences.

    ANS: C   PG: 102   TYP: knowledge

Chapter 4

88. _____ describes a state in which ties attaching the individual to others in the society are weak.
    a. Egoistic
    b. Altruistic
    c. Anomic
    d. Fatalistic

    ANS: A   PG: 103   TYP: knowledge

89. _____ is the opposite of egoistic.
    a. Anomic
    b. Fatalistic
    c. Altruistic
    d. Retreatist

    ANS: C   PG: 103   TYP: comprehension

90. Often members of ingroups and outgroups clash over symbols. The _____ was the focus of many conflicts between Israelis and Palestinians.
    a. wall or barrier
    b. hijab
    c. passport
    d. color black

    ANS: A   PG: 103   TYP: knowledge

91. Which one of the following characteristics does not apply to ingroup-outgroup relationships?
    a. Boundaries between the two groups are sharp.
    b. There is little interaction between ingroup-outgroup members.
    c. Ingroup and outgroup members know a lot about one another.
    d. Often one group has superior economic or political status over the other.

    ANS: C   PG: 103   TYP: comprehension

92. The social ties of the chronically ill are characterized as _____ when family, friends, and other acquaintances avoid interacting with them.
   a. egoistic
   b. altruistic
   c. anomic
   d. fatalistic

   ANS: A   PG: 103   TYP: application

93. _____ describes a state in which there is no hope of change.
   a. Anomic
   b. Fatalistic
   c. Altruistic
   d. Egoistic

   ANS: B   PG: 103   TYP: knowledge   SOURCE: study guide

94. The Palestinian suicide bomber/martyr is motivated by
   a. despair.
   b. poverty.
   c. revenge for acts committed by Israelis.
   d. religious fervor.

   ANS: C   PG: 104   TYP: comprehension

95. Suicide bombers/martyrs are glorified and lionized by the Palestinian population. This fact suggests that these suicides can be classified as
   a. anomic.
   b. fatalistic.
   c. altruistic.
   d. egoistic.

   ANS: C   PG: 104   TYP: application

Chapter 4

96. About 86 percent of Palestinian suicide bombers/martyrs are single. This fact suggests that, on some level, their social ties are
    a. anomic.
    b. fatalistic.
    c. altruistic.
    d. egoistic.

    ANS: D   PG: 104   TYP: application

97. Examples of _____ include magazines, newspapers, commercials, radio broadcasts, and cartoon characters.
    a. significant symbols
    b. mass media
    c. primary groups
    d. total institutions

    ANS: B   PG: 104   TYP: application   SOURCE: new

98. _____ are forms of communication designed to reach large audiences without requiring face-to-face contact between those conveying and receiving the messages.
    a. Significant symbols
    b. Mass media
    c. Primary groups
    d. Total institutions

    ANS: B   PG: 104   TYP: comprehension   SOURCE: new

99. Which area of the world is most likely to have the highest Internet penetration rates?
    a. North America
    b. Middle East
    c. Africa
    d. Asia

    ANS: A   PG: 105   TYP: knowledge   SOURCE: study guide

100. Which area of the world is most likely to have the lowest Internet penetration rates?
    a. North America
    b. Middle East
    c. Africa
    d. Asia

    ANS: C   PG: 105   TYP: knowledge   SOURCE: new

101. _____ is the most watched children's show, airing in 120 countries.
    a. Barney
    b. Mr. Rogers
    c. Sesame Stories
    d. Sesame Street

    ANS: D   PG: 105   TYP: knowledge   SOURCE: new

102. _____ is the United States city with the largest Jewish population in the world.
    a. Miami
    b. New York
    c. San Francisco
    d. Boston

    ANS: B   PG: 109   TYP: knowledge   SOURCE: study guide

103. Government-instigated massacres and persecution against Jews is known as
    a. cultural genocide.
    b. a pogrom.
    c. institutional completeness.
    d. material culture.

    ANS: B   PG: 109   TYP: knowledge

104. During _____ of the life cycle, consistent and predictable care is most critical.
    a. Stage 6, Young adulthood
    b. Stage 5, Adolescence
    c. Stage 4, Ages 6-12
    d. Stage 1, Infancy

    ANS: D   PG: 107   TYP: comprehension   SOURCE: new

Chapter 4

105. _____ of the life cycle is characterized by rapid body growth.
    a. Stage 6, Young adulthood
    b. Stage 5, Adolescence
    c. Stage 4, Ages 6-12
    d. Stage 1, Infancy

    ANS: B   PG: 107   TYP: comprehension   SOURCE: new

106. Ideally, during _____ of the life cycle, people make an effort to guide and help establish the next generation.
    a. Stage 6, Young adulthood
    b. Stage 7, Middle Age
    c. Stage 8, Old Age
    d. Stage 5, Young adulthood

    ANS: B   PG: 107   TYP: comprehension   SOURCE: new

107. The birth rate is highest in which one of the following areas?
    a. Gaza
    b. West Bank
    c. Israel
    d. Jordan

    ANS: A   PG: 108   TYP: knowledge   SOURCE: new

108. The fertility rate is lowest in which one of the following areas?
    a. Gaza
    b. West Bank
    c. Israel
    d. Jordan

    ANS: C   PG: 108   TYP: knowledge   SOURCE: new

109. The largest percentage of the 65 and older population is found in which one of the following areas?
    a. Gaza
    b. West Bank
    c. Israel
    d. Jordan

    ANS: C   PG: 108   TYP: knowledge   SOURCE: new

110. The percentage of the population living in poverty is highest in which one of the following areas?
    a. Gaza
    b. West Bank
    c. Israel
    d. Jordan

    ANS: A   PG: 108   TYP: knowledge

111. The country with the largest number of Jews residing in it is
    a. Gaza.
    b. West Bank.
    c. the United States.
    d. Israel.

    ANS: C   PG: 109   TYP: knowledge   SOURCE: new

112. People who choose to participate in a process or program designed to remake them undergo _____ resocialization.
    a. systematic, voluntary
    b. involuntary
    c. informal, systematic
    d. voluntary, informal

    ANS: A   PG: 109   TYP: comprehension

Chapter 4

113. Mental hospitals, concentration camps, and boarding schools are
    a. voluntary organizations.
    b. outgroups.
    c. primary groups.
    d. total institutions.

    ANS: D   PG: 110   TYP: application

114. _____ is the process of discarding values and behaviors unsuited to new circumstances and replacing them with new, more appropriate values and norms.
    a. Reflexive thinking
    b. Role-taking
    c. Ethnocentrism
    d. Resocialization

    ANS: D   PG: 109   TYP: comprehension

115. Homes for the blind, indigent, and elderly are examples of
    a. engrams.
    b. collective settings.
    c. primary groups.
    d. total institutions.

    ANS: D   PG: 110   TYP: application

116. Which one of the following examples is a case of involuntary or imposed resocialization?
    a. A person seeks treatment to correct a problem.
    b. A college graduate enrolls in medical school.
    c. A person is forced to undergo a program to rehabilitate him or her.
    d. A person enlists in the army to acquire a technical skill.

    ANS: C   PG: 110   TYP: application

117. _____ wrote *Asylums: Essays on the Social Situation of Mental Patients and Other Inmates*.
   a. Erving Goffman
   b. George Herbert Mead
   c. Charles Horton Cooley
   d. Jean Piaget

   ANS: A   PG: 110   TYP: knowledge

118. Upon entering a total institution, inmates experience a
   a. sense of euphoria.
   b. deep, initial break with past roles.
   c. new beginning.
   d. sense of deep relief.

   ANS: B   PG: 110   TYP: comprehension

119. It is easier to resocialize a person if learning a new behavior
   a. is connected to making another party happy.
   b. requires a person to be subservient to another.
   c. leads to a sense of self-worth and competence.
   d. does not take much personal effort.

   ANS: C   PG: 111   TYP: comprehension

Multiple Choice Questions on the Web

1. Socialization ends
   a. around age six.
   b. during the teenage years.
   c. in middle adulthood.
   d. at death.

   ANS: D   PG: 86   TYP: comprehension

Chapter 4

2. Mary was born with blue eyes and blond hair. These characteristics describe
   a. socialization.
   b. internalization.
   c. nature.
   d. nurture.

   ANS: C   PG: 86   TYP: application

3. Cases of extreme isolation teach us that people need
   a. caretakers free of speaking or hearing impairments.
   b. a certain amount of "space."
   c. their physical needs met.
   d. meaningful social contact with others.

   ANS: D   PG: 87   TYP: comprehension

4. Which of the following statements is *true* about memory?
   a. For the most part, scientists know how memory works.
   b. Engrams store 'actual' records of past events.
   c. Fortunately, a person can participate in society without memory.
   d. We take it for granted that people have important social information stored in memory.

   ANS: D   PG: 91   TYP: knowledge

5. Author David Grossman observed that the Palestinian children in a West Bank refugee camp were taught to say the name of a former Arab town when asked their place of birth. Some children in the camp were also named after former Arab cities and towns. This example shows how _____ is passed on and recast from one generation to the next.
   a. symbolic gesture
   b. reflexive thinking
   c. collective memory
   d. an engram

   ANS: C   PG: 93   TYP: concept application

6. The stage at which children pretend to be significant others is the
   a. preparatory stage.
   b. play stage.
   c. game stage.
   d. looking-glass self stage.

   ANS: B   PG: 96   TYP: comprehension

7. Israeli children repeat that "Jerusalem is the capital of Israel" before they even understand what the statement means. The children are in the _____ stage.
   a. preparatory
   b. role-taking
   c. play
   d. game

   ANS: A   PG: 95   TYP: application

8. According the theory of the looking-glass self, _____ is critical to self-awareness.
   a. imitation
   b. imagining others' reactions
   c. rejection of others' opinions
   d. independent thought

   ANS: B   PG: 97   TYP: knowledge

9. Groups that are characterized by face-to-face contact and strong emotional ties among members are
   a. intimate groups.
   b. primary groups.
   c. outgroups.
   d. secondary groups.

   ANS: B   PG: 100   TYP: comprehension

Chapter 4

10. The country with the largest Jewish population in the world is
    a. Russia.
    b. the United States.
    c. Israel.
    d. Germany.

    ANS: B   PG: 109   TYP: knowledge

True/False Questions

1. The Israeli-Palestinian conflict has lasted for 20 years.

    ANS: False   PG: 85   SOURCE: study guide

2. Socialization is a life-long process.

    ANS: True   PG: 86

3. Human infants are born with the biological potential to learn any language.

    ANS: True   PG: 86

4. In the first weeks of life, babies are able to babble the sounds needed to speak any language.

    ANS: True   PG: 86   SOURCE: study guide

5. Nature, as opposed to nurture, is the more important factor in socialization.

    ANS: False   PG: 86

6. Socialization depends on meaningful interaction experiences with others.

    ANS: True   PG: 87

7. The West Bank Barrier separates the West Bank from Israel.

    ANS: True   PG: 88   SOURCE: new

8. Gaza and the West Bank are geographically separate territories.

    ANS: True   PG: 88   SOURCE: new

9. The political party Fatah is backed by Syria and Iran.

    ANS: False   PG: 89   SOURCE: study guide

10. Meaningful social contact and stimulation from others are important at any age.

    ANS: True   PG: 90

11. Memories are stored in engrams (physical traces in the brain), just as films are stored on videocassette tapes.

    ANS: False   PG: 91

12. The Nazi Holocaust is the event that gave a desperate urgency to what is known as the Jewish return movement.

    ANS: True   PG: 92

13. Language is a particularly important significant symbol.

    ANS: True   PG: 93   SOURCE: study guide

14. The "me" is the social self; the "I" is the spontaneous self.

    ANS: True   PG: 94

Chapter 4

15. During the preparatory stage, children practice taking the role of the significant other.

    ANS: False   PG: 94

16. During the game stage, children learn to take the role of the significant other.

    ANS: False   PG: 96   SOURCE: study guide

17. Through play, children learn to organize their behavior around the generalized other.

    ANS: False   PG: 96   SOURCE: new

18. Piaget maintained that reasoning abilities cannot be hurried.

    ANS: True   PG: 98

19. Piaget's ideas about how children develop increasingly sophisticated levels of reasoning stemmed from his study of water snails.

    ANS: True   PG: 98

20. Sociologists classify the family and the military unit as primary groups.

    ANS: True   PG: 100   SOURCE: new

21. If their primary groups remain intact, children can emerge from widespread turmoil, violence, and destruction in relatively good psychological condition.

    ANS: True   PG: 101   SOURCE: study guide

22. Military units train their recruits to think of their own personal safety over that of the group.

    ANS: False   PG: 101

23. The majority of Jews that live in Israel are native to the land.

    ANS: False   PG: 101

24. "Israeli Palestinian" is the label the Israeli government applies to the Palestinians living in Israel that did not leave in 1948.

    ANS: False   PG: 102   SOURCE: new

25. Unless exempt, Israeli men serve on active duty for at least one month every year until they are 51 years old.

    ANS: True   PG: 103

26. Israeli women are exempt from military service.

    ANS: False   PG: 103

27. From a sociological point of view, suicide is the severing of relationships.

    ANS: True   PG: 103   SOURCE: study guide

28. For suicide bombers/martyrs, despair is the factor that best explains their willingness to die.

    ANS: False   PG: 104

29. More than 80 percent of suicide bombers/martyrs are unmarried.

    ANS: True   PG: 104   SOURCE: study guide

30. In Israel and the Palestinian Territories, Sesame Street airs as Sesame Stories.

    ANS: True   PG: 105   SOURCE: new

Chapter 4

31. Sesame Street airs in about 20 countries worldwide.

    ANS: False   PG: 96   SOURCE: new

32. The infant mortality rate is higher among the Israeli population than among the Palestinian population.

    ANS: False   PG: 108

33. A greater percentage of Israelis than Palestinians are age 65 and over.

    ANS: True   PG: 108

34. If all goes well, in Stage 8 (Old Age), a person comes to accept the life he or she has lived.

    ANS: True   PG: 108   SOURCE: study guide

35. The "total" character of total institutions is symbolized by barriers to social interaction, such as locked doors, fences, and high walls.

    ANS: True   PG: 110

36. Total institutions seek to increase the inmates' interactions with those on the outside.

    ANS: False   PG: 110

37. Mental hospitals, concentration camps, and boarding schools are primary groups.

    ANS: False   PG: 110   SOURCE: study guide

38. Palestinians and Israelis have relied largely on resocialization measures that attempt to force the other side to change.

    ANS: True   PG: 111

Concept Application (also in study guide)

Consider the concepts listed below. Match one or more of the concepts with each scenario. Explain your choices.

a. Collective memory
b. Nature
c. Nurture
d. Resocialization
e. Total institutions
f. Anomic social relationships
g. Altruistic social relationships

Scenario 1
"In 1910, two French surgeons wrote about their successful operation on an 8-year-old boy who had been blind since birth because of cataracts. When the boy's eyes were healed, they removed the bandages, eager to discover how well the child could see. Waving a hand in front of the boy's physically perfect eyes, they asked him what he saw. He replied weakly, 'I don't know.' 'Don't you see it moving?' they asked. 'I don't know,' was his only reply. The boy's eyes were clearly not following the slowly moving hand. What he saw was only a varying brightness in front of him. He was then allowed to touch the hand. As it began to move, he cried out in a voice of triumph: 'It's moving!' He could feel it move, and even, as he said, 'hear it move,' but he still needed laboriously to learn to see it move" (Zajonc 1993:22).

ANS: B, C, D

Scenario 2
"Let me say to you, the Palestinians, we are destined to live together on the same soil in the same land. We the soldiers who have returned from battles stained with blood; we who have seen our relatives and friends killed before our eyes; we who have attended their funerals and cannot look into the eyes of their parents; we who have come from a land where parents bury their children; we who have fought against you, the Palestinians" (Rabin 1993:A7).

ANS: A

Scenario 3

"Genetic endowments may set limits for the height or intelligence that individuals can attain, but their actual height or intelligence also depends upon how they are raised. The increasing height of the American population over the past several generations reflects the change in nutritional conditions and probably the diminution in childhood illnesses more than a genetic selection" (Lidz 1976:40).

    ANS: B, C

Scenario 4

"Hospitals with hundreds, even thousands of inpatients, maintain schedules aimed at ensuring that every patient receives essential care, and the staff must fit the needs and daily activities of dying patients into the hospital's schedule. They tend to require all patients, whether terminal or not, to give up virtually all personal control over the little things that make up their day-to-day lives. The kinds of personal items that can make a big difference, such as your own pillow from home, are often not allowed. Visits by children may be curtailed, and having a pet stay with a dying person is prohibited. Activities, such as walking, eating, bathing, and any physical exercise will proceed according to an established routine" (Anderson 1991:144).

    ANS: D, E

Scenario 5

Some events are experienced by great numbers of people, diverse in interest, age, race, ethnicity, lifestyle and life chances, gender, language, and place, who temporarily become bound together by a historical moment. The January 28, 1986, Space Shuttle Challenger disaster was such a moment. Collectively, the country grieved, and not for the first time. Many still vividly remember—and will quickly confess, when the subject comes up—exactly where they were, what they were doing, and how they felt when they heard about the tragedy. The initial shock was perpetuated by the television replays of the Challenger's final seconds, by the anguished faces of the astronauts' families and other onlookers huddled in disbelief on bleachers at the launch pad, by the news analyses, and then by the official investigation of the Presidential Commission (Vaughn 1996:xi).

    ANS: A

Scenario 6

"Around 400 volunteers signed up in Tehran to sacrifice their lives in "occupied Islamic countries" on Wednesday night, inspired by a fatwa from a top hardline cleric giving religious backing to suicide missions. Wednesday's registration session was the latest by a group called the Committee for the Commemoration of Martyrs of the Global Islamic Campaign, which says it has enrolled 35,000 volunteers nationwide for possible attacks since last year... 'As a Muslim, it is my duty to sacrifice my life for oppressed Palestinian children,' said Maryam Partovi, 31, a mother of two. A banner hanging over the main entrance quoted Khamenei as saying, 'Sacrificing oneself for religion and national interest is the height of honour and bravery.'"

ANS: G

Short Essay Questions

1. Why are Israel and the Palestinian Territories paired with the concept socialization?

2. What is socialization?

3. Distinguish between nature and nurture.

4. How do extreme cases of isolation underscore the importance of socialization? Choose one of the following cases to illustrate: (a) Anna and Isabelle; (b) children orphaned as a result of the Holocaust; (c) Spitz's study of orphanages for children of prison mothers; and (d) the elderly in nursing homes.

5. On the basis of Anna and Isabelle's case histories, what conclusions did Kingsley Davis reach about the effects of prolonged isolation?

6. What are the basic dynamics underlying the century-long struggle between Palestinian Arabs and Jews? What kinds of issues must be resolved if the peace process is to move forward?

7. What is the social importance of memory?

8. Define collective memory. How is collective memory passed on?

Chapter 4

9. What are significant symbols?

10. Distinguish between the "I" and the "me." How does the "me" develop?

11. What is role-taking? What are the stages by which children come to learn to take the role of others?

12. According to Charles Horton Cooley's "Looking Glass-Self" theory, how does a sense of self develop?

13. What central concept underlies Piaget's theory of cognitive development? What are the four stages of cognitive development?

14. What are agents of socialization?

15. What are primary groups? How are they important agents of socialization?

16. What characteristics make a military unit a primary group?

17. What are ingroups and outgroups? What is their sociological significance?

18. How does Emile Durkheim define suicide? What are the four types?

19. How might Durkheim classify the ties that bind Palestinian suicide bombers/martyrs to the group?

20. What is the mass media? How does it affect the sense of self and individuals' relationships to others?

21. Why is *Sesame Street* called *Sesame Stories* in Israel and the Palestinian Territories?

22. Briefly summarize the eight stages of life cycle.

23. What is resocialization? What are the types of resocialization?

24. What are total institutions? What mechanisms do total institutions use to resocialize inmates?

25. Under what conditions are people least likely to resist resocialization?

Comprehensive Essay Questions

1. After reading about the century-long conflict between Palestinians and Israelis, which term—suicide bomber or martyr—better captures the underlying dynamics of this dramatic act?

2. Discuss at least three ways that long-standing conflicts between groups are passed down from one generation to another.

3. Think about a personal acquaintance or celebrity who has committed suicide. Use Durkheim's theory of suicide to analyze the relationships that were severed by the act.

Chapter 5

Social Interaction

Multiple-Choice Questions

1. The Democratic Republic of the Congo is located in _____ Africa.
    a. northern
    b. west
    c. the southern tip of
    d. central

    ANS: D   PG: 117   TYP: knowledge

2. The Congo is emphasized in Chapter 5 ("Social Interaction) because
    a. HIV originated in the Congo.
    b. HIV "traveled" from Europe to the Congo.
    c. a blood sample frozen in 1959 and stored in a Congo blood bank provides evidence that HIV existed before the 1980s.
    d. HIV traveled from the Congo to Cuba to the United States.

    ANS: C   PG: 117   TYP: knowledge   SOURCE: study guide

3. AIDS researchers believe that the story of HIV/AIDS started in which one of the following African countries?
    a. Cameroon
    b. Democratic Republic of the Congo
    c. The Belgian Congo
    d. Zaire

    ANS: A   PG: 117   TYP: knowledge   SOURCE: new

4. AIDS researchers believe that the global epidemic known as HIV/AIDS started in which one of the following years?
   a. 1930
   b. 1960
   c. 1980
   d. 1989

   ANS: A   PG: 117   TYP: knowledge   SOURCE: new

5. The global story of the transmission of HIV/AIDS revolves around the theme of
   a. social interaction.
   b. significant others.
   c. homosexuality.
   d. heterosexuality.

   ANS: A   PG: 117   TYP: comprehension

6. To get at the _____ of HIV/AIDS, sociologists ask, "What circumstances drew people from different counties and continents to the Congo?"
   a. global story
   b. solidarity
   c. back stage
   d. front stage

   ANS: A   PG: 118   TYP: knowledge   SOURCE: new

7. Since 1959, the estimated number of worldwide HIV/AIDS cases has risen from one known case to _____ known cases.
   a. 1 billion
   b. 55 million
   c. 10 million
   d. 5 million

   ANS: B   PG: 117   TYP: knowledge

8. Situations in which at least two people communicate and respond through language and symbolic gestures to affect one another's thinking and behavior are termed
   a. social intervention.
   b. social interaction.
   c. social manipulation.
   d. impression management.

   ANS: B   PG: 118   TYP: comprehension

9. _____ wrote *The Division of Labor in Society*.
   a. Karl Marx
   b. Max Weber
   c. Emile Durkheim
   d. C. Wright Mills

   ANS: C   PG: 118   TYP: knowledge   SOURCE: study guide

10. *The Division of Labor in Society* offers a framework for understanding
    a. the forces underlying global-scale interactions.
    b. front stage-back stage behavior.
    c. the dramaturgical perspective.
    d. the exact cause of HIV and AIDS.

    ANS: A   PG: 118   TYP: application   SOURCE: new

11. Division of labor refers to specialization with respect to all *but* which one of the following?
    a. the work required to complete a specific task
    b. raw materials
    c. parts needed to produce a product
    d. mechanical solidarity

    ANS: D   PG: 118   TYP: comprehension

12. In *The Division of Labor*, Durkheim observed that an increase in _____ intensified the demand for resources.
    a. population size and density
    b. capital
    c. division of labor
    d. specialization

    ANS: A   PG: 118   TYP: comprehension

13. In what year was an HIV-infected blood sample found in a Congo blood bank?
    a. 1920
    b. 1946
    c. 1959
    d. 1972

    ANS: C   PG: 117   TYP: knowledge   SOURCE: new

14. The Congo was once a colony of
    a. the United States.
    b. France.
    c. Italy.
    d. Belgium.

    ANS: D   PG: 119   TYP: knowledge

15. King Leopold II claimed the Congo as his private property. His reign over the land has been described as
    a. important to the economic progress of the Belgian Congo.
    b. the vilest scramble for loot that ever disfigured the history of human conscience and geographical location.
    c. putting the Congo and its people in the modern world.
    d. the event that led to the formation of a democratic form of government.

    ANS: B   PG: 119   TYP: knowledge   SOURCE: study guide

Chapter 5

16. The _____ River is known as the "river that swallows all rivers" or Central Africa.
    a. Sudan
    b. Congo
    c. Ugandan
    d. Tanzania

    ANS: B		PG: 120		TYP: knowledge		SOURCE: new

17. Emile Durkheim used the general term _____ to describe the ties that bind people to one another in a society.
    a. social interaction
    b. solidarity
    c. context
    d. content

    ANS: B		PG: 121		TYP: comprehension		SOURCE: study guide

18. Solidarity is a term used by Durkheim to refer to
    a. a characteristic of hunting and gathering societies.
    b. the ties that bind people to one another in a society.
    c. specialization of work tasks.
    d. mechanization.

    ANS: B		PG: 121		TYP: comprehension

19. _____ derives from a simple division of labor.
    a. Mechanical solidarity
    b. Organic solidarity
    c. Specialization
    d. Global interdependence

    ANS: A		PG: 121		TYP: comprehension

20. A simple division of labor causes people to be
    a. extremely different from one another.
    b. suspicious of one another.
    c. reflexive thinkers.
    d. more alike than different.

    ANS: D		PG: 121		TYP: comprehension

Social Interaction

21. The Mbuti pygmies are a hunting and gathering people who share
    a. an exploitive value system.
    b. a forest-oriented value system.
    c. a capitalist value system.
    d. a Muslim faith.

    ANS: B   PG: 121   TYP: knowledge

22. "For the Mbuti, the forest is sacred. It is the very source of their existence... Young or old, male or female... the Mbuti talk, shout, whisper, and sing to the forest, addressing it as mother or father or both." This description of the Mbuti and their forest-centered values represents an example of
    a. mechanical solidarity.
    b. organic solidarity.
    c. the division of labor.
    d. role strain.

    ANS: A   PG: 121   TYP: application

23. Social order and cohesion based on a common conscience or uniform thinking and behavior is
    a. organic solidarity.
    b. mechanical solidarity.
    c. division of labor.
    d. social interaction.

    ANS: B   PG: 121   TYP: comprehension

24. In societies characterized by mechanical solidarity, the ties that bind people together are based primarily on
    a. kinship and religion.
    b. occupation.
    c. agriculture and friendship.
    d. social status and the division of labor.

    ANS: A   PG: 121   TYP: comprehension

Chapter 5

25. _____ interactions mean that people interact with one another for a specific reason, not to get to know each other.
    a. Front stage
    b. Back stage
    c. Common conscience
    d. Instrumental

    ANS: D   PG: 122   TYP: comprehension   SOURCE: new

26. Durkheim wrote that a person's "first duty is to resemble everybody else—to not have anything personal about one's core beliefs and actions." Durkheim was writing about
    a. the division of labor.
    b. specialization.
    c. mechanical solidarity.
    d. organic solidarity.

    ANS: C   PG: 121   TYP: comprehension   SOURCE: study guide

27. In societies characterized by organic solidarity, the ties that bind individuals to one another are based primarily on
    a. kinship.
    b. religion.
    c. specialized roles.
    d. a shared way of life.

    ANS: C   PG: 122   TYP: comprehension

28. In societies characterized by_____, people relate to one another in terms of their specialized roles.
    a. mechanical solidarity
    b. organic solidarity
    c. the division of labor
    d. role strain

    ANS: B   PG: 122   TYP: comprehension

29. A complex division of labor _____ among people.
    a. increases differences
    b. increases similarities
    c. decreases differences
    d. decreases interdependence

    ANS: A   PG: 122   TYP: comprehension

30. Which one of the following words corresponds to organic solidarity?
    a. similarity
    b. conflict
    c. specialized roles
    d. common conscience

    ANS: C   PG: 122   TYP: comprehension

31. In societies characterized by _____, social ties remain strong because people need one another to survive.
    a. mechanical solidarity
    b. common conscience
    c. organic solidarity
    d. role strain

    ANS: C   PG: 122   TYP: comprehension

32. In societies characterized by _____, people find that they must depend on others that they do not know personally. Social ties remain strong because people need one another.
    a. imperialism
    b. organic solidarity
    c. mechanical solidarity
    d. colonization

    ANS: C   PG: 122   TYP: comprehension

Chapter 5

33. In *Division of Labor*, Durkheim argued that societies become more vulnerable as the division of labor becomes more complex and specialized. He was particularly concerned about the kinds of events that
    a. promote self-sufficiency.
    b. increase independence among people.
    c. increase differences among people.
    d. break down people's ability to connect to one another in meaningful ways through their labor.

    ANS: D   PG: 122   TYP: comprehension

34. According to Durkheim, the vulnerability of societies _____ as the division of labor becomes more complex and specialized.
    a. decreases
    b. remains the same
    c. increases
    d. increases but eventually decreases

    ANS: C   PG: 122   TYP: comprehension   SOURCE: study guide

35. Which of the following events was not defined by Durkheim as causing disruptions to the division of labor in industrial societies?
    a. industrial and commercial crisis
    b. strikes
    c. extreme job specialization
    d. positions filled on the basis of achieved characteristics

    ANS: D   PG: 122   TYP: comprehension

36. HIV's origin must be placed in the context of
    a. sexual practices of African people.
    b. European colonial rule of Africa.
    c. bizarre African cultural practices.
    d. the European failure to civilize the people of the Congo.

    ANS: B   PG: 122   TYP: comprehension   SOURCE: new

37. The biographies of Joel Goddard (a laid-off Ford worker) and an African fisherman who escapes a colonial patrol demanding he meet a rubber quota are both shaped by
   a. role strain.
   b. role conflict.
   c. scapegoating.
   d. disruptions to the division of labor.

   ANS: D   PG: 122   TYP: comprehension   SOURCE: new

38. Which one of the following disruptions to the division of labor occurs when workers are so isolated that few people grasp the workings and consequences of the overall enterprise?
   a. job specialization
   b. industrial and commercial crises
   c. inefficient management of worker talents
   d. forced division of labor

   ANS: A   PG: 122   TYP: application   SOURCE: study guide

39. Historically, disease patterns are affected by
   a. economic and social isolation.
   b. the extent to which a society depends on Western medicine.
   c. changes in population density and transportation patterns.
   d. the quality of health care professionals.

   ANS: C   PG: 125   TYP: comprehension

40. According to UN data, the countries with the largest percentages of adults with HIV/AIDS are
   a. Asian.
   b. North American.
   c. Sub-Saharan African.
   d. Eastern European and former Soviet Union countries.

   ANS: C   PG: 126   TYP: knowledge   SOURCE: new

Chapter 5

41. The purpose of the 1885 Berlin West African Conference was to
    a. divide the African continent among colonial powers.
    b. set up trade regulations between Africa and Europe.
    c. plan World War I.
    d. end slavery.

    ANS: A   PG: 118   TYP: knowledge

42. After achieving independence in 1960, the Belgian Congo became
    a. the Democratic Republic of Congo.
    b. the Congo.
    c. Zaire.
    d. the Congo Republic.

    ANS: C   PG: 124   TYP: knowledge   SOURCE: study guide

43. The Congo is referred to as the site of
    a. the worst AIDS/HIV epidemic in Africa.
    b. the richest African country.
    c. innovation against HIV.
    d. Africa's First World War.

    ANS: D   PG: 124   TYP: knowledge

44. Sociologists use the word *social status* to mean
    a. a role.
    b. a rank.
    c. prestige.
    d. a position in a social structure.

    ANS: D   PG: 125   TYP: comprehension

45. In which of the following countries was the medical condition HIV/AIDS was *first* noticed in the late 1980s?
    a. the United States
    b. People's Republic of China
    c. Belgium
    d. Haiti

    ANS: B   PG: 126   TYP: knowledge   SOURCE: study guide

46. _____ consists of two or more people interacting and interrelating in specific, expected ways, regardless of their unique personalities.
    a. Role set
    b. Impression management
    c. Social structure
    d. Social behavior

    ANS: C   PG: 125   TYP: comprehension

47. Joel Goddard is a laid-off Ford worker, a male, a father, an unemployed individual, and a husband. This sentence describes Goddard's
    a. achieved statuses.
    b. ascribed statuses.
    c. status set.
    d. social structure.

    ANS: C   PG: 125   TYP: application   SOURCE: new

48. Ascribed statuses result from
    a. chance.
    b. effort.
    c. ability.
    d. choice.

    ANS: A   PG: 127   TYP: comprehension   SOURCE: new

49. Achieved statuses result from
    a. chance.
    b. luck.
    c. fate.
    d. ability.

    ANS: D   PG: 127   TYP: comprehension   SOURCE: new

Chapter 5

50. Sometimes one status in a status set is so important to a person's social identity, it overshadows all other statuses a person occupies. That "so important" status is known as a(n) _____ status.
    a. achieved
    b. ascribed
    c. master
    d. premier

    ANS: C   PG: 127   TYP: comprehension   SOURCE: new

51. Between 1884 and 1960, black Congolese and other Africans who migrated to the Belgian colony were least likely to occupy which one of following positions?
    a. steamboat captain
    b. porter
    c. low- to mid-level technical staff
    d. rubber gatherers

    ANS: A   PG: 127   TYP: comprehension   SOURCE: new

52. The distinction between role and status is subtle: people _____ statuses and _____ roles.
    a. occupy; enact
    b. enact; occupy
    c. choose; take on
    d. take on; choose

    ANS: A   PG: 128   TYP: comprehension

53. A(n) _____ is behavior expected of a status in relation to another social status.
    a. attribution
    b. role
    c. obligation
    d. right

    ANS: B   PG: 128   TYP: comprehension

54. When physicians knowingly perform unnecessary surgery, overmedicate, engage in sexual relations with patients, or break confidentiality, they have
    a. failed to meet role obligations.
    b. experienced role strain.
    c. no right to demand patient cooperation.
    d. achieved role conflict.

    ANS: A   PG: 128   TYP: application   SOURCE: new; study guide

55. When patients do not give honest answers to questions their physicians ask, and they do not comply with treatment plans, they have
    a. failed to meet role obligations.
    b. experienced role strain.
    c. no right to demand patient cooperation.
    d. achieved role conflict.

    ANS: A   PG: 128   TYP: application   SOURCE: new

56. The _____ associated with a role define(s) what a person assuming that role can demand or expect from others.
    a. role set
    b. social structure
    c. rights
    d. obligations

    ANS: C   PG: 128   TYP: comprehension

57. Role _____ is a predicament in which contradictory expectations are associated with a single role.
    a. conflict
    b. reversal
    c. enactment
    d. strain

    ANS: D   PG: 128   TYP: comprehension

Chapter 5

58. Role _____ is a predicament in which expectations associated with two or more roles in a role set contradict one another.
    a. conflict
    b. reversal
    c. enactment
    d. strain

    ANS: A   PG: 128   TYP: comprehension

59. As a patient, Tosen has a(n) _____ to make and keep an appointment, to comply with the treatment plan, and to want to get better.
    a. role strain
    b. obligation
    c. right
    d. role conflict

    ANS: B   PG: 128   TYP: application

60. When a professor fails to prepare for class,
    a. students' rights are violated.
    b. students' obligations are violated.
    c. students do not have to uphold their obligation to study.
    d. social structures collapse.

    ANS: A   PG: 128   TYP: application

61. Which one of the following generalizations is least characteristic of Western-style medicine?
    a. Western physicians rely heavily on technological tools to diagnose and treat illness.
    b. The major objective of the patient-physician interaction is to determine the exact physiological problem.
    c. Tremendous effort is devoted to finding a technological solution to illness.
    d. When diagnosing illness, Western physicians attach considerable importance to the patient's social relationships and psychological distress.

    ANS: D   PG: 129   TYP: comprehension   SOURCE: study guide

62. One of the most grisly policies of _____ rule over the Congo was to sever the right hands of any Congolese people who refused to gather rubber.
    a. Laurent Kabila's
    b. Mobutu's
    c. King Leopold's
    d. Joseph Kabila's

    ANS: C   PG: 128   TYP: knowledge   SOURCE: new

63. Western medicine is shaped by a profound cultural belief in
    a. the body's ability to heal on its own.
    b. the ability of technology to solve medical problems.
    c. self-medication.
    d. alternative medicine.

    ANS: B   PG: 129   TYP: knowledge

64. The United States, with less than 5 percent of the world's population, consumes an estimated _____ percent of the world's pharmaceutical supply.
    a. 20
    b. 33
    c. 44
    d. 55

    ANS: C   PG: 129   TYP: knowledge

65. As a patient, Shelby has an obligation to follow her doctor's treatment plan. However, her prescribed drug makes her feel very drowsy, preventing her from carrying out her role as a mother. Shelby feels she is not alert enough to properly care for her daughter. Shelby is experiencing
    a. role strain.
    b. status inconsistency.
    c. a role set.
    d. role conflict.

    ANS: D   PG: 128   TYP: application

Chapter 5

66. In contrast to Western-oriented physicians, traditional healers
    a. fail to recognize the organic and physical aspects of disease.
    b. rely on technology to treat patients.
    c. are "quacks."
    d. attach considerable importance to social relationships and psychological distress.

    ANS: D   PG: 129   TYP: comprehension

67. Which one of the following traits distinguishes Western-trained physicians from traditional healers?
    a. Healers concentrate on finding a cure, not on the relief of symptoms.
    b. Healers rely on drugs, not on surgery, to cure a condition.
    c. Healers attach considerable importance to factors other than biology, such as social relationships.
    d. Healers are ineffective at relieving symptoms.

    ANS: C   PG: 128   TYP: comprehension

68. Western-trained physicians working in the Congo's urban hospitals are
    a. more successful than traditional healers.
    b. less likely to succeed if they consider other models of sickness.
    c. likely to achieve better health outcomes if the patient's relatives are kept on the sidelines.
    d. most successful when they tolerate, respect, and consider other models of illness.

    ANS: D   PG: 129   TYP: knowledge

69. The _____ model corresponds to the perspective in which social interaction is viewed as though it is taking place in a theater.
    a. dramaturgical
    b. historical
    c. cultural strain
    d. division of labor

    ANS: A   PG: 130   TYP: comprehension   SOURCE: study guide

Social Interaction

70. On the first day of class, Professor Smith always wears a tie to convey that he is serious about his job. On the other hand, he gives out his home number as a way of letting students know that he is approachable. Professor Smith is engaged in
    a. backstage behavior.
    b. impression management.
    c. role strain.
    d. role conflict.

    ANS: B   PG: 130   TYP: application   SOURCE: study guide

71. Which one of the following statements about impression management is true?
    a. Most people do not engage in impression management.
    b. Impression management can be constructive.
    c. Most people manipulate their audiences in deliberately deceitful ways.
    d. If people spoke and behaved as they pleased, relationships would become more open.

    ANS: B   PG: 131   TYP: comprehension   SOURCE: new

72. _____ is a useful concept for understanding the dilemma that sexual partners face when one partner suggests using a condom as a precautionary condition of sexual intercourse.
    a. Role
    b. Impression management
    c. Social structure
    d. Role strain

    ANS: B   PG: 131   TYP: application   SOURCE: new ; study guide

73. _____ is the sociologist associated with the dramaturgical model of social interaction.
    a. Erving Goffman
    b. Emile Durkheim
    c. Randy Shilts
    d. Neil Postman

    ANS: A   PG: 131   TYP: knowledge   SOURCE: new

Chapter 5

74. In the *Colonial Disease*, Maryinez Lyons argues that it "is vital to understand the profound importance and depth of this Congolese belief regarding cause and treatment" of disease. What is that belief?
    a. The Western physician is superior to the African healer.
    b. Technologies, such as CAT scans and vaccines, are crucial to treating disease.
    c. Curing disease is more important than preventing it.
    d. Chronic illnesses, such as sleeping sickness, are man made.

    ANS: D   PG: 130   TYP: concept   SOURCE: new

75. In the backstage, people
    a. are on their best behavior.
    b. "let their hair down."
    c. behave appropriately.
    d. follow the "rules."

    ANS: B   PG: 133   TYP: comprehension

76. For the most part, impression management is
    a. manipulative and deceitful.
    b. a premeditated line of action.
    c. a normal feature of social interaction.
    d. something sincere people never do.

    ANS: C   PG: 131   TYP: comprehension

77. From a sociological point of view, restaurant kitchen employees who eat food from customers' plates are engaging in _____ behavior.
    a. frontstage
    b. backstage
    c. upfront
    d. negligent

    ANS: B   PG: 131   TYP: application   SOURCE: study guide

78. The front stage is the area
    a. out of the audience's sight.
    b. where people take care to create and maintain expected images and behavior.
    c. where individuals can "let their hair down."
    d. that people take great care to conceal from the audience.

    ANS: B   PG: 131   TYP: comprehension

79. The _____ is the region visible to an "audience."
    a. backstage
    b. frontstage
    c. middle stage
    d. off stage

    ANS: B   PG: 131   TYP: comprehension

80. King Leopold presented his interests in the Congo to the public as purely philanthropic. Among other things, he used the International African Association as a front for his profit-making ventures. He promised to establish medic posts and scientific centers. In reality, he used the most brutal methods to take everything from the Congolese people. By presenting himself as philanthropist, Leopold engaged in
    a. frontstage behavior.
    b. solidarity.
    c. impression management.
    d. backstage behavior.

    ANS: C   PG: 131   TYP: application   SOURCE: new

81. Tyrone states, "When I do not think a police officer is around, I drive 90 to 95 miles per hour on the highway. I weave in and out of lanes, and I tailgate. I keep a radar detector on so I know when to drive more slowly and more safely." Tyrone is describing
    a. role strain.
    b. role conflict.
    c. backstage behavior.
    d. frontstage behavior.

    ANS: C   PG: 132   TYP: application

Chapter 5

82. _____ is considered one of the world's earliest and best success stories in overcoming HIV.
    a. The Democratic Republic of Congo
    b. Zimbabwe
    c. Kenya
    d. Uganda

    ANS: D   PG: 132   TYP: knowledge

83. Uganda is considered a success story with regard to lowering the prevalence of HIV/AIDS. The country did this by
    a. prohibiting media campaigns to increase AIDS awareness.
    b. asking faith-based leaders to condemn those with AIDS.
    c. banning condoms.
    d. establishing Africa's first confidential voluntary counseling and testing service.

    ANS: D   PG: 132   TYP: knowledge   SOURCE: new

84. Attributing cause to _____ factors functions to reduce uncertainty about the source and spread of disease.
    a. dispositional
    b. situational
    c. backstage
    d. contextual

    ANS: A   PG: 133   TYP: comprehension   SOURCE: study guide

85. Don does poorly on a test. He attributes his failure to his heavy work schedule. Don's explanation focuses on
    a. situational factors.
    b. dispositional factors.
    c. genetic disposition.
    d. historical forces.

    ANS: A   PG: 133   TYP: application

86. Don's professor believes that Don failed his exam because he doesn't care about school. The professor's explanation focuses on
    a. situational factors.
    b. dispositional factors.
    c. genetic disposition.
    d. historical forces.

    ANS: B   PG: 133   TYP: application

87. Ramona claims she failed a biology exam because her professor can't explain the subject matter and asks tricky questions. Ramona is attributing her failure to
    a. role strain.
    b. role conflict.
    c. dispositional factors.
    d. situational factors.

    ANS: D   PG: 133   TYP: application

88. A theoretical approach that helps us understand how we arrive at our everyday explanations of behavior is
    a. role theory.
    b. the dramaturgical approach.
    c. attribution theory.
    d. game theory.

    ANS: C   PG: 133   TYP: comprehension

89. Dispositional traits include
    a. bad luck.
    b. personality traits.
    c. environmental factors.
    d. chance.

    ANS: B   PG: 133   TYP: comprehension

90. Situational factors include
    a. bad luck.
    b. mood.
    c. innate ability.
    d. personal shortcomings.

    ANS: A   PG: 133   TYP: comprehension

91. For the most part, people tend to explain their own *failures* by referring to
    a. situational factors.
    b. dispositional factors.
    c. genetic factors.
    d. personal shortcomings.

    ANS: A   PG: 133   TYP: application

92. Bad luck is an example of
    a. a situational factor.
    b. a dispositional factor.
    c. a genetic factor.
    d. historical forces.

    ANS: A   PG: 133   TYP: comprehension

93. Isiah argues that HIV-infected people earned their disease as a penalty for their perverse, indulgent, and illegal behaviors. Isiah is attributing HIV to
    a. dispositional factors.
    b. situational factors.
    c. role conflict.
    d. role strain.

    ANS: A   PG: 133   TYP: application   SOURCE: study guide

94. The Thomas theorem states: If people define situations as real, they are
    a. usually not real.
    b. real in their consequences.
    c. constructed realities.
    d. imaginary.

    ANS: B   PG: 133   TYP: application   SOURCE: new

95. In sociological terms, a(n) _____ is a person or a group that is assigned blame for conditions that threaten a community's sense of well-being or shake the foundations of a trusted institution.
    a. attribution
    b. target
    c. scapegoat
    d. disposed person

    ANS: C   PG: 134   TYP: comprehension   SOURCE: study guide

96. Official definitions of AIDS have all but which of the following consequences?
    a. They affect the way in which the condition is defined.
    b. They influence statistics about who has AIDS.
    c. They affect the content of the physician-patient relationship (e.g., whether the physician asks a patient to be HIV-tested).
    d. They encourage people in low-risk groups to agree to random blood tests for HIV infection.

    ANS: D   PG: 135   TYP: knowledge

97. We now know that 50 percent of _____ were HIV-infected before the first case of AIDS appeared in this group.
    a. homosexuals
    b. hemophiliacs
    c. Haitians
    d. drug users

    ANS: B   PG: 136   TYP: knowledge   SOURCE: study guide

98. Until 1993, the official definition of AIDS did not include HIV-related gynecological disorders, such as cervical cancer, as one of the conditions that constituted a diagnosis of AIDS. This example shows
    a. AIDS is "moving" beyond homosexuals.
    b. high-risk sexual activity is related to cervical cancer.
    c. gynecologists were slow to learn about HIV's effects on women.
    d. that attribution about who "should" have AIDS affects the way AIDS is defined.

    ANS: D   PG: 135   TYP: comprehension

Chapter 5

99. The U.S. supplies about _____ percent of the world's blood and blood products.
    a. 10
    b. 15
    c. 25
    d. 60

    ANS: D   PG: 136   TYP: knowledge   SOURCE: study guide

100. In 1981, the year HIV was discovered and that scientists first learned that it was in the blood supply, Japan imported _____ percent of its blood and blood products from the U.S.
    a. 20
    b. 40
    c. 70
    d. 98

    ANS: D   PG: 136   TYP: knowledge

101. _____ are the most dependable method for determining the number of HIV-infected persons.
    a. Educated guesses
    b. Questionnaires
    c. Participant observations
    d. Random samplings of blood

    ANS: D   PG: 137   TYP: knowledge

102. Upon learning that someone is HIV-positive, situational thinkers would react by
    a. saying the diagnosis is a penalty for perverse behavior.
    b. connecting the condition to "gay" behavior.
    c. reminding the person that the origin of HIV lies with bizarre African rituals.
    d. considering the historical and social circumstances that put this person at risk.

    ANS: D   PG: 135   TYP: application

103. AIDS stands for Acquired Immunodeficiency Syndrome. Acquired means that the disease
    a. develops after birth from contact with a disease-causing agent.
    b. is the result of factors over which people have no control.
    c. is the result of a genetic predisposition.
    d. symptoms vary from person to person.

    ANS: A   PG: 143   TYP: knowledge   SOURCE: new

104. An HIV-infected person receives a diagnosis of AIDS after
    a. testing positive twice.
    b. 10 years, regardless of whether or not he or she is sick.
    c. a doctor determines the cause of the infection.
    d. developing one of the 25 CDC-defined AIDS indicator illnesses.

    ANS: D   PG: 143   TYP: knowledge   SOURCE: new

Multiple Choice Questions on the Web

1. Focusing on the Congo and its relationship to other countries helps us to
    a. identify exactly who is responsible for AIDS.
    b. understand how AIDS became a global epidemic.
    c. understand why Africa is the "cradle of AIDS."
    d. understand why AIDS is a predominantly homosexual disease in the U.S and throughout the world.

    ANS: B   PG: 117   TYP: comprehension

2. _____ gives us a general framework for understanding both global interdependence and conditions that cause large-scale upheaval.
    a. *The Division of Labor*, by Emile Durkheim
    b. *The Sociological Imagination*, by C. Wright Mills
    c. *Das Kapitol*, by Karl Marx
    d. *The Communist Manifesto*, by Karl Marx

    ANS: A   PG: 118   TYP: knowledge

Chapter 5

3. Ultimately, the Europeans vigorously colonized much of Asia, Africa, and the Pacific in the late nineteenth and early twentieth centuries because of
   a. their superior intellect.
   b. a need to help the less "civilized" peoples.
   c. a growing demand for resources and low cost (even free) labor.
   d. the human need to explore the unknown.

   ANS: C   PG: 119   TYP: knowledge

4. Which one of the following phrases does not correspond to mechanical solidarity?
   a. uniform thinking
   b. common conscience
   c. interdependence and cooperation
   d. simple division of labor

   ANS: C   PG: 121   TYP: comprehension

5. The common conscience of the Mbuti revolves around
   a. the sea.
   b. the forest.
   c. mines.
   d. nature in general.

   ANS: B   PG: 121   TYP: knowledge

6. Examples of _____ include doctor-patient, professor-student, a family, and a large corporation.
   a. social status
   b. social structure
   c. organic solidarity
   d. mechanical solidarity

   ANS: B   PG: 122   TYP: application

Social Interaction

7. Between 1884 and 1960, white Belgian males were most likely to occupy which one of the following positions?
   a. steamboat captain
   b. porter
   c. low- to mid-level technical staff
   d. rubber gatherers

   ANS: A   PG: 127   TYP: comprehension

8. Jerome and Rhonda are military doctors. As physicians, they have an obligation to preserve life. At the same time, they are employed to care for patients who are often deliberately placed in health-threatening situations. The predicament represents an example of role
   a. strain.
   b. conflict.
   c. obligation.
   d. rights.

   ANS: A   PG: 128   TYP: application

9. People usually attribute cause to either dispositional traits or situational factors. Dispositional factors include which one of the following?
   a. bad luck
   b. social facts
   c. personal effort
   d. larger social forces

   ANS: C   PG: 133   TYP: knowledge

10. The fact that U.S. blood companies failed to test the blood already stored in their inventories after agreeing to screen for HIV infection suggests that they were motivated by
    a. a wish to induce worldwide panic.
    b. ignorance.
    c. limitations in technologies.
    d. profit.

    ANS: D   PG: 135   TYP: comprehension

Chapter 5

True/False Questions

1. HIV's origin cannot be understood apart from European colonial rule of Africa.

    ANS: True   PG: 117   SOURCE: new; study guide

2. AIDS researchers believe that the story of this global epidemic started in southeastern Cameroon around 1981 when the virus "jumped" from a chimpanzee to a human host.

    ANS: False   PG: 117   SOURCE: new

3. The purpose of the West Africa Conference in 1885 was to divide Africa among competing European powers.

    ANS: True   PG: 118   SOURCE: new; study guide

4. King Leopold was considered a benevolent ruler that looked after the best interests of the Congolese people.

    ANS: False   PG: 117   SOURCE: new

5. The capital city of the Belgian Congo was Leopoldville.

    ANS: True   PG: 120   SOURCE: new

6. The Mbuti pygmies share a forest-oriented value system.

    ANS: True   PG: 121   SOURCE: study guide

7. A society with a complex division of labor is characterized by organic solidarity.

    ANS: True   PG: 121

8. In societies characterized by mechanical solidarity, people relate to one another in terms of their specialized roles in the division of labor.

   ANS: True   PG: 122   SOURCE: new

9. By 1980, there was a Belgium-Congo air flight, which increased opportunities for interaction.

   ANS: False   PG: 120   SOURCE: new

10. Sociologists define social status as rank of prestige.

    ANS: False   PG: 125   SOURCE: study guide

11. There is no doubt that the first case of HIV originated in what is now the DRC.

    ANS: False   PG: 125   SOURCE: new

12. Travel is a potent force in the emergence of disease.

    ANS: True   PG: 125   SOURCE: new

13. In all regions of the world, "men having sex with men" is considered a main mode of HIV transmission.

    ANS: False   PG: 126   SOURCE: new

14. People enact statuses and occupy roles.

    ANS: False   PG: 127

15. In the United States, 40 percent of airline pilots are female.

    ANS: False   PG: 127   SOURCE: new; study guide

Chapter 5

16. In the United States, 45 percent of child care providers are male.

    ANS: False   PG: 127   SOURCE: new

17. Role strain is a predicament in which the expectations associated with two or more roles contradict one another.

    ANS: False   PG: 128

18. The United States, with 5 percent of the world's population, consumes 44 percent of the world's pharmaceutical supply.

    ANS: True   PG: 129

19. One of the most grisly policies of Leopold's rule was to sever the right hands of Congolese that refused to gather rubber.

    ANS: True   PG: 129   SOURCE: new

20. Traditional healers attach almost no importance to the physical aspects of diseases.

    ANS: False   PG: 129

21. The front stage is the area where individuals can "let their hair down."

    ANS: False   PG: 131

22. Upon learning their health status, nine of ten HIV-infected people do not donate blood.

    ANS: False   PG: 133   SOURCE: new; study guide

23. Impression management is always manipulative and deceitful.

    ANS: False   PG: 130

24. In Africa, sleeping sickness was considered the AIDS of the early 20th century.

    ANS: True   PG: 130   SOURCE: new

25. The Democratic Republic of the Congo is considered a success story in overcoming the HIV epidemic.

    ANS: False   PG: 132   SOURCE: new

26. Twenty percent of blood donors claim that they would have answered screening questions differently in a more private setting.

    ANS: True   PG: 133   SOURCE: study guide

27. When evaluating the causes of their own failures, people tend to favor situational factors.

    ANS: True   PG: 133   SOURCE: study guide

28. When evaluating causes of their own successes, people tend to favor dispositional factors.

    ANS: True   PG: 133

29. Dispositional factors are forces outside an individual's control.

    ANS: False   PG: 133   SOURCE: new

30. Attributions about who should have AIDS affects the way AIDS is defined and diagnosed.

    ANS: True   PG: 135   SOURCE: study guide

31. We know that 50 percent of hemophiliacs were HIV-infected by Factor VIII treatments before the first case of AIDS appeared in that group.

    ANS: True   PG: 136

Chapter 5

32. The United States is the world's largest supplier of plasma and blood products.

    ANS: True   PG: 136

33. Since 1993, HIV-positive women with cervical cancer are diagnosed as having AIDS.

    ANS: True   PG: 135

34. We simply do not know how many people are infected with HIV in the United States or worldwide.

    ANS: True   PG: 136   SOURCE; study guide

Concept Application (also in study guide)

Consider the concepts listed below. Match one or more of the concept with each scenario. Explain your choices.

   a. Dispositional traits
   b. Front stage
   c. Impression management
   d. Role strain
   e. Situational factors
   f. Social interactions

Scenario 1
   "Ten minutes after William Andrews succumbed to the poisonous concoction injected into his arm, Dr. Robert Jones performed a task from which he said he would never quite recover. He entered the chamber of death, checked the condemned man's vital signs, and confirmed that he was, in fact, dead.
   "The medical director for the Utah State Prison system did not witness the July 1992 execution, but his limited role so troubled him that he decided never again to have anything to do with a state-ordered killing.
   'It was much more stressful, much more disconcerting than I though it would be,' Jones says. 'I literally slept for a whole day afterward, and I thought, 'That's an experience in life that you don't want to have to go through again… Physicians usually try to preserve life, not end it.'

"As a prison doctor, Jones sits at the uncomfortable intersection of medicine and criminal justice. His dilemma highlights an ethical debate that is raging in the medical community: should doctors, who take the Hippocratic Oath not to harm their patients, take part in carrying out the death penalty? When state laws and regulations require physicians to be present at executions—as in California, where doctors watch the heart monitor that charts the prisoner's final moments in the gas chamber—should the physician comply?" (Stolberg 1994:E1).

ANS: D

Scenario 2

"Janet's sister, Pam, and brother, Nicholas, along with their own spouses and children, had a hard time understanding what was happening to their mother. It took them longer than it took Janet to catch on because their mother managed to do a superb job of keeping up appearances during the quarter of an hour or so each week when they spoke with her on the phone. And because they didn't want anything major to be the matter either, they weren't able to take Janet's worrying seriously for quite a long time" (Nelson and Nelson 1996:44).

ANS: B, C

Scenario 3

"Almost everybody, at some point in life, will avoid uncomfortable truths, 'edit' their own memories, mislead others, and even sometimes tell out-and-out falsehoods. And almost everybody feels uncomfortable about lying repeatedly. As Barbara wrestles with this problem, she has put herself in her dad's shoes and acknowledged that she would feel very uncomfortable if it turned out that someone was lying to her. Even so, she also knows from experience that the price of avoiding a lie can sometimes be just as high as the price of telling one.

"While people will agree that one ought to tell the truth whenever possible, it's not so easy to say precisely why that's so. To understand better whether and when it's morally okay to break the rule against lying, it's necessary to figure out just what's at stake in telling the truth or failing to do so" (Nelson and Nelson 1996:25).

ANS: C

Chapter 5

Scenario 4

"I use a wheelchair because I was paralyzed by polio 40 years ago. One of my first trips out of the hospital back then was to a supermarket. I remember I was rolling down an aisle when a kid saw me. He stopped dead in his tracks and pointed. 'Mommy,' he said in a loud voice.....and in a loud voice, 'Mommy, look at the broken man'" (Gallagher 1992).

    ANS: A

Scenario 5

"Lauren M. Cook had been participating in reenactments of famous Civil War battles for two years, and she took the hobby seriously. She spent thousands of dollars buying Civil War period clothing. She bound her breasts under her uniform so no one would know she was a woman. She even tried to adopt male mannerisms to aid her disguise. 'I would always squint,' she said. 'Women's eyes are larger than men's, so they really give you away'" (Marcus 2002).

    ANS: C

Short Essay Questions

1. Why is the Democratic Republic of the Congo the country of emphasis for the topic of social interaction?

2. What is social interaction? How do sociologists approach the study of social interaction?

3. How did Durkheim define the division of labor? How is the division of labor related to colonization?

4. How did the Democratic Republic of Congo, especially Leopoldville, become part of the global economy?

5. Distinguish between organic and mechanical solidarity.

6. What kinds of disruptions to the division of labor break down the abilities of people to connect with one another in meaningful ways through their labor?

7. How did the European-imposed forced division of labor contribute to the origin of AIDS/HIV?

8. How is the activation and spread of HIV connected to the unprecedented mixing of people from all over the world?

9. Who is responsible for triggering and transmitting HIV? Explain your answer.

10. What is a social status? How is it related to social structure?

11. How are the concepts of status, role, rights, and obligations related?

12. Distinguish between ascribed, achieved, and master statuses?

13. Distinguish between role strain and role conflict?

14. Does the idea of role imply totally predictable behavior? Explain.

15. What are the broad differences between Africa and Congolese regarding the causes and treatment of diseases?

16. What is impression management? What interaction dilemmas are associated with impression management?

17. Apply the concept of impression management to King Leopold and his interest in the Congo.

18. What is the difference between backstage and frontstage? Use these concepts to analyze answers blood donors' give to screening questions?

19. People usually attribute cause to either dispositional traits or situational factors. What is the difference between the two factors? Give an example of each.

20. What is a scapegoat? Under what conditions is a person or group likely to be made a scapegoat?

21. What problems are associated with using dispositional traits to explain the cause of AIDS and to diagnose AIDS cases?

22. How does someone get a diagnosis of AIDS? Give an example of how the definition of AIDS shapes understanding of who has AIDS?

23. What must take place before we can truly understand the cause of HIV and AIDS?

Comprehensive Essay Questions

1. Consider the information in Chapter 6. Imagine that you are asked to give a 30-minute presentation on the social origins of AIDS/HIV. What information would you be sure to include in your presentation? Why?

2. How did AIDS/HIV become a global problem in the span of less than 45 years?

Chapter 6

Formal Organizations

Multiple-Choice Questions

1. From a sociological perspective, formal organizations
    a. cannot be studied apart from the people who create them.
    b. have a life that depends on the people that belong to them.
    c. continue to exist even as their members die, quit, or return.
    d. are coordinating mechanisms without clear objectives.

    ANS: C   PG: 142   TYP: comprehension

2. The McDonald's corporation has franchises in approximately _____ countries.
    a. 55
    b. 120
    c. 220
    d. 300

    ANS: B   PG: 143   TYP: knowledge

3. From a sociological point of view, a formal organization is
    a. a legally recognized group of people.
    b. a coordinating mechanism created by people to achieve stated objectives.
    c. the building in which people meet.
    d. a money making enterprise.

    ANS: B   PG: 144   TYP: comprehension   SOURCE: study guide

4. Which of the following is the best example of a formal organization?
   a. the class of '95
   b. shoppers in a mall
   c. Wal-Mart
   d. the country of India

   ANS: C   PG: 144   TYP: application   SOURCE: study guide

5. Sociologists classify formal organizations as
   a. primary groups.
   b. secondary groups.
   c. multinational organizations.
   d. global corporations.

   ANS: B   PG: 144   TYP: comprehension   SOURCE: new

6. Primary groups are characterized by
   a. weak ties.
   b. objectivity.
   c. face-to-face contact.
   d. impersonal associations.

   ANS: C   PG: 144   TYP: comprehension   SOURCE: new

7. Family, military units, and peer groups are examples of
   a. primary groups.
   b. secondary groups.
   c. utilitarian organizations.
   d. coercive organizations.

   ANS: A   PG: 144   TYP: comprehension   SOURCE: new

8. Which one of the following is a secondary group?
   a. a family
   b. a basketball team
   c. a military unit
   d. a class of college students

   ANS: D   PG: 144   TYP: comprehension   SOURCE: new

9. If relationships between people are limited to a specific activity and setting, the people are part of a(n)
   a. primary group.
   b. secondary group.
   c. outgroup.
   d. ingroup.

   ANS: B   PG: 144   TYP: comprehension   SOURCE: new; study guide

10. The human biography can be described as a series of encounters with _____ — born in a hospital, educated in a school system, loaned money by a bank and so on.
    a. primary groups
    b. formal organizations
    c. coercive organizations
    d. government agencies

    ANS: B   PG: 144   TYP: comprehension   SOURCE: new

11. _____ draw in people who give time, talent, or treasure to support mutual interests, meet important human needs, or achieve a not-for-profit goal.
    a. Voluntary organizations
    b. Coercive organizations
    c. Utilitarian organizations
    d. Bureaucracies

    ANS: A   PG: 145   TYP: comprehension   SOURCE: new

12. _____ draw in people that have no choice but to participate.
    a. Voluntary organizations
    b. Coercive organizations
    c. Utilitarian organizations
    d. Bureaucracies

    ANS: B   PG: 145   TYP: comprehension   SOURCE: new

Chapter 6

13. _____ draw in people seeking material gain in the form of pay, health benefits, or a new status.
    a. Voluntary organizations
    b. Coercive organizations
    c. Utilitarian organizations
    d. Bureaucracies

    ANS: C   PG: 145   TYP: comprehension   SOURCE: new; study guide

14. McDonald's is an example of a(n)
    a. voluntary organization.
    b. coercive organization.
    c. utilitarian organization.
    d. bureaucracy.

    ANS: C   PG: 145   TYP: application   SOURCE: new

15. Organizations dedicated to compulsory socialization and resocialization, such as elementary schools and prisons are examples of
    a. voluntary organizations.
    b. coercive organizations.
    c. utilitarian organizations.
    d. bureaucracies.

    ANS: B   PG: 145   TYP: comprehension   SOURCE: new

16. A coordinating mechanism created by people to achieve stated objectives is a(n)
    a. assembly line.
    b. ideal type.
    c. formal organization.
    d. expert power.

    ANS: C   PG: 144   TYP: comprehension   SOURCE: new

Formal Organizations

17. A perfectly rational organization is a(n)
    a. informal organization.
    b. bureaucracy.
    c. formal organization.
    d. oligarchy.

    ANS: B   PG: 145   TYP: comprehension

18. An ideal type is
    a. a desirable standard.
    b. a standard against which real cases can be compared.
    c. a list of traits that guarantee that things run perfectly.
    d. the actual way in which an organization operates.

    ANS: B   PG: 146   TYP: comprehension

19. According to standard operating procedures, every customer at McDonald's is greeted with the words, "Welcome to McDonald's. May I take your order?" The practice corresponds with which characteristic of a bureaucracy?
    a. a clean-cut division of labor
    b. positions filled on the basis of qualification
    c. personnel treat "clients" as cases
    d. authority belongs to the position

    ANS: C   PG: 146   TYP: application   SOURCE: study guide

20. In writing about bureaucracies, Weber emphasizes that authority is located in
    a. the personal qualities a leader possesses.
    b. the position a person occupies in the division of labor.
    c. the masses.
    d. unions.

    ANS: B   PG: 146   TYP: comprehension

Chapter 6

21. A McDonald's manager has authority over employees only when they are on the time clock. This practice reflects which one of the following features of bureaucracy?
    a. a clear-cut division of labor
    b. organizational personnel treat clients as cases
    c. authority belongs to the position, not the person
    d. positions are filled on the basis of qualification

    ANS: C   PG: 146   TYP: application

22. An employee that gives friends free food and soft drinks when the manager is not looking represents an example of
    a. the informal dimension of organizations.
    b. the formal dimension of organizations.
    c. oligarchy.
    d. trained incapacity.

    ANS: A   PG: 147   TYP: application

23. The "on-paper" workings of an organization correspond with
    a. an oligarchy.
    b. an ideal type.
    c. the informal dimension of organizations.
    d. the formal dimension of organizations.

    ANS: D   PG: 147   TYP: application

24. One requirement for buying a McDonald's franchise is that an applicant must have $200,000 of unborrowed cash on hand. This requirement represents which one of the following features of a bureaucracy?
    a. a clear-cut division of labor
    b. organizational personnel treat clients as cases
    c. authority belongs to the position, not the person
    d. positions are filled on the basis of objective criteria

    ANS: D   PG: 146   TYP: application   SOURCE: new

25. In a British-based McDonald's court case, employees testified that they routinely witnessed managers and employees watering down soft drinks and failing to throw away food that had been dropped on the floor. These observations relate to
    a. oligarchy.
    b. the ideal type.
    c. the informal dimensions of organizations.
    d. the formal dimension of organizations.

    ANS: C   PG: 147   TYP: application   SOURCE: study guide

26. The _____ dimension of organizations consists of the official written guidelines, rules, regulations, and policies.
    a. formal
    b. informal
    c. scientific
    d. traditional

    ANS: A   PG: 147   TYP: comprehension

27. The informal dimension of an organization consists of
    a. written guidelines.
    b. policies that define the goals of the organization.
    c. worker-generated norms about the pace of production.
    d. an organizational chart.

    ANS: C   PG: 147   TYP: comprehension

28. McDonald's 600-page operations and training manual (that specifies everything from where sauces should be placed on buns to how thick pickle slices should be) would be of interest to sociologists studying
    a. oligarchy.
    b. expert authority.
    c. the informal dimensions of organizations.
    d. the formal dimensions of organizations.

    ANS: D   PG: 147   TYP: application

Chapter 6

29. Which of the following is an example of an informal dimension of an organization?
    a. Each office or position in the organization is assigned a specific task toward accomplishing organizational goals.
    b. Positions are filled on the basis of qualifications determined by objective criteria.
    c. Organizational personnel treat clients as cases and without emotions.
    d. Bosses expect employees to do work unrelated to their official job descriptions.

    ANS: D   PG: 147   TYP: application

30. Theoretically, in a bureaucracy,
    a. authority belongs to the person.
    b. positions are filled on the basis of connections.
    c. authority resides in the personalities of people holding important positions.
    d. personnel treat clients as cases and without emotion.

    ANS: D   PG: 146   TYP: comprehension   SOURCE: study guide

31. Worker-generated norms that govern output or physical effort are part of the
    a. informal dimension of organizations.
    b. formal dimension of organizations.
    c. rules and policies that define the goals of the organization.
    d. coordinating organizations.

    ANS: A   PG: 147   TYP: application

32. _____ is a process by which thought and action rooted in emotion, superstition, respect for mysterious forces, and tradition are replaced by value-rational thought and action.
    a. Externality cost
    b. Rationalization
    c. Bureaucracy
    d. Oligarchy

    ANS: B   PG: 147   TYP: knowledge

33. Weber defined rationalization as a process whereby thought and action rooted in emotion are replaced by
    a. value-rational thought and action.
    b. mysterious forces.
    c. tradition.
    d. instrumental action.

    ANS: A   PG: 147   TYP: comprehension

34. A "rate buster," or someone working faster than any employee, would be of interest to sociologists studying
    a. oligarchy.
    b. trained incapacity.
    c. the informal dimensions of organizations.
    d. the formal dimensions of organizations.

    ANS: C   PG: 147   TYP: comprehension

35. "Rivers are something to dam; swamps are something to drain; lakes are sewers to use for corporate waste." These ideas about nature reflect _____ action.
    a. instrumental
    b. value-rational
    c. traditional
    d. effective

    ANS: B   PG: 148   TYP: application

36. Egg suppliers regularly deprive hens of food and water for as long as two weeks, as the practice increases egg production. This view of chickens and their needs reflects
    a. instrumental action.
    b. value-rational action.
    c. effective action.
    d. traditional action.

    ANS: B   PG: 148   TYP: application

Chapter 6

37. From a value-rational point of view, nature is something to be
    a. conserved.
    b. respected.
    c. held in awe.
    d. used to make a profit.

    ANS: D   PG: 148   TYP: application   SOURCE: study guide

38. In *Dominion: The Power of Man, the Suffering of Animals, and the Call to Mercy*, Matthew Scully wrote that "humans have a moral responsibility to treat the animals in our care with kindness, empathy, and thoughtfulness." Scully's plea makes a case for social action that is
    a. value-rational.
    b. emotion-driven.
    c. logical.
    d. instrumental.

    ANS: B   PG: 148   TYP: application   SOURCE: new

39. Weber made several important qualifications regarding value-rational thought and action. Which of the following is one of them?
    a. Rationalization refers to the way people actually think.
    b. Rationalization refers to the ways in which daily life is organized to accommodate large numbers of people.
    c. Organizations cannot accommodate large numbers of people.
    d. On a personal level, people have no experience with rationalization.

    ANS: B   PG: 148   TYP: comprehension

40. According to the Pizza Hut Web site, the company needs a herd of 250,000 dairy cows producing at full capacity 365 days a year to fill the company's demand for cheese toppings. This view of cows reflects _____ action.
    a. instrumental
    b. value-rational
    c. traditional
    d. effective

    ANS: B   PG: 148   TYP: application

41. The problem with value-rational action is that
    a. decision makers spend too much time evaluating the various means of achieving a valued goal.
    b. people's thought and behavior is influenced by emotion and superstition.
    c. the valued goal can become so all-important that people lose sight of the negative consequences that can arise from the methods used to reach that goal.
    d. decision makers spend too much time trying to anticipate the unforeseen consequences of value-rational action.

    ANS: C   PG: 148   TYP: comprehension

42. _____ is the sociologist that coined the term "McDonaldization of society."
    a. Max Weber
    b. George Ritzer
    c. Emile Durkheim
    d. Elizabeth Coser

    ANS: B   PG: 149   TYP: knowledge

43. Filling soft drinks from dispensers that automatically shut off represents which dimension of McDonaldization?
    a. efficiency
    b. quantification
    c. predictability
    d. control

    ANS: D   PG: 149   TYP: application

44. A hamburger purchased in a Wyoming Wendy's and a hamburger purchased in a German Wendy's has the same appearance and taste. This phenomenon represents which feature of McDonaldization?
    a. efficiency
    b. predictability
    c. control
    d. quantification

    ANS: B   PG: 149   TYP: application   SOURCE: study guide

Chapter 6

45. Mohammed works in a fast food restaurant. When he fills drink orders, the dispenser automatically fills the cup with ice and soft drinks and shuts itself off. This is an example of what McDonaldization principle?
    a. efficiency
    b. quantification and calculation
    c. predictability
    d. control

    ANS: D   PG: 149   TYP: application

46. The McDonaldization of society involved four principles. These principles are
    a. efficiency, quantification, predictability, and control.
    b. alienation, oligarchy, bureaucracy, and expert authority.
    c. traditional, value-rational, instrumental, and purposeful action.
    d. trained incapacity, informate, automate, and technology.

    ANS: A   PG: 150   TYP: comprehension

47. Antonio hears an ad on the radio claiming that it is possible to earn an MBA degree in one year by going to school one night per week and meeting with a study group for two hours each week. This is an example of what McDonaldization principle?
    a. efficiency
    b. quantification and calculation
    c. predictability
    d. control

    ANS: B   PG: 149   TYP: application

48. _____ are enterprises that own, control, or license production and service facilities in countries other than the one in which their headquarters is located.
    a. Organizations
    b. Bureaucracies
    c. Oligarchies
    d. Multinational corporations

    ANS: D   PG: 151   TYP: comprehension

49. Which of the following is one of the strategies McDonald's used to become a global giant?
    a. raise production costs
    b. reduce the number of products that it offers customers
    c. create new markets
    d. accept cash only

    ANS: C   PG: 150   TYP: comprehension

50. Order takers at a fast food restaurant ask every customer whether he or she would like to "supersize" their drink or meal. This strategy is an example of
    a. lowering production costs.
    b. creating new products.
    c. creating new markets.
    d. suggestive selling.

    ANS: D   PG: 150   TYP: application

51. While it may seem rational to create and produce uniform potatoes, the overuse of pesticides to produce them is irrational. This statement applies to which one of the following concepts?
    a. iron cage of rationality
    b. instrumental action
    c. bureaucracy
    d. quantification and calculation

    ANS: A   PG: 150   TYP: application

52. The term "iron cage of irrationality" is used to describe the
    a. informal dimension of organizations.
    b. problems of oligarchy.
    c. formal dimension of organizations.
    d. irrationalities that supposedly rational systems generate.

    ANS: D   PG: 150   TYP: comprehension

53. Outside of North America, what region of the world is *least likely* to have a McDonald's?
    a. Asia
    b. South America
    c. Europe
    d. Western and Central Africa

    ANS: D   PG: 152   TYP: knowledge   SOURCE: study guide

54. The first McDonald's opened in what year?
    a. 1940
    b. 1955
    c. 1980
    d. 1992

    ANS: B   PG: 152   TYP: knowledge   SOURCE: new

55. Taken together, the annual revenues of the top 10 global corporations is $2.3 trillion. Only _____ countries in the world have a gross national product that exceeds this amount.
    a. 100
    b. 60
    c. 20
    d. 5

    ANS: D   PG: 153   TYP: knowledge

56. The world's largest global corporation in 2006 was
    a. General Electric.
    b. IBM.
    c. Exxon/Mobil.
    d. Wal-Mart.

    ANS: C   PG: 153   TYP: knowledge

57. Which one of the following countries would *least* likely be the headquarters to one of the world's 500 largest multinational corporations?
    a. the United States
    b. Japan
    c. Germany
    d. South Korea

    ANS: D   PG: 153   TYP: knowledge

58. Nine of the world's ten largest global corporations are
    a. retail and insurance companies.
    b. defense and pharmaceutical companies.
    c. automobile and oil companies.
    d. retail and automobile companies.

    ANS: C   PG: 153   TYP: knowledge   SOURCE: new

59. With the help of science, the fast food industry has been able to produce a uniform-looking and uniform-tasting potato. However, this potato comes at a cost—it requires heavy doses of chemicals that pollute land and surrounding waters. Sociologists call this a(n) _____ cost.
    a. externality
    b. social
    c. environmental
    d. secret

    ANS: A   PG: 155   TYP: application

60. Which one of the following is an example of an externality cost?
    a. the cost of labor
    b. the cost of materials to produce a product
    c. the cost of operating a manufacturing plant
    d. the cost of restoring contaminated and barren land

    ANS: D   PG:155   TYP: application   SOURCE: study guide

61. Virtually all major fast food companies have introduced low-fat foods on their menus, and most have proved unpopular with consumers. This shows that multinationals, such as McDonald's, are
    a. responsible for the obesity crisis.
    b. not doing enough to inform consumers about the importance of a healthy diet.
    c. responding to consumer tastes for items higher in calories and fat.
    d. contributing to social inequality.

    ANS: C   PG: 155   TYP: comprehension

Chapter 6

62. Magie Richard is the citizen who took on Shell Chemicals and got results. The defining event in her decision to become an activist occurred when
    a. Shell officials threatened her life.
    b. a Shell pipeline exploded, killing an elderly woman and a teenage boy mowing the woman's lawn.
    c. her grandchildren died from a rare bacterial infection.
    d. she decided to make taking on Shell a college class project.

    ANS: B   PG: 156   TYP: knowledge

63. An estimated 3 percent of plastic bags used to carry home groceries and other items end up in creeks, rivers, lakes, and oceans where ducks, turtles, and other wildlife choke on the plastic debris that they mistake for food. Sociologists consider this situation
    a. the McDonaldization of society.
    b. the informal dimension of organizations.
    c. externality costs.
    d. oligarchy.

    ANS: C   PG: 155   TYP: application   SOURCE: new

64. In her book *In the Age of the Smart Machine*, Zuboff distinguished between work environments that promote trained incapacity and those that promote
    a. freedom of expression.
    b. empowering behavior.
    c. a clear division of labor.
    d. flextime.

    ANS: B   PG: 158   TYP: knowledge

65. _____ means to use computers to increase workers' speed or to keep an eye on their job performance.
    a. Trained incapacity
    b. Automate
    c. Informate
    d. Professionalization

    ANS: C   PG: 158   TYP: comprehension

210

66. If workers are trained to do their jobs only under normal circumstances and to respond mechanically, they risk developing
    a. instrumental logic.
    b. trained incapacity.
    c. apathy.
    d. a bureaucratic mentality.

    ANS: B   PG: 158   TYP: application

67. _____ means to use computers to empower workers with a decision-making tool.
    a. Trained incapacity
    b. Automate
    c. Informate
    d. Professionalization

    ANS: C   PG: 158   TYP: comprehension

68. If management uses the computer to "check up" on workers, it is using the computer as an _____ tool.
    a. informating
    b. automating
    c. updating
    d. empowering

    ANS: B   PG: 158   TYP: comprehension

69. Trained incapacity is
    a. an inability to recognize the informal rules governing behavior.
    b. an ability to respond to unusual circumstances.
    c. an inability to recognize when official rules and procedures are outmoded.
    d. an ability to anticipate "what-if" scenarios.

    ANS: C   PG: 158   TYP: comprehension

Chapter 6

70. A worker says, "Sometimes, I am amazed when I realize that we stare at the computer screen even when it has gone down." This comment suggests that in that organization, computers are used as
    a. an automating tool.
    b. an informating tool.
    c. a coordinating mechanism.
    d. a technological resource.

    ANS: A   PG: 158   TYP: application   SOURCE: study guide

71. When management chooses to use computers to increase workers' speed as a source of surveillance, they are using the computer as
    a. an automating tool.
    b. an informating tool.
    c. a learning tool.
    d. a technological resource.

    ANS: A   PG: 158   TYP: comprehension

72. "I was trained for one particular job. During training, they just told me, 'here are the valves you are supposed to turn.'" This statement is a good example of
    a. trained incapacity.
    b. oligarchy.
    c. professionalization.
    d. rationalization.

    ANS: A   PG: 158   TYP: application

73. Workers at a manufacturing plant had no knowledge of the production process as a whole or the rationale behind any of the rules and procedures. Most workers reported that they were trained to master certain steps but not to handle the machinery under all conditions. Such a situation is an example of
    a. trained incapacity.
    b. expert authority.
    c. oligarchy.
    d. rationalization.

    ANS: A   PG: 158   TYP: application

74. Most workers at chemical plants have little understanding of the materials they work with, especially of how the chemicals might react under unusual circumstances. This fact points to a problem related to
   a. rationalization.
   b. formal aspects of organizations.
   c. statistical measures of performance.
   d. trained incapacity.

   ANS: D   PG: 158   TYP: application

75. If occupational safety is measured by the number of accidents that occur on the job, then the _____ industry has one of the lowest accident rates of all industries.
   a. construction
   b. logging
   c. chemical
   d. trucking

   ANS: C   PG: 159   TYP: comprehension   SOURCE: study guide

76. Encouraging employees to concentrate on achieving good scores and to ignore problems generated by their drive to score well illustrates the problem with
   a. statistical measures of performance.
   b. trained incapacity.
   c. oligarchy.
   d. expert power.

   ANS: A   PG: 159   TYP: application

77. Managers that require employees to work off the clock in order to meet profit goals are influenced by
   a. trained incapacity.
   b. bureaucratic red tape.
   c. statistical measures of performance.
   d. oligarchy.

   ANS: C   PG: 158   TYP: application

Chapter 6

78. June works as a cashier. Her productivity is judged according to the number of items passed over a scanner per hour. She is being rated according to
    a. statistical measures of performance.
    b. trained incapacity.
    c. informal policies.
    d. an oligarchy.

    ANS: A   PG: 158   TYP: application   SOURCE: study guide

79. Blau and Schoenherr maintain that experts
    a. are trained by the organization for which they work.
    b. receive their training in colleges and universities.
    c. are subjected to direct supervision.
    d. are micro-managed employees.

    ANS: B   PG: 159   TYP: application

80. University of California researchers created a technology to produce growth hormones to treat dwarfism. Corporations market the product as a solution for people dissatisfied with their height. This situation speaks to the problem of
    a. trained incapacity.
    b. statistical measures of performance.
    c. the informal dimension of organizations.
    d. expert knowledge and responsibility.

    ANS: D   PG: 159   TYP: application

81. McDonald's evaluators pose as customers and conduct each year more than 500,000 unannounced visits at its 31,000 restaurants. The company also uses a checklist of 500 performance measures to evaluate each of its restaurants. This practice represents
    a. the informal aspects of organizations.
    b. statistical measures of performance.
    c. expert authority.
    d. the iron cage of rationality.

    ANS: B   PG: 158   TYP: application   SOURCE: new

214

82. A student writes, "At my place of work, sales staff is rewarded according to a point system. When a customer applies for and is accepted for a store credit card, the salesperson receives 1,000 points." The student is writing about
    a. trained incapacity.
    b. statistical measures of performance.
    c. the informal dimension of organizations.
    d. expert knowledge and responsibility.

    ANS: B   PG: 160   TYP: application   SOURCE: new

83. Robert Michels wrote, "One of the most bizarre features of any advanced industrial society in our time is that the cardinal choices have to be made by a handful of men. And by cardinal choices, I mean those that determine whether we live or die." Michels was referring to a phenomenon known as
    a. expert power.
    b. oligarchy.
    c. trained incapacity.
    d. rationalization.

    ANS: B   PG: 159   TYP: application

84. When decision-making power is concentrated in the hands of a few people that hold the top positions in an organizational hierarchy, the result is a state of
    a. oligarchy.
    b. alienation.
    c. disenchantment.
    d. trained capacity.

    ANS: A   PG: 159   TYP: comprehension

85. _____ is a trend in which organizations hire experts as consultants or full-time employees.
    a. Professionalization
    b. Rationalization
    c. Oligarchy
    d. Bureaucracy

    ANS: A   PG: 160   TYP: knowledge

Chapter 6

86. McDonald's employs about 500,000 people in its corporate offices. It is impossible for that many people to come together to discuss issues that affect daily operations. This shortcoming reflects the principles of
    a. oligarchy.
    b. bureaucracy.
    c. expert power.
    d. McDonaldization.

    ANS: A   PG: 160   TYP: application   SOURCE: study guide

87. _____ makes it impossible for all members of a multinational organization to participate in important decisions.
    a. Size
    b. Time
    c. Trained incapacity
    d. Alienation

    ANS: A   PG: 160   TYP: comprehension

88. Oligarchy is
    a. the concentration of decision-making power in the hands of a few people.
    b. expert power.
    c. a body of persons organized and classified according to rank.
    d. government run by the clergy.

    ANS: A   PG: 160   TYP: comprehension

89. The danger of oligarchy is that those who make decisions may
    a. run the organization as a bureaucracy.
    b. not have the necessary background to understand the full implications of their decisions.
    c. rely on informal mechanisms to get things done.
    d. suffer from disenchantment of the world.

    ANS: B   PG: 160   TYP: comprehension   SOURCE: study guide

90. A chemist working for a large corporation has the training to design a pesticide, but he or she is not trained to consider the abilities and limitations of the consumers who use it. This situation speaks to the problems associated with
    a. automating technologies.
    b. oligarchy.
    c. statistical measures of performance.
    d. expert knowledge and responsibility.

    ANS: D   PG: 161   TYP: application

91. _____ is a state in which human life is dominated by the forces of human inventions.
    a. Alienation
    b. Oligarchy
    c. Professionalization
    d. Bureaucracy

    ANS: A   PG: 161   TYP: knowledge

92. In *Dominion: The Power of Man, the Suffering of Animals, and the Call to Mercy*, Matthew Scully speaks to how the mass processing of animals for meat for human consumption impairs our moral responsibility to treat animals in our care with kindness, empathy, and thoughtfulness. Scully's concerns relate to the concept of
    a. oligarchy.
    b. expert power.
    c. professionalization.
    d. alienation.

    ANS: D   PG: 162   TYP: application

93. Karl Marx believed that increased control over nature is accompanied by
    a. disenchantment.
    b. anomie.
    c. alienation.
    d. trained incapacity.

    ANS: C   PG: 161   TYP: comprehension

Chapter 6

94. Fertilizers, herbicides, pesticides, and chemically treated seeds give people control over nature because they eliminate the need to fight weeds, and they prevent pests from destroying crops. Yet heavy reliance on chemical technologies causes the soil to erode and become less productive. This dilemma represents a case of
    a. alienation.
    b. trained incapacity.
    c. oligarchy.
    d. optimum technology.

    ANS: A   PG: 161   TYP: application   SOURCE: study guide

95. Although chemicals have reduced the physical demands involved in producing goods, they have negatively impacted society by
    a. helping people to produce unprecedented amounts of food.
    b. eliminating the need to fight weeds with hoes.
    c. undermining the practice of planting crops in rows.
    d. leading to the loss of knowledge about how to control insects and disease without chemicals.

    ANS: D   PG: 162   TYP: knowledge

96. Which one of the following circumstances is <u>not</u> an example of alienation?
    a. Families are forced to move where work is available.
    b. Workers are treated as economic components, rather than as active, creative, and social beings.
    c. Employees use technology as informating tools.
    d. No person can claim a product as the unique result of his or her labor.

    ANS: C   PG: 162   TYP: comprehension

97. Workers are _____ because they produce not for themselves or for known consumers but, rather, produce for an abstract, impersonal market.
    a. alienated from the process
    b. professionalized
    c. formally trained
    d. obsolete

    ANS: A   PG: 160   TYP: application   SOURCE: new

98. Employers that specify exactly how workers should look, behave, and speak are contributing to
    a. informal dimensions of control.
    b. a safe work environment.
    c. informating the workplace.
    d. alienation from self.

    ANS: D   PG: 163   TYP: application   SOURCE: study guide

99. _____ is a state in which human life is dominated by the forces of human invention.
    a. Trained incapacity
    b. Alienation
    c. Oligarchy
    d. Professionalism

    ANS: B   PG: 161   TYP: comprehension

100. Karl Marx believed that, for the most part, workers are treated as economic components rather than active, creative, and social beings. This description suggests that Marx was concerned about
    a. bureaucracy.
    b. informal dimensions of organizations.
    c. statistical measures of performance.
    d. alienation in the workplace.

    ANS: D   PG: 161   TYP: application

101. Workers are alienated from _____ because home and work environments are separate.
    a. the process of production
    b. the product
    c. the family
    d. the self

    ANS: C   PG: 162   TYP: application   SOURCE: study guide

Chapter 6

102. Because employers own the factory buildings, the tools, the machines, and the labor of workers, the workers are alienated from
    a. the process of production.
    b. the product.
    c. the family.
    d. the self.

    ANS: A   PG: 161   TYP: application   SOURCE: study guide

Multiple Choice Questions on the Web

1. _____ are impersonal associations among people who interact with a specific purpose.
    a. Primary groups
    b. Secondary groups
    c. Outgroups
    d. Ingroups

    ANS: B   PG: 144   TYP: comprehension   SOURCE: new

2. Community service centers, politically-oriented groups, religious organizations, historical societies, and sports associations are examples of
    a. voluntary organizations.
    b. coercive organizations.
    c. utilitarian organizations.
    d. bureaucracies.

    ANS: A   PG: 145   TYP: application   SOURCE: new

3. A bureaucracy is a(n)
    a. completely rational organization that uses the most efficient means to achieve a valued goal.
    b. organization that plans and manages on a global scale.
    c. commercial, industrial, and professional entity.
    d. government establishment characterized by red tape.

    ANS: A   PG: 145   TYP: comprehension

4. The official written guidelines, rules, regulations, and policies that define the goals of the organization are part of
    a. the informal dimension.
    b. the formal dimension.
    c. the social network.
    d. worker-generated norms.

    ANS: B   PG: 147   TYP: comprehension

5. People living in a value-rational environment typically know little about their surroundings and come to rely on _____ when something goes wrong.
    a. religion
    b. specialists or experts
    c. their instincts
    d. chance

    ANS: B   PG: 149   TYP: comprehension

6. In the mid-1960s, McDonald's replaced in-store peeling and slicing appliances with a system of flash-freezing half-cooked potatoes. This strategy is an example of
    a. lowering production costs.
    b. creating new products.
    c. creating new markets.
    d. suggestive selling.

    ANS: A   PG: 150   TYP: application

7. Hidden costs to the environment, workers, and consumers that are associated with using or making a product but that are not figured into its price are
    a. externality costs.
    b. entrepreneurial costs.
    c. reality checks.
    d. façade of legitimacy costs.

    ANS: A   PG: 155   TYP: knowledge

8. A fast-food service restaurant keeps statistics on the amount of milkshakes sold per gallon of shake mix used as a way of monitoring workers' performance. This recordkeeping represents
   a. the informal dimension of organizations.
   b. oligarchy.
   c. statistical measures of performance.
   d. alienation.

   ANS: C PG: 158 TYP: application

9. A danger of _____ is that those who make decisions may not have the necessary background to understand the full implications of their decisions.
   a. oligarchy
   b. automating the work environment
   c. informal aspects of organization
   d. alienation

   ANS: A PG: 160 TYP: comprehension

10. Carmen works between 6 pm and 2 am six days a week. Thus, she is not home for dinner and is still sleeping when her husband leaves for work and her kids leave for school. Marx would argue that such a situation leaves Carmen alienated from
    a. the self.
    b. the family.
    c. the product.
    d. the process of production.

    ANS: B PG: 162 TYP: application

True/False Questions

1. Formal organizations have a life that extends beyond the people that comprise them.

   ANS: True PG: 143 SOURCE: study guide

2. In this chapter, we emphasize McDonald's because it is the worst fast food organization in the United States.

   ANS: False PG: 143

3. Ronald McDonald is the most recognized personality in the world after Santa Claus.

   ANS: True   PG: 143   SOURCE: new

4. Secondary groups can range in size from small to extremely large.

   ANS: True   PG: 144   SOURCE: new; study guide

5. Groups are considered primary when relationships are limited to certain activities and settings.

   ANS: False   PG: 144   SOURCE: new

6. Members of secondary groups can form primary groups if they expand their relationships beyond the task at hand.

   ANS: True   PG: 143   SOURCE: new

7. Organizational problems occur when employees fail to follow official policies *or* follow them too rigidly.

   ANS: True   PG: 147   SOURCE: new; study guide

8. The ideal is a standard against which real cases can be measured.

   ANS: True   PG: 146

9. Actual behavior in organizations departs from the ideal.

   ANS: True   PG: 146   SOURCE: study guide

10. From a strictly bureaucratic point of view, emotion interferes with the efficient delivery of goods and services.

    ANS: True   PG: 146

Chapter 6

11. An ideal type is equivalent to a caricature.

    ANS: True   PG: 146

12. Rationalization assumes greater understanding and knowledge about the surrounding environment.

    ANS: False   PG: 148

13. The McDonaldization of society involves four principles: efficiency, quantification, predictability, and ethics.

    ANS: False   PG: 151   SOURCE: new

14. Multinational corporations plan, produce, and sell on a national scale.

    ANS: False   PG: 151   SOURCE: study guide

15. The fourth meal is one strategy that fast food restaurants use to sell more products.

    ANS: True   PG: 151   SOURCE: new

16. Multinational corporations are headquartered disproportionately in the United States, Japan, and Western Europe.

    ANS: True   PG: 152   SOURCE: study guide

17. Market researchers have found that when customers defer payment until a later date, they are likely to spend more at the time of purchase.

    ANS: True   PG: 150

18. Only 30 countries in the world have a gross national product that exceeds Exxon Mobil's annual revenue of $339 billion.

    ANS: True   PG: 153   SOURCE: new

19. In theory, a truly global corporation should have some kind of economic relationship with every country in the world.

    ANS: True   PG: 153   SOURCE: new

20. France is one of the five countries in the world with GNP that exceeds the annual combined revenues of the top 10 global corporations.

    ANS: False   PG: 153   SOURCE: new; study guide

21. Germany is one of the five countries in the world with GNP that exceeds the annual combined revenues of the top 10 global corporations.

    ANS: True   PG: 153   SOURCE: new

22. Despite the fast food industry's effort to market healthier choices, consumers clearly prefer high calorie menu items.

    ANS: True   PG: 155   SOURCE: new

23. To informate means to use the computer as a source of surveillance.

    ANS: False   PG: 158   SOURCE: study guide

24. Statistical measures of performance are rarely used in the fast food industry.

    ANS: False   PG: 158   SOURCE: new

25. Blau and Schoenherr maintain that experts hired by an organization have little control over the application of the information, service, or invention they provide to the organization.

    ANS: True   PG: 161

26. Karl Marx is the theorist associated with the concept *alienation*.

    ANS: True   PG: 161   SOURCE: study guide

Chapter 6

27. Workers are alienated from the product when their roles in producing it are limited.

    ANS: True   PG: 161

28. Oligarchy means rule by the many.

    ANS: False   PG: 159   SOURCE: study guide

29. Most formal organizations can be classified as bureaucracies.

    ANS: True   PG: 164   SOURCE: new

30. One organization trend guided by traditional action is the McDonaldization of society.

    ANS: False   PG: 153   SOURCE: new

Concept Application (also in study guide)

Consider the concepts listed below. Match one or more of the concepts with each scenario. Explain your choices.
- a. Automate
- b. Externality costs
- c. Informal dimensions of organizations
- d. Multinational corporation
- e. Value-rational

Scenario 1
"Is IBM Japan an American or a Japanese company? Its workforce of 20,000 is Japanese, but its equity holders are American. Even so, over the past decade, IBM Japan has provided, on average, three times more tax revenue to the Japanese government than has Fujitsu. What is its nationality? Or what about Honda's operation in Ohio? Or Texas Instruments' memory-chip activities in Japan? Are they 'American' products? If so, what about the cellular phones sold in Tokyo that contain components made in the United States by American workers who are employed by the U.S. division of a Japanese company? Sony has facilities in Dotham, Alabama, from which it sends audio tapes and video tapes to Europe. What is the nationality of these products or the operation that makes them?" (Ohmae 1990:10).

    ANS: D

Scenario 2

"A number of employees (5%) respond to perceived injustices by not performing their required tasks. One incident involved a male stockroom worker at a retail store who claimed he was paid less than others in similar positions. After an unsuccessful attempt to discuss the matter with his supervisor, the worker decided to deal with the conflict in his own way: 'I didn't really want to quit, so I goofed off a lot. I didn't do anything unless I was specifically asked to. When working at night, I would listen to music for hours and do nothing.... If I was goofing off and saw the manager, I would act as if I was really doing something'" (Tucker 1993:37).

ANS: C

Scenario 3

"Scientifically, the atomic bomb was an advance into unknown territory, but militarily, it was simply a more cost-effective way of attaining a goal that was already a central part of strategy: a means of producing the results achieved at Hamburg and Dresden cheaply and reliably every time the weapon was used [for example, a quarter million bombs were used to destroy the city of Dresden]. Even at the time, the $2 billion cost of the Manhattan Project was dwarfed by the cost of trying to destroy cities the hard way, using conventional bombs" (Dyer 1985:96).

ANS: E

Scenario 4

"The same kind of computer technology that enables employers to keep track of workers' backgrounds also makes it possible for them to quantify and monitor work performance. Anyone who works on a video display terminal, electronic telephone console, or other computer-based equipment, including laser scanner cash registers, is subject to constant monitoring.

"Although the stated aim of monitoring workers is to improve productivity and service, the effect can be to turn checkstands into pressure cookers. 'Computers are wonderful for many things,' says Beverly Crownover, president of Local 1532 of United Food and Commercial Workers in Santa Rosa, California. 'But when they're used to monitor how many items a cashier scans per minute, it's like a whip. There's incredible pressure on workers'" (UFCW Action 1993:135).

ANS: A

Scenario 5

"The cost of stress to the American workplace has been estimated at between $150 billion and $180 billion a year. Stress-related illness accounts for millions of lost working days each year, and the number is rising. One study found that in 1980, no occupational disease claims were related to stress; in 1990, 10 percent of them were. A 1993 study by Commerce Clearing House reports that unscheduled absences can cost U.S. employers more than $500 per employee per year. Experts believe that stress accounts for 12 percent of all workers' compensation claims" (Wright and Smye 1996:7).

ANS: B

Short Essay Questions

1. Why is the McDonald's corporation the focus of a chapter on formal organizations?

2. What is a formal organization?

3. Distinguish between primary and secondary groups? Name and define the three kinds of secondary groups that exist.

4. What is a bureaucracy? Is McDonald's a bureaucracy? Explain.

5. How is studying a bureaucracy as an ideal type useful?

6. Distinguish between formal and informal dimensions of organizations.

7. What is value-rational thought? Why was Max Weber especially concerned with value-rational action?

8. Define rationalization. How does the example of factory farms relate to rationalization? What are the positive and negative outcomes of rationalization?

9. What is McDonaldization of society?

10. Explain the iron cage of rationality.

11. How do organizations, such as McDonald's, reach beyond local markets to regional, national, and global markets?

12. Define multinational corporation. In what ways are multinational corporations engines of progress? In what ways are they engines of destruction?

13. How do sociologists demonstrate the size and, by extension, power of global corporations? Give examples.

14. What are externality costs?

15. How does the case of Margie Eugene Richard, who took on Shell Chemical, illustrate the power of informed consumers?

16. What is trained incapacity? Give an example from Shoshana Zuboff's *In the Age of the Smart Machine* of a work environment that promotes trained incapacity. Contrast that work environment with one that promotes empowering behavior.

17. How do organizations use statistical measures of performance? What are some of the problems that can accompany such measures? Give examples of statistical measures of performance at McDonald's.

18. What is expert power? How can expert power be problematic?

19. Define oligarchy. Why does oligarchy seem to be an inevitable feature of large organizations?

20. How did Karl Marx define alienation? What are the four levels of alienation? Give examples of each type.

Chapter 6

Comprehensive Essay Questions

1. Imagine you were called into an organization and asked to identify its strengths and weaknesses. What concepts discussed in Chapter 6 could you use to frame an analysis?

2. Think about an organization you have worked for or an organization on which you depend. What features of organizations discussed in Chapter 6 come to mind when you think of that organization?

3. What is the McDonaldization of society? Give an example of an organization (other than a fast food organization) that follows the four principles of McDonaldization.

Chapter 7

Deviance, Conformity, and Social Control

Multiple-Choice Questions

1. The sociological contribution to understanding deviant behavior is the emphasis on
    a. the individual as a deviant.
    b. unchanging and universal definitions of deviance.
    c. the context under which deviant behavior occurs.
    d. conformity.

    ANS: C   PG: 168   TYP: comprehension   SOURCE: study guide

2. The People's Republic of China represents an interesting case for studying issues of deviance, conformity, and social control because
    a. since July 1, 1997, Hong Kong has imposed its system of social control on China.
    b. many of the behaviors that constituted deviance during the Cultural Revolution no longer apply today.
    c. China is attempting to model its system of social control after the U.S. system.
    d. China has a model system of social control.

    ANS: B   PG: 169   TYP: knowledge

3. The number one destination of Chinese students studying abroad is
    a. the European Union.
    b. the United States.
    c. the Soviet Union.
    d. North Korea.

    ANS: B   PG: 169   TYP: knowledge

Chapter 7

4. _____ is any behavior or appearance that is socially challenged because it departs from the norms and expectations of the group.
    a. Deviance
    b. Conformity
    c. Social control
    d. Corporate power

    ANS: A   PG: 170   TYP: comprehension

5. _____ is any behavior or appearance that follows and maintains the standards of a group.
    a. Deviance
    b. Conformity
    c. Social control
    d. Power

    ANS: B   PG: 170   TYP: comprehension   SOURCE: study guide

6. _____ includes the methods used to teach, persuade, or force people to comply with norms and expectations.
    a. Social control
    b. Deviance
    c. Conformity
    d. Context

    ANS: A   PG: 170   TYP: knowledge

7. The only characteristic common to all forms of deviance is the fact that
    a. they invoke formal sanctions.
    b. everyone in the society is offended by the behavior.
    c. the behaviors are considered deviant across time and place.
    d. some social audience regards the act or appearance as deviant.

    ANS: D   PG: 170   TYP: comprehension

8. The Cultural Revolution occurred from
   a. 1929-1939.
   b. 1944-1954.
   c. 1988-1999.
   d. 1966-1976.

   ANS: D   PG: 169   TYP: knowledge

9. People who violate _____ are usually punished severely; they are ostracized, institutionalized in prisons or mental hospitals, and sometimes even executed.
   a. folkways
   b. mores
   c. rituals
   d. mechanisms of social control

   ANS: B   PG: 170   TYP: comprehension

10. Which one of the following characteristics applies to the concept of mores?
    a. essential to the well-being of a group
    b. one of many ways to do things
    c. routine matters
    d. details of life

    ANS: A   PG: 171   TYP: comprehension   SOURCE: study guide

11. Which one of the following words does not apply to the concept of a folkway?
    a. essential
    b. customary
    c. routine
    d. superficial

    ANS: A   PG: 170   TYP: comprehension

Chapter 7

12. When guests depart in the People's Republic of China, the Chinese host walks them out to their vehicle and then stands and waves until the visitors are out of sight. This behavior is an example of a
    a. folkway.
    b. more.
    c. sanction.
    d. mechanism of social control.

    ANS: A   PG: 171   TYP: application

13. People that violate _____ experience reactions on the order of frowns or remarks or disapproval.
    a. folkways
    b. mores
    c. sanctions
    d. norms

    ANS: A   PG: 171   TYP: comprehension   SOURCE: new

14. For most people, "the rule to do as all do suffices." This was sociologist William Sumner's explanation for why most people adhere to
    a. established folkways and mores.
    b. informal and formal sanctions.
    c. negative and positive sanctions.
    d. innovation and ritualism.

    ANS: A   PG: 171   TYP: comprehension   SOURCE: new

15. During the Cultural Revolution, the dominant _____ rejected special social status and the accumulation of worldly possessions.
    a. folkways
    b. sanctions
    c. mores
    d. innovators

    ANS: C   PG: 171   TYP: comprehension   SOURCE: new

16. In general, Chinese preschoolers are taught to
    a. suppress individual impulses.
    b. play competitively with other children.
    c. be independent.
    d. assume flexible roles in the classroom.

    ANS: A   PG: 171   TYP: comprehension

17. A preschool teacher comments, "Why do small children in the United States go to the bathroom separately? It is much easier to have everyone go at the same time." This comment is most likely coming from a teacher working in
    a. China.
    b. Taiwan.
    c. Japan.
    d. South Korea.

    ANS: A   PG: 172   TYP: application   SOURCE: study guide

18. Chinese preschool teachers tend to discipline their four-year-olds by
    a. stopping them from misbehaving before they know they are about to misbehave.
    b. allowing the children to "police" themselves.
    c. rewarding them with small toys whenever they are good.
    d. punishing them harshly whenever they break a rule.

    ANS: A   PG: 172   TYP: knowledge

19. In comparison to American preschools, Chinese preschools are
    a. loosely structured.
    b. socially-minded.
    c. self-directed.
    d. materialistic.

    ANS: B   PG: 172   TYP: comprehension

Chapter 7

20. In contrast to preschoolers in China, preschoolers in the United States are taught to
    a. attune themselves to group enterprises.
    b. suppress individual talents.
    c. cooperate with other children.
    d. cultivate individual interests.

    ANS: D   PG: 172   TYP: knowledge

21. When researchers showed American parents and teachers films portraying daily life in Chinese preschools, Americans were particularly disturbed by the
    a. lack of toys.
    b. bathroom scene.
    c. drabness of the classroom.
    d. rough treatment accorded Chinese preschoolers.

    ANS: B   PG: 173   TYP: application

22. Americans that watched the film about preschool in Chinese culture regarded the Chinese preschools as
    a. chaotic.
    b. undisciplined.
    c. promoting self-centeredness.
    d. too rigid.

    ANS: D   PG: 173   TYP: comprehension

23. A teacher asks her class, "Who would like to paint? Who would like to work on a puzzle?" This exchange is most typical of preschools in
    a. China.
    b. Taiwan.
    c. Japan.
    d. the United States.

    ANS: D   PG: 172   TYP: application

236

Deviance, Conformity, and Social Control

24. Chinese that watched the film showing life in a typical American preschool regarded the preschool as
   a. chaotic.
   b. group-oriented.
   c. overly restrictive.
   d. rigid.

   ANS: A   PG: 173   TYP: comprehension

25. Ideally, conformity should be
   a. imposed.
   b. established through informal negative sanctions.
   c. voluntary.
   d. established through a formal reward system.

   ANS: C   PG: 172   TYP: comprehension

26. _____ is a reaction or response of approval or disapproval to another's behavior or appearance.
   a. Deviance
   b. Conformity
   c. Retreatism
   d. A sanction

   ANS: D   PG: 173   TYP: comprehension

27. Ridicule, imprisonment, and withdrawal of affection are examples of _____ sanctions.
   a. informal
   b. positive
   c. negative
   d. formal

   ANS: C   PG: 171   TYP: application   SOURCE: new

28. Six-year-old Martha picks up her toys and puts them away. Her father smiles and pats her on the back. The smile and pat represent a _____ sanction.
    a. positive formal
    b. negative formal
    c. negative informal
    d. positive informal

    ANS: D   PG: 173   TYP: application   SOURCE: study guide

29. Which one of the following is an informal sanction?
    a. medals
    b. diplomas
    c. a frown
    d. the death penalty

    ANS: C   PG: 174   TYP: application   SOURCE: new

30. Informal sanctions are
    a. backed by the force of law.
    b. spontaneous and unofficial expressions of approval or disapproval.
    c. group-generated expressions of approval or disapproval.
    d. systematic laws, rules, and regulations.

    ANS: B   PG: 173   TYP: application

31. Adolescents at a middle school tease a girl because she has yet to shave her legs. The teasing represents an example of a _____ sanction.
    a. positive formal
    b. negative formal
    c. negative informal
    d. positive informal

    ANS: C   PG: 173   TYP: application

Deviance, Conformity, and Social Control

32. Jeremy wore barrettes to nursery school. One day, a boy repeatedly told Jeremy that "only girls wear barrettes." The incident shows how _____ work as mechanisms of social control.
    a. formal positive sanctions
    b. informal positive sanctions
    c. formal negative sanctions
    d. informal negative sanctions

    ANS: D   PG: 173   TYP: application

33. Which one of the 50 states has the highest incarceration rate?
    a. Minnesota
    b. Texas
    c. Louisiana
    d. California

    ANS: C   PG: 175   TYP: knowledge

34. Which on the following countries has the highest incarceration rate?
    a. the United States
    b. Nigeria
    c. Sudan
    d. India

    ANS: A   PG: 175   TYP: knowledge   SOURCE: new

35. The pillory was a _____ popular in Europe between 1275 and 1870.
    a. more
    b. folkway
    c. negative sanction
    d. positive sanction

    ANS: C   PG: 176   TYP: application   SOURCE: new

Chapter 7

36. _____ is a method employed to prevent information from reaching some audience.
   a. Censorship
   b. Surveillance
   c. A negative sanction
   d. A positive sanction

   ANS: A   PG: 175   TYP: comprehension

37. A Harvard Law School study identified _____ as the country with the most extensive internet censorship in the world.
   a. South Korea
   b. the United States
   c. China
   d. Romania

   ANS: C   PG: 176   TYP: knowledge   SOURCE: study guide

38. A Harvard Law School study found that the Chinese government blocked Internet users' access to Web sites sponsored by *Time Magazine, National Public Radio,* and the *Washington Post*. This mechanism of social control is known as
   a. deviance.
   b. censorship.
   c. surveillance.
   d. conformity.

   ANS: B   PG: 176   TYP: application

39. The Chinese government blocks access to the following Web sites: *Time Magazine*, National Public Radio, and the *Washington Post*. That government is engaging is
   a. surveillance.
   b. conformity.
   c. innovation.
   d. censorship

   ANS: D   PG: 176   TYP: application   SOURCE : new

40. The Chinese government launched a _____ campaign to monitor the estimated 220 billion text messages that 300 million Chinese send to each other each year.
    a. surveillance
    b. conformity
    c. innovation
    d. censorship

    ANS: A   PG: 177   TYP: application   SOURCE: new

41. Telephone tapping, interception of letters, observations via closed circuit television, and electronic monitoring are examples of
    a. censorship.
    b. surveillance.
    c. conformity.
    d. deviance.

    ANS: B   PG: 176   TYP: application

42. The U.S. Department of Justice asked meter readers, cable installers, and telephone repair people to report suspicious activities they might notice while serving customers. This qualifies as a form of
    a. censorship.
    b. surveillance.
    c. conformity.
    d. deviance.

    ANS: B   PG: 176   TYP: application   SOURCE: study guide

43. Durkheim argued that deviance would be present, even in a "community of saints in an exemplary and perfect monastery." This statement suggests that
    a. deviance and crime are distinct concepts.
    b. those in power define what is deviant.
    c. there are some societies in which deviance does not exist.
    d. deviance is present in all societies.

    ANS: D   PG: 177   TYP: comprehension

Chapter 7

44. Durkheim argued that, even among the exemplary, some seemingly insignificant act or appearance will be greeted as deviant, even criminal, because "it is impossible for everyone to be alike if only because each of us cannot stand in the same spot." This argument explains why Durkheim believed that
    a. deviance and crime are distinct concepts.
    b. those in power define what is deviant.
    c. there are some societies in which deviance does not exist.
    d. deviance is present in all societies.

    ANS: D   PG: 177   TYP: comprehension   SOURCE: new

45. Wearing eyeglasses in China during the Cultural Revolution was deviant because it represented all but which one of the following?
    a. special status
    b. abandonment of revolutionary spirit
    c. a physical defect
    d. resistance to the Great Leap Forward

    ANS: C   PG: 177   TYP: comprehension

46. Which one of the following statements best corresponds with Durkheim's perspective on deviance?
    a. It is impossible for any society to be entirely free of deviance.
    b. Behavior that is unthinkable when an individual is acting on his or her own may be executed without hesitation when carried out under orders.
    c. When people become criminals, they do so because of contacts with criminal patterns and because of isolation from non-criminal patterns.
    d. Deviance is a consequence not of a particular behavior but of the application of rules and sanctions.

    ANS: A   PG: 177   TYP: comprehension

47. Durkheim's theory of deviance (crime) is written from a _____ perspective.
    a. functionalist
    b. conflict
    c. symbolic interactionist
    d. social action

    ANS: A   PG: 177   TYP: comprehension   SOURCE: study guide

48. A student writes, "I used to sell drugs. I was very careful. I watched who I sold to and didn't take any new customers. I was never caught." This student can be classified as
    a. a conformist.
    b. a secret deviant.
    c. falsely accused.
    d. a pure deviant.

    ANS: B   PG: 178   TYP: application

49. Durkheim's theory of deviance (crime) does not address which one of the following questions?
    a. Why is deviance present in every society?
    b. How can almost any behavior qualify as deviant?
    c. Who decides that a particular activity or appearance is deviant?
    d. How is deviance functional for society?

    ANS: C   PG: 178   TYP: application   SOURCE: study guide

50. Howard Becker wrote
    a. *The Presentation of Self.*
    b. *The Functions of Deviance.*
    c. *Asylums.*
    d. *Outsiders: Studies on the Sociology of Deviance.*

    ANS: D   PG: 178   TYP: knowledge

51. *Outsiders: Studies on the Sociology of Deviance* was written by which one of the following?
    a. Erving Goffman
    b. Emile Durkheim
    c. Howard Becker
    d. Joel Best

    ANS: C   PG: 177   TYP: knowledge   SOURCE: new

Chapter 7

52. Kai Erikson wrote, "The critical variable in the study of deviance, then, is the social audience rather than the individual actor since the social audience decides whether or not a behavior is deviant." This statement best corresponds with which theory of deviance?
    a. functionalist
    b. labeling theory
    c. differential association
    d. structural strain theory

    ANS B   PG: 178   TYP: application

53. The _____ was chairman Mao Zedong's response to the Great Leap Forward.
    a. Four Olds
    b. Five Year Plan
    c. Cultural Revolution
    d. Special Economic Zones project

    ANS: C   PG: 179   TYP: comprehension

54. The "Great Leap Forward" was Mao's plan, which
    a. pushed the country into the 21st century.
    b. was supported by the United States.
    c. created economic surpluses and generated prosperity.
    d. failed miserably.

    ANS: D   PG: 179   TYP: knowledge   SOURCE: study guide

55. The _____ was Mao's plan that was designed to mobilize the masses and transform China from a country of poverty to a land of agricultural abundance in five short years.
    a. Five Year Plan
    b. Great Leap Forward
    c. Cultural Revolution
    d. Special Economic Zones Project

    ANS: B   PG: 179   TYP: knowledge

Deviance, Conformity, and Social Control

56. The forces behind the _____ help us to understand more clearly why making money was considered a crime against the state during the Cultural Revolution.
    a. population explosion in China
    b. Great Leap Forward
    c. post-Mao era
    d. Industrial Revolution

    ANS: B   PG: 179   TYP: knowledge

57. _____ are people that have broken the rules and are caught, punished, and labeled as outsiders.
    a. Conformists
    b. Secret deviants
    c. The falsely accused
    d. Pure deviants

    ANS: D   PG: 178   TYP: comprehension

58. _____ are people that have not violated rules of a group and are treated accordingly.
    a. Conformists
    b. Secret deviants
    c. The falsely accused
    d. Pure deviants

    ANS: A   PG: 178   TYP: comprehension

59. A person takes on a(n) _____ when his or her deviant status becomes more important than any other status he or she occupies.
    a. label of secret deviant
    b. master status of deviant
    c. informal status
    d. label of confederate

    ANS: B   PG: 178   TYP: comprehension

Chapter 7

60. Which one of the following is an assumption underlying the labeling theory?
    a. Definitions of deviance are consistent across cultural settings.
    b. Rules are enforced uniformly and consistently.
    c. Deviants are those whose behavior people have noticed, labeled as such, and applied sanctions.
    d. Deviant behavior is learned in the same way conforming behavior is learned.

    ANS: C   PG: 178   TYP: comprehension   SOURCE: new

61. Labeling theorists suggest that for every rule a social group creates, four categories of people exist. Which one of the following is not one of those categories?
    a. conformist
    b. pure deviants
    c. falsely accused
    d. defendants

    ANS: D   PG: 178   TYP: comprehension

62. A U.S. Bureau of Justice survey of crime victims documented that almost 58 percent of crime victims do not report the crime to police. This suggests that there are large numbers of _____ in U.S. society.
    a. conformists
    b. pure deviants
    c. secret deviants
    d. falsely accused

    ANS: C   PG: 179   TYP: application   SOURCE: study guide

63. _____ are people who have not broken the rules but are treated as if they have.
    a. The falsely accused
    b. Innovators
    c. Secret deviants
    d. Conformists

    ANS: A   PG: 179   TYP: comprehension   SOURCE: new

Deviance, Conformity, and Social Control

64. Prison populations include pure deviants and
    a. ritualists.
    b. the falsely accused.
    c. conformists.
    d. secret deviants.

    ANS: B   PG: 179   TYP: application

65. Reseachers Michael L. Radelet and Adam Bedau reviewed more than 800 cases of innocent people being convicted of capital crimes, and they found that 56 had
    a. made false confessions.
    b. had received early parole.
    c. admitted guilt.
    d. no jury trial.

    ANS: A   PG: 179   TYP: knowledge

66. _____ are likely to be accused of a crime when the well-being of a country or group is threatened.
    a. Pure deviants
    b. The falsely accused
    c. Secret deviants
    d. Conformists

    ANS: B   PG: 179   TYP: comprehension

67. _____ are people who have broken the rules but whose violation goes unnoticed.
    a. Pure deviants
    b. The falsely accused
    c. Secret deviants
    d. Conformists

    ANS: C   PG: 178   TYP: comprehension

Chapter 7

68. A campaign to identify, investigate, and correct behavior that is believed to undermine a group or a country is known as
    a. a moral event.
    b. ethnic cleansing.
    c. a witch hunt.
    d. target practice.

    ANS: C   PG: 179   TYP: comprehension   SOURCE: study guide

69. After September 11, 2001, Muslims and Arab Americans have been caught up in a criminal investigation of historical proportions. From a sociological point of view, this criminal investigation qualifies as
    a. a moral event.
    b. ethnic cleansing.
    c. a witch hunt.
    d. target practice.

    ANS: C   PG: 179   TYP: application

70. In the United States, police efforts are largely directed at controlling
    a. corporate crime.
    b. white collar crime.
    c. crimes against individuals and property.
    d. the behavior of the middle class.

    ANS: C   PG: 180   TYP: comprehension   SOURCE: new

71. The plight of the falsely accused is of particular interest to
    a. functionalists.
    b. labeling theorists.
    c. structural strain theorists.
    d. differential association theorists.

    ANS: B   PG: 178   TYP: application

72. Under which of the following circumstances is a person least likely to be falsely accused of committing a crime?
    a. times of economic crisis
    b. during a health crisis (or epidemic)
    c. times of rapid economic growth
    d. when an important institution is threatened

    ANS: C   PG: 179   TYP: comprehension   SOURCE: study guide

73. The existence of the falsely accused underscores the fact that the study of deviance must consider
    a. the personality of deviance.
    b. formal sanctions.
    c. the socialization process.
    d. the role of rule makers and rule enforcers.

    ANS: D   PG: 180   TYP: application

74. Labeling theorist _____ recommended that researchers pay particular attention to rule makers and rule enforcers.
    a. Emile Durkheim
    b. Howard Becker
    c. Robert K. Merton
    d. J.L. Simmons

    ANS: B   PG: 180   TYP: knowledge

75. When labeling theorists study deviance, they focus least on
    a. the context.
    b. the rule makers.
    c. the rule enforcers.
    d. the rule that is broken.

    ANS: D   PG: 180   TYP: comprehension

Chapter 7

76. In January 2000, Republican Governor George Ryan placed a moratorium on executions in the state of Illinois. He did this because he believed that
    a. the state had no right to take a life.
    b. the legal process was so flawed that it must be shut down until repaired.
    c. the death penalty was immoral.
    d. the voters in his state supported a moratorium.

    ANS: B   PG: 181   TYP: comprehension

77. Former Governor George Ryan argued that "our capital system is haunted by the demon of error—error in determining guilt and error in determining who among the guilty deserve to die." Ryan focuses our attention on which one of the following parties?
    a. the criminal
    b. rule makers and rule enforcers
    c. the guilty
    d. the innocent

    ANS: B   PG: 180   TYP: application   SOURCE: new; study guide

78. The internment of 110,000 people of Japanese descent, which took place in the United States during World War II is an example of
    a. a crime.
    b. an informal mechanism of social control.
    c. a structural strain.
    d. a witch hunt.

    ANS: D   PG: 180   TYP: application

79. By placing a moratorium on executions in Illinois and commuting the death sentences to life without parole for 167 inmates, Republican Governor George Ryan has forced many to ask which of the following questions?
    a. Does the state have the right to take a person's life?
    b. Is life in prison a better option than execution?
    c. How many of the 3,557 persons on death row are falsely accused?
    d. Should the U.S. government abolish the death penalty?

    ANS: C   PG: 181   TYP: comprehension

80. Sutherland and Cressy wrote about "crimes committed by persons of respectability and high social status in the course of their occupations." They were writing about
    a. corporate crime.
    b. white-collar crime.
    c. deviance.
    d. the falsely accused.

    ANS: B   PG: 180   TYP: comprehension

81. In 2004, _____ percent of all people sentenced to U.S. federal prisons were classified as white-collar criminals, compared with 54 percent classified as drug offenders.
    a. 50
    b. 30
    c. 10
    d. less than one

    ANS: D   PG: 182   TYP: knowledge

82. In the case of _____, offenders occupy positions in the organization that permit them to carry out illegal activities discreetly.
    a. white-collar crime
    b. the falsely accused
    c. deviance
    d. witch hunts

    ANS: A   PG: 180   TYP: comprehension

83. Janice Tucker, who works for Lab, Inc., pleaded guilty to submitting false lab analyses of contamination at "clean up" sites. Lab, Inc. charged companies $6,000 for these analyses. Tucker submitted false results because she wanted return business. She committed a(n)
    a. corporate crime.
    b. act of retreatism.
    c. white-collar crime.
    d. act of rebellion.

    ANS: C   PG: 180   TYP: application

Chapter 7

84. USX corporation, the nation's largest steelmaker, illegally discharged waste water from its Gary, Indiana, plant into the Great Calumet River. This is an example of
    a. retreatism.
    b. secret deviance.
    c. white-collar crime.
    d. corporate crime.

    ANS: D   PG: 180   TYP: application

85. Which one of the following helps us to understand how millions of Chinese cooperated to carry out Mao Zedong's mission of finding and purging those deemed responsible for failure of the Great Leap Forward.
    a. Stanley Milgram's *Obedience to Authority*
    b. Howard Becker's master status of deviant.
    c. Robert K. Merton's theory of structural strain
    d. Edward Sutherland's theory of differential association.

    ANS: A   PG: 183   TYP: application   SOURCE: new

86. In research, a person working in cooperation with an experimenter is known as
    a. the control agent.
    b. a confederate.
    c. the experimented-on.
    d. a double agent.

    ANS: B   PG: 183   TYP: knowledge

87. _____ is the researcher who conducted the classic study *Obedience to Authority*.
    a. Stanley Milgram
    b. Emile Durkheim
    c. Howard Becker
    d. Erving Goffman

    ANS: A   PG: 182   TYP: knowledge   SOURCE: study guide

88. Since 1949, Chinese leaders in power have adhered to which one of the following codes?
    a. In any circumstances and at any cost, political power must be retained in its totality.
    b. Chinese that attend college in the United States are not allowed to take courses in political and social theory.
    c. Sports undermine the principles of communism.
    d. Intellectuals are unimportant to the success of the country.

    ANS: A   PG: 182   TYP: knowledge

89. Stanley Milgram wrote, "The person who, with inner conviction, loathes stealing, killing, and assault may find himself committing these acts with relative ease." Under what conditions does Milgram believe this happens?
    a. when no one is watching
    b. when under the influence of alcohol
    c. when the person's life is threatened
    d. when commanded by an authority

    ANS: C   PG: 183   TYP: comprehension

90. In Stanley Milgram's classic experiment, *Obedience to Authority*, he discovered that obedience was founded on
    a. the firm command of a person with a status that gave minimal authority over a subject recruited to participate in the study.
    b. the subject's fear of being punished physically if he or she disobeyed.
    c. the subject's dislike of the learner's physical characteristics.
    d. the subject's firm belief that learning is enhanced when failure is punished.

    ANS: A   PG: 183   TYP: knowledge

91. When constructionists study the process by which a group or behavior is defined as a problem to society, they focus on
    a. the valued goals and the means to achieve those goals.
    b. the rule breaker, rule maker, and rule enforcers.
    c. responses to structural strain.
    d. who makes the claims, whose claims are heard, and how audiences respond.

    ANS: D   PG: 185   TYP: comprehension   SOURCE: study guide

Chapter 7

92. Staff Sergeant Ivan Frederick testified that when at the Abu Ghraib Prison "I questioned some of the things that I saw....such as leaving inmates in their cells with no clothes or in female underpants—and the answer I got was 'This is how military intelligence wants it done.'" The dynamics Frederick described best correspond with
    a. Stanley Milgram's *Obedience to Authority*.
    b. Howard Becker's master status of deviant.
    c. Robert K. Merton's theory of structural strain.
    d. Edward Sutherland's theory of differential association.

    ANS: A   PG: 183   TYP: application   SOURCE: new

93. The Chinese government issued the report "The Human Rights Record of the United States" because
    a. it believes that the United States is a model with regard to human rights.
    b. the U.S. asked for an independent evaluation of its human rights record.
    c. it wanted to show that its human rights record is better than the U.S record.
    d. the U.S. issues Country Reports on Human Rights Practices each year for 190 countries but does not critique its own record.

    ANS: D   PG: 185   TYP: comprehension   SOURCE: study guide

94. To call AIDS a moral problem is to locate its cause in the goodness or badness of human action and to suggest that a solution depends on changing evil ways. To call it a medical problem is to locate its cause in the biological workings of the mind or body and to suggest that a solution rests with a drug, a vaccine, or surgery. This contrast in perspective shows
    a. labels, examples, and orientation are important because they tend to evoke a particular cause and a particular solution.
    b. the harm that results when AIDS is defined as a medical problem.
    c. that there is no right way to talk about AIDS.
    d. that it is difficult to generate profiles describing why people have AIDS.

    ANS: A   PG: 185   TYP: application

95. Structural strain occurs when
    a. the valued goals have clear boundaries.
    b. the legitimate opportunities to achieve valued goals are open to everyone.
    c. the means to achieve goals are unclear.
    d. a large segment of the population is young.

    ANS: C   PG: 186   TYP: comprehension

96. According to Robert K. Merton, structural strain exists in the United States because
    a. opportunities are open to all.
    b. people must go to college in order to become successful.
    c. American culture places a high value on social advancement for all its members, regardless of the circumstances into which they are born.
    d. the legitimate means to achieve the culturally-valued goals are clearly defined.

    ANS: C   PG: 186   TYP: knowledge

97. Special Economic Zones are designated areas within the People's Republic of China that
    a. operate on the socialist model.
    b. use prison populations to perform labor.
    c. are designed to make no profit.
    d. enjoy capitalist privileges.

    ANS: D   PG: 186   TYP: knowledge

98. _____ percent of all athletes who play college basketball have a chance to play in the professional ranks.
    a. Approximately 50
    b. 25
    c. About 10
    d. Fewer than 2

    ANS: D   PG: 186   TYP: application

99. Which of the following phrases best summarizes "innovation"?
    a. Win by the rules of the game.
    b. I don't like the game or the rules.
    c. Change the rules to win the game.
    d. Follow the rules even if you don't win.

    ANS: C   PG: 187   TYP: application   SOURCE: new

Chapter 7

100. Retreatism is a response to structural strain that involves
    a. creating new goals and the means to achieving them.
    b. accepting both cultural goals and legitimate means to achieving them.
    c. accepting cultural goals but rejecting the means to achieving them.
    d. rejecting cultural goals and the legitimate means to achieving them.

    ANS: D   PG: 187   TYP: comprehension

101. According to Merton's typology of responses associated with structural strain, a college graduate who takes a job bagging groceries would be classified as a
    a. secret deviant.
    b. conformist.
    c. ritualist.
    d. retreatist.

    ANS: C   PG: 187   TYP: application

102. One reason boys are valued more in China is that
    a. sons are less likely to move away from their parents when they marry.
    b. sons are easier to raise than daughters.
    c. sons cost less money to raise.
    d. sons and their families are expected to care for parents in their old age.

    ANS: D   PG: 188   TYP: knowledge

103. For couples planning to have children, one major source of structural strain in China rests with
    a. culturally-valued goals that favor girls over boys.
    b. limited access to birth control technology.
    c. the number of legitimate opportunities to have children, especially a son.
    d. an overemphasis on economic success.

    ANS: C   PG: 188   TYP: application

104. "Don't aim high, and you won't be disappointed" is an attitude that represents the thinking of
    a. retreatists.
    b. ritualists.
    c. innovators.
    d. conformists.

    ANS: B   PG: 187   TYP: application

105. According to Merton's typology of responses associated with structural strain, couples in China would be classified as retreatists if they
    a. decided to abort a baby because it was a girl.
    b. disagreed with the one-child policy.
    c. claimed ethnic minority status in order to have more than one child.
    d. hid the birth of baby girls from party officials.

    ANS: D   PG: 188   TYP: application

106. In China, those most likely to be innovators are those
    a. whose first child is a son.
    b. who have no preferences as to the sex of their child.
    c. who are firmly committed to upholding laws related to birth control
    d. who prefer a male child over a female one.

    ANS: D   PG: 188   TYP: application

107. Which one of the following responses to childbearing would constitute a ritualist in China?
    a. Upon the birth of a girl baby, the parents arrange to have a midwife kill the infant.
    b. A couple decides to have children until they have a boy.
    c. A couple claims minority status.
    d. A couple disagrees with government policies on family size, but they limit their family to one child anyway.

    ANS: D   PG: 188   TYP: application

Chapter 7

108. The students who participated in the 1989 demonstration in Tiananmen Square were accused of "bourgeois liberalization." This means they were guilty of
    a. following capitalist principles.
    b. draft evasion.
    c. the wanton expression of individual freedom.
    d. slandering Chairman Mao.

    ANS: C   PG: 190   TYP: knowledge   SOURCE: study guide

109. The theory of differential association focuses on
    a. how a person comes to learn the norms of a deviant subculture.
    b. how an act comes to be labeled as deviant.
    c. the function of deviance.
    d. obedience to authority.

    ANS: A   PG: 190   TYP: comprehension

110. "When persons become criminals, they do so because of contacts with criminal patterns and also because of isolation from non-criminal patterns." This statement represents an essential assumption that underlies _____ theories.
    a. structural strain
    b. differential association
    c. labeling
    d. constructionist

    ANS: B   PG: 190   TYP: application

111. Which one of the following statements is *most* closely associated with differential association theory?
    a. It is impossible for any society to be entirely free of deviance.
    b. Behavior that is unthinkable in an individual who is acting on his or her own may be executed without hesitation when carried out under orders.
    c. When people become criminals, they do so because of contacts with criminal patterns and because of isolation from non-criminal patterns.
    d. Deviance is a consequence not of a particular behavior but of the application of rules and sanctions.

    ANS: C   PG: 190   TYP: comprehension

112. Which theory underlies the Chinese philosophy that rehabilitation is the purpose of punishment?
   a. structural strain
   b. differential association
   c. labeling
   d. claims making

   ANS: B   PG: 190   TYP: application

113. "A deviant individual, whether a thief or revisionist, becomes deviant because of 'bad' education or association with 'bad' influences." This statement represents the essential assumptions underlying
   a. structural strain theory.
   b. differential association theory.
   c. labeling theory.
   d. constructionist theory.

   ANS: B   PG: 190   TYP: application

114. A university professor in the People's Republic of China states that "it is a very challenging job here on campus to learn about advanced technologies and the very interesting ideas and value systems from the outside world and, at the same time, to keep our own traditions." The professor is expressing concern about
   a. labeling.
   b. differential association.
   c. structural strain.
   d. obedience to authority.

   ANS: B   PG: 190   TYP: application

115. Sociologist Terry Williams finds that to become a successful drug dealer, a youth must learn a number of skills: pleasing the boss, meeting goals, and getting along with associates. These specific findings support
   a. labeling theory.
   b. differential association.
   c. structural strain.
   d. the constructionist approach.

   ANS: B   PG: 190   TYP: application

Chapter 7

116. The _____ is one major factor supporting the rigid system of social control in China.
    a. for-profit prison industry in China
    b. rebellious nature of the Chinese people
    c. size of the Chinese population
    d. apathetic nature of the Chinese people

    ANS: C   PG: 191   TYP: knowledge

117. Roughly, one of every _____ people alive in the world lives in the People's Republic of China.
    a. five
    b. two
    c. ten
    d. twenty

    ANS: A   PG: 191   TYP: knowledge   SOURCE: study guide

118. China has approximately _____ percent of the world's arable land and _____ percent of the world's population.
    a. 20; 7
    b. 10; 2
    c. 30; 15
    d. 6; 20

    ANS: D   PG: 191   TYP: knowledge

119. The population of China is approximately
    a. 500 million.
    b. 750 million.
    c. 1.3 billion.
    d. 2 billion.

    ANS: C   PG: 191   TYP: knowledge

Deviance, Conformity, and Social Control

120. The *habitable* land area of China is approximately
    a. the size of the United States.
    b. the size of Europe, North America, and South America combined.
    c. half the size of the United States.
    d. the size of the African continent.

    ANS: C   PG: 191   TYP: knowledge   SOURCE: study guide

For the following questions, use one from the following responses to match each statement with the appropriate theory of deviance.

    a. Functionalist perspective (as represented by Emile Durkheim)
    b. Labeling theory
    c. Differential association
    d. Constructionist approach
    e. Structural strain

121. Deviance, especially the ritual of identifying and exposing wrongdoing, determining a punishment, and carrying out a punishment, is an emotional experience that binds together members of groups and establishes a sense of community.

    ANS: A   PG: 177

122. Claims makers play important roles in defining deviance and responses to it.

    ANS: D   PG: 184

123. Deviance is likely to be high when the legitimate opportunities for meeting the culturally-valued goals are closed to a significant portion of people.

    ANS: E   PG: 186

124. Criminal behavior is learned.

    ANS: C   PG: 190

Chapter 7

125. Deviance depends on whether people notice it.

   ANS: B   PG: 178

Multiple Choice Questions on the Web

1. We pay special attention to the People's Republic of China in Chapter 7 because changes in views about _____ illustrate the contextual nature of deviance.
   a. profit-making activities
   b. the role of preschool
   c. individuality
   d. guilt and innocence

   ANS: A   PG: 169   TYP: knowledge

2. From a sociological point of view, deviance is
   a. any unlawful activity.
   b. behavior considered criminal.
   c. any behavior or physical appearance that is socially challenged or condemned.
   d. a disturbance located in the social structure.

   ANS: C   PG: 170   TYP: comprehension

3. What event occurred in China between 1966 and 1976?
   a. The Great Leap Forward
   b. The Cultural Revolution
   c. The Opium Wars
   d. Colonialization

   ANS: B   PG: 170   TYP: knowledge   SOURCE: new

4. Mores are norms that
   a. people define as pivotal to the well-being of the group.
   b. describe customary and routine ways of doing things.
   c. govern the details of life (e.g., when to eat).
   d. people are most able to conceive of changing.

   ANS: A   PG: 171   TYP: comprehension

5. U.S. parents who viewed films of Chinese preschools criticized them for
   a. being chaotic and undisciplined.
   b. promoting self-centeredness.
   c. depending on material items.
   d. making children drab, colorless, and robot-like.

   ANS: D   PG: 173   TYP: knowledge

6. Which one of the following countries has the highest incarceration rate in the world?
   a. South Africa
   b. the United States
   c. China
   d. Russia

   ANS: B   PG: 174   TYP: knowledge

7. U.S. government officials delayed for seven months the release of a congressional report concerning 9-11. When the report was released, some sections related to Saudi Arabia were blackened out. This mechanism of social control is known as
   a. deviance.
   b. censorship.
   c. surveillance.
   d. conformity.

   ANS: B   PG: 176   TYP: application

8. Howard Becker wrote, "No one really knows how much this phenomenon exists, but the amount is very sizable, much more than we are apt to think." Becker was writing about
   a. secret deviants.
   b. innovators.
   c. conformists.
   d. witch-hunts.

   ANS: A   PG: 178   TYP: comprehension

Chapter 7

9. Labeling theorists maintain that determining whether an act is deviant is dependent on all but which one of the following?
    a. whether people notice it
    b. whether people react to it as a violation
    c. whether the deviant act was actually committed by the accused person
    d. whether sanctions are applied

    ANS: C   PG: 178   TYP: comprehension

10. Stanley Milgram's study on obedience to authority offers insights as to how
    a. the falsely accused restore their reputations.
    b. people in positions of authority manage to get others to accept their definitions of deviance.
    c. deviance can exist even in seemingly perfect societies.
    d. drugs, such as cocaine, have come to be defined as illegal.

    ANS: B   PG: 180   TYP: comprehension

True/False Questions

1. The sociological contribution to deviance is that it focuses on the deviant individual.

    ANS: False   PG: 168   SOURCE: study guide

2. Almost any behavior or appearance can qualify as deviant under the right circumstances.

    ANS: True   PG: 168

3. China's current leaders were in their teens or early 20s during the Cultural Revolution.

    ANS: True   PG: 169   SOURCE: new

4. The Cultural Revolution occurred between 1966 and 1976.

    ANS: True   PG: 169   SOURCE: study guide

5. During the Chinese Cultural Revolution, wearing eyeglasses was considered deviant.

   ANS: True   PG: 169

6. We acknowledge the previous legality of cocaine in the United States whenever we ask for a "coke."

   ANS: True   PG: 170   SOURCE: study guide

7. In the United States, cocaine has always been an illegal substance.

   ANS: False   PG: 170

8. Conceptions of what is deviant vary across time and place.

   ANS: True   PG: 170   SOURCE: study guide

9. In China, individualism is the illusion of being different.

   ANS: True   PG: 171   SOURCE: new

10. Folkways are norms that apply to the routine aspects of life.

    ANS: True   PG: 171   SOURCE: new

11. In the United States, preschoolers are likely to be corrected after they do something wrong.

    ANS: True   PG: 172   SOURCE: new

12. Ridicule is a formal sanction.

    ANS: False   PG: 173   SOURCE: study guide

13. Sanctions can be positive or negative.

    ANS: True   PG: 173   SOURCE: new

Chapter 7

14. China has one of the highest incarceration rates in the world.

    ANS: False   PG: 174   SOURCE: new

15. The United States has the highest incarceration rate in the world.

    ANS: True   PG: 174   SOURCE: new; study guide

16. Censorship and surveillance are methods of social control.

    ANS: True   PG: 175

17. According to a Gallup poll, about five percent of Americans favor special security checks on any person of Arab descent.

    ANS: False   PG: 177

18. Today, no one in China can speak critically of the Communist leadership.

    ANS: False   PG: 176   SOURCE: new

19. According to Emile Durkheim, deviance will be present even in a community of saints.

    ANS: True   PG: 177   SOURCE: study guide

20. Labeling theorists maintain that a rule breaker is deviant even if no one notices the violation.

    ANS: False   PG: 178

21. Secret deviants have broken no rules but are treated as if they have.

    ANS: False   PG: 178

22. Mao used the Cultural Revolution as an attempt to eliminate anyone that opposed his policies.

    ANS: True   PG: 179

23. In the U.S., about 90 percent of crime victims report the crime to police.

    ANS: False   PG: 179   SOURCE: study guide

24. By all accounts, the Great Leap Forward was a success.

    ANS: False   PG: 179   SOURCE: new

25. Prison populations contain the falsely accused within their ranks.

    ANS: True   PG: 179

26. People are likely to be falsely accused of a crime when the well-being of a country or a group is threatened.

    ANS: True   PG: 179   SOURCE: new

27. During WWII, the internment of more than 110,000 people of Japanese descent is an example of a witch hunt.

    ANS: True   PG: 180

28. Governor George Ryan ordered a moratorium on executions in his state after discovering that 13 death row inmates were found innocent by DNA evidence.

    ANS: True   PG: 181

29. Sociologists are just as concerned with those who make and enforce laws as they are with those who violate them.

    ANS: True   PG: 182   SOURCE: new

Chapter 7

30. Stanley Milgram's study *Obedience to Authority* is relevant to understanding the Cultural Revolution and Abu Ghraib.

    ANS: True   PG: 184   SOURCE: new; study guide

31. The Chinese government seeks to emulate the human rights record of the United States.

    ANS: False   PG: 185   SOURCE: new

32. The U.S. State Department classifies China's human rights record as poor.

    ANS: True   PG: 185   SOURCE: study guide

33. Setting up picket lines or calling for a boycott are examples of claims-making activities.

    ANS: True   PG: 185

34. Structural strain does not exist in the United States.

    ANS: False   PG: 186

35. According to Merton, the lowest social classes clearly face the greatest pressure to engage in "innovation."

    ANS: True   PG: 187

36. Approximately 25 percent of athletes who play Division I college basketball have a chance of playing in the NBA.

    ANS: False   PG: 187

37. In his theory of structural strain, Robert K. Merton maintains that the upper classes face the greatest pressure to "innovate."

    ANS: False   PG: 187

38. One source of structural strain in China relates to the number of legitimate opportunities open to married couples to have children.

    ANS: True   PG: 188

39. The sex imbalance in China favors girls.

    ANS: False   PG: 189   SOURCE: new

40. There are no exceptions to the one-child policy in China.

    ANS: False   PG: 190

41. The Chinese believe that a deviant individual becomes deviant because of "bad" influences.

    ANS: True   PG: 190

42. One in every 10 people in the world live in China.

    ANS: False   PG: 191

43. After Tiananmen Square, public protests have been nonexistent in China.

    ANS: False   PG: 191

Concept Application (also in study guide)

Consider the concepts listed below. Match one of more of the concepts with each scenario. Explain your choices.

   a. Claims makers
   b. Falsely accused
   c. Mores
   d. Secret deviants
   e. White-collar crimes

Chapter 7

Scenario 1

"The Tobacco Institute was founded in 1958, even before the first Surgeon General's report on the health risks of smoking, to represent the interests of tobacco companies to lawmakers. Once financed by a dozen companies, it now works for only five—Philip Morris, R. J. Reynolds, Lorillard, Liggett, and American Brands—but its twofold mission remains the same: to persuade federal, state, and local authorities to lay off and to sell the virtues of the industry to the American public. A staff of lobbyists handles the first task and Ms. Dawson, at 32, the second. The job description is fairly typical for a trade organization—to develop and articulate the industry position on any given issue, then make sure the message reaches the public. But this is no typical industry" (Janofsky 1994:8F).

ANS: A

Scenario 2

"Boesky told the government about his insider trading activities, not only with me but with at least one other well-known investment banker. Beyond that, he detailed various schemes, concocted with those in the highest circles of power, to circumvent SEC regulations and tax laws. Said Carroll, 'He has played fast and loose with the rules that govern our markets, with the effect of manipulating the outcome of financial transactions measured in the hundreds of millions of dollars" (Levine and Hoffer 1991:346).

ANS: E

Scenario 3

"The small-time criminals are everywhere. Maybe they're sneaking into more than one theater in the local Cineplex or grabbing a handful of yogurt peanuts from the grocery store bin and eating all the evidence before getting to the check-out stand or making personal long-distance calls from work" (Tomashoff 1993:E1).

ANS: D

Scenario 4

"Death sentences for people who later prove to be innocent are less unusual than is commonly supposed. Just in the last five months, four once-condemned prisoners have been released after spending years on death row. Two of them, in Alabama and Texas, turned out to have been convicted on fabricated evidence and perjured testimony; the third, in Texas, was convicted because of evidence that was withheld; the fourth, in Maryland, was exonerated by DNA analysis, a technology that was unavailable at the time of his trial" (*The New Yorker* 1993:14).

ANS: B

Scenario 5

"Can a court force an unwilling person to give up part of his or her body (e.g., bone marrow, a kidney) to a relative who needs that body part to survive? That was the question recently brought before the court of common pleas in Allegheny County, Pennsylvania. The common law has consistently held that one human being is under no legal obligation to give aid or take action to save another human being or to rescue one. The court said that such a rule, although revolting in a moral sense, is founded upon the very essence of a free society, and while other societies may view things differently, our society has as its first principle respect for the individual—and society and government exist to protect that individual from being invaded and hurt by another" (Chayet 1983).

ANS: C

Short Essay Questions

1. Why focus on China in conjunction with concepts of deviance, conformity, and social control?

2. What is deviance? How is it related to conformity and social control?

3. Is it possible to generate a list of deviant behaviors? Why or why not?

4. Distinguish between folkways and mores. Give examples of each concept.

5. What important cultural lessons are incorporated into the daily activities of Chinese and American preschoolers? How do parents from each culture react to the other's system?

6. What are the major mechanisms of social control? Give examples of each.

7. According to Durkheim, why is crime a "normal" and necessary phenomenon?

8. What are the major assumptions that guide labeling theory? How do these assumptions relate to the following categories: conformists, pure deviant, secret deviant, and falsely accused?

9. Under which circumstances are people most likely to be falsely accused of a crime?

10. What are witch hunts? Why do they occur? Give an example of witch hunt.

11. Define white-collar crime and corporate crime. Why are white-collar and corporate criminals less likely to be caught than so-called common criminals?

12. In Milgram's classic experiment *Obedience to Authority*, why did a significant number of volunteers come to accept an authority's definition of deviance and administer shocks even though these shocks caused obvious harm to confederates?

13. Who are claims makers? What factors determine a claim maker's success?

14. Describe the constructionist approach to analyzing claims makers and claims making activities.

15. What is structural strain? What are the sources of structural strain in the United States?

16. What are the responses to structural strain?

17. Identify one source of structural strain in China. Use Merton's typology of responses to consider how people in China respond to this strain.

18. Summarize the major assumptions underlying the theory of differential association. How does this assumption relate to the mechanisms of social control in China?

19. What larger historical and geographical factors shape China's one-child policy?

Comprehensive Essay Questions

1. Explain the following statement: "Almost any behavior or appearance can qualify as deviant under the right circumstances."

2. Identify a deviant behavior in the news. Which sociological theories help to explain that behavior?

Chapter 8

Social Stratification

Multiple-Choice Questions

1. Approximately _____ million people in the world are worth at least $1 million (excluding the value of their homes).
   a. 8.3
   b. 20
   c. 50.3
   d. 100

   ANS: A   PG: 199   TYP: knowledge

2. Which one of the following countries has the lowest poverty rate in the world?
   a. Mexico
   b. Haiti
   c. Taiwan
   d. North Korea

   ANS: C   PG: 199   TYP: knowledge   SOURCE: study guide

3. About one in every _____ people on the planet does not have a decent place to go to the bathroom
   a. 100
   b. 20
   c. 10
   d. 3

   ANS: D   PG: 199   TYP: knowledge   SOURCE: new

Chapter 8

4. Which one of the following questions would be of *least* interest to a sociologist studying the world's richest and poorest peoples?
    a. How does one explain the disparity between the richest 8.3 million and the poorest 1.2 billion?
    b. Why should so few in the world enjoy great wealth while so many struggle to live on the equivalent of $1 per day?
    c. Can the free enterprise system and globalization correct dramatic inequalities between the world's richest and poorest peoples?
    d. How might we instill a work ethic in the poorest 1.2 billion?

    ANS: D   PG: 199   TYP: comprehension

5. Social stratification is _____ process in which individuals, groups, and places are categorized and ranked on a scale of social worth.
    a. a random
    b. an arbitrary
    c. a systematic
    d. an automatic

    ANS: C   PG: 200   TYP: comprehension

6. _____ include(s) everything from the chance to stay alive during the first year of life to the chance to go to college.
    a. Social stratification
    b. Life chances
    c. Apartheid
    d. Social status

    ANS: B   PG: 200   TYP: comprehension

7. The systematic process by which individuals, groups, and places are ranked on a scale of social worth is
    a. social stratification.
    b. symbolic stratification.
    c. apartheid.
    d. social structure.

    ANS: A   PG: 200   TYP: comprehension   SOURCE: study guide

8. Class and caste systems of stratification differ with regard to all but which one of the following?
   a. ease of mobility
   b. relative importance of achieved and ascribed characteristics
   c. restrictions placed on interaction between people considered unequal
   d. status value assigned to positions

   ANS: D   PG: 207   TYP: comprehension   SOURCE: new

9. About one third of the world's population does not have a decent place to go the bathroom. One solution to this problem is
   a. the arborloo.
   b. the port-o-let.
   c. cheaply-made ceramic toilets.
   d. plastic bags.

   ANS: A   PG: 201   TYP: knowledge   SOURCE: new

10. A baby born in _____ has one of the best chances of surviving its first year of life.
    a. the United States
    b. Sweden
    c. Italy
    d. Singapore

    ANS: B   PG: 202   TYP: knowledge   SOURCE: study guide

11. A baby born in _____ has one of the worst chances of surviving the first year of life.
    a. China
    b. Mexico
    c. Afghanistan
    d. Vietnam

    ANS: C   PG: 202   TYP: knowledge

Chapter 8

12. Consumers living in the highest-income countries account for _____ percent of total private consumption.
    a. 98
    b. 86
    c. 50
    d. 25

    ANS: B   PG: 203   TYP: knowledge

13. In the United States, babies classified as _____ have the worst chance of surviving the first year of life.
    a. white
    b. black
    c. Hispanic
    d. Asian

    ANS: B   PG: 203   TYP: knowledge   SOURCE: new

14. The world's poorest 1.2 billion (i.e., the poorest fifth) people account for _____ percent of total private consumption.
    a. 40
    b. 25
    c. 10
    d. less than 2

    ANS: D   PG: 202   TYP: knowledge

15. Which of the following is an achieved characteristic?
    a. wrinkles
    b. skin color
    c. occupation
    d. reproductive capacity

    ANS: C   PG: 200   TYP: application   SOURCE: new; study guide

16. An achieved characteristic is an attribute that people
    a. inherit at birth.
    b. develop over time.
    c. possess through no fault or effort of their own.
    d. acquire through some combination of choice, effort, and ability.

    ANS: D   PG: 200   TYP: comprehension

17. Sociologists are particularly interested in situations in which _____ are assigned different status value.
    a. achieved characteristics
    b. eye colors
    c. roles
    d. ascribed characteristics

    ANS: D   PG: 201   TYP: comprehension

18. For sociologists, one important dimension of any stratification system is the extent to which people "are treated as members of a category, irrespective of their individual merits." This statement suggests that sociologists are particularly interested in
    a. achieved characteristics.
    b. class systems of stratification.
    c. ascribed characteristics.
    d. status value.

    ANS: C   PG: 202   TYP: comprehension   SOURCE: new

19. People assign _____ when they regard some features of a characteristic as more valuable or worthy than other features.
    a. life chances
    b. status value
    c. social class
    d. social stratification

    ANS: B   PG: 201   TYP: comprehension   SOURCE: study guide

Chapter 8

20. The compensation guidelines for the September 11, 2001, attacks assigned least value to which category?
    a. Married persons 30 and under with two children and an annual income of $225,000
    b. Single mothers age 30 and over earning $20,000
    c. Single, childless person age 65 and older with an annual income of $10,000
    d. Married person 30 and over, no children, earning $100,000

    ANS: C   PG: 202   TYP: comprehension

21. In the United States, for every $1,000 earned by the poorest 10 percent, the richest 10 percent earn _____.
    a. $2,200
    b. $5,000
    c. $16,000
    d. $20,000

    ANS: C   PG: 204   TYP: knowledge

22. Caste systems of stratification are characterized by <u>all</u> but which one of the following adjectives?
    a. rigid
    b. closed
    c. restricted
    d. fluid

    ANS: D   PG: 205   TYP: comprehension   SOURCE: study guide

23. In a caste system of social stratification,
    a. inequality is not systematic.
    b. there is a systematic connection between ascribed characteristics and life chances.
    c. people can change their class position through hard work.
    d. talent, merit, and ability determine a person's life chances.

    ANS: B   PG: 205   TYP: comprehension

24. Apartheid is an example of
    a. a caste system of stratification.
    b. a class system of stratification.
    c. an ideal type of social stratification.
    d. intergenerational mobility.

    ANS: A   PG: 206   TYP: application   SOURCE: study guide

25. Class systems of stratification are characterized as
    a. rigid.
    b. closed.
    c. restricted.
    d. fluid.

    ANS: D   PG: 206   TYP: comprehension

26. Apartheid is a system of social stratification in which
    a. every aspect of life is regulated according to racial classification.
    b. whites imposed a separate but equal policy on the nonwhite peoples.
    c. class elements dominate.
    d. nonwhites enforce the system of racial inequality.

    ANS: A   PG: 206   TYP: knowledge

27. In comparison to class systems, caste systems of stratification
    a. are extremely rigid.
    b. rank people on the basis of achievements.
    c. have few barriers to social interaction among people from different strata.
    d. allow marriage between people of different strata.

    ANS: A   PG: 206   TYP: comprehension

28. Ideally, in a class system of stratification,
    a. life chances are inherited.
    b. people rise and fall on the strength of their abilities.
    c. there is no intergenerational mobility.
    d. inequality is systematic.

    ANS: B   PG: 206   TYP: comprehension

Chapter 8

29. A person who changes his or her class position through marriage, graduation, inheritance, or job promotions is experiencing
    a. vertical mobility.
    b. horizontal mobility.
    c. caste mobility.
    d. downward mobility.

    ANS: A   PG: 206   TYP: application   SOURCE: study guide

30. _____ mobility is a gain or loss of rank, such as when an accountant becomes unemployed.
    a. Vertical
    b. Intergenerational
    c. Horizontal
    d. Social

    ANS: A   PG: 206   TYP: comprehension

31. Intragenerational mobility is movement
    a. that results in a loss of rank or status.
    b. that cannot be anticipated early.
    c. upward or downward during an individual's lifetime.
    d. upward or downward over two or more generations.

    ANS: C   PG: 206   TYP: comprehension

32. When a son or daughter goes into an occupation that is higher or lower in rank and prestige than a parent's occupation, sociologists label that mobility
    a. intragenerational.
    b. intergenerational.
    c. downward.
    d. upward.

    ANS: B   PG: 207   TYP: application   SOURCE: new

Social Stratification

33. In the United States, dental assistants are likely to be which one the following?
    a. male and white
    b. Hispanic and male
    c. Hispanic and female
    d. white and female

    ANS: D   PG: 207   TYP: comprehension   SOURCE: new

34. In the United States, concrete finishers and cement masons are likely to be which one the following?
    a. male and white
    b. Hispanic and male
    c. Hispanic and female
    d. white and female

    ANS: B   PG: 207   TYP: comprehension   SOURCE: new; study guide

35. Income profiles for households classified as white, black, and Hispanic show that
    a. black and Hispanic households compare favorably with white households.
    b. black and Hispanic households are disproportionately concentrated in lower-income categories.
    c. income distribution is not affected by type of household.
    d. low paying and low prestige occupations are equally distributed in <u>all</u> household types.

    ANS: B   PG: 207   TYP: comprehension

36. If the United States had a true class system, the percentages of households classified as white, black, and Hispanic in each income category would be
    a. smaller for white households than for the other two household types.
    b. the same across all households.
    c. greater for black households than for white or Hispanic households.
    d. greater for Hispanic and black households than for white households.

    ANS: B   PG: 207   TYP: comprehension

37. Most systems of stratification, including the U.S. system, are
    a. class systems.
    b. caste systems.
    c. a combination of class and caste systems.
    d. intragenerational class systems.

    ANS: C   PG: 206   TYP: comprehension

38. The fact that income and occupation are connected to race means that we must conclude that the United States is, at best,
    a. a class system.
    b. a caste system.
    c. a mixture of class and caste systems.
    d. unstratified.

    ANS: C   PG: 207   TYP: comprehension

39. Eighty-five percent of Americans believe that "it is possible in America to pretty much be who you want to be." The high percentage suggests that most American believe the United States is
    a. classless.
    b. a caste system.
    c. a class system.
    d. a combination of caste and class.

    ANS: C   PG: 206   TYP: application

40. Which racial category has the greatest percentage of households in the lowest income category?
    a. black
    b. white
    c. Hispanic
    d. Asian

    ANS: A   PG: 207   TYP: knowledge

41. If 25 percent of professional baseball players were classified as black or Hispanic, and if the on-field positions were filled without regard to race or ethnicity, we should expect _____ percent of pitchers to be black or Hispanic.
    a. 25
    b. 3
    c. 10
    d. 50

    ANS: A   PG: 206   TYP: application

42. According to the functionalist perspective, the unequal distribution of rewards is necessary in order to
    a. ensure that the most functionally important occupations are filled by the best-qualified people.
    b. make the least functionally important occupations attractive to the masses.
    c. justify denying some people the opportunity to achieve functionally important occupations.
    d. make the system as democratic as possible.

    ANS: A   PG: 210   TYP: comprehension

43. Davis and Moore argue that the more functionally unique an occupation, the greater its functional importance. *Functionally unique* means that
    a. few other people can perform the same occupation.
    b. just about anyone can do the job.
    c. the occupation has an unusual name.
    d. few people want to do the job.

    ANS: A   PG: 211   TYP: comprehension

44. In analyzing social stratification, functionalists ask
    a. who benefits from social stratification and at whose expense.
    b. how do people of different social statuses interact.
    c. why some positions in society are more valued than other positions.
    d. why the disadvantaged lack the work ethic needed to advance.

    ANS: C   PG: 210   TYP: comprehension   SOURCE: study guide

Chapter 8

45. Critics of the functional perspective on social stratification argue that this approach falls short because
    a. one must assume that social stratification exists in all societies.
    b. workers who perform the same jobs tend to receive equal pay regardless of their race or sex.
    c. salary reflects an occupation's contribution to society.
    d. it is difficult to determine the functional importance of an occupation.

    ANS: D   PG: 212   TYP: knowledge

46. Which one of the following factors does *not* interfere with a stratification system's ability to attract the most qualified people to fill the most important positions?
    a. capable individuals are overlooked or not granted access to training
    b. parents' influence and wealth determine the status their children attain
    c. elite groups control the avenues of training
    d. the best qualified and most capable people apply for the functionally unique positions

    ANS: D   PG: 211   TYP: comprehension

47. Comparable worth means
    a. that when men and women work in the same firms in the same occupation, they must not be paid differently.
    b. that when occupational categories are agreed to be equivalently valuable within a firm, the compensation must be equivalent across those categories.
    c. male and female dominated occupations should be valued equally.
    d. men and women can be paid differently, even if they are in the same occupation.

    ANS: B   PG: 212   TYP: comprehension

48. The question "Why should full-time workers at a child care center (a traditionally female occupation) receive a median weekly salary of $333, while a person working as an auto mechanic (a traditionally male occupation) earns $578?" relates to issues of
    a. pay equity.
    b. comparable worth.
    c. functional uniqueness.
    d. status consciousness.

    ANS: B   PG: 212   TYP: application   SOURCE: study guide

Social Stratification

49. Which one of the following questions do conflict theorists ask to highlight the problems with the functional perspective of social stratification?
    a. How can we attract the best qualified people to fill the most functionally important positions?
    b. Will the most qualified people be attracted to the less functionally important occupations?
    c. How much inequality in salary is really necessary to ensure that people choose the most important positions in society?
    d. Why do the disadvantaged lack the motivation to acquire the training needed to fill the most important positions in society?

    ANS: C   PG: 213   TYP: comprehension

50. The Pew Hispanic Center estimates that there are at least 12 million undocumented workers living in the United States. Without this source of "cheap labor," fruits and vegetables would rot in the fields, toddlers in Manhattan would be without nannies, towels in hotels would go unlaundered, and bedpans and trays would go uncollected. This situation illustrates
    a. functional uniqueness.
    b. comparable worth.
    c. the functions of poverty.
    d. status consciousness.

    ANS: C   PG: 209   TYP: application

51. Poor people purchase goods and services that would otherwise go unused, such as day-old bread, used cars, and second-hand clothes. Such purchases speak to
    a. functional uniqueness.
    b. comparable worth.
    c. the functions of poverty.
    d. status consciousness.

    ANS: C   PG: 209   TYP: application   SOURCE: new

Chapter 8

52. Many businesses, governmental agencies, and nonprofit organizations exist to serve poor people or to monitor their behavior. This arrangement is an example of
    a. functional uniqueness.
    b. comparable worth.
    c. the functions of poverty.
    d. status consciousness.

    ANS: C   PG: 209   TYP: application   SOURCE: new; study guide

53. While only 51 Filipino troops serve as part of the U.S.-led coalition in Iraq, more than 4,000 serve food, clean toilets, and fill other support staff positions. Without them, the U.S. military would be hard-pressed. This arrangement illustrates
    a. functional uniqueness.
    b. comparable worth.
    c. the functions of poverty.
    d. status consciousness.

    ANS: C   PG: 210   TYP: application

54. According to world-system theorists, capitalism has come to dominate the world economy because
    a. under this system, governments control economic activities.
    b. it is the only economic system in the world.
    c. of the ways in which capitalists respond to changes in the economy, especially to economic stagnation.
    d. national interests take precedence over corporate interests.

    ANS: C   PG: 214   TYP: comprehension   SOURCE: study guide

55. Which one of the following countries would world-system theorists classify as a core economy?
    a. People's Republic of China
    b. India
    c. Japan
    d. Hong Kong

    ANS: C   PG: 214   TYP: application

56. An overwhelming majority of Fortune 500 corporations are headquartered in countries with economies classified as
   a. low-income.
   b. semiperipheral.
   c. peripheral.
   d. core.

   ANS: D   PG: 214   TYP: application

57. Vietnam is a country that world-system theorists would classify as a _____ economy.
   a. capitalist
   b. semiperipheral
   c. peripheral
   d. core

   ANS: C   PG: 215   TYP: knowledge

58. Japan, Germany, the United States, Canada, Italy, and the United Kingdom possess _____ economies.
   a. semiperipheral
   b. core
   c. peripheral
   d. transitional

   ANS: B   PG: 214   TYP: application   SOURCE: study guide

59. The Vietnamese economy is very vulnerable to price fluctuations. For example, the country managed to become the third largest producer of coffee beans when prices were around $3.00 per pound, only later to see the price drop to less than 50 cents. The vulnerability explains why Vietnam is classified as a _____ economy.
   a. core
   b. peripheral
   c. semiperipheral
   d. middle-income

   ANS: B   PG: 215   TYP: application

Chapter 8

60. As defined by the U.S. Department of Commerce, the 10 emerging markets possess _____ economies.
    a. semiperipheral
    b. core
    c. peripheral
    d. transitional

    ANS: A   PG: 215   TYP: application

61. Which one of the following is one of the 10 emerging markets as defined by the U.S. Department of Commerce?
    a. Canada
    b. Vietnam
    c. South Korea
    d. Japan

    ANS: C   PG: 215   TYP: application   SOURCE : new

62. The world economy is at least _____ years old.
    a. 500
    b. 250
    c. 100
    d. 50

    ANS: A   PG: 213   TYP: knowledge

63. Many successful people view government and society as irrelevant or, worse, a hindrance to their good fortune; instead, they attribute their success to their own character and individual performance. This viewpoint represents the _____ theory of wealth creation.
    a. "great man"
    b. societal-created
    c. narcissistic
    d. free ride

    ANS: A   PG: 213   TYP: comprehension   SOURCE: study guide

64. _____ economies include the wealthiest, most highly diversified economies with strong, stable governments.
   a. Core
   b. Peripheral
   c. Semiperipheral
   d. Extractive

   ANS: A   PG: 214   TYP: comprehension

65. _____ economies operate on the fringes of the world economy.
   a. Core
   b. Peripheral
   c. Semiperipheral
   d. Service

   ANS: B   PG: 214   TYP: comprehension

66. _____ is a form of domination in which a foreign power uses its superior military force to impose its political, economic, social, and cultural institutions on an indigenous population with the aim of dominating their resources, labor, and markets.
   a. Neocolonialism
   b. Social stratification
   c. Conflict
   d. Colonialism

   ANS: D   PG: 216   TYP: knowledge

67. _____ is the term for continuing economic dependence on former colonial powers.
   a. Neocolonialism
   b. Social stratification
   c. Conflict
   d. Colonialism

   ANS: A   PG: 217   TYP: knowledge   SOURCE: study guide

Chapter 8

68. _____ percent of the African continent was once controlled by colonial power.
   a. 25
   b. 50
   c. 75
   d. 90

   ANS: D   PG: 217   TYP: knowledge

69. "As leaders, we have a duty. . . to all the world's people, especially the most vulnerable and, in particular, the children of the world, to whom the future belongs." These words reflect the spirit of which global initiative?
   a. Holt International
   b. USA AID
   c. the Millennium Development Project
   d. Micro-lending

   ANS: C   PG: 217   TYP: knowledge   SOURCE: new

70. The bulk of U.S. foreign assistance to the world's poorest countries goes toward all *but* which one of the following?
   a. development
   b. crisis intervention
   c. military training and financing
   d. narcotics control

   ANS: A   PG: 219   TYP: knowledge   SOURCE: new; study guide

71. World-system theorists argue that continuous economic expansion on a global scale is
   a. capitalist-driven.
   b. socialist-driven.
   c. coming to an end.
   d. totalitarianism.

   ANS: A   PG: 219   TYP: comprehension

Social Stratification

72. Which one of the following statements regarding tariffs is false?
    a. Tariffs raise the price of less expensive imported goods so that they cost as much or more than domestic versions.
    b. Tariffs benefit workers in the protected market.
    c. Tariffs are usually lowest on luxury items and highest on essential items, such as shoes and clothes.
    d. The Millenium Development Project has called for the elimination of tariffs on the products imported from the poorest economies.

    ANS: B   PG: 219   TYP: application   SOURCE: new

73. _____ is the flow of the most educated people from poor to rich economies.
    a. Subsidized education
    b. Out-migration
    c. In-migration
    d. Brain drain

    ANS: D   PG: 215   TYP: application   SOURCE: new; study guide

74. The British Medical Association wrote, "All countries must strive to attain self-sufficiency in their health care workforce without generating adverse consequences for other countries." The Association was responding to
    a. subsidized education
    b. out-migration
    c. in-migration
    d. brain drain

    ANS: D   PG: 215   TYP: application   SOURCE: new

75. _____ depends on many factors, including relationship to the means of production, source of income, access to consumer goods, status group, and marketable abilities.
    a. Brain drain
    b. Social class
    c. Social stratification
    d. Global migration

    ANS: B   PG: 215   TYP: comprehension   SOURCE: new

Chapter 8

76. Karl Marx believed that _____ was the most important engine of change.
    a. technology
    b. societal need
    c. class struggle
    d. ideology

    ANS: C   PG: 221   TYP: comprehension   SOURCE: study guide

77. In *The Communist Manifesto*, Marx focused on the two social classes he believed would usher society out of capitalism and into another era. These two classes were
    a. landlords and peasants.
    b. the bourgeoisie and the proletariat.
    c. capitalists and landowners.
    d. finance aristocracy and the peasant class.

    ANS: B   PG: 221   TYP: comprehension

78. The negatively privileged property classes include all <u>but</u> which one of the following?
    a. completely unskilled persons
    b. those dependent on seasonal employment
    c. those at the bottom of the class system
    d. the bourgeoisie

    ANS: D   PG: 222   TYP: comprehension

79. According to Max Weber, persons completely unskilled, lacking property, and dependent on seasonal or sporadic employment constitute the
    a. negatively privileged property class.
    b. ascribed property class.
    c. marketless class.
    d. negatively privileged status group.

    ANS: A   PG: 222   TYP: knowledge

80. In the United States in any given month, an estimated _____ percent of the U.S. population lives in poverty.
    a. 5 to 8
    b. 13 to 16
    c. 20 to 23
    d. 40 to 43

    ANS: B   PG: 222   TYP: knowledge

81. According to Max Weber's terminology, Promise Keepers, United Auto Workers, and Kurdistan Workers Party are
    a. positively privileged property classes.
    b. status groups.
    c. political parties.
    d. negatively privileged property classes.

    ANS: C   PG: 223   TYP: application

82. Weber's ideas about social class inspire sociologists to
    a. study the people who comprise the middle class.
    b. compare the situation of the wealthiest with that of the poorest.
    c. study class conflict as an agent of change.
    d. think of social class as determined by one's relationship to the means of production.

    ANS: B   PG: 224   TYP: knowledge   SOURCE: study guide

83. The 1.2 billion people that live on the equivalent of $1 per day represent the
    a. negatively privileged property class.
    b. semiperipheral class.
    c. functionally unique.
    d. positively privileged property class.

    ANS: A   PG: 223   TYP: application

Chapter 8

84. The richest 8.3 million people in the world represent the
    a. negatively privileged property class.
    b. semiperipheral class.
    c. functionally unique.
    d. positively privileged property class.

    ANS: D   PG: 222   TYP: application

85. Extreme wealth is the most excessive form of wealth. The term applies to a minority of people, perhaps as few as the richest _____ people in the world.
    a. 800
    b. 100 million
    c. 1.2 billion
    d. 2.4 billion

    ANS: A   PG: 224   TYP: knowledge   SOURCE: new

86. Extreme poverty is the most severe form of poverty in which people cannot afford the basic human necessities (food, water, clothes, and shelter). This term applies to about how many people in the world?
    a. 800,000
    b. 100 million
    c. 1.2 billion
    d. 2.4 billion

    ANS: C   PG: 224   TYP: knowledge   SOURCE: new

87. The _____ are the most visible and most publicized underclass in the United States.
    a. Appalachian poor
    b. migrant poor
    c. inner city poor
    d. rural poor

    ANS: C   PG: 224   TYP: knowledge

88. Which one of the following characteristics does not fit the profile of the urban underclass?
    a. homogeneous
    b. at the very bottom of the economic hierarchy
    c. consisting of families and individuals
    d. inner city based

    ANS: A   PG: 224   TYP: comprehension

89. _____ are people with exceptional behaviors and practices that enable them to get better results than their neighbors with the exact same resources.
    a. Conformists
    b. Positive deviants
    c. Microlenders
    d. The upper class

    ANS: B   PG: 225   TYP: comprehension   SOURCE: new

90. A researcher connected to the Save the Children organization observed Vietnamese mothers using alternative food sources available to everyone (they were going to the rice paddies to harvest tiny shrimp and crabs, and they were picking sweet potato greens—considered low-class food—and mixing both food sources with rice). As a result, their children were not malnourished. The mothers are considered
    a. positive deviants.
    b. positively privileged.
    c. negatively privileged.
    d. part of the urban underclass

    ANS: A   PG: 225   TYP: comprehension   SOURCE: new

91. In the United States, 48 of the 50 counties with the highest poverty rates are considered
    a. urban.
    b. rural.
    c. suburban.
    d. inner city.

    ANS: B   PG: 227   TYP: comprehension   SOURCE: new

Chapter 8

92. In numerical terms, people in the United States classified as _____ represent the racial group with the largest number of people living in poverty.
    a. black
    b. Native American
    c. white
    d. Asian

    ANS: C   PG: 227   TYP: comprehension   SOURCE: new

Multiple Choice Questions on the Web

1. About _____ people live on less than $1 per day.
    a. 100 million
    b. 800 million
    c. 1.2 billion
    d. 2 billion

    ANS: C   PG: 199   TYP: knowledge

2. _____ are attributes that people have at birth, develop over time, or possess through no effort or fault of their own.
    a. Achieved characteristics
    b. Status values
    c. Ascribed characteristics
    d. Social stratification

    ANS: C   PG: 200   TYP: comprehension

3. Under apartheid, one's racial category determined where and with whom one could "live, work, eat, travel, play, learn, sleep, and be buried." According to this description, Apartheid is a(n) _____ system of social stratification.
    a. mixed
    b. caste
    c. class
    d. achieved

    ANS: B   PG: 205   TYP: application   SOURCE: new

Social Stratification

4. Mary worked as a secretary for 25 years. Her daughter Jane works as a biological engineer. The difference in status is known as
   a. intergenerational mobility.
   b. intragenerational mobility.
   c. horizontal mobility.
   d. status mobility.

   ANS: A   PG: 206   TYP: application

5. Joe and Jane are on a coed softball team. Jane plays left field, and Joe plays short stop. The coach has assigned them to these positions because she believes that men can naturally field and throw better than women. Based on this information alone, we can make the case that the coach is operating according to a(n)
   a. caste system of stratification.
   b. class system of stratification.
   c. combination of class and caste systems of social stratification.
   d. open system of social stratification.

   ANS: A   PG: 206   TYP: application

6. From a functionalist perspective, social inequality
   a. causes people in the entry-level jobs to work harder.
   b. ensures that the best-qualified people will fill the most demanding positions.
   c. increases the motivation level of all workers.
   d. guarantees that the least-qualified people will not seek the most important jobs.

   ANS: B   PG: 211   TYP: comprehension

7. Which one the following is considered a structural response to reducing global inequality?
   a. transferring wealth through foreign aid and fair trade policies
   b. inviting skilled workers from poor countries to work in the United States
   c. building fences between the world's richest and poorest countries
   d. sending missionaries to the world's poorest countries

   ANS: A   PG: 217   TYP: comprehension   SOURCE: new

Chapter 8

8. The British Medical Association wrote, "Developed countries must assist developing countries in expanding their capacity to train and retain physicians and nurses, which will enable them to become self-sufficient." The Association was responding to
    a. subsidized education.
    b. out-migration.
    c. in-migration.
    d. brain drain.

    ANS: D   PG: 215   TYP: application   SOURCE: new

9. A(n)_____ is an amorphous group of persons held together by virtue of a lifestyle and the level of social esteem and honor others accord them.
    a. primary group
    b. ingroup
    c. status group
    d. functionally unique group

    ANS: C   PG: 222   TYP: comprehension

10. A researcher connected with the Save the Children organization observed Vietnamese mothers feeding their children when they had diarrhea, a behavior that was contrary to traditional practice by
    a. positive deviants.
    b. the positively privileged.
    c. the negatively privileged.
    d. part of the urban underclass.

    ANS: A   PG: 222   TYP: comprehension   SOURCE: new

True/False Questions

1. Ninety percent of the world's richest people live in the United States.

    ANS: False   PG: 199   SOURCE: new

2. About one-third of the world's people do not have a decent place to go to the bathroom.

    ANS: True   PG: 199   SOURCE: new

3. Ascribed characteristics are attributes people cannot easily change.

    ANS: True   PG: 200   SOURCE: new; study guide

4. Ascribed characteristics are attributes people can easily change.

    ANS: False   PG: 200

5. Ascribed characteristics involve some combination of choice, effort, and ability.

    ANS: False   PG: 200

6. Inequality exists both across countries and within countries.

    ANS: True   PG: 203   SOURCE: study guide

7. A baby born in the United States has the best chance in the world of surviving its first year of life.

    ANS: False   PG: 202   SOURCE: study guide

8. A baby born in Angola has one of the worst chances in the world of surviving the first year of life.

    ANS: True   PG: 202

9. Apartheid, South Africa's system of social stratification, was abolished (in a legal sense) in 1994.

    ANS: True   PG: 206   SOURCE: study guide

10. In a true class system, ascribed characteristics determine one's social class.

    ANS: False   PG: 206

Chapter 8

11. Theoretically, in class systems of stratification, people rise and fall on the strength of their abilities.

    ANS: True   PG: 206

12. In a true class system, there is no inequality.

    ANS: False   PG: 206   SOURCE: study guide

13. Systems of stratification are usually a combination of class and caste.

    ANS: True   PG: 206

14. All evidence indicates that the United States possesses a true class system.

    ANS: False   PG: 206

15. Most Americans believe that in the United States, it is possible to be pretty much who you want to be.

    ANS: True   PG: 207   SOURCE: new

16. In the United States, chances are good that a dental assistant is a female classified as white.

    ANS: True   PG: 207   SOURCE: new; study guide

17. In the United States, chances are good that a firefighter is a male classified as Hispanic.

    ANS: False   PG: 207   SOURCE: new

18. Functionalists argue that social stratification is necessary for attracting the best qualified to the most important positions.

    ANS: True   PG: 208   SOURCE: new

Social Stratification

19. U.S. consumers—about 4.6 percent of the world's population—buy almost 50 percent of the 800 million diamond stones produced per year.

    ANS: True   PG: 209   SOURCE: new

20. The Wal-Mart CEO earns 6,000 times the salary of the Chinese factory worker who makes products sold in the CEO's stores.

    ANS: True   PG: 213   SOURCE: study guide

21. Brazil is classified as a core economy.

    ANS: False   PG: 214

22. Nike sport shoe is the largest indirect employer in Vietnam.

    ANS: True   PG: 215

23. One hundred and thirty countries gained independence from a colonial power during the twentieth century.

    ANS: True   PG: 216

24. The United States is the largest donor in absolute foreign aid dollar.

    ANS: True   PG: 217   SOURCE: new; study guide

25. When foreign aid is measured as a percentage of Gross National Income, the United States is the world's largest donor.

    ANS: False   PG: 217   SOURCE: new

26. Tariffs are usually lowest on luxury items and highest on essential items, such as shoes and clothing, especially the cheaper varieties.

    ANS: True   PG: 219   SOURCE: new

Chapter 8

27. Social class is difficult to define.

    ANS: True   PG: 220   SOURCE: new; study guide

28. Karl Marx wrote *The Communist Manifesto* with Emile Durkheim.

    ANS: False   PG: 221

29. During a 48-month period—between January 1, 1996 and December 3, 1999—two percent of the U.S. population stayed poor.

    ANS: True   PG: 222

30. In numerical terms, people classified as black represent the largest racial category living in poverty.

    ANS: False   PG: 217   SOURCE: new; study guide

Concept Application (also in study guide)

Consider the concepts listed below. Match one or more of the concepts with each scenario. Explain your choices.

   a. Ascribed characteristics
   b. Intergenerational mobility
   c. Life chances
   d. Negatively privileged property class
   e. Social stratification
   f. Status group
   g. Status value
   h. Upward mobility
   i. Vertical mobility

Scenario 1
   "Do blondes have more fun? Social scientists have yet to nail down the answer. But economists now have good reason to believe that blondes make more money—or at least the trim, attractive ones do. New studies show that men and women (with any hair color) who are rated by survey interviewers as below average in attractiveness typically earn 10 to 20 percent less than those rated above average".

"One is tempted to write off the results as proof that idle econometricians are the Devil's helpers. But the findings from Daniel Hamermesh of the University of Texas and Jeff Biddle of Michigan State are complemented by other research showing that obese women are also at a considerable earnings disadvantage. And they could figure prominently in the very serious business of deciding who is protected by the three-year-old Americans with Disabilities Act" (Passell 1994:C2).

ANS: G, C, A

Scenario 2

"The Brinks Hotel was another American symbol in Saigon. It was a bachelor officer's headquarters, an American world that Vietnamese need not enter unless, of course, it was to clean the rooms or to cook or to provide some other form of service. It stood high over Saigon and its hovels, a world of Americans eating American food, watching American movies, and just to make sure that there was a sense of home, on the roof terrace there was always a great charcoal grill on which to barbecue thick American steaks flown in especially to that end" (Halberstam 1987:618-19).

ANS: F

Scenario 3

"These children [of people who make enough money to live a privileged life] learn to live with choices—more clothes, a wider range of food, a greater number of games and toys—that other boys and girls may never be able to imagine. They learn to grow fond of or resolutely ignore dolls and more dolls, large dollhouses, and all sorts of utensils and furniture to go in [these dollhouses, as well as] enough Lego sets to build yet another house for the adults in the family. They learn to take for granted enormous playrooms filled to the brim with trains, helicopters, boats, punching bags, Monopoly sets.... They learn to assume instruction—not only at school, but at home—for tennis, for swimming, for dancing, for horse riding. And they learn often enough to feel competent at those sports, in control of themselves while playing them, and, not least, able to move smoothly from one to the other" (Coles 1978:26).

ANS: C, E

Scenario 4

"Wanting out is a common ambition in small towns all over America. In 1951, there were three ways to realize it. One was to get a job in the big city—in my case, either Kansas City or St. Louis, at the edges of the imaginable world. At sixteen, I was too young for this, and besides, I had no idea of what I could do."

"A second way—chosen by four men from the class ahead of me—was to enlist in a branch of military service or volunteer for the draft. That would get you even farther from home and pile up educational benefits under the GI Bill."

"A third alternative to work and military service was just beginning to open up to people—mostly men—of my class and region: college" (Davis 1996:14).

ANS: H, I, B

Scenario 5
"The deeper message of Edin's book concerns the material hardships that most welfare families still endure. Eight in 10 had severe housing problems. One in six had recently been homeless. One-third had run out of food sometime in the previous year. And conditions didn't really improve for those who appear to have moved up one step to an entry-level job. In examining the budgets of 165 working mothers, Edin found them even more likely than those on welfare to be unable to pay their bills. 'I thought they might be the same, but not worse,' she says" (DePerle 1997:34).

ANS: D

Short Essay Questions

1. As members of the world's richest country, what questions about wealth distribution are we obligated to ask?

2. Why does the social stratification chapter emphasize the world's richest and poorest peoples?

3. What is the connection between social stratification and life chances?

4. Distinguish between achieved and ascribed characteristics.

5. What does *status value* mean?

6. What characteristics distinguish a caste from a class system of stratification?

7. Use infant mortality and consumption patterns as examples of how life chances vary across countries.

8. How do sociologists describe life chances within countries?

9. Explain the basic dynamics of apartheid.

10. Is the United States a class system? Why or why not?

11. Are caste and class systems distinct types of stratification systems? Explain.

12. In what ways is inequality in the United States systematic?

13. How do the "functions of poverty" help us to understand whose needs are being met by a system that pays so many so little for their labor?

14. How do functionalists (Davis and Moore) explain social stratification?

15. Explain the conflict position on Davis and Moore's theory.

16. From a world system perspective, how has capitalism come to dominate the global network of economic relationships?

17. Distinguish among core, peripheral, and semiperipheral economies. Give an example of a country that fits each of these three economies.

18. What are some of the structural responses to global inequality? Are those responses taking place? How effective are those responses?

19. Distinguish between colonialism and neocolonialism.

20. Summarize how Marx approached social class in his writings. What are the contemporary applications for Marx's ideas?

Chapter 8

21. How does Max Weber use the concept of social class? What are the contemporary applications?

22. How is class ranking complicated by status groups and parties?

23. What general structural changes in the American economy have created the urban and other underclasses?

Comprehensive Essay Questions

1. Imagine you are one of the world's 800 billionaires. How might you justify your wealth in comparison to the world's 2.1 billion poorest?

2. List your achieved and ascribed statuses. Have your ascribed characteristics affected your achievements? If yes, in what way? If no, why not?

Chapter 9

Race and Ethnicity

Multiple-Choice Questions

1. The peopling of the United States is one of the great dramas of human history. It involved all but which one of the following?
    a. the conquest of Native peoples
    b. the annexation of Mexican territory
    c. an influx of involuntary immigrants
    d. a long-standing tradition of open immigration policies

    ANS: D   PG: 233   TYP: knowledge

2. The _____ census was the first census in U.S. history that allowed people to claim more than one of six official racial categories.
    a. 1960
    b. 1970
    c. 1990
    d. 2000

    ANS: D   PG: 235   TYP: knowledge

3. On the 2000 census, for the first time in the history of the United States, people
    a. had to choose to belong to a single racial category.
    b. of mixed racial heritage had to choose the race of their father as their own race.
    c. could identify themselves as belonging to more than one official racial category.
    d. could refuse to identify their race.

    ANS: C   PG: 235   TYP: knowledge

Chapter 9

4. _____ is a vast collectivity of people more or less bound together by shared and selected history, ancestries, and physical features.
   a. Assimilation
   b. Race
   c. Segregation
   d. A minority group

   ANS: C   PG: 234   TYP: comprehension   SOURCE: new; study guide

5. In regard to race, most (if not all) biologists and social scientists have come to agree that
   a. race is a biologically based fact.
   b. race is not a biological fact.
   c. has no real social significance.
   d. race is a product of the 19th century.

   ANS: B   PG: 234   TYP: comprehension   SOURCE: new

6. By _____, the first formal laws emerged stating that an African immigrant could serve a master "for the rest of his natural life."
   a. 1492
   b. 1640
   c. 1776
   d. 1886

   ANS: B   PG: 233   TYP: knowledge

7. Which one of the following is *not* one of the six official racial categories in the United States?
   a. white
   b. Hispanic
   c. Native Hawaiian or other Pacific Islander
   d. American Indian or Alaskan Native

   ANS: B   PG: 233   TYP: comprehension

8. In the U.S. today, there are _____ race categories if we include single and multiple race responses.
   a. 63
   b. 103
   c. 213
   d. 13

   ANS: A   PG: 236   TYP: knowledge   SOURCE: study guide

9. When given the chance to identify with more than one race, _____ percent of U.S. residents do so.
   a. Less than five
   b. 15
   c. 20
   d. 30

   ANS: A   PG: 236   TYP: knowledge   SOURCE: new

10. In 1910, approximately _____ percent of the "negro" population was classified as Mulatto.
    a. 10
    b. 20
    c. 40
    d. 50

    ANS: B   PG: 237   TYP: knowledge

11. Race and ethnic identities
    a. are biologically based.
    b. are static.
    c. shift over time.
    d. are limited to five or six categories.

    ANS: C   PG: 235   TYP: comprehension   SOURCE: new

Chapter 9

12. It is significant that the U.S. definition for which one of the following racial categories omits the words *original peoples*?
    a. American Indian
    b. Asian
    c. black or African-American
    d. white

    ANS: C　　PG: 235　　TYP: comprehension　　SOURCE: new

13. Assigning people to one racial category has many shortcomings. Which one of the following is *not* one of these shortcomings?
    a. There is no sharp dividing line to separate physical characteristics associated with race.
    b. Millions of people in the world possess physical traits that make it impossible to place them into just one category.
    c. Rules and guidelines for placing people into categories are vague, contradictory, and ever-changing.
    d. More than 25 percent of the U.S. population describe themselves as more than one race.

    ANS: D　　PG: 236　　TYP: comprehension

14. Under the U.S. system of racial classification, people with ancestors from Pakistan and Siberia are expected to identify themselves as
    a. Asian.
    b. Native American.
    c. black.
    d. white.

    ANS: A　　PG: 235　　TYP: knowledge　　SOURCE: study guide

15. At one time in South Africa, the government board that oversaw racial classification used a pencil test to classify individuals as white or black. If a pencil fell out of the person's hair, he or she was classified as white. This classification strategy suggests that
    a. race is a biologically based concept.
    b. race has no real social significance. .
    c. the lack of a clear dividing line does not stop people from creating one.
    d. racial classification systems do work.

    ANS: C　　PG: 236　　TYP: comprehension　　SOURCE: new

16. In the United States, as many as 2,000 distinct cultural groups make up the Native American category. This fact speaks to
    a. the practice of forcing under one umbrella term a large amount of people that vary in language and culture.
    b. the sharp dividing line separating one racial category from another.
    c. the biological significance of race.
    d. the need for more racial categories.

    ANS: A   PG: 236   TYP: comprehension   SOURCE: new

17. In the United States, the Census Bureau classifies everyone within its borders as belonging to one of _____ official ethnic categories.
    a. two
    b. three
    c. four
    d. five

    ANS: A   PG: 237   TYP: knowledge

18. In the United States, "a person of Mexican, Puerto Rican, Cuban, or Central or South American culture or origin" is known as
    a. a conquistador.
    b. a Pacific Islander.
    c. a Hispanic.
    d. non-white.

    ANS: C   PG: 237   TYP: comprehension   SOURCE: study guide

19. The official definition of Hispanic used in the United States
    a. considers the complex history and intermixing of people in Latin America.
    b. acknowledges the diversity of people who are considered Hispanic.
    c. divides the U.S. population into two ethnic categories: Hispanic and non-Hispanic.
    d. considers Hispanics as one of five official categories.

    ANS: C   PG: 237   TYP: knowledge

Chapter 9

20. According to the U.S. system of racial classification, Hispanics can or should be classified as
    a. white.
    b. black.
    c. Native American.
    d. any race.

    ANS: D   PG: 238   TYP: comprehension

21. _____ is the larger social setting in which racial and ethnic categories are recognized, constricted, and challenged.
    a. Chance
    b. Context
    c. Choice
    d. Conscious

    ANS: B   PG: 239   TYP: comprehension   SOURCE: study guide

22. _____ relates to those things not subject to human will, choice, or effort.
    a. Chance
    b. Context
    c. Choice
    d. Conscious

    ANS: A   PG: 239   TYP: comprehension

23. According to the U.S. Census Bureau, a person with one Hispanic and one non-Hispanic parent
    a. can claim both heritages.
    b. shares the ethnicity of the female parent.
    c. is Hispanic.
    d. is non-Hispanic.

    ANS: B   PG: 238   TYP: comprehension

Race and Ethnicity

24. Most of the U.S. population classified as Hispanic are likely to classify themselves as also belonging to which one of the following racial categories?
    a. white
    b. black
    c. American Indian
    d. Asian

    ANS: A   PG: 239   TYP: knowledge

25. According to the information presented in Chapter 9 (Race and Ethnicity), we can conclude that race is
    a. an inherited trait (like hair color).
    b. a biological fact.
    c. a result of the system of racial classification.
    d. a scientific fact.

    ANS: C   PG: 237   TYP: comprehension

26. The origins of an ideology that supports the U.S. belief in racial purity can be traced to
    a. slavery.
    b. reconstruction.
    c. the Civil War.
    d. the Jim Crow era.

    ANS: A   PG: 240   TYP: knowledge   SOURCE: study guide

27. Tiger Woods' mother is half Thai, one-quarter Chinese, and one-quarter white. His father is half black, one-quarter Chinese, and one-quarter American Indian. Tiger appears "black." Tiger's physical appearance reflects the importance of _____ in regard to racial classification.
    a. chance
    b. context
    c. choice
    d. consciousness

    ANS: A   PG: 239   TYP: application

Chapter 9

28. We do not choose our biological parents nor can we control the physical characteristics we inherit from them. These facts speak to the role of _____ in determining race and ethnicity.
   a. chance
   b. choice
   c. context
   d. understanding

   ANS: A   PG: 239   TYP: application

29. At one time in the United States, people could go into a "white" church if they could run a comb through their hair without it snagging. This situation speaks to the importance of _____ in determining race.
   a. chance
   b. choice
   c. context
   d. choice in context

   ANS: C   PG: 239   TYP: application

30. Sexual relationships between enslaved women and their master produced not only "mixed race" offspring but also sons and daughters. Yet the system of racial classification assigned the offspring of these unions to the race of the mother. This situation speaks to the importance of _____ in determining race.
   a. chance
   b. choice
   c. context
   d. choice in context

   ANS: C   PG: 239   TYP: application

31. Black Americans, whether they are native-born or immigrants, are pressured to identify as black, not as an ethnic group. This situation reflects the lack of
   a. chance.
   b. choice.
   c. context.
   d. choice in context.

   ANS: B   PG: 239   TYP: application   SOURCE: study guide

Race and Ethnicity

32. Africans forced to immigrate as enslaved people from hundreds of cultures emerged from their experiences as a single _____ category.
    a. racial
    b. ancestry
    c. ethnic
    d. language

    ANS: A   PG: 251   TYP: comprehension

33. According to the U.S. system of racial classification, people of Middle Eastern and Arab ancestries are classified as
    a. Asian.
    b. black.
    c. white.
    d. Other.

    ANS: C   PG: 241   TYP: comprehension

34. The U.S. Bureau of the Census has explored the possibility of creating a new racial category for people of _____ ancestry.
    a. German
    b. Arab-Middle Eastern
    c. Spanish
    d. Brazilian

    ANS: B   PG: 241   TYP: comprehension

35. The U.S. Bureau of the Census decided <u>not</u> to create an "Arab" or "Middle Eastern" racial or ethnic category because
    a. such a category would be too large in size.
    b. there is little agreement about the geographic meaning of Middle Eastern.
    c. Arab is an ethnic category and not a race.
    d. most Arab and Middle Eastern people identify as "white."

    ANS: B   PG: 241   TYP: comprehension   SOURCE: new

Chapter 9

36. The only source of data we have on the size of Arab or Middle Eastern populations in the United States comes from
    a. FBI records.
    b. birth and death certificates.
    c. the ancestry question on the census.
    d. driver's licenses.

    ANS: C   PG: 241   TYP: knowledge   SOURCE: study guide

37. The U.S. definition of Arab classifies some people as Arab who do not see themselves as such. Which one of the following is an example of such a people?
    a. Kurds
    b. Iraqis
    c. Saudis
    d. Kuwaitis

    ANS: A   PG: 241   TYP: knowledge   SOURCE: new

38. Some social critics maintain that the U.S. government classifies people of Middle Eastern and Arab ancestry as "white" because
    a. most Middle Easterners self-classify themselves as white.
    b. the Middle East holds important symbolic values that whites hope to associate with their "race."
    c. this ancestry group doesn't fit clearly into the "black" category.
    d. the dominant population classifies Middle Easterners as "white."

    ANS: B   PG: 241   TYP: comprehension

39. An estimated _____ percent of Arab-Americans are Christian.
    a. 5
    b. 25
    c. 50
    d. 75

    ANS: D   PG: 242   TYP: knowledge

40. Which region of the world has the largest percentage of its labor force comprised of foreign born individuals?
    a. the United States
    b. Europe
    c. the Persian Gulf
    d. Canada

    ANS: C   PG: 241   TYP: knowledge   SOURCE: new

41. Tiger Woods' physical appearance is a result of
    a. choice.
    b. context.
    c. chance.
    d. choice in context.

    ANS: C   PG: 239   TYP: application   SOURCE: new

42. In his autobiography, Barak Obama wrote, "When people, black or white, who don't know me well discover my [mixed racial] background (and it usually is a discovery, for I ceased to advertise my mother's race at the age of twelve or thirteen when I began to suspect that by doing so I was ingratiating myself to whites), I see the split-second adjustments they have to make." Obama's observation speaks to the role of
    a. choice.
    b. context.
    c. chance.
    d. choice in context.

    ANS: A   PG: 240   TYP: application   SOURCE: new

43. In an interview, Tiger Woods remarked, "In this country, I'm looked at as being black. When I go to Thailand, I'm considered Thai. It's very interesting. And when I go to Japan, I'm considered Asian. I don't know why it is, but it just is." Woods' observations speak to the importance of
    a. choice.
    b. context.
    c. chance.
    d. choice in context.

    ANS: B   PG: 240   TYP: application   SOURCE: new

Chapter 9

44. About 33.5 million foreign-born residents live in the United States. That number represents _____ percent of the total population.
    a. 5
    b. 12
    c. 20
    d. 30

    ANS: B   PG: 298   TYP: knowledge

45. Which one of the following states is most likely to have the largest percentage of foreign-born living within its borders?
    a. Texas
    b. New Jersey
    c. Florida
    d. California

    ANS: D   PG: 243   TYP: knowledge   SOURCE: study guide

46. Which characteristic applies to the Arab population?
    a. Arabs represent 30 percent of the population in Dearborn, Michigan.
    b. An estimated 25 percent of the Arab population is Christian.
    c. Approximately 100 million people in the United States have Arab ancestry.
    d. People classified as Iraqi account for over 60 percent of the Arab population in the United States.

    ANS: A   PG: 240   TYP: knowledge   SOURCE: new; study guide

47. Which one of the following cities has the largest percentage of foreign-born residents?
    a. Rome
    b. San Francisco
    c. Paris
    d. Miami

    ANS: D   PG: 243   TYP: knowledge   SOURCE: new

48. If we take a long view of U.S. history, we can see that the top 10 countries from which people have immigrated include all but which one of the following?
    a. Germany
    b. the Philippines
    c. Vietnam
    d. Ireland

    ANS: C   PG: 244   TYP: knowledge

49. Under the Immigration Act of 1924, a quota system set numerical limits on immigration based on national origin. Immigrants from which region of the world were <u>most</u> affected by this Act?
    a. western Europe
    b. southern, central, and eastern Europe
    c. Asia
    d. Latin America

    ANS: C   PG: 244   TYP: knowledge

50. The _____ permitted illegal workers in the United States to apply for amnesty and legal status.
    a. Immigration Act of 1924
    b. Chinese Exclusion Act of 1924
    c. Bracero Program
    d. Immigration and Reform Act of 1986

    ANS: D   PG: 245   TYP: knowledge

51. Which one of the following states has attracted 25 percent of all immigrants that have ever come to America?
    a. Alaska
    b. Texas
    c. California
    d. New Mexico

    ANS: C   PG: 243   TYP: knowledge

52. The Bracero Program, which began in 1942, allowed _____ to work legally in the United States to relieve labor shortages in rural areas and to bolster the American work force during World War II.
    a. Mexicans
    b. Italians
    c. Japanese
    d. Africans

    ANS: A   PG: 244   TYP: knowledge   SOURCE: study guide

53. Which one of the following immigration acts permitted illegal workers to apply for amnesty if they could prove they had worked in the U.S. for at least 90 days?
    a. The Bracero Program
    b. Immigration Act of 1924
    c. Immigration and Reform Act of 1986
    d. Chinese Exception Act of 1822

    ANS: C   PG: 245   TYP: knowledge

54. Sixty-five percent of the 63.1 million total immigrants to the United States since 1820 have come from five countries. Which one of the following countries has sent the greatest overall numbers of immigrants?
    a. Mexico
    b. the United Kingdom
    c. Russia
    d. Germany

    ANS: D   PG: 244   TYP: knowledge   SOURCE: new

55. Which one of the following statements about minority status is *false*?
    a. A minority may be the numerical majority in a society.
    b. Minorities do not enjoy the freedom or the privilege to move within the society in the same way that members of the dominant group do.
    c. People that belong to a minority group are treated as a category, not as individuals.
    d. Minority status is a sociological term that applies exclusively to racial and ethnic groups.

    ANS: D   PG: 247   TYP: comprehension

56. "When I use checks, credit cards, or cash, I can count on my skin color not to work against the appearance that I am financially reliable." This statement illustrates an example of
    a. privileges that members of dominant groups enjoy and take for granted.
    b. privileges that members of dominant groups have earned.
    c. adaptation to dominant culture.
    d. the workings of capitalist societies.

    ANS: A   PG: 248   TYP: application   SOURCE: study guide

57. The most controversial quality identified as a characteristic of a minority group is that
    a. people who belong to such a group are treated as members of a category.
    b. minority status is based on numbers.
    c. a minority group may be the majority of the population.
    d. membership is involuntary; if people are free to leave the group, they do not constitute a minority.

    ANS: D   PG: 247   TYP: knowledge

58. The key characteristic determining minority status is
    a. size relative to the dominant group.
    b. voluntary emigration.
    c. lack of access to and control over valued resources.
    d. physical appearance distinct from the majority of people in the society.

    ANS: C   PG: 247   TYP: comprehension   SOURCE: study guide

59. _____ are subgroups within a society that can be distinguished from members of the dominant group by visible identifying characteristics.
    a. Stigmatized groups
    b. Minority groups
    c. The foreign born
    d. The native born

    ANS: B   PG: 247   TYP: comprehension   SOURCE: new

Chapter 9

60. Which one of the following countries has a minority group within its borders that is a numerical majority?
    a. South Africa
    b. Canada
    c. the United States
    d. Israel

    ANS: A   PG: 248   TYP: knowledge

61. Strictly speaking, under sociologist Louis Wirth's conception of a minority, a very light-skinned person of African and German descent who can pass as white is
    a. still a minority.
    b. not a minority.
    c. a privileged minority.
    d. a voluntary minority.

    ANS: B   PG: 247   TYP: application

62. The process by which ethnic and racial distinctions between groups disappear is
    a. assimilation.
    b. cultivation.
    c. institutionalization.
    d. socialization.

    ANS: A   PG: 249   TYP: comprehension

63. In _____ assimilation, members of a minority, ethnic, or racial group adapt to the ways of the dominant group.
    a. melting pot
    b. absorption
    c. involuntary
    d. voluntary

    ANS: B   PG: 249   TYP: comprehension

64. _____ is the physical and/or social separation of categories of people from one another.
   a. Absorption assimilation
   b. Involuntary migration
   c. Segregation
   d. Melting pot assimilation

   ANS: C   PG: 249   TYP: comprehension

65. Which one of the following groups has the best chance of living a long life in the United States?
   a. black males
   b. white women
   c. white men
   d. Asian females

   ANS: D   PG: 247   TYP: comprehension   SOURCE: new

66. Which one of the following groups has the lowest chance of having health insurance?
   a. Asians
   b. Native Americans
   c. blacks
   d. whites

   ANS: B   PG: 247   TYP: knowledge   SOURCE: new

67. Which one of the following groups has the greatest chance of going to prison?
   a. black males
   b. Asian males
   c. Native American males
   d. white males

   ANS: A   PG: 247   TYP: knowledge   SOURCE: new

Chapter 9

68. _____ is an example of an involuntary minority.
    a. German-Americans
    b. African-Americans
    c. Italian-Americans
    d. Chinese-Americans

    ANS: B   PG: 250   TYP: application

69. Melting pot assimilation
    a. is a one-sided process in which a minority group is absorbed into the dominant culture.
    b. exists when a minority group identifies with the dominant culture.
    c. occurs when a minority group procreates with those of a dominant group.
    d. is a new process of cultural blending in which the groups involved accept new behaviors and values from one another.

    ANS: D   PG: 250   TYP: comprehension

70. Ethnic and racial groups that did not choose to be part of a country are
    a. voluntary minorities.
    b. involuntary minorities.
    c. political refugees.
    d. labor migrants.

    ANS: B   PG: 250   TYP: comprehension

71. The concept of melting pot assimilation can be applied to the experiences of
    a. the various African ethnic groups brought to the United States as slaves.
    b. the various Hispanic groups that have settled in the United States.
    c. international labor migrants in Germany.
    d. East and West Germans after the fall of the Berlin Wall.

    ANS: A   PG: 251   TYP: application

72. _____ assimilation produces a newly blended cultural system.
    a. Melting pot
    b. Absorption
    c. Involuntary
    d. Voluntary

    ANS: A   PG: 250   TYP: comprehension

73. _____ occurs when all of the important and meaningful primary relationships (dating, play, school, and fraternity groups) are confined largely to people of the same racial and ethnic groups.
    a. Assimilation
    b. Stratification
    c. Segregation
    d. Acculturation

    ANS: C   PG: 250   TYP: comprehension

74. Ideologies
    a. are accurate accounts and explanations of why things are as they are.
    b. are supported by rigorous analysis.
    c. support the interests of minority groups.
    d. are beliefs that are not challenged or subjected to scrutiny by the people that hold them.

    ANS: D   PG: 252   TYP: comprehension

75. Former Los Angeles police chief Daryl Gates argues that many blacks have died from restraining chokeholds because their veins and arteries do not open up as fast as they do on normal people. Sociologists classify this argument as an example of
    a. institutionalized discrimination.
    b. a hate crime.
    c. racist ideology.
    d. discrimination.

    ANS: C   PG: 252   TYP: comprehension   SOURCE: study guide

Chapter 9

76. The Jim Crow laws were enacted in the _____ and were overturned in the _____.
    a. 1880s; 1960s
    b. 1960s; 1980s
    c. 1770s; 1990s
    d. 1880s; 1920s

    ANS: A		PG: 253		TYP: knowledge

77. One possible explanation for black-white differences in tipping can be traced to the fact that
    a. blacks deliberately leave poor tips.
    b. blacks are angry at whites for slavery.
    c. until recently, blacks have not been allowed to work as waiters and waitresses.
    d. blacks are exercising reverse discrimination.

    ANS: C		PG: 252		TYP: comprehension

78. "No person or corporation shall require any white female nurse to nurse in wards or rooms in hospitals, either public or private, in which Negro men are placed." This Alabama law is an example of _____ laws.
    a. Civil Rights
    b. Jim Crow
    c. Civil War era
    d. Integration

    ANS: B		PG: 253		TYP: application

79. "All marriages of white persons with Negroes, Mulattos, Mongolians, or Malaya hereafter contracted in the State of Wyoming are and shall be illegal and void." This Wyoming law is an example of _____ laws.
    a. Civil Rights
    b. Jim Crow
    c. Civil War era
    d. Integration

    ANS: B		PG: 253		TYP: application		SOURCE: study guide

80. Sociologist Larry T. Reynolds observes that using the term *race* as a concept for classifying humans is a product of
    a. the 1960s.
    b. the eleventh century.
    c. the 1700s.
    d. the 1400s.

    ANS: C   PG: 252   TYP: knowledge

81. People who embrace _____ believe that something in the biological makeup of an ethnic or racial group explains or justifies its subordinate or superior status.
    a. integration
    b. segregation
    c. racist ideology
    d. assimilation

    ANS: C   PG: 252   TYP: comprehension

82. Which one of the following theories best explains why black male athletes dominate the sport of basketball?
    a. The black male athletes' ability can be traced to the fact that slave owners bred their ancestors to be strong.
    b. The black male athlete has an extra muscle in his leg.
    c. Blacks are just better athletes, plain and simple.
    d. Black athletes' energy is channeled toward money-making sports, such as basketball.

    ANS: D   PG: 255   TYP: comprehension

83. When prejudiced people encounter a minority person that contradicts stereotypes, usually
    a. they come to see the group in a new light.
    b. the stereotype is discredited.
    c. they see that person as an "exception to the rule."
    d. they fail to notice the person.

    ANS: C   PG: 253   TYP: application

84. Which of the following characteristics does not apply to the concept of prejudice?
    a. a rigid and unfavorable judgment about an outgroup
    b. contradictory evidence weakens the unfavorable judgment
    c. supported by stereotypes
    d. applied to anyone who is a member of the outgroup

    ANS: B   PG: 253   TYP: comprehension

85. "People experience their prejudices as irresistible products of their own observations; to them, their observations permit no other conclusions." This statement highlights the dynamics of
    a. institutional racism.
    b. hate crimes.
    c. racism.
    d. selective perception.

    ANS: D   PG: 253   TYP: application

86. Bill notes that black athletes dominate the sport of basketball and uses that as evidence of natural leaping ability. At the same time, he does not use the same kind of logic to explain why white athletes dominate gymnastics. Bill is guilty of
    a. selective perception.
    b. assimilation.
    c. institutionalized discrimination.
    d. non-prejudiced discrimination.

    ANS: A   PG: 253   TYP: application   SOURCE: study guide

87. Many people believe that white men can't jump and are slow based on their observations of the relatively small number of white men who play professional basketball. This belief is derived from which one of the following processes?
    a. selective perception
    b. assimilation
    c. institutionalized discrimination
    d. structural strain

    ANS: A   PG: 253   TYP: application

88. When prejudiced people notice only those behaviors that support stereotypes about a particular minority group, they are engaging in
    a. discrimination.
    b. selective perception.
    c. a hate crime.
    d. visualization.

    ANS: B   PG: 253   TYP: comprehension

89. The distinction between prejudice and discrimination is that
    a. prejudice is a behavior, and discrimination is an attitude.
    b. prejudice is an attitude, and discrimination is a behavior.
    c. prejudice is an ideology, and discrimination is an attitude.
    d. prejudice is an attitude, and discrimination is an ideology.

    ANS: B   PG: 254   TYP: comprehension

90. Merton's nickname for prejudiced nondiscriminators is
    a. all-weather liberals.
    b. fair-weather liberals.
    c. timid bigots.
    d. active bigots.

    ANS: C   PG: 256   TYP: application

91. _____ are likely to initiate hate crimes.
    a. Fair-weather liberals
    b. All-weather liberals
    c. Timid bigots
    d. Active bigots

    ANS: D   PG: 256   TYP: knowledge

Chapter 9

92. Mary's supervisor tells her that the only way to prevent theft is to follow black customers as they shop. Mary complies because she does not want to lose her job. Mary is a
    a. nonprejudiced nondiscriminator.
    b. nonprejudiced discriminator.
    c. prejudiced nondiscriminator.
    d. prejudiced discriminator.

    ANS: B   PG: 254   TYP: application

93. Within a one month period after 9-11, there were 326 different media reports of hate-based incidents against people who appeared to be of Arab or Middle Eastern descent. These crimes were most likely committed by
    a. nonprejudiced nondiscriminators.
    b. nonprejudiced discriminators.
    c. prejudiced nondiscriminators.
    d. prejudiced discriminators.

    ANS: D   PG: 256   TYP: application

94. Jerome admits that "whenever someone would break out the inevitable 'black joke,' I would be angered, but I didn't want to jeopardize my own social standing by speaking up." Jerome's behavior and conflicting attitude represents that of a(n)
    a. nonprejudiced nondiscriminator.
    b. nonprejudiced discriminator.
    c. prejudiced nondiscriminator.
    d. prejudiced discriminator.

    ANS: B   PG: 254   TYP: application

95. _____ is unequal treatment (intentional or unintentional) on the basis of ascribed attributes, such as race and gender.
    a. Discrimination
    b. Prejudice
    c. Racism
    d. Stereotyping

    ANS: A   PG: 254   TYP: comprehension

96. _____ is the established and customary way of doing things in society that keeps minority members in a disadvantaged position.
    a. Systematic discrimination
    b. Corporate discrimination
    c. Normative discrimination
    d. Institutionalized discrimination

    ANS: D   PG: 258   TYP: comprehension   SOURCE: study guide

97. The U.S. Department of Justice has identified at least 33 real estate companies in nine states whose agents steer African Americans away from predominantly white areas and into predominantly minority areas. In sociological terms, this practice is an example of
    a. individual discrimination.
    b. a racist ideology.
    c. institutionalized discrimination.
    d. prejudice.

    ANS: C   PG: 258   TYP: application

98. The First National Bank in New Mexico unfairly denied loans to Hispanic applicants by applying more stringent standards to the Hispanic applicants than to similarly situated Anglo applicants. This practice represents a case of
    a. individual discrimination.
    b. racist ideology.
    c. institutional discrimination.
    d. prejudice.

    ANS: C   PG: 258   TYP: application

99. The sociologist _____ wrote *Stigma: Notes on the Management of Spoiled Identity*.
    a. Robert K. Merton
    b. Erving Goffman
    c. Raymond Breton
    d. Louis Wirth

    ANS: B   PG: 258   TYP: knowledge

100. According to sociologist Erving Goffman, the very anticipation of contact can cause the "normals" and the stigmatized to try to avoid one another. This is because the two parties
    a. wish to resist the social pressures pushing them to interact with one another.
    b. wish to avoid discomfort, rejection, and suspicions they encounter from people in the other group.
    c. believe they cannot form a relationship that matches the "ideal" kind of relationship portrayed in the media.
    d. have experienced negative reactions from everyone they have encountered in the other group.

    ANS: B   PG: 258   TYP: application

101. A stigma is considered discrediting because
    a. it damages the possessor's reputation.
    b. it means the person cannot get financial credit.
    c. it overshadows all other attributes that a person might possess.
    d. it draws attention to other positive and negative characteristics.

    ANS: C   PG: 258   TYP: comprehension   SOURCE: study guide

102. When studying stigmas, Goffman maintained that the primary focus should be on
    a. interaction between the stigmatized and the "normals."
    b. the attribute that is defined as the stigma.
    c. the three types of stigmas.
    d. "normals."

    ANS: A   PG: 259   TYP: comprehension

103. Goffman used the term "normal" to mean
    a. healthy.
    b. well-adjusted.
    c. those who possess no discrediting attribute.
    d. free of pathology.

    ANS: C   PG: 258   TYP: comprehension

104. Which one of the following is not a characteristic of mixed contacts?
    a. Sometimes the stigmatized and the "normals" avoid each other.
    b. The stigmatized are sure that everyone they meet will view them in a negative light.
    c. "Normals" often view accomplishments by the stigmatized as signs of remarkable and noteworthy capacities.
    d. Stigmatized persons experience invasions of privacy.

    ANS: B   PG: 259   TYP: comprehension

105. In the Kolts Report written in response to the Rodney King beating, investigators found that
    a. nearly all deputies in the Los Angeles County Sheriff's Department were disrespectful to people while on duty.
    b. about one in every four deputies behaved in outrageous ways.
    c. only a very small proportion of deputies (about 1 percent) were identified as problem officers.
    d. white male deputies worked different shifts than female and other minority deputies.

    ANS: C   PG: 260   TYP: knowledge

106. Which one of the following statements describes how minorities respond to stigmatization?
    a. Minorities are passive victims.
    b. Minorities respond in predictable, aggressive ways.
    c. Minorities claim "discrimination" even when it doesn't exist.
    d. Minorities respond in a variety of ways to being treated as members of a category.

    ANS: D   PG: 261   TYP: comprehension

Multiple Choice Questions on the Web

1. In the United States, the Census Bureau classifies everyone within its borders as belonging to one of _____ official "race" categories (including "other").
    a. two
    b. three
    c. six
    d. ten

    ANS: C   PG: 235   TYP: knowledge

Chapter 9

2. Which one of the following statements is *false* about the U.S. system of racial classification?
   a. A parent and his or her biological children can be classified as two different races.
   b. People of Arab, North African, and Middle Eastern descent are classified as black.
   c. *Hispanic* is not a race.
   d. The U.S. population is divided into two ethnic groups: Hispanic and non-Hispanic.

   ANS: B   PG: 235   TYP: knowledge

3. The label *Hispanic* is confusing because it forces people to identify themselves with conquistadors and settlers from
   a. Britain.
   b. Brazil.
   c. Spain.
   d. Portugal.

   ANS: C   PG: 237   TYP: knowledge

4. U.S. Secretary of State Colin Powell has written that he is the son of Jamaican immigrants and has African, English, Irish, Scottish, Jewish, and Arawak Indian ancestries. Yet, he is more often than not described as "black." This situation reflects the importance of _____ to racial classification.
   a. chance
   b. context
   c. choice
   d. consciousness

   ANS: B   PG: 240   TYP: application

5. The Hispanic designation lumps together a variety of people into a single _____ category.
   a. racial
   b. ancestry
   c. ethnic
   d. language

   ANS: C   PG: 237   TYP: comprehension

6. Pop star Michael Jackson altered his physical appearance in such a way that he appears white. Jackson's efforts reflect the importance of _____ to racial classification.
    a. chance
    b. context
    c. choice
    d. consciousness

    ANS: C   PG: 239   TYP: application

7. _____ is a situation in which a dominant group defines some subgroup of people in racial or ethnic terms, thereby forcing that subgroup to become, appear, or feel more ethnic than they might otherwise be.
    a. Designated ethnicity
    b. Ethnicity
    c. Foreign ethnicity
    d. Involuntary ethnicity

    ANS: D   PG: 250   TYP: comprehension   SOURCE: study guide

8. The _____ of 1882 prohibited the entry of Chinese laborers and, later, all Chinese into the United States.
    a. Labor Prohibition Act
    b. Chinese Exclusion Act
    c. Immigration and Reform Act
    d. East Asia Exclusion Act

    ANS: B   PG: 244   TYP: knowledge

9. Which one of the following groups is <u>most</u> likely to be a voluntary minority?
    a. Native Americans
    b. Mexican-Americans
    c. Native Hawaiians
    d. Korean-Americans

    ANS: D   PG: 250   TYP: comprehension   SOURCE : study guide

Chapter 9

10. "It shall be unlawful for colored people to frequent any park owned or maintained by the city for the benefit, use, and enjoyment of white persons . . . and unlawful for any white person to frequent any park owned or maintained by the city for the use and benefit of colored persons." This Georgia law is an example of _____ laws.
    a. Civil Rights
    b. Jim Crow
    c. Civil War era
    d. Integration

    ANS: B   PG: 253   TYP: application

True-False Questions

1. At one time, California belonged to Mexico.

    ANS: True   PG: 233

2. Under the U.S. system of racial classification, parents and their biological children can belong to different races.

    ANS: True   PG: 232   SOURCE: study guide

3. The U.S. government defines "black or African American" as a person having origins in any of the original peoples of Africa.

    ANS: False   PG: 235   SOURCE: new

4. About 20 percent of the U.S. population claim membership in two or more races.

    ANS: False   PG: 236

5. The federal government classifies those who identify with more than one race as multiracial.

    ANS: False   PG: 235

6. Physical boundaries separating one racial category from another are clear and definite.

   ANS: False   PG: 236   SOURCE: study guide

7. Intermixture between the races became more common after 1967.

   ANS: False   PG: 237

8. Hispanics can be of any race.

   ANS: True   PG: 235   SOURCE: study guide

9. In the United States, *Hispanic* is considered to be a racial category.

   ANS: False   PG: 237   SOURCE: new

10. Individual choice regarding race is constrained by chance and context.

    ANS: True   PG: 239   SOURCE: study guide

11. In the United States, most people that are classified as Hispanic classify themselves as white.

    ANS: True   PG: 239

12. In the United States, the biological facts of ancestry have no bearing on the system of racial classification.

    ANS: True   PG: 239   SOURCE: new, study guide

13. The U.S. Census Bureau allows respondents to list up to five ancestries to answer the question, "What is this person's ancestry or ethnic origin?"

    ANS: False   PG: 241   SOURCE: new

14. In the United States, Tiger Woods is looked upon as being black; in Japan, he is considered Asian.

    ANS: True   PG: 241

15. Japan and Germany welcome immigrants as permanent residents and citizens.

    ANS: False   PG: 242   SOURCE: new; study guide

16. Approximately 50 percent of the foreign-born living in the United States were born in an Asian country.

    ANS: False   PG: 243

17. Since 1920, five of the top 10 countries from which people have immigrated to the United States are in Western Europe.

    ANS: True   PG: 244

18. The Immigration Act of 1924 established a quota system that set numerical limits on immigration that varied by national origin.

    ANS: True   PG: 244   SOURCE: new

19. Someone born on American soil to two parents with illegal immigration status is considered a U.S. citizen.

    ANS: True   PG: 242   SOURCE: study guide

20. After the 9-11 attacks, an executive order was put in place that expedited citizenship wherein anyone foreign-born that served any amount of time in the military was immediately eligible to become a citizen of the United States.

    ANS: True   PG: 246   SOURCE: new

21. The key to minority status is smaller numbers relative to the majority population.

    ANS: False   PG: 247

22. People who belong to a minority group are treated as members of a category.

    ANS: True   PG: 247   SOURCE: study guide

23. There are two kinds of assimilation: absorption assimilation and melting pot assimilation.

    ANS: True   PG: 249   SOURCE: new

24. The melting pot concept of assimilation helps to explain how the various African ethnic groups that were imported to the U.S. as slaves became one racial group.

    ANS: True   PG: 251

25. Discrimination is a behavior; prejudice is an attitude.

    ANS: True   PG: 254

26. Racial classification was the cornerstone of the Jim Crow laws enacted in the 1880s.

    ANS: True   PG: 253   SOURCE: study guide

27. The Jim Crow laws mandated busing as a means of ending segregation.

    ANS: False   PG: 253

28. No hate crimes seem to involve blacks attacking whites.

    ANS: False   PG: 257   SOURCE: study guide

29. Institutionalized discrimination can exist even if most members are not prejudiced.

    ANS: True   PG: 258

Chapter 9

30. The concepts of race and ethnicity cannot be understood apart from systems of racial and ethnic classifications.

    ANS: True   PG: 258   SOURCE: new

Concept Application (also in study guide)

Consider the concepts listed below. Match one of more of the concepts with each scenario. Explain your choices.

   a. Institutionalized discrimination
   b. Involuntary minorities
   c. Melting pot assimilation
   d. Mixed contacts
   e. Selective perception
   f. Stereotypes
   g. Stigma

Scenario 1
"In the book, an American Asian woman finds her white beau attractive because he is from Connecticut, not Canton. He is tall and lanky; he does not have skinny arms like her brothers and father. He is commanding and gets what he wants. Asian men, however, are not depicted as commanding but as arrogant and chauvinistic. My Asian father has never treated my mother arrogantly. He is not short or uncommunicative either. My father is tall with broad shoulders, a physical attribute inherited by both my brother and me. We have his strong jaw line, too. And I have a dimple on my chin like actor Kirk Douglas. An American Asian woman acquaintance made a comment that my brother and I were unlike 'typical' Asian men because we are tall and muscular. Her own brother is tall and muscular! It gets worse. Two strangers from Latin America, on two separate occasions, asked me if I was 'mixed.' Both refused to believe that I was 100% Asian because I did not fit their stereotype of what an Asian should look like. One even referred to my 'big' eyes'" (Wang 1994:20).

    ANS: E, G, D, F

Scenario 2

"…[I]ntegration can be seen as a two-way process in which the dominant and subordinate sectors interact to forge a new entity, in much the same way as different paints in a bucket. Under integration, the best elements of both the majority and minority culture are merged into a single and coherent national framework across a range of practices, including intermarriage and education" (Fleras and Elliott 1992:62).

    ANS: C

Scenario 3

"Finally, the category 'Native American' is an artifice of the colonial collision. It is composed of multiple socio-cultural groups who share a colonial history as Indians. They, too, were marginalized in and excluded from full and equal participation in mainstream American institutions and practices. First, there was the military conquest of the Native Americans and their subsequent removal to reservations. But, almost from their first interactions, Native Americans sought education from the United States government. In more than one-quarter of the approximately four hundred treaties entered into by the United States government between 1778 and 1871, education was one of the specific services Native Americans requested in exchange for their lands. But in the formalized education provided by the United States, Native American students were forced to embrace Western ideas and culture, whose price was the repression and denial of their own cultures. Many students were forced into a cultural no-man's land where they remained torn between two worlds. Most students simply dropped out of the system" (Hogue 1996:9).

    ANS: B

Scenario 4

"The Tuskegee study began in 1932 when the Public Health Service (and later the Centers for Disease Control) decided to follow 400 black men with syphilis without treating them. The subjects, who were recruited from churches and clinics throughout the South, were told only that they had 'bad blood'" (Stryker 1997: E4).

    ANS: A

Scenario 5

"As soon as I walked into the students' center, I knew I'd gone to the wrong place. Just about everyone there looked really ethnic-African American, Asian, Native American, Latino. And there I was, this white-looking guy. A few other students looked kind of white, too, but at least their names tags made up for it: last names like 'Chan' or 'Lee' or 'Wong.' What's my last name? Jewish. Great.

Chapter 9

I stood around feeling really out of place until this other student began talking to me. He was African American. 'So, what are you?' he asked me right away. I was relieved to tell him my mom was Chinese, like I was explaining myself. 'Oh, OK, yeah, you can sort of see it,' he said, after eyeing me carefully. 'But would you look at some of the guys here? I don't know what they're supposed to be. I left a little later and never went back" (Hess 1997).

ANS: D

Short Essay Questions

1. Explain how the peopling of the United States is a global story.

2. Why is it important to focus on the U.S. system of racial and ethnic classification?

3. Is race a biological fact? Explain.

4. What is ethnicity?

5. Name the 6 official single race categories as designated by the U.S. Census Bureau. How did the system of racial classification change for the 2000 Census?

6. What are the problems associated with assigning people to racial categories?

7. What is the total number of multiple-race categories in the United States? What percentage of Americans identify with more than one race?

8. Describe the U.S. system of ethnic classification. Why is the label *Hispanic* confusing?

9. Is Hispanic a race? Explain.

10. Define chance, choice, and context. How is race a product of these factors?

11. How is ethnicity a product of chance, choice, and context?

12. Why does the United States not include Arab or Middle Eastern as a racial category?

13. Why are people of Middle Eastern and Arab ancestry classified as white?

14. Why is the 2003 Census population brief on Arab populations within the United States historic?

15. What percentage of the U.S. population is foreign-born? Who are the foreign-born?

16. Give two examples of how race and ethnicity have been connected to U.S. immigration policy?

17. Immigration has always inspired debate in the United States. Why?

18. What are minority groups? What are the essential characteristics of all minority groups?

19. Distinguish between absorption assimilation and melting pot assimilation.

20. What are racist ideologies? Give at least two examples showing how racist ideologies are used to justify one group's domination over another.

21. How do systems of racial classification coincide with discrimination?

22. What are the reasons black athletes dominate some sports, such as basketball and are virtually invisible in others?

23. What is a stereotype? How are stereotypes perpetuated and reinforced?

24. According to Robert K. Merton, what is the relationship between prejudice and discrimination?

Chapter 9

25. Distinguish between individual discrimination and institutional discrimination. Give examples.

26. What is a stigma? How is this concept relevant to issues of race and ethnicity?

27. What are mixed contacts? How do stigmas dominate the course of interaction between the stigmatized and the "normals"?

28. How do the stigmatized respond to people who treat them as members of a category?

Comprehensive Essay Questions

1. How is the history of the United States a global story?

2. If you were asked to give a seminar to improve race relations in a community, what three ideas or concepts in this chapter would you be sure to emphasize? Explain why you would emphasize these three.

3. Consider Goffman's concepts of stigma and mixed contacts. Describe a mixed contact that you have observed where the interaction proceeded according to the possibilities outlined by Goffman. If you cannot think of an example that fits Goffman's model, describe an interaction that does not fit the model, and explain why Goffman's principles did not apply.

Chapter 10

Gender

Multiple-Choice Questions

1. When sociologists study gender, they focus on male-female differences that are
   a. socially created.
   b. biologically based.
   c. innate in nature.
   d. sex appropriate.

   ANS: A   PG: 266   TYP: comprehension   SOURCE: new

2. American Samoa is the focus of the gender chapter because that society
   a. makes the greatest distinctions between males and females.
   b. makes the least distinctions between males and females.
   c. channels male energy into pursuing football careers.
   d. channels female energy into pursuing cheerleading careers.

   ANS: C   PG: 267   TYP: comprehension   SOURCE: new; study guide

3. In American Samoa and other Pacific island areas, people recognize _____ genders.
   a. two
   b. three
   c. four
   d. five

   ANS: B   PG: 267   TYP: comprehension   SOURCE: new

4. It is remarkable that American Samoa, with a population of 65,000, can claim 200 men that play professional or division I level college _____ in the United States.
   a. soccer
   b. basketball
   c. football
   d. tennis

   ANS: C   PG: 267   TYP: comprehension   SOURCE: new

5. In American Samoa, 90 percent of those who work in health service occupations are
   a. male.
   b. female.
   c. immigrants.
   d. minorities.

   ANS: B   PG: 267   TYP: knowledge   SOURCE: new

6. A person's sex is determined first and foremost on the basis of
   a. distribution of facial and body hair.
   b. secondary sex characteristics.
   c. primary sex characteristics.
   d. social expectations.

   ANS: C   PG: 268   TYP: comprehension   SOURCE: study guide

7. _____ are considered primary sex characteristics.
   a. Reproductive organs
   b. Facial and body hair
   c. Voice qualities
   d. Chromosomes

   ANS: A   PG: 268   TYP: comprehension

8. _____ determines a baby's sex.
   a. Predestination
   b. Chance
   c. The male biological parent
   d. The female biological parent

   ANS: C   PG: 268   TYP: knowledge

Gender

9. Each biological parent contributes a sex chromosome; the mother contributes a(n) _____ chromosome and the father a(n) _____ chromosome.
   a. y; y
   b. x; y
   c. x; y or x
   d. x or y; x

   ANS: C   PG: 268   TYP: knowledge

10. We know from cases of _____ that a person's primary sex characteristics may not match his or her sex chromosomes.
    a. homosexuals
    b. female athletes who have failed sex tests
    c. the gender polarized
    d. male weightlifters

    ANS: B   PG: 268   TYP: knowledge

11. From a sociological point of view, sex is _____ and gender is _____.
    a. a biologically based classification scheme; a socially constructed phenomenon
    b. a socially constructed phenomenon; a feminist creation
    c. a classification scheme; a continuum
    d. a socially constructed phenomenon; a biological construction

    ANS: A   PG: 269   TYP: comprehension   SOURCE: study guide

12. _____ are considered secondary sex characteristics.
    a. Reproductive organs
    b. Facial and body hair
    c. Chromosomes
    d. Hormones

    ANS: B   PG: 269   TYP: comprehension

Chapter 10

13. Sociologist define _____ as social distinctions based on culturally conceived and learned ideas about appropriate behavior and appearances for males and for females.
    a. sex
    b. gender
    c. sexuality
    d. primary sex characteristics

    ANS: B   PG: 269   TYP: comprehension

14. Biological sex is not a clear-cut category because the intersexed exist. The intersexed are people
    a. with some mixture of male and female biological characteristics.
    b. bisexual in orientation.
    c. who are professed homosexuals.
    d. who are trapped in the body of a sex they do not want to be.

    ANS: A   PG: 268   TYP: comprehension

15. The *Diagnostic and Statistical Manual of Mental Disorders* estimates that _____ in 30,000 people born as a male has/have a gender identity disorder.
    a. 1
    b. 10
    c. 100
    d. 1,000

    ANS: A   PG: 269   TYP: knowledge

16. Spanish hurdler Maria Jose Martinez Patino lost her right to compete in amateur and Olympic events because she failed the sex tests. Martinez challenged that decision. In the end, the IAAF ruled that Martinez
    a. was a "man."
    b. was intersexed.
    c. would have to compete with men in the future.
    d. possessed no special advantages over other female competitors.

    ANS: D   PG: 269   TYP: knowledge   SOURCE: study guide

17. _____ are people whose primary sex characteristics do not match the sex they perceive and know themselves to be.
    a. The intersexed
    b. Transsexuals
    c. Endocrinologists
    d. True hermaphrodites

    ANS: B   PG: 268   TYP: comprehension

18. Transsexuals motivated to undergo a sex change are labeled as _____ transsexuals.
    a. intersexed
    b. high-intensity
    c. desperate
    d. sex-confirmation

    ANS: B   PG: 268   TYP: knowledge

19. _____ are physical traits not essential to reproduction.
    a. Primary sex characteristics
    b. Secondary sex characteristics
    c. Chromosomal sex characteristics
    d. Genders

    ANS: B   PG: 269   TYP: comprehension   SOURCE: study guide

20. _____ are considered secondary sex characteristics.
    a. Reproductive organs
    b. Distribution patterns of facial and body hair
    c. Chromosomes
    d. Hormones

    ANS: B   PG: 269   TYP: comprehension

21. To achieve the ideal foot length of 4 to 6 inches, Chinese girls from the 10th to the mid-20th centuries endured foot binding. The practice involved breaking the four smallest toes on each foot and binding them toward the heels so the feet could no longer grow. This situation suggests that
    a. gender ideals do not exist in reality, but that does not stop people from trying to achieve them.
    b. Chinese women (more than women of other nationalities) will do anything to achieve an ideal.
    c. gender ideals are realistic standards that women can meet.
    d. gender ideals are biologically based realities.

    ANS: A   PG: 268   TYP: application   SOURCE: new

22. _____ is the physical, behavioral, and mental or emotional traits believed to be characteristic of females.
    a. A secondary sex characteristic
    b. Gender
    c. Femininity
    d. A primary sex characteristic

    ANS: C   PG: 270   TYP: comprehension

23. Breast development, quality of voice, and skeletal form are considered
    a. primary sex characteristics.
    b. secondary sex characteristics.
    c. gender characteristics.
    d. reproductive characteristics.

    ANS: B   PG: 269   TYP: comprehension

24. When the painter Paul Gauguin visited Tahiti in 1891, he emphasized that there is "something virile in the women and something feminine in the men." His observations suggest that
    a. Tahiti was a backward society.
    b. homosexuality was acceptable in that society.
    c. there is a fixed line separating maleness from femaleness.
    d. the United States (and Europe) had made women into artificial creations.

    ANS: D   PG: 271   TYP: application

25. _____ is the physical, behavioral, and mental or emotional characteristics believed to be characteristic of males.
    a. A secondary sex characteristic
    b. Gender
    c. Masculinity
    d. A primary sex characteristic

    ANS: C   PG: 270   TYP: comprehension   SOURCE: study guide

26. In American Samoa, ideal standards of beauty for women center around
    a. eyebrows.
    b. long hair.
    c. shoe size.
    d. legs.

    ANS: B   PG: 271   TYP: knowledge

27. In pre-Christian Samoa, ideal standards signifying manhood centered around
    a. speed and agility.
    b. hair.
    c. body tattooing.
    d. muscles.

    ANS: C   PG: 271   TYP: knowledge   SOURCE: study guide

28. The fact that women in the United States conform to norms specifying that women have hairless bodies suggests that
    a. most women are hairless.
    b. women who do not conform are defective females.
    c. many seemingly biological differences between men and women are socially constructed.
    d. women are biologically distinct from men.

    ANS: C   PG: 271   TYP: comprehension

Chapter 10

29. Before the Christianization of Samoa, the transition from boyhood to manhood was accompanied by
    a. a religious ceremony that lasted for 3 days.
    b. a time of isolation in the wilderness.
    c. separation from females for one year.
    d. a long, painful process of body tattooing from the waist to below the knees.

    ANS: D   PG: 271   TYP: knowledge

30. Before the Christianization of Samoa, _____ did not merely signify manhood; it was manhood.
    a. short hair
    b. facial hair
    c. tattooing
    d. shaving

    ANS: C   PG: 271   TYP: knowledge

31. Sandra Bem wrote that a person's sex is connected to "virtually every aspect of human experience, including modes of dress, social roles, and even ways of expressing emotion and experiencing sexual desire." Bem was writing about
    a. primary sex characteristics.
    b. gender polarization.
    c. genetic and chromosomal sex.
    d. the intersexed.

    ANS: B   PG: 272   TYP: application   SOURCE: study guide

32. The organizing of social life around the male-female distinction is
    a. gender polarization.
    b. gender response.
    c. hormonal segregation.
    d. biological imperative.

    ANS: A   PG: 273   TYP: comprehension

33. A college student is asked, "How would your life be different if you were a member of the opposite sex?" He replies, "I would not have to appear to be in control of every situation." His response suggests that
    a. men can feel constrained by their gender roles.
    b. his life would change in negative ways.
    c. women are naturally flighty.
    d. he would be more conscious of his physical appearance.

    ANS: A   PG: 273   TYP: application

34. College students make gender-schematic decisions about possible majors if they ask, even subconsciously,
    a. "Would my parent approve of this major?"
    b. "Will this major lead to a high paying job?"
    c. "Are the professors who teach the classes feminists?"
    d. "What is the 'sex' of this major?"

    ANS: D   PG: 273   TYP: comprehension

35. A woman consciously or unconsciously decides that the man she dates must be bigger, taller, and stronger than she is. Her decision can be classified as
    a. feminist.
    b. natural.
    c. anti-feminist.
    d. gender-schematic.

    ANS: D   PG: 273   TYP: application   SOURCE: study guide

36. A man decides, consciously or unconsciously, that the woman he dates must be shorter and younger than he is. This decision can be classified as
    a. gender-schematic.
    b. natural.
    c. biologically based.
    d. feminist.

    ANS: A   PG: 273   TYP: application

Chapter 10

37. Gender-schematic decisions are influenced by considerations related to
    a. undoing gender stereotypes.
    b. self-fulfillment.
    c. society's polarized definitions of masculinity and femininity.
    d. intersexuality.

    ANS: C   PG: 273   TYP: comprehension

38. Which college major listed below is the most male-dominated?
    a. computer and information science
    b. library science
    c. mathematics
    d. psychology

    ANS: A   PG: 273   TYP: knowledge

39. Which college major listed below is the most female-dominated?
    a. library science
    b. parks and recreation
    c. theological studies
    d. psychology

    ANS: A   PG: 273   TYP: knowledge

40. In the United States, the average life expectancy for women is approximately _____ years longer than that for men.
    a. 2
    b. 6
    c. 10
    d. 15

    ANS: B   PG: 274   TYP: knowledge

41. Michael notes, "There is an unwritten rule my friends and I follow: if you are going to touch me, make it hurt." Michael is identifying a
    a. rite of passage.
    b. primary sex characteristic.
    c. feeling rule.
    d. universal norm.

    ANS: C   PG: 274   TYP: application   SOURCE: study guide

Gender

42. Corey states, "It's all right for two guys to be friends, but I can't picture two guys holding hands and not having some sexual feelings for each other." Corey is identifying a
    a. distinction between genders.
    b. feeling rule.
    c. universal norm.
    d. natural reaction.

    ANS: B   PG: 274   TYP: application

43. _____ are internal bodily sensations that we experience in relationships with other people.
    a. Feeling rules
    b. Social emotions
    c. Friendships
    d. Same-sex emotions

    ANS: B   PG: 274   TYP: knowledge

44. _____ are norms specifying appropriate ways to express internal bodily sensations that we experience in relationships with other people.
    a. Feeling rules
    b. Social emotions
    c. Friendships
    d. Same-sex emotions

    ANS: A   PG: 274   TYP: knowledge

45. Which one of the following statements is *false* regarding people's reactions to gender ideals of masculinity and femininity?
    a. People can resist gender ideals even as they use them to evaluate themselves and others.
    b. People can resist gender ideals even while conforming.
    c. Most people find ways to subvert gender ideals through deception, secret agreements with others, impression management, or outright challenges.
    d. For the most part, human beings passively accept gender ideals regarding masculinity and femininity.

    ANS: D   PG: 274   TYP: comprehension

46. The closest word we have to *fà-afafines* in American society is
    a. male.
    b. transvestite.
    c. transsexual.
    d. intersexed.

    ANS: B   PG: 276   TYP: knowledge

47. In American Samoa, *fà-afafines* are
    a. biological females who have taken on "men's ways."
    b. males with tattoos covering the lower body.
    c. females with tattoos covering the lower body.
    d. males who have taken on the "way of women."

    ANS: D   PG: 276   TYP: comprehension   SOURCE: study guide

48. *Fà-afafine* literally means
    a. transvestite.
    b. intersexual.
    c. in the way of women.
    d. unusual to a fault.

    ANS: C   PG: 276   TYP: knowledge   SOURCE: new

49. Which of the following characteristics about Samoa society helps explain how *fà-afafines* became commonplace in contemporary Samoa?
    a. Samoans make sharp distinctions between males and females.
    b. Close and physically affectionate relations with same-sex people are prohibited.
    c. The declining status of the *aumaga* has left men without a clear sense of purpose.
    d. Because there is widespread unemployment in Samoa, men take on *fà-afafine* roles for status.

    ANS: D   PG: 277   TYP: comprehension

50. The two largest employers in American Samoa are
    a. the military and banks.
    b. tourism and tuna canneries.
    c. the government and tuna canneries.
    d. GM and McDonald's.

    ANS: C   PG: 277   TYP: knowledge   SOURCE: study guide

51. Anthropologist Jeanette Mageo argues that *fa-afafines* could not have become commonplace in Samoa unless something about that society supported
    a. gender blurring.
    b. homosexuality.
    c. gender polarization.
    d. gender-schematic decisions.

    ANS: A   PG: 277   TYP: comprehension

52. When child development specialist Beverly Fagot studied children in play groups at age 12 months and then at age 24 months, she found
    a. significant sex differences between the interaction styles of 12-month-old boys and girls.
    b. no significant sex differences between the interaction styles of 24-month-old boys and girls.
    c. that teachers interacted with toddlers in gender-polarized ways.
    d. that teachers responded positively toward girls when they behaved assertively and positively toward boys when they communicated in gentle ways.

    ANS: C   PG: 278   TYP: knowledge

53. Which one of the following statements about early childhood teachers is false?
    a. Teachers are more accepting of girls' cross-gender behavior and explorations than of boys' cross-gender behaviors and exploration.
    b. Teachers believe that boys who behave like sissies are at greater risk than girls of growing up to be homosexuals.
    c. Teachers are more accepting of boys' cross-gender behaviors and exploration than of girls' cross-gender behavior and exploration.
    d. Teachers believe that girls who behave like tom-boys are at less risk of growing up to be homosexual.

    ANS: C   PG: 278   TYP: comprehension   SOURCE: study guide

Chapter 10

54. Which statement best reflects the "socialization perspective" of gender differences?
    a. A person's position in the social structure can channel his or her behavior in a stereotypical male or female direction.
    b. There is a close correspondence between primary sex characteristics and athletic ability.
    c. An undetermined but significant portion of male-female differences are products of the ways in which males and females are treated.
    d. Differences between men and women can be traced to their daily work experiences.

    ANS: C   PG: 278   TYP: comprehension

55. Socialization theorists argue that the socialization process explains
    a. away seemingly biologically-based differences.
    b. a very small proportion of male/female differences.
    c. an undetermined but significant proportion of male/female differences.
    d. almost 70 percent of male/female differences.

    ANS: C   PG: 278   TYP: comprehension

56. In American Samoa, the _____ occupation has the highest percentage of male workers.
    a. finance and real estate
    b. machine operator
    c. construction trade
    d. personal service worker

    ANS: C   PG: 278   TYP: knowledge

57. In American Samoa, the _____ occupation has the highest percentage of female workers.
    a. secretarial
    b. personal service
    c. transportation and material moving
    d. finance, insurance, and real estate

    ANS: A   PG: 278   TYP: knowledge

58. Research suggests that early childhood teachers are more accepting of girls' cross-gender behaviors and explorations than they are of such behaviors from boys. Apparently, teachers believe that boys who behave like "sissies" are at greater risk of growing up to be homosexual and to be psychologically ill-adjusted than are girls who behave like "tomboys." The practice speaks to which one of the following dynamics?
    a. the dynamics of socialization
    b. innate differences between boys and girls
    c. biologically based differences between boys and girls
    d. gender neutral approaches to education

    ANS: A PG: 278 TYP: application SOURCE: new

59. An estimated _____ percent of girls between the ages of 3 and 11 in the United States have Barbie dolls.
    a. 20
    b. 40
    c. 70
    d. 95

    ANS: D PG: 279 TYP: knowledge

60. Mattel markets "Barbie" as a(n)
    a. aspirational doll.
    b. doll with traditional values.
    c. doll with feminist values.
    d. intersexed toy.

    ANS: A PG: 279 TYP: knowledge SOURCE: study guide

61. Action toys for boys include X-Men, Street Fighter, and Mortal Kombat. These toys are marketed as
    a. aspirational dolls.
    b. dolls with traditional values.
    c. dolls with feminist values.
    d. intersexed toys.

    ANS: A PG: 279 TYP: knowledge SOURCE: new

Chapter 10

62. Which one of the following learned body language characteristics applies to males?
   a. sitting or standing with legs positioned away from the body.
   b. affiliative facial expression
   c. sitting with legs crossed at the ankles
   d. lowered gaze and constricted body

   ANS: A   PG: 279   TYP: application   SOURCE: new ; study guide

63. Which one of the following learned body language characteristics applies to females?
   a. sitting or standing with legs positioned away from the body.
   b. hands in pockets
   c. sitting with legs crossed at the ankles
   d. direct gaze

   ANS: C   PG: 279   TYP: application   SOURCE: new

64. About one in every _____ American Samoan male high school graduate leaves the island to play football in the United States.
   a. 50
   b. 20
   c. 9
   d. 4

   ANS: C   PG: 282   TYP: knowledge

65. Which one of the following factors explains why Samoan males are so successful at football?
   a. Football represents an opportunity to succeed in a place where 99 percent of jobs are connected to the tuna industry.
   b. High school football is very unpopular in Samoa.
   c. The sport was introduced to the island in the late 1990s.
   d. Samoan football players who enjoy success in the United States fuel interest of young Samoan males.

   ANS: D   PG: 282   TYP: comprehension

66. _____ is the process of introducing products into the market by using advertising and sales campaigns that promise consumers they will achieve gender ideals if they buy them.
    a. Selective marketing
    b. Gender-schematic marketing
    c. The commercialization of gender ideals
    d. Gender polarization

    ANS: C   PG: 282   TYP: comprehension

67. One way marketers convince people to buy products is to play on their insecurities about whether they meet or maintain (as they age) appearances that conform to gender ideals. This strategy applies to
    a. selective marketing.
    b. gender-schematic marketing.
    c. the commercialization of gender ideals.
    d. gender polarization.

    ANS: C   PG: 282   TYP: comprehension   SOURCE: new

68. _____ is/are the established and customary rules, policies, and day-to-day practices that affect a person's life chances.
    a. Structural constraints
    b. Ideologies
    c. Selective perceptions
    d. Ethgender

    ANS: A   PG: 283   TYP: comprehension   SOURCE: study guide

69. The female market is saturated with products. Thus, marketers must search for a new market, which is directed at men. The problem for marketers is how to sell men products that have been traditionally viewed as feminine. One strategy is to
    a. promote female products as better than male products.
    b. advertise the feminizing qualities of the product.
    c. "masculinize" feminine products.
    d. sell gender-neutral products.

    ANS: C   PG: 282   TYP: comprehension   SOURCE: new

Chapter 10

70. The theme of _____ is addressed in sociologist Renee R. Anspach's research on physicians and nurses working in neonatal intensive care units.
    a. socialization
    b. structural constraints
    c. sexist ideology
    d. reverse discrimination

    ANS: B   PG: 284   TYP: comprehension

71. Sociologist Renee R. Anspach found that physicians caring for babies in neonatal intensive care units tended to _____ to determine how well infants were doing.
    a. draw on technical information
    b. look for interactional clues
    c. consider a baby's level of alertness
    d. consider a baby's responsiveness to touch

    ANS: A   PG: 284   TYP: application   SOURCE: study guide

72. Which one of the following occupations is not among the 20 leading occupations of employed women?
    a. retail and personal sales
    b. secretaries
    c. cashiers
    d. college professors

    ANS: D   PG: 285   TYP: knowledge

73. In her study of neonatal intensive care units, Renee R. Anspach found that nurses and doctors used different criteria to answer the question, "How can you tell if an infant is doing well or poorly?" Specifically, she found that in comparison with physicians, nurses tended to draw on _____ to answer that question.
    a. technical or measurable information
    b. physical examination
    c. interactional clues
    d. medical paradigms

    ANS: C   PG: 284   TYP: comprehension

74. Women choose specialties and fields that require them to work with young children, that involve supervising other women, or that are otherwise considered feminine. This practice is an example of
    a. a structural constraint.
    b. ideology.
    c. selective perception.
    d. ethgender.

    ANS: A   PG: 284   TYP: application

75. Women comprise approximately _____ percent of the workforce that is engaged in nursing, home health, teaching preschoolers, and taking care of children.
    a. 70
    b. 80
    c. 90
    d. 100

    ANS: C   PG: 284   TYP: comprehension   SOURCE: new

76. Men comprise approximately _____ percent of the workforce that is engaged in construction, labor, carpentry, and maintenance.
    a. 70
    b. 80
    c. 90
    d. 10

    ANS: C   PG: 284   TYP: comprehension   SOURCE: new

77. In their discussion of male-female relationships, John and Mary come to the conclusion that men are prisoners of their hormones and simply not capable of forming meaningful relationships. Their argument is grounded in
    a. socialization theory.
    b. an understanding of situational constraints.
    c. the scientific method.
    d. sexist ideology.

    ANS: D   PG: 286   TYP: application

Chapter 10

78. Sexist ideologies are structured around several notions. Which one of the following is not one of those notions?
    a. People can be classified into two categories: male and female.
    b. There is a close correspondence between a person's sex and other characteristics, such as emotional makeup.
    c. Primary sex characteristics explain social and other inequalities.
    d. Secondary sex characteristics are ultimately social constructions.

    ANS: D   PG: 286   TYP: comprehension

79. The belief that one sex—and by extension, one gender—is superior to another and that this superiority justifies inequalities between sexes is known as
    a. structuralism.
    b. sexism.
    c. feminism.
    d. gender bias.

    ANS: B   PG: 284   TYP: comprehension   SOURCE: new

80. A U.S. Department of Defense directive states that homosexuality is incompatible with military service. This directive is grounded in
    a. socialization theory.
    b. an understanding of situational constraints.
    c. the scientific method.
    d. sexism.

    ANS: D   PG: 286   TYP: application

81. Which one of the following countries allows openly gay men and lesbians to serve in the military?
    a. Italy
    b. Saudi Arabia
    c. the United States
    d. North Korea

    ANS: A   PG: 287   TYP: knowledge   SOURCE: new

82. According to a Zogby poll, ___ percent of U.S. soldiers from Iraq and Afghanistan indicated that they were comfortable interacting with gay colleagues.
    a. 5
    b. 20
    c. 40
    d. 75

    ANS: D   PG: 287   TYP: knowledge   SOURCE: new

83. According to a Zogby poll, ___ percent of U.S. soldiers from Iraq and Afghanistan indicated that they were extremely uncomfortable interacting with gay colleagues.
    a. 5
    b. 20
    c. 40
    d. 75

    ANS: A   PG: 287   TYP: knowledge   SOURCE: new; study guide

84. In which of the following areas of life are men, as a group, most likely to be disadvantaged relative to women?
    a. income
    b. life expectancy
    c. career opportunities
    d. occupational status

    ANS: B   PG: 287   TYP: comprehension   SOURCE: new

85. Which age group of women has the lowest income gap with men?
    a. 16-24 years of age
    b. 25-34 years of age
    c. 35-44 years of age
    d. 45 to 54 years of age

    ANS: A   PG: 289   TYP: knowledge   SOURCE: new

Chapter 10

86. Women living in the United States are asked, "Do you consider yourself a feminist?" ____ in four women answer yes.
    a. One
    b. Two
    c. Three
    d. Four

    ANS: A   PG: 289   TYP: knowledge   SOURCE: new

87. When women living in the United States are told that a feminist is someone who believes in social, political, and economic equality of the sexes and are then asked, "Do you consider yourself a feminist?" ____ percent of women answer yes.
    a. 20
    b. 40
    c. 65
    d. 100

    ANS: C   PG: 289   TYP: knowledge   SOURCE: new

88. From a sociological point of view, a _____ is a perspective that advocates equality between men and women.
    a. sexist
    b. structuralist
    c. feminist
    d. socialist

    ANS: C   PG: 289   TYP: knowledge   SOURCE: new

89. Sociologists take a _____ perspective when they emphasize in their research and teaching such themes as a right to bodily integrity and autonomy, access to safe contraceptives, the right to choose, and freedom from sexual harassment.
    a. sexist
    b. structuralist
    c. feminist
    d. socialist

    ANS: C   PG: 289   TYP: knowledge   SOURCE: new; study guide

90. Sociologists Floya Anthias and Nira Yuval-Davis argue that "Women are a special focus of state concerns as a social category with a specific role." That role is
   a. spouse.
   b. nurturer.
   c. human reproduction.
   d. homemaker.

   ANS: C   PG: 292   TYP: knowledge

91. Approximately _____ percent of U.S. Senators are women.
   a. 5
   b. 17
   c. 25
   d. 50

   ANS: B   PG: 292   TYP: knowledge

92. Sociologists Floya Anthias and Nira Yuval-Davis introduce the term *ethgender* to refer to people who share the same sex, race, and ethnicity. They are particularly interested in the connection between ethgender and
   a. daily workplace experiences.
   b. certain areas of life (especially human reproduction) over which governments exercise control.
   c. aspirational dolls.
   d. life and death decisions about whether to withdraw medical care.

   ANS: B   PG: 292   TYP: concept

93. The focus of the suit filed by the abandoned Filipinos is
   a. the establishment of whether the sexual relationships between the servicemen and local women were consensual.
   b. the support of an estimated 8,600 children fathered by U.S. servicemen.
   c. to establish the Navy's direct role in the local bar and sex industry.
   d. to keep the military base in the Philippines.

   ANS: B   PG: 294   TYP: knowledge

Chapter 10

94. In her studies of male-female body language, Mills found
    a. male body language includes many affiliative clues.
    b. female body language is characterized by serious facial expressions.
    c. females create an overall impression of power, dominance, and high status.
    d. women tend to constrict their arms and legs, sit in attentive upright postures, and frequently lower their eyes.

    ANS: D   PG: 282   TYP: application

Use the following set of responses to answer the following questions. For each statement, decide which factor is being emphasized.

   a. Socialization
   b. Structural constraints
   c. Sexist ideology

95. The different social and physical demands and skills required of men and women when performing their various jobs helps them to channel their abilities in sex-appropriate directions.

    ANS: B   PG: 284

96. Ideas linking primary sex characteristics with behavior and ability perpetuate gender differences and inequality.

    ANS: C   PG: 286

97. One's position in the division of labor serves as an interpretive lens that channels perception and behavior.

    ANS: B   PG: 351

98. Norms governing body language are learned.

    ANS: A   PG: 278

Gender

99. An undetermined but significant portion of male-female differences are products of the ways in which males and females are treated.

    ANS: A   PG: 278

100. If we take a long view of women's wages (a 15-year period), we find that the average woman earns _____ percent of what men do during that same time period.
    a. 38
    b. 50
    c. 65
    d. 82

    ANS: A   PG: 289   TYP: knowledge   SOURCE: study guide

Multiple Choice Questions on the Web

1. In American Samoa, 90 percent of those in construction trades are
    a. male.
    b. female.
    c. immigrants.
    d. minorities.

    ANS: A   PG: 267   TYP: knowledge   SOURCE: new

2. _____ is a biological concept, whereas _____ is a social construct.
    a. Gender; sex
    b. Sexuality; gender
    c. Sex; chromosomal sex
    d. Sex; gender

    ANS: D   PG: 269   TYP: comprehension

Chapter 10

3. To the ideal waistline of 13-18 inches, women have worn corsets and even had their lower ribs removed. This situation suggests that
   a. gender ideals do not exist in reality, but that does not stop people from trying to achieve them.
   b. Chinese women (more than other nationalities of women) will do anything to achieve an ideal.
   c. gender ideals are realistic standards that women can meet.
   d. gender ideals are biologically based realities.

   ANS: A   PG: 268   TYP: application   SOURCE: new

4. An elementary school student is asked, "How would your life be different if you were a member of the opposite sex?" He replies, "I would have to shave my whole body." His response implies that he thinks in terms of
   a. feminist principles.
   b. gender polarization.
   c. a biological model of sex differences.
   d. gender convergence.

   ANS: B   PG: 273   TYP: application

5. Sociologists find gender a useful concept because
   a. people of the same sex look and behave in uniform ways.
   b. a society's gender expectations are central to people's lives whether they conform rigidly or resist.
   c. people vary in the extent to which they meet their society's gender expectations.
   d. ideas about appropriate behavior for males and females do not change.

   ANS: B   PG: 274   TYP: comprehension

6. Football was introduced to the island in 1969, after _____ decided that public schools should field football teams.
   a. a Samoan government official
   b. the U.S. president
   c. the Samoan president
   d. a U.S. government official

   ANS: D   PG: 282   TYP: knowledge

7. Which statement would sociologists that are focusing on structural constraints use to explain gender differences?
   a. A person's position in a social structure can channel behavior in sex-appropriate directions.
   b. Children's toys figure prominently in the socialization process.
   c. There is a close correspondence between primary sex characteristics and athletic capability.
   d. Gender inequalities have a physical basis.

   ANS: A   PG: 284   TYP: comprehension

8. Men comprise approximately _____ percent of the workforce engaged in nursing, home health, teaching preschoolers, and taking care of children.
   a. 1
   b. 10
   c. 40
   d. 50

   ANS: A   PG: 284   TYP: comprehension   SOURCE: new

9. Which one of the following countries bans openly gay men and lesbians from serving in the military?
   a. Italy
   b. South Africa
   c. the United States
   d. Israel

   ANS: C   PG: 287   TYP: comprehension   SOURCE: new

10. Ethgender refers to
    a. people who share or are believed to share the same race, sex, and ethnicity.
    b. people who have the same legal relationship with a political entity.
    c. people who are naturalized citizens of a state.
    d. women who share the same ethnicity.

    ANS: A   PG: 292   TYP: comprehension

Chapter 10

True-False Questions

1. In America, Samoa, and other Pacific Island areas, people recognize four genders.

    ANS: False   PG: 267   SOURCE: new

2. Even attractive men and women fall short (or will eventually fall short) of gender ideals.

    ANS: True   PG: 270   SOURCE: new

3. Biological sex is not a clear-cut category.

    ANS: True   PG: 268   SOURCE: study guide

4. Gender is a biologically based distinction.

    ANS: False   PG: 269

5. "Sex" and "gender" are interchangeable terms.

    ANS: False   PG: 269

6. The biological father's contribution of an x or a y chromosome determines the baby's sex.

    ANS: True   PG: 268   SOURCE: study guide

7. The practice of body tattooing has disappeared in American Samoa.

    ANS: False   PG: 272

8. Ninety percent of Bachelor's degrees in Library Science are awarded to males.

    ANS: False   PG: 274   SOURCE: study guide

9. Many women buy shoes that are too narrow and wear high heels in spite of foot, back, and neck pain.

   ANS: True   PG: 274   SOURCE: new

10. Samoans (relative to people in the United States) make sharp and clear distinctions between males and females.

    ANS: False   PG: 267   SOURCE: new

11. Sociologists are interested in the extent to which sex differences are socially induced.

    ANS: True   PG: 278

12. As a group, males have a longer life expectancy than females.

    ANS: False   PG: 273   SOURCE: study guide

13. Sociologists would label Barbie as an aspirational doll.

    ANS: True   PG: 282

14. The *fa-afafines* in American Samoa imitate popular foreign female vocalists, such as Britney Spears or Madonna.

    ANS: True   PG: 276   SOURCE: study guide

15. An estimated 60 percent of girls between age 3 and 11 in the United States have Barbie dolls.

    ANS: False   PG: 279

16. In American Samoa, the two largest employers are the tuna canneries and the U.S. government.

    ANS: True   PG: 277   SOURCE: study guide

Chapter 10

17. Transvestitism was practiced in pre-Christian Samoa.

    ANS: False   PG: 277

18. The unemployment rate is 12 percent in American Samoa.

    ANS: True   PG: 277

19. A lowered gaze and constricted body signal deference.

    ANS: True   PG: 281   SOURCE: new; study guide

20. In the United States, there is a commercial product on the market to improve almost every female body part or body function.

    ANS: True   PG: 282   SOURCE: study guide

21. From a marketing perspective, the male segment of the commercial market is saturated.

    ANS: False   PG: 283

22. Compared to men, women are disproportionately channeled into lower-paying, dead-end jobs.

    ANS: True   PG: 285

23. Of the 435 members that comprise the U.S. House of Representatives, 15 percent are women.

    ANS: True   PG: 292

24. The fertility rate of women on public assistance is higher than the fertility rate of women not on such assistance.

    ANS: False   PG: 293   SOURCE: study guide

25. Scientific evidence shows that homosexuality is incompatible with military service.

    ANS: False   PG: 287

26. Many poor women that live near overseas military bases see a relationship with a U.S. serviceman as their only way out of poverty.

    ANS: True   PG: 294

27. Evidence to date suggests that openly gay soldiers in the British military serve without any problems.

    ANS: True   PG: 287   SOURCE: new

28. The British military recruits soldiers at gay pride events.

    ANS: True   PG: 287   SOURCE: new; study guide

29. The U.S. military has discharged more than 11,000 servicemen and women under its "Don't Ask, Don't Tell Policy."

    ANS: True   PG: 287   SOURCE: new

30. If we consider male-female wage differences over a lifetime, the average woman earn about 38 percent of what a man earns.

    ANS: True   PG: 294   SOURCE: new

Concept Application (also in study guide)

Consider the concepts listed below. Match one or more of the concepts with each scenario. Explain your choices.
    a. Femininity (or feminine characteristics)
    b. Gender
    c. Gender polarization
    d. Structural constraints
    e. Intersexuals

Chapter 10

Scenario 1

"Women were widely excluded from the jury service until a few decades ago, many years after it was no longer permissible to exclude blacks as a group, and it was not until 1975 that the Supreme Court ruled that states had to maintain a representative jury pool that included women" (Greenhouse 1994:A10).

ANS: D

Scenario 2

High-heeled shoes are still meant predominantly for posing, as Miss America does in her swimsuit. She keeps her legs together, one knee gently bent. Pictures of women in bathing suits with heeled legs astride make a more up-to-date, but not necessarily a more feminist, statement.

High heels have never been made for comfort or for ease of movement. Their first wearers spoke of themselves as "mounted" or "propped" upon them; they were strictly court wear and constituted proof that one intended no physical exertion and need make none.

The Chinese had long known footwear that had the same effect, with wooden pillars under the arch of each shoe so that wearers required one or even two servants to help them totter along. Women had their feet deformed, by binding them into tiny, almost useless fists, which were shod in embroidered bootees. (Visser 1994:38)

ANS: A

Scenario 3

"Women in professional jobs have workplace issues like the glass ceiling and the mommy track. But now there is one for secretaries: rug-ranking. 'If the secretary's pay is based on her boss' status, not on the content of her job, that's rug-ranking—treating her as a perk like the size of his office or the quality of the carpet on his floor,' said N. Elizabeth Fried, a labor consultant based in Dublin, Ohio. 'Secretaries are the only ones in the corporate world whose pay is directly linked to the boss. Instead of a career path of their own, most secretaries have had a hitch-your-wagon-to-a-star reward system" (Lewin 1994:A1).

ANS: D

Scenario 4

"Family work was structured around gender and age…Women were responsible for the farmyard economy of milking, rearing of young animals, poultry, butter making, and frequently the cultivation of vegetables as well…Animal husbandry, the buying and selling of animals, and most fieldwork (e.g., plowing, burrowing) and structural yard work (e.g., building, repairing) requiring heavy effort was undertaken by the male 'farmer'" (O'Hara 2001).

ANS: C

Scenario 5
"[There] are rare cases in which babies are born whose sexual gender is ambiguous or indeterminate…Sexually ambiguous infants, who either appear to be female but are biologically male or appear to be male but are biologically female are sometimes called pseudohermaphrodites" (Scarboro 1991:339).

    ANS: E

Short Essay Questions

1. Why is American Samoa the focus of a chapter on gender?

2. Distinguish between primary and secondary sex characteristics. Is sex (the biological concept of male and female) a clear-cut distinction?

3. Define gender. Why do sociologists find the concept of "gender" useful?

4. What is gender polarization? Give an example.

5. Define gender-schematic and gender polarization. How are they connected? Explain how gender-schematic decisions and sexual desire affect educational choices and sexual desire.

6. Explain the following statement: "People of the same sex vary in the extent to which they meet their society's gender expectations."

7. What are *fà-afafines*? What characteristics of Samoan society support this gender blurring?

8. How does socialization operate to teach people about society's gender expectations?

9. What socialization mechanisms are at work in American Samoa to encourage interest and success in football among males?

10. What does the commercialization of gender ideals mean? Give at least one example.

11. How do structural constraints help to explain male-female differences? Specifically, how does one's position in the social structure channel behavior in stereotypically male or female directions?

12. What is sexist ideology? How is sexist ideology reflected in military policy toward homosexuals?

13. What is feminism? Give examples of the variety of feminist positions.

14. What is ethgender?

15. Name five areas of women's lives over which the state may choose to exercise control.

Comprehensive Essay Questions

1. Distinguish between sex and gender. How does gender influence the appearance of male/female "biological" differences?

2. Sociologists are most interested in the extent to which sex differences are socially created. Describe at least three ways sex differences are socially created.

3. Imagine you had the chance to introduce three policies to reduce gender inequalities at your university or place of employment. What areas would you emphasize? How would you make changes?

Chapter 11

Economics and Politics

Multiple-Choice Questions

1. Iraq is situated in a region of the world holding _____ of the world's known oil reserves.
    a. 10 percent
    b. half
    c. two-thirds
    d. 90 percent

    ANS: C   PG: 299   TYP: knowledge

2. The United States represents about _____ percent of the world's population, yet it consumes _____ percent of the world's annual oil production.
    a. 20; 50
    b. 15; 35
    c. 10; 25
    d. 5; 25

    ANS: D   PG: 299   TYP: knowledge

3. The Bush administration invaded Iraq with the intention of establishing a _____ in the heart of the Middle East.
    a. democracy
    b. totalitarian state
    c. centrally planned economy
    d. communist government

    ANS: A   PG: 299   TYP: knowledge   SOURCE: new; study guide

Chapter 11

4. _____ are institutions that coordinate human activity to produce, distribute, and consume goods and services.
   a. Economic systems
   b. Political systems
   c. Educational systems
   d. Religions

   ANS: A   PG: 300   TYP: comprehension

5. Which one of the following would be classified as a "service"?
   a. growing food
   b. manufacturing clothing
   c. providing transportation
   d. building computer hardware

   ANS: C   PG: 300   TYP: application

6. Which one of the following would be classified as "goods"?
   a. entertainment
   b. transportation
   c. financial services
   d. clothing

   ANS: D   PG: 300   TYP: application   SOURCE: study guide

7. The first agricultural revolution is believed to have taken place approximately _____ years ago.
   a. 1,000
   b. 5,000
   c. 7,000
   d. 10,000

   ANS: D   PG: 300   TYP: knowledge

8. _____ include(s) activities performed by others that result in no tangible product, such as entertainment, transportation, and personal care.
    a. Services
    b. Goods
    c. Products
    d. Economics

    ANS: A   PG: 300   TYP: comprehension   SOURCE: new

9. "Domestication" means that
    a. plants and animals have been brought under human control.
    b. the housekeeping occupation came into being.
    c. food sources became unpredictable.
    d. economic activity became separated from the household.

    ANS: A   PG: 300   TYP: comprehension

10. The most important agricultural revolution in history took place more than 10,000 years ago and coincided with the
    a. rise of hunting and gathering societies.
    b. domestication of plants and animals.
    c. invention of the scratch plow.
    d. invention of the wheel.

    ANS: B   PG: 370   TYP: knowledge

11. On the most basic level, the existence of _____ enables a society to support nonfood occupations, such as musicians and craftsmen.
    a. metal
    b. a food surplus
    c. automation
    d. industrialization

    ANS: B   PG: 300   TYP: comprehension

12. Irrigation systems, the windmill, the tractor, and pesticides are innovations that triggered
    a. domestication.
    b. agricultural revolutions.
    c. the service economy.
    d. democracy.

    ANS: B   PG: 300   TYP: comprehension   SOURCE: new

13. The innovation that turned the hand loom into a power loom, the horse-drawn carriage into the steam engine, and the blacksmith's hammer into a power machine is
    a. capitalism.
    b. domestication.
    c. mechanization.
    d. the computer chip.

    ANS: C   PG: 301   TYP: application   SOURCE: study guide

14. Many of the great Sumerian legacies, such as writing, irrigation, and the wheel are adaptive responses to
    a. the Tigris and Euphrates Rivers.
    b. domestication.
    c. the Nile River.
    d. the Industrial Revolution.

    ANS: A   PG: 301   TYP: knowledge

15. Biblical scholars identify the _____ region as the setting for the flood linked to Noah's Ark.
    a. Tigris-Euphrates
    b. Sudan
    c. Nile
    b. Indus

    ANS: A   PG: 301   TYP: knowledge

16. _____ is a form of domination in which one country imposes its political, economic, social, and cultural institutions on an indigenous population and the land the indigenous population occupies.
    a. Mechanization
    b. Colonialization
    c. Industrialization
    d. Revolution

    ANS: B   PG: 301   TYP: comprehension

17. Silicon chips, fiber optics, and satellites are technologies associated with the
    a. agricultural revolution.
    b. domestication revolution.
    c. Industrial Revolution.
    d. post-industrial revolution.

    ANS: D   PG: 303   TYP: application

18. Eleven countries belong to the Organization of Petroleum Exporting Companies (OPEC). ____ of them are former colonies of a European power.
    a. Two
    b. Five
    c. Eight
    d. Ten

    ANS: D   PG: 300   TYP: knowlede   SOURCE: new

19. The skills needed for jobs in the _____ revolve around interpersonal communication, reading, writing, and calculating.
    a. agricultural sector
    b. manufacturing sector
    c. postindustrial economy
    d. secondary economy

    ANS: C   PG: 300   TYP: comprehension   SOURCE: new

Chapter 11

20. Which one of the following is not a characteristic of capitalism?
    a. private ownership of property
    b. profit-driven
    c. governed by law of supply and demand
    d. government-regulated economies

    ANS: D   PG: 305   TYP: comprehension

21. _____ is a cornerstone of the socialist economic system.
    a. Private property
    b. Self-interest
    c. Public ownership
    d. Profit

    ANS: C   PG: 305   TYP: comprehension

22. The term _____ was first used in the early 19th century in response to the excessive poverty and inequality that accompanied the Industrial Revolution.
    a. socialism
    b. capitalism
    c. domestication
    d. democracy

    ANS: A   PG: 300   TYP: comprehension   SOURCE: new

23. _____ maintain that banks, credit lending institutions, modes of transportation, and the media should be state-owned.
    a. Capitalists
    b. Socialists
    c. Economists
    d. Theologians

    ANS: B   PG: 300   TYP: application   SOURCE: new

Economics and Politics

24. Under a system of private ownership, _____ own the means of production.
    a. individuals
    b. unions
    c. governments
    d. communes

    ANS: A   PG: 305   TYP: comprehension   SOURCE: study guide

25. The extent of colonization during the twentieth century is exemplified by the fact that _____ countries gained independence from their "mother countries."
    a. 50
    b. 80
    c. 100
    d. 130

    ANS: D   PG: 302   TYP: knowledge

26. _____ economies are defined by the manipulation of numbers, words, images, and other symbols.
    a. Colonial
    b. Agricultural
    c. Postindustrial
    d. Industrial

    ANS: C   PG: 302   TYP: comprehension

27. "When consumer demand for an item increases, prices rise." This principle applies to
    a. socialist forms of economic activity.
    b. the laws of supply and demand.
    c. mechanization.
    d. the division of labor.

    ANS: B   PG: 305   TYP: application

Chapter 11

28. _____ is an essential characteristic of socialist systems.
   a. Public ownership of the means of production
   b. Private ownership of the means of production
   c. The law of supply and demand
   d. A consumer-driven economy

   ANS: A	PG: 305	TYP: comprehension

29. Which one of the following economies is not officially classified as socialist or Communist?
   a. North Korea
   b. Brazil
   c. Vietnam
   d. Cuba

   ANS: B	PG: 306	TYP: comprehension

30. Saddam Hussein came to power in Iraq in
   a. 1930.
   b. 1949.
   c. 1955.
   d. 1979.

   ANS: D	PG: 306	TYP: knowledge

31. Iraq's economy is heavily dependent on
   a. agriculture.
   b. the service sector.
   c. oil revenues.
   d. migrant labor.

   ANS: C	PG: 307	TYP: comprehension	SOURCE: study guide

32. The _____ resulted in more than a million casualties between 1980 and 1988.
   a. Gulf War II
   b. Gulf War I
   c. Iran-Iraq War
   d. Oil-for-Food Program

   ANS: C	PG: 306	TYP: knowledge

33. According to world-system theorists, capitalism has come to dominate the world economy because
    a. under this system, governments control economic activities.
    b. it is the only economic system in the world.
    c. of the ways in which capitalists respond to changes in the economy, especially to economic stagnation.
    d. national interests take precedence over corporate interests.

    ANS: C   PG: 307   TYP: comprehension

34. An overwhelming majority of Fortune 500 corporations are headquartered in countries with economies classified as
    a. low-income.
    b. semiperipheral.
    c. peripheral.
    d. core.

    ANS: D   PG: 308   TYP: application

35. Iraq is a country that world-system theorists would classify as a _____ economy.
    a. capitalist
    b. semiperipheral
    c. peripheral
    d. core

    ANS: C   PG: 307   TYP: knowledge

36. Japan, Germany, the United States, Canada, Italy, and the United Kingdom possess _____ economies.
    a. semiperipheral
    b. core
    c. peripheral
    d. transitional

    ANS: B   PG: 308   TYP: application

Chapter 11

37. The Vietnamese economy is very vulnerable to price fluctuations. For example, the country managed to become the third largest producer of coffee beans when prices were around $3.00 per pound only to see the price drop to less than 50 cents. The vulnerability explains why Vietnam is classified as a _____ economy.
    a. core
    b. peripheral
    c. semiperipheral
    d. middle-income

    ANS: B   PG: 307   TYP: application

38. _____ economies include the wealthiest, most highly diversified economies with strong, stable governments.
    a. Core
    b. Peripheral
    c. Semiperipheral
    d. Industrial

    ANS: A   PG: 307   TYP: comprehension

39. Iraq's debt began accumulating with the
    a. Gulf War I.
    b. Iran-Iraq War.
    c. Gulf War II.
    d. Six-Day War.

    ANS: B   PG: 307   TYP: knowledge

40. Iraq's Oil-for-Food program was administered by
    a. the United Nations.
    b. the United States.
    c. the European community.
    d. OPEC.

    ANS: A   PG: 308   TYP: knowledge

41. Which one of the following is a characteristic of an extremely oil revenue dependent economy?
    a. strong domestic manufacturing sector
    b. a currency that is undervalued
    c. heavily taxed citizens
    d. corruption and political rivalries among those controlling the oil

    ANS: D   PG: 307   TYP: comprehension   SOURCE: study guide

42. UN Security Council Resolution 661 issued after Saddam Hussein invaded Kuwait in 1990 asked countries
    a. not to export oil to Iraq.
    b. to cut all trade relations with Iraq.
    c. to import only medical supplies and food stuffs from Iraq.
    d. not to import products originating in Iraq.

    ANS: D   PG: 307   TYP: comprehension

43. Which one of the following countries has the highest per capita GDP in the world?
    a. Luxembourg
    b. the United States
    c. Israel
    d. Germany

    ANS: A   PG: 308   TYP: knowledge

44. In the United States, practically all gains in household income since 1975 have gone to the top _____ percent of households.
    a. 5
    b. 20
    c. 40
    d. 50

    ANS: B   PG: 308   TYP: knowledge

Chapter 11

45. The CIA World Factbook states that in the United States, "those at the bottom lack the education and the professional/technical skills of those at the top, and more and more fail to get comparable pay raises, health insurance coverage, and other benefits." The World Factbook is describing a(n)
    a. tiertiary economy.
    b. emerging economy.
    c. a collapsing economy.
    d. two-tier labor market.

    ANS: D   PG: 308   TYP: comprehension

46. The U.S. economy can be classified as all but which of one of the following?
    a. market-oriented
    b. capitalist
    c. socialist
    d. dominated by private enterprise

    ANS: C   PG: 308   TYP: comprehension

47. The primary sector of the economy includes economic activities
    a. that generate or extract raw materials from the natural environment.
    b. that transform raw materials into manufactured goods.
    c. related to delivering services.
    d. related to the creation and distribution of information.

    ANS: A   PG: 309   TYP: comprehension   SOURCE: study guide

48. The secondary sector of the economy includes economic activities
    a. that generate or extract raw materials from the natural environment.
    b. that transform raw materials into manufactured goods.
    c. related to delivering services.
    d. related to the creation and distribution of information.

    ANS: B   PG: 310   TYP: comprehension

49. In the United States, the tertiary sector of the economy accounts for _____ percent of the GDP.
    a. 20
    b. 40
    c. 60
    d. 87

    ANS: D   PG: 310   TYP: knowledge

50. Which one of the following occupations is <u>not</u> projected to be among the five fastest-growing occupations between now and 2014?
    a. medical assistants
    b. physician assistants
    c. manufacturing workers
    b. computer software engineers

    ANS: C   PG: 310   TYP: comprehension   SOURCE: new

51. Customer service jobs are in which one of the following economic sectors?
    a. primary
    b. tertiary
    c. secondary
    d. manufacturing

    ANS: B   PG: 309   TYP: application   SOURCE: new

52. Which sector of the economy contributes the most to the GDP of the United States?
    a. primary
    b. secondary
    c. tertiary
    d. manufacturing

    ANS: C   PG: 310   TYP: knowledge   SOURCE: study guide

Chapter 11

53. Most people in the United States work in the _____ sector of the economy.
    a. primary
    b. secondary
    c. tertiary
    d. manufacturing

    ANS: C   PG: 310   TYP: knowledge

54. The five occupations estimated to have the largest job growth between now and 2014 are in which sector of the American economy?
    a. primary
    b. secondary
    c. tertiary
    b. manufacturing

    ANS: C   PG: 310   TYP: knowledge

55. A(n) _____ exists when a handful of producers dominate a market.
    a. monopoly
    b. oligopoly
    c. conglomerate
    d. bureaucracy

    ANS: B   PG: 309   TYP: application

56. Chris works as a customer service representative. Her job is in the _____ sector of the economy.
    a. primary
    b. secondary
    c. tertiary
    d. peripheral

    ANS: C   PG: 310   TYP: comprehension   SOURCE: study guide

Economics and Politics

57. When a single producer dominates a market, a(n) _____ exists.
    a. oligopoly
    b. conglomerate
    c. oligarchy
    d. monopoly

    ANS: D   PG: 309   TYP: comprehension

58. If one argues that a handful of oil companies—Exxon Mobile, Royal Dutch Shell, BP, Chevron, and Conoco Phillips—dominate the oil market in the United States, they are suggesting that a(n) _____ exists.
    a. oligopoly
    b. conglomerate
    c. oligarchy
    d. monopoly

    ANS: B   PG: 309   TYP: application   SOURCE: new

59. Agricultural activity accounts for _____ percent of the GDP of the United States.
    a. 1
    b. 15
    c. 40
    d. 60

    ANS: A   PG: 310   TYP: comprehension

60. Manufacturing accounts for _____ percent of the GDP of the United States.
    a. 1
    b. 12
    c. 40
    d. 60

    ANS: B   PG: 310   TYP: comprehension   SOURCE: new

61. The U.S. tertiary sector accounts for _____ percent of the GDP of the United States.
    a. 1
    b. 15
    c. 40
    d. 87

    ANS: D   PG: 310   TYP: comprehension   SOURCE: new

Chapter 11

62. In the United States, union membership varies by state. Which one of the following states has the greatest percentage of workers represented by unions?
    a. Hawaii
    b. Florida
    c. Kentucky
    d. Ohio

    ANS: A   PG: 310   TYP: knowledge   SOURCE: study guide

63. Which one of the following factors does not help to explain the drop in union membership?
    a. increased significance of the manufacturing sector
    b. increased percentage of females in the workforce
    c. increased global competition
    d. increased number of jobs with no union tradition

    ANS: A   PG: 311   TYP: comprehension

64. Approximately _____ of the U.S. workforce have memberships in unions.
    a. 12
    b. 25
    c. 30
    d. 50

    ANS: A   PG: 311   TYP: knowledge

65. The United States produces approximately 2.1 billion barrels of crude oil each year. That amount accounts for approximately _____ percent of the United States' annual crude oil needs.
    a. 20
    b. 40
    c. 60
    d. 80

    ANS: B   PG: 312   TYP: knowledge

Economics and Politics

66. The United States has an estimated 20.2 billion barrels of proven oil reserves. At the current rate of production, these reserves will last about _____ years.
   a. 10
   b. 20
   c. 40
   d. 100

   ANS: A   PG: 312   TYP: comprehension

67. The worldwide demand for oil and minerals is expected to increase because two countries, which are home to 2.5 billion people, are experiencing dramatic economic growth. These two countries are
   a. Brazil and Mexico.
   b. Iraq and Vietnam.
   c. India and China.
   d. Japan and Canada.

   ANS: C   PG: 312   TYP: comprehension   SOURCE: study guide

68. As the world demand for energy increases, the United States must address a critical question. That question is:
   a. Can the United States find more sources of oil within its borders?
   b. Can Iraq's oil meet the U.S. demand for it?
   c. How can the United States take control of more oil?
   d. How can a country with 4.6 percent of the world's population continue to consume 40 percent of the world's energy resources?

   ANS: D   PG: 313   TYP: comprehension

69. _____ debt results from spending sprees and impulse buying.
   a. Safe
   b. Survival
   c. Stupid
   d. National

   ANS: C   PG: 313   TYP: knowledge

395

Chapter 11

70. _____ debt is secured debt; collateral, such as a house, is associated with this debt.
    a. Safe
    b. Survival
    c. Stupid
    d. National

    ANS: A   PG: 313   TYP: knowledge   SOURCE: new

71. _____ debt is debt acquired from using credit cards to pay living expenses associated with food, rent, and transportation.
    a. Safe
    b. Survival
    c. Stupid
    d. National

    ANS: B   PG: 313   TYP: knowledge   SOURCE: new

72. The two top foreign holders of U.S. debt are
    a. Spain and South Africa.
    b. Germany and Italy.
    c. Mexico and Canada.
    d. China and Japan.

    ANS: D   PG: 313   TYP: knowledge   SOURCE: study guide

73. Automatic teller machines (ATMs) were first introduced in the
    a. 1950s.
    b. 1970s.
    c. 1980s.
    d. 1990s.

    ANS: B   PG: 311   TYP: knowledge

Economics and Politics

74. The difference between the dollar value of goods and services imported and exported is known as
    a. the national debt.
    b. the trade deficit/surplus.
    c. odious debt.
    d. consumer debt.

    ANS: B   PG: 313   TYP: knowledge

75. _____ relate to the use of and access to power.
    a. Economic institutions
    b. Political institutions
    c. Educational institutions
    d. Religions

    ANS: B   PG: 314   TYP: comprehension

76. The United States represents 4.6 percent of the world's population, yet it consumes _____ percent of the world's total energy resources.
    a. 40
    b. 60
    c. 70
    d. 90

    ANS: A   PG: 313   TYP: knowledge

77. _____ is the probability that an individual can achieve his or her will even against another individual's opposition.
    a. A life chance
    b. Politics
    c. Rationalization
    d. Power

    ANS: D   PG: 314   TYP: comprehension

Chapter 11

78. A "chief," "king," or "queen" possesses power based on which form of authority?
    a. traditional
    b. charismatic
    c. legal-rational
    d. socialistic

    ANS: A   PG: 314   TYP: comprehension   SOURCE: study guide

79. Which one of the following persons held/holds power grounded on traditional authority?
    a. Richard Nixon
    b. Queen Elizabeth II
    c. Martin Luther King, Jr.
    d. Al Gore

    ANS: B   PG: 314   TYP: application

80. _____ leaders often emerge during times of profound crisis.
    a. Traditional
    b. Charismatic
    c. Legal-rational
    d. Socialistic

    ANS: B   PG: 315   TYP: application

81. Leaders who, by virtue of their special qualities, have the ability to unleash revolutionary changes possess _____ authority.
    a. traditional
    b. charismatic
    c. legal-rational
    d. political

    ANS: B   PG: 315   TYP: comprehension

82. Which one of the following persons held/holds power grounded on charismatic authority?
    a. Richard Nixon
    b. Queen Elizabeth II
    c. Adolf Hitler
    d. Dick Cheney

    ANS: C   PG: 315   TYP: application   SOURCE: new

83. _____ authority rests on a system of impersonal rules that formally specify the qualifications for occupying a powerful position.
   a. Traditional
   b. Charismatic
   c. Legal-rational
   d. Political

   ANS: C   PG: 315   TYP: comprehension

84. _____ is a system of government in which power is vested in the citizen body or "the people."
   a. Capitalism
   b. Democracy
   c. Totalitarianism
   d. Authoritarianism

   ANS: B   PG: 315   TYP: knowledge   SOURCE: study guide

85. Attraction and devotion to a leader cannot sustain a community indefinitely: the object of these emotions is mortal. This statement applies to _____ authority.
   a. charismatic
   b. traditional
   c. legal-rational
   d. democratic

   ANS: A   PG: 315   TYP: application

86. _____ governments are products of the twentieth century because a technology exists that allows a few people in power to control the behavior of the masses.
   a. Totalitarianism
   b. Democratic
   c. Authoritarian
   d. Charismatic

   ANS: A   PG: 317   TYP: comprehension

87. Authoritarian governments are defined by which one of the following characteristics?
    a. an unchallenged official ideology
    b. a vision of the perfect society
    c. some outside power plays a role in bringing the leader to power
    d. citizens have the right to vote

    ANS: C   PG: 317   TYP: comprehension

88. Sir Winston Churchill once said that _____ "is the worst form of government except for all others that we have tried."
    a. communism
    b. authoritarianism
    c. democracy
    d. totalitarianism

    ANS: C   PG: 315   TYP: comprehension   SOURCE: new

89. China under Mao Zedong, a leader who espoused overthrowing capitalist and foreign influence, can be classified as a(n) _____ government.
    a. democratic
    b. authoritarian
    c. totalitarian
    d. representative

    ANS: C   PG: 315   TYP: application

90. Totalitarianism is a system of government characterized by
    a. multiple political parties vying for power.
    b. tolerance for dissent.
    c. an unchallenged official ideology.
    d. independent media.

    ANS: C   PG: 315   TYP: comprehension   SOURCE: new

91. Which one of the following historical figures headed a totalitarian system of government?
    a. Joseph Stalin
    b. Saddam Hussein
    c. William Jefferson Clinton
    d. Castro

    ANS: A   PG: 315   TYP: application   SOURCE : new

92. Named after a U.S. Ambassador to the United States in the 1980s, the Kirkpatrick Doctrine maintained that the U.S. would support _____ regimes because they are less dangerous to the American way of life.
    a. tertiary
    b. authoritarian
    c. totalitarian
    d. representative

    ANS: B   PG: 318   TYP: comprehension

93. _____ means "rule of the deity."
    a. Theocracy
    b. Democracy
    c. Fundamentalism
    d. Authoritarianism

    ANS: A   PG: 318   TYP: comprehension

94. _____ is a form of government in which political authority is in the hands of religious leaders or a theologically trained elite.
    a. Theocracy
    b. Democracy
    c. Totalitarianism
    d. Authoritarianism

    ANS: A   PG: 318   TYP: comprehension   SOURCE: study guide

Chapter 11

95. The Vatican under the Pope, Afghanistan under the Taliban, and Iran under Supreme Ayatollah Ali Hoseni-Khamenei are all examples of _____ forms of government.
    a. totalitarian
    b. democratic
    c. authoritarian
    d. theocratic

    ANS: D   PG: 318   TYP: application

96. The overlapping interests of the political, military, and corporate elite can be traced to which one of the following events?
    a. World War II
    b. the Industrial Revolution
    c. the breakup of the Soviet Union
    d. the Vietnam War

    ANS: A   PG: 320   TYP: knowledge

97. C. Wright Mills wrote, "The power to make decisions of national and international consequence is now so clearly seated in political, military, and economic institutions that other areas of society seem off to the side." Mills was writing about
    a. monopolies.
    b. the power elite.
    c. a pluralist society.
    d. conglomerates.

    ANS: B   PG: 320   TYP: comprehension   SOURCE: study guide

98. The _____ model suggests that a relatively low number of people make decisions that have consequences affecting millions of people worldwide.
    a. democratic
    b. power elite
    c. pluralist
    d. socialist

    ANS: B   PG: 320   TYP: comprehension

99. Which one of the following presidents was the first to warn the American people about the military-industrial complex?
    a. George W. Bush
    b. George H. W. Bush
    c. Dwight D. Eisenhower
    d. Thomas Jefferson

    ANS: C   PG: 319   TYP: knowledge

100. Each year, the U.S. Department of Defense issues approximately _____ contracts with 2,000 businesses.
    a. 10,000
    b. 100,000
    c. 30 million
    d. 60 million

    ANS: D   PG: 320   TYP: knowledge

101. In the United States, the National Association of Realtors, the National Auto Dealers Association, and the Association of Trial Lawyers of America contribute to political campaigns and are known as
    a. monopolies.
    b. primary sector industries.
    c. special interest groups.
    d. political action committees.

    ANS: D   PG: 322   TYP: application   SOURCE: study guide

102. The _____ model views politics as an arena of compromises, alliances, and negotiations among many competing special interest groups.
    a. power elite
    b. pluralist
    c. socialist
    d. capitalist

    ANS: B   PG: 321   TYP: comprehension   SOURCE: study guide

103. MoveOn.org, Swift Vets, and POWs for Truth are classified as
    a. PACs.
    b. 527 groups.
    c. conglomerates.
    d. the power elite.

    ANS: B   PG: 322   TYP: application

104. _____ percent of Iraqi marriages are between first and second cousins.
    a. Seventy
    b. Fifty
    c. Twenty
    d. Five

    ANS: B   PG: 322   TYP: knowledge

105. The divorce rate among those Iraqis who marry first or second cousins is _____ percent.
    a. 2
    b. 10
    c. 20
    d. 30

    ANS: A   PG: 322   TYP: knowledge

106. Some scholars argue that extraordinarily strong family bonds complicate the road to democracy in Iraq because democracies depend on
    a. weak family ties.
    b. different perspectives.
    c. individuals who value public good over family obligations.
    d. special interest groups.

    ANS: C   PG: 322   TYP: comprehension

107. Which empire yields the most hits on the Google search engine?
    a. American
    b. British
    c. Roman
    d. Mayan

    ANS: A   PG: 323   TYP: knowledge

108. A group of countries under the direct control of a foreign power or government such that the dominant power shapes political, economic, and cultural development is a(n)
    a. monopoly.
    b. conglomerate.
    c. PAC.
    d. empire.

    ANS: D   PG: 322   TYP: comprehension

109. One U.S. Pentagon official pointed out in a news briefing that "the sheer size of this campaign has never been seen before, never been contemplated before." *This* campaign was the
    a. 1990 oil embargo against Iraq.
    b. Food-for-Oil program in Iraq.
    c. shock and awe campaign in Iraq.
    d. democratization of Iraq.

    ANS: C   PG: 324   TYP: comprehension   SOURCE: study guide

110. _____ are groups that participate in armed rebellion against an established authority, government, or administration with the hope that those in power will pull out.
    a. Colonizers
    b. PACs
    c. Revolutionaries
    d. Insurgents

    ANS: D   PG: 324   TYP: comprehension   SOURCE: study guide

Chapter 11

Multiple Choice Questions on the Web

1. _____ is the country that holds the largest amount of proven oil reserves in the world.
   a. Iraq
   b. Saudi Arabia
   c. Kuwait
   d. Afghanistan

   ANS: B   PG: 299   TYP: knowledge

2. _____ include(s) any product that is manufactured, grown, or extracted from the earth.
   a. Services
   b. Goods
   c. Products
   d. Economics

   ANS: B   PG: 300   TYP: comprehension

3. Which one of the following rivers is located in Iraq?
   a. Tigris-Euphrates
   b. Congo
   c. Nile
   d. Indus

   ANS: B   PG: 301   TYP: knowledge

4. Economic ideals are
   a. the best ways of organizing economic activities.
   b. standards against which real economic systems can be compared.
   c. capitalist-driven.
   d. proven profit-generating strategies.

   ANS: B   PG: 304   TYP: comprehension

Economics and Politics

5. "A strong tertiary sector" of the economy means that economic activity related to_____ is very important.
   a. extracting raw materials
   b. drilling for oil
   c. transforming raw materials into manufactured goods
   d. delivering services

   ANS: D   PG: 310   TYP: comprehension

6. Many of the world's largest companies are _____; that is, they own "smaller" corporations acquired through merger or acquisition.
   a. oligopolies
   b. conglomerates
   c. oligarchies
   d. monopolies

   ANS: B   PG: 309   TYP: comprehension

7. In the sociological sense of the word, a charismatic leader is
   a. a popular person.
   b. demanding to the point of insisting that followers make extraordinary sacrifices.
   c. an attractive, likable person.
   d. someone who is continually in our thoughts.

   ANS: B   PG: 315   TYP: comprehension

8. Which one of the following characteristics does not apply to theocracies?
   a. separation of church and state
   b. divine laws and practices and guiding principles
   c. political authority is in the hands of religious leaders
   d. leaders are devoted to religious principles

   ANS: A   PG: 318   TYP: comprehension

Chapter 11

9. According to Mills, the interests of the government, military, and corporations became deeply intertwined when the power elite
   a. realized that each could only thrive under a democracy.
   b. decided that church and state should be separate.
   c. decided that oil was the engine of industrialization.
   d. decided a permanent war industry was needed to fight communism.

   ANS: D   PG: 320   TYP: knowledge

10. The purpose of the _____ was to "shatter Iraq physically, emotionally, and psychologically" such that the people lost their will to fight.
    a. occupation of Iraq
    b. shock and awe campaign in Iraq
    c. liberation of Iraq
    d. oil embargo

    ANS: B   PG: 324   TYP: comprehension

True-False Questions

1. When invading Iraq, the Bush administration was clear on its intention to change the political system in Iraq from a dictatorship to a democracy.

   ANS: True   PG: 299   SOURCE: new; study guide

2. When invading Iraq, the Bush administration was clear on its intention to change the economy of Iraq from a free market to a centrally-planned system.

   ANS: False   PG: 299   SOURCE: new

3. Iraq is situated in a region of the world that holds 90 percent of the world's known oil reserves.

   ANS: False   PG: 299   SOURCE: new

4. The Tigris-Euphrates Rivers lie within the political boundaries of Iraq.

   ANS: True   PG: 300

5. Many agricultural revolutions have taken place over the course of human history.

   ANS: True   PG: 300   SOURCE: study guide

6. The Industrial Revolution cannot be separated from colonization.

   ANS: True   PG: 299   SOURCE: new

7. In post-industrial societies, the skills needed for jobs revolve around interpersonal communication, reading, writing, and calculating.

   ANS: True   PG: 302

8. Socialist systems are governed by the laws of supply and demand.

   ANS: False   PG: 305

9. No economic system, even the U.S. system, fully realizes capitalist principles.

   ANS: True   PG: 304   SOURCE: study guide

10. No economic system fully realizes socialist principles.

    ANS: True   PG: 304

11. The People's Republic of China, Cuba, North Korea, and Vietnam allow no activities that generate personal wealth.

    ANS: False   PG: 306

12. Because of its oil wealth, Iraq is classified as a core economy.

    ANS: False   PG: 307   SOURCE: study guide

Chapter 11

13. Since 1979, Iraq's main export has been oil.

    ANS: False   PG: 307

14. The UN Food-for-Oil Program succeeded in keeping oil revenues in the hands of the Iraqi people.

    ANS: False   PG: 308

15. The U.S. has the most powerful, diverse, and technologically advanced economy in the world.

    ANS: True   PG: 308   SOURCE: study guide

16. Luxembourg has the highest per capita GDP in the world.

    ANS: True   PG: 308

17. The secondary sector consists of economic activities that involve the creation and distribution of information.

    ANS: False   PG: 310

18. The United States has the largest and most technologically powerful economy in the world.

    ANS: True   PG: 308   SOURCE: new; study guide

19. Exxon-Mobile is considered a conglomerate because it owns smaller corporations and subsidiaries.

    ANS: True   PG: 309   SOURCE: new

20. The primary sector of an economy generates or extracts raw materials from the natural environment.

    ANS: True   PG: 309   SOURCE: new

21. A monopoly exists when a handful of producers dominate a market.

    ANS: False   PG: 309   SOURCE: study guide

22. The agricultural sector of the American economy accounts for about 1 percent of U.S. GDP.

    ANS: True   PG: 310

23. North Carolina is one of five states in which union affiliation among workers is less that 5 percent.

    ANS: True   PG: 311   SOURCE: new

24. Saudi Arabia is the top supplier of petroleum products to the United States.

    ANS: False   PG: 313

25. Charismatic leaders often emerge during times of profound crisis.

    ANS: True   PG: 315

26. The source of a charismatic leader's authority lies in the "goodness" of that leader's vision.

    ANS: False   PG: 315

27. In the United States, Hispanics stand out as the category most likely to vote.

    ANS: False   PG: 316   SOURCE: study guide

28. Since Saddam Hussein came to power in 1978, the United States government has both supported and opposed him.

    ANS: True   PG: 318

Chapter 11

29. In a theocracy, church and state are one in the same.

   ANS: True   PG: 318

30. P.A.C. stands for Political Action Committee.

   ANS: True   PG: 322   SOURCE: study guide

31. In the United States, 527 groups are tax-exempt advocacy organizations that seek to influence federal elections.

   ANS: True   PG: 322

32. Israel is the largest buyer of arms in the world.

   ANS: False   PG: 324   SOURCE: study guide

33. Fifty percent of Iraq's marriages are between first and second cousins.

   ANS: True   PG: 322

Concept Application (also in study guide)

Consider the concepts listed below. Match one or more of the concepts with each scenario. Explain your choices.

   a. Semiperipheral economy
   b. Peripheral economy
   c. Conglomerate
   d. Primary sector
   e. Secondary sector
   f. Special interest groups

Scenario 1

"In less than three decades, Taiwan has become a major economic player not only in the economy of the Pacific Rim but [also] in the global system as well. Foreign investors have played a vital role in Taiwan's economic development. For example, a mass buyer, like Sears or K-Mart, would visit Taiwanese factories and order goods in bulk for sale under the chain's brand name. A company like Arrow shirts or U.S. Shoe would supply samples to several factories and then contract with the factory that offered the best deal in terms of cost and quality. The "Made in Taiwan" label spread worldwide, even if no one outside Taiwan knew a single Taiwanese company that produced the products" (Goldstein 1991).

ANS: A

Scenario 2

At the urging of Chiquita Brands, a unit of the American Financial Corporation and the world's largest banana producer, the Clinton Administration is seeking to overturn an agreement that guarantees small Caribbean banana farmers special access to the European Union market.

"Why is America doing this to us?" Mr. Prosper, 53, asked as his crop was being boxed at a weighing station here the other day. "This is a little place, and this is all that we know and what we depend on. We have nothing else and we hurt nobody, but now they want to take even this from us."

Much as in neighboring Dominica and St. Vincent and the Grenadines, one-quarter of the labor force in this country of 145,000 people is employed in the banana industry, either growing, processing, or shipping the fruit. In contrast to Central America, where workers paid as little as $2 a day grow most of Chiquita's bananas, Caribbean banana workers are mostly independent growers who own the small plot they farm (Rohter 1997:A6).

ANS: B

Scenario 3

A notable feature of the biggest recent mergers is that the firms dominating this process are not media companies in a strict sense: Disney is avowedly a "family entertainment communication company" in the business of selling theme parks, toys, movies, and videos. Its focus, in the words of CEO Michael Eisner, is on the provision of "non-political entertainment and sports." Time Warner has a similarly wide spectrum of business interests and a comparable marketing orientation. Disney and Time Warner are what Herbert Schiller calls "pop cultural corporate behemoths."

Westinghouse, by contrast, has long been primarily a nuclear power and weapons producer, with its media interests generating only 10 percent of sales revenue. With the Westinghouse takeover of CBS, two of the three top networks are controlled by large firms in the politically sensitive nuclear power/weapons industries (the other is NBC's owner General Electric, which along with Westinghouse is one of the top 15 U.S. defense contractors). (Herman 1996)

ANS: C

Chapter 11

Scenario 4

"A mainstay of the mining industry is gold, which is being extracted from the West faster than ever before, says France. About 85 percent of the gold extracted in the West ends up in jewelry, the rest going into products such as electronics." (DiSilvesto 1996)

    ANS: D, E

Scenario 5

"As more private sector organizations learn to use the tools of the political campaign industry, a broad range of corporations, associations, unions, and non-profits are playing a larger, more aggressive role in the shaping of public opinion on matters they deem important…. A study conducted by the Annenberg Public Policy Center of the University of Pennsylvania estimated that during the 1995-96 election cycle, one-third of the total dollars spent on advertising in federal elections was attributable to "issue" advocacy efforts." (Faucheux 1998)

    ANS: F

Short Essay Questions

1. Why focus on Iraq in conjunction with the topics of economics and politics?

2. Define economic system. Name three revolutions that have shaped economic systems.

3. Why are the domestication of plants and animals and the invention of the scratch plow considered revolutionary?

4. Name one of the most fundamental features of the Industrial Revolution. Why is this feature fundamental?

5. What do we mean when we say that the Industrial Revolution cannot be separated from European colonization? Use oil as an example.

6. What is a Postindustrial society?

7. What characteristics distinguish a capitalist economic system from a socialist one?

8. From a world system perspective, how has capitalism come to dominate the global network of economic relationships?

9. Distinguish among core, peripheral, and semiperipheral economies.

10. Explain why Iraq would be considered a peripheral economy.

11. Which country is considered to have the strongest and most diverse economy in the world? Why?

12. What contributions do the primary, secondary, and tertiary sectors of the U.S. economy make to the GDP? Which sector contributes the largest share? Explain.

13. What is the difference between a monopoly and an oligopoly?

14. What is a conglomerate? Give an example.

15. What do we mean when we say that the United States is an oil- and mineral-dependent economy?

16. Describe the various kinds of debt that exist in the U.S. economy.

17. Define political system.

18. What is authority? How many types of authority did Weber identify? Give examples of each kind of authority.

19. What are the essential characteristics of a democracy?

20. How do we distinguish between totalitarian and authoritarian governments?

21. What is a theocracy?

22. What is the power elite? Who comprises the power elite in the United States?

23. Does C. Wright Mills believe that there are any significant constraints on the decision-making powers of the power-elite? Why or why not?

24. Explain the pluralist model of power.

25. What are PACs and 527 groups? Give examples.

26. Define empire, imperialistic power, hegemony, and militaristic power.

27. What are some examples of U.S. power and influence in the world?

28. What are insurgents?

Comprehensive Essay Questions

1. Suppose you were the director of a career placement office at a university. You have invited seniors to a seminar about the future of employment in the United States. What kind of information would you present?

2. If someone from a foreign country asked you to describe economic and political life in the United States, what points would you be sure to emphasize?

3. Is the United States an imperialist power?

Chapter 12

Family and Aging

Multiple-Choice Questions

1. In Japan, the average number of children that women bear in their lifetime is
   a. 1.2
   b. 2.1
   c. 3.0
   d. 3.4

   ANS: A   PG: 331   TYP: comprehension

2. Which one of the following is true about Japan relative to United States?
   a. Japan has a higher fertility rate.
   b. In Japan, more children live in single parent households.
   c. The teen birth rate is lower in Japan.
   d. Fewer elderly in Japan live with adult children.

   ANS: C   PG: 331   TYP: comprehension   SOURCE: new

3. In the United States, approximately ____ percent of children live with a single parent.
   a. 10
   b. 15
   c. 28
   d. 48

   ANS: C   PG: 331   TYP: knowledge

Chapter 12

4. Japan's _____ is a major national concern.
   a. high death rate
   b. low dependency ratio
   c. low fertility rate
   d. high infant mortality rate

   ANS: C   PG: 331   TYP: knowledge   SOURCE: study guide

5. Relative to Japan, the United States has
   a. lower infant mortality.
   b. lower rate of reported child abuse cases.
   c. lower percentage of marriage beginning as cohabitation.
   d. higher total fertility rate.

   ANS: D   PG: 331   TYP: knowledge   SOURCE: new

6. In Japan, _____ percent of persons age 65 and older live with their adult children.
   a. 20
   b. 30
   c. 50
   d. 70

   ANS: C   PG: 331   TYP: knowledge

7. The average number of children that a woman bears in her lifetime is known as the
   a. fertility rate.
   b. crude birth rate.
   c. age-specific birth rate.
   d. infant mortality rate.

   ANS: A   PG: 332   TYP: comprehension

8. An aging population is a label attached to a situation in which
   a. the number of elderly is increasing in a society.
   b. one out of every three people is 65 and over.
   c. the youth outnumber the elderly population.
   d. the percentage of the population age 65 and older is increasing relative to other age groups.

   ANS: D   PG: 331   TYP: comprehension   SOURCE: study guide

9. Which one of the following represents an example of tertiary kin?
   a. mother
   b. mother's mother
   c. brother's daughter's son
   d. father's sister

   ANS: C   PG: 332   TYP: comprehension

10. Which one of the following represents an example of secondary kin?
    a. father
    b. father's father
    c. mother's sister's son
    d. brother's daughter's son's son

    ANS: B   PG: 332   TYP: comprehension

11. Which one of the following factors explains why Japan has one of the oldest populations in the world?
    a. long life expectancy
    b. high total fertility rate
    c. low immigration rate
    d. effective contraceptives

    ANS: A   PG: 331   TYP: comprehension   SOURCE: new

12. _____ is one way people limit the number of kin relatives.
    a. Conscious decisions
    b. Contraceptives
    c. Selective forgetting
    d. An unconscious decision

    ANS: C   PG: 332   TYP: comprehension

13. Which one of the following constitutes primary kin?
    a. mother, father, sister, brother
    b. mother's mother, mother's father, sister's son
    c. brother's daughter's son
    d. brother's daughter's son's son

    ANS: A   PG: 332   TYP: comprehension   SOURCE: study guide

14. Which one of the following female-dominated occupations is associated with the lowest hourly wage?
    a. pre-kindergarten and kindergarten teacher
    b. LPN
    c. nursing aides
    d. child care workers (private households)

    ANS: D   PG: 339   TYP: knowledge

15. At her wedding, Julie met her brother's daughter's son. Julie met a
    a. primary relative.
    b. secondary relative.
    c. tertiary relative.
    d. quadiary relative.

    ANS: C   PG: 332   TYP: comprehension

16. Hector argues that he is marrying Maria for love. His choice of spouse can be classified as
    a. arranged.
    b. romantic.
    c. endogamy.
    d. exogamy.

    ANS: B   PG: 333   TYP: application

17. Sara marries someone of the same religion as herself. She has followed the norm of
    a. patrilocal groups.
    b. endogamy.
    c. exogamy.
    d. monogamy.

    ANS: B   PG: 333   TYP: application

18. When family residence is neolocal, that means the
    a. wife lives with or near her husband's family.
    b. husband lives with or near his wife's family.
    c. husband and wife live apart from each other.
    d. husband and wife's residence is separate from their parents.

    ANS: D   PG: 333   TYP: knowledge

19. In at least 90 countries in the world, the fertility rate is below _____, the rate needed to replace those members that die.
    a. 1.8
    b. 2.1
    c. 3.2
    d. 4.0

    ANS: B   PG: 335   TYP: knowledge

20. It is estimated that between _____ percent of children born are not the biological children of the men that believe they have fathered these children.
    a. 1 and 2
    b. 2 and 10
    c. 11 and 15
    d. 25 and 30

    ANS: B   PG: 335   TYP: knowledge

21. A functionalist would argue that families are structured to
    a. devalue reproductive work.
    b. maintain and perpetuate social inequalities.
    c. replace the members of society who die.
    d. foster racial divisions and boundaries.

    ANS: C   PG: 335   TYP: comprehension   SOURCE: study guide

22. On average, _____ births per woman is required if a society is to replace itself.
    a. 1.0 – 1.3
    b. 2.03 – 2.11
    c. 3.03 – 3.31
    d. 3.0

    ANS: B   PG: 335   TYP: comprehension

Chapter 12

23. The family passes on social privileges and social disadvantages to its members, thereby perpetuating the system of inequality. This viewpoint coincides with which one of the following sociological perspectives?
    a. symbolic interaction
    b. conflict theory
    c. functionalist
    d. structural strain theory

    ANS: B   PG: 335   TYP: comprehension   SOURCE: new

24. Japan has a much lower rate of child and domestic abuse than the United States because in Japan
    a. harmony is valued.
    b. many cases go unreported.
    c. family relationships are more harmonious.
    d. the nuclear family is valued.

    ANS: B   PG: 337   TYP: comprehension

25. _____ is the author of *The Origin of Family, Private Property, and the State*.
    a. Frederich Engles
    b. Karl Marx
    c. Emile Durkheim
    d. Max Weber

    ANS: A   PG: 338   TYP: knowledge

26. Which one of the following countries has one of the lowest fertility rates in the world?
    a. Japan
    b. the United States
    c. Russia
    d. Spain

    ANS: D   PG: 338   TYP: knowledge

Family and Aging

27. Which one of the following countries has one of the <u>highest</u> fertility rates in the world?
    a. Yemen
    b. Hong Kong
    c. Japan
    d. Italy

    ANS: A   PG: 338   TYP: application   SOURCE: study guide

28. The "means of existence, food, clothing, and shelter and tools" relates to
    a. productive work.
    b. reproductive work.
    c. life chances.
    d. work.

    ANS: A   PG: 338   TYP: application

29. Child bearing, care giving, managing households, and educating children fall under the category of
    a. productive work.
    b. reproductive work.
    c. life chances.
    d. housework.

    ANS: B   PG: 338   TYP: application

30. Ji-wu lives in a household where his father is unemployed, but his mother works 35 hours per week at a job she has held for five years. According to the U.S. Census Bureau, Ji-wu lives in a household with
    a. a dead-beat dad.
    b. poverty-level income.
    c. insecure parental employment.
    d. secure parental employment.

    ANS: D   PG: 337   TYP: application   SOURCE: study guide

Chapter 12

31. In the United States, children classified as _____ are most likely to live in secure parental employment households.
    a. Hispanic
    b. Native American
    c. Black
    d. White, non-Hispanic

    ANS: D   PG: 337   TYP: application

32. A child lives in a household with secure parental employment. This means the child lives with at least one parent or guardian who is employed _____ hours per week.
    a. 10
    b. 20
    c. 35
    d. 40

    ANS: C   PG: 337   TYP: knowledge

33. The highest fertility rates in the world are between _____ children per woman.
    a. 5 and 6
    b. 6 and 7
    c. 7 and 8
    d. 9 and 10

    ANS: C   PG: 338   TYP: knowledge

34. A husband, his wife, and their two-year-old son are traveling by plane. The husband is holding his screaming son. A male passenger turns around and remarks, "Why doesn't the mother take care of the baby?" The passenger is conveying his belief that women do the _____ work.
    a. reproductive
    b. productive
    c. life chance
    d. fertility

    ANS: A   PG: 340   TYP: application

35. At one time (before 1967), the United States had laws prohibiting marriages between people classified as white and black. Those laws enforced
    a. polyandry.
    b. monogamy.
    c. endogamy.
    d. exogamy.

    ANS: C   PG: 341   TYP: application

36. In Japan, 95.5 percent of marriages involve brides and grooms both classified as Japanese. The pattern of marrying within one's own ethnic group is known as
    a. exogamy.
    b. monogamy.
    c. endogamy.
    d. polyandry.

    ANS: C   PG: 342   TYP: application

37. In the United States, the practice of dividing family members along racial lines began with
    a. independence.
    b. the Revolutionary War.
    c. the arrival of Christopher Columbus.
    d. slavery.

    ANS: D   PG: 341   TYP: comprehension

38. DNA evidence suggests that _____ fathered at least one child with Sally Hemings, an enslaved woman Thomas Jefferson owned.
    a. a Jefferson male
    b. Thomas Jefferson
    c. a non-Jefferson male
    d. a white farm hand

    ANS: A   PG: 341   TYP: comprehension

Chapter 12

39. Endogamy refers to norms requiring or encouraging people to choose partners
    a. outside their immediate family.
    b. of the opposite sex.
    c. who share the same race.
    d. of a different religion.

    ANS: C   PG: 342   TYP: comprehension

40. In the United States, race and ethnic categories persist because most people "choose" partners that they believe belong to their own racial category. This practice is known as
    a. polyandry
    b. monogamy
    c. endogamy
    d. exogamy

    ANS: C   PG: 342   TYP: application

41. Currently, Japan issues to foreigners 50,000 work visas per year. Demographers project this number must increase to _____ per year to prevent its population from shrinking.
    a. 5 million
    b. 1.2 million
    c. 640,000
    d. 100,000

    ANS: C   PG: 342   TYP: knowledge

42. Sociologist Kingsley Davis traced the initial rise in the divorce rate in the United States to the breadwinner system and specifically to
    a. the two-income system.
    b. increased employment opportunities for women.
    c. the shift of economic production to outside the home.
    d. women's entry into the labor market.

    ANS: C   PG: 345   TYP: comprehension   SOURCE: study guide

43. Sociologist Kingsley Davis called the new economic arrangement between husband and wife that emerged as a result of industrialization the
    a. traditional household.
    b. isolated family.
    c. breadwinner system.
    d. nuclear family.

    ANS: C   PG: 343   TYP: comprehension

44. The breadwinner system is an outcome of an economic arrangement. That arrangement is
    a. socialism.
    b. agriculture-based economy.
    c. information- or service-based economy.
    d. capitalism (Industrial Revolution).

    ANS: D   PG: 343   TYP: comprehension   SOURCE: study guide

45. The heyday of the breadwinner system in the United States was
    a. between 1860 and 1920.
    b. between 1920 and 1960.
    c. in the 1950s.
    d. in the 1970s and 1980s.

    ANS: A   PG: 344   TYP: knowledge

46. The breadwinner system that Davis described did not last because it placed too much strain on husbands and wives. The strain stemmed from all but <u>one</u> of the following sources:
    a. never before had the roles of husband and wife been so distant.
    b. never before had women played such an indirect role in producing what the family consumed.
    c. never before had men had it so easy relative to the role of women.
    d. never before had men had to bear the sole responsibility of supporting the family.

    ANS: C   PG: 344   TYP: application

Chapter 12

47. Sociologist Kingsley Davis argues that once the divorce rate reached a certain threshold, more married women seriously considered seeking employment to protect themselves in case of divorce. That threshold was _____ percent.
    a. 5
    b. 10
    c. 20
    d. 50

    ANS: C   PG: 345   TYP: knowledge   SOURCE: study guide

48. We know that the Industrial Revolution separated the workplace from the home and altered the division of labor between men and women. More specifically,
    a. the woman came to produce most of what her family consumed.
    b. the economic value of women and children increased.
    c. the man became the link between the family and the wider market economy.
    d. the man's role changed from stressful to carefree.

    ANS: C   PG: 343   TYP: comprehension

49. Under this system, "the man's economic role became, in one sense, more important to the family, for he was the link between the family and the wider market economy." *This* system is
    a. the extended family.
    b. the dual income family.
    c. the breadwinner system.
    d. traditional households.

    ANS: C   PG: 343   TYP: application   SOURCE: study guide

50. Kingsley Davis believed that married women became motivated to seek work outside the household for all <u>but</u> which one of the following reasons?
    a. changes in child bearing experiences
    b. boredom with children and housework
    c. increases in life expectancy
    d. rising divorce rates

    ANS: B   PG: 345   TYP: comprehension

Family and Aging

51. The Tokyo Metropolitan government launched Family Bonding Day in response to the many problems it believes are connected to
    a. the aging population.
    b. the high mortality rate.
    c. declining fertility.
    d. the high divorce rate.

    ANS: C   PG: 346   TYP: knowledge

52. The dramatic drop in the fertility rate in Japan can be attributed to all but which one of the following factors?
    a. the fall of the *ie* family system
    b. the rise of the breadwinner system
    c. decreased employment opportunities for women
    d. the rise of the "parasite single"

    ANS: C   PG: 348+   TYP: comprehension

53. The *ie* family system in Japan was abolished during what time period?
    a. after WWI
    b. in 1898 with the rise of the Domestic Relations and Inheritance Laws
    c. after WWII, when the U.S. occupied Japan
    d. during the economic crisis of the 1990s

    ANS: C   PG: 348   TYP: knowledge

54. Which one of the following occupying powers abolished the *ie* family system in Japan?
    a. Britain
    b. China
    c. Germany
    d. the United States

    ANS: D   PG: 348   TYP: comprehension   SOURCE: study guide

429

55. Under the *ie* system,
    a. a daughter was viewed as a permanent family member until she married.
    b. a bride was known as the "bride of the family," not the bride of her husband.
    c. a wife served and obeyed her parents.
    d. a married woman was responsible for caring for her parents.

    ANS: B   PG: 347   TYP: comprehension

56. An author of an article in *The New York Times Magazine* wrote, "In the U.S., you are supposed to be with your boyfriend or husband all the time. In Japan, women have their ways of having fun and men have their ways. You are not expected to bring a date everywhere, and you don't feel excluded if you are not involved with someone." These statements suggest that
    a. Japanese have low sex drives.
    b. Japanese women are feminists.
    c. Japan lacks a couple's culture.
    d. Japanese couples are developmentally delayed.

    ANS: C   PG: 349   TYP: knowledge

57. In Japan, the population of working single adults (22 and older) that live with their parents while contributing little to household expenses is known as
    a. the baby boomlet.
    b. spoiled singles.
    c. parasite singles.
    d. mama's boys and girls.

    ANS: C   PG: 349   TYP: comprehension   SOURCE: study guide

58. *Juku* is a Japanese term for
    a. the single life.
    b. a childless life.
    c. cram schools.
    d. welfare-reform.

    ANS: C   PG: 350   TYP: knowledge

Family and Aging

59. The *juku* pressure is stressful for everyone involved, but especially for
    a. children.
    b. fathers.
    c. grandparents.
    d. mothers.

    ANS: D   PG: 350   TYP: comprehension

60. Sociologist Kaku Sechiyama argues that the key to establishing a work environment that is supportive of women is to
    a. establish an equal opportunity/affirmative action program.
    b. pay women *not* to have children.
    c. adopt the U.S. employment model.
    d. create a system that imposes housework, child rearing, and elder care duties on men.

    ANS: D   PG: 350   TYP: comprehension   SOURCE: study guide

61. In Japan, junior colleges train young women to be
    a. skilled, gracious, and responsible homemakers.
    b. entry-level employees.
    c. secretaries.
    d. eldercare providers.

    ANS: A   PG: 350   TYP: comprehension

62. Sociologist Randall Collins maintains that the ideology of _____ is at the heart of sexual stratification.
    a. sexual property
    b. gender polarization
    c. sexism
    d. capitalism

    ANS: A   PG: 351   TYP: comprehension   SOURCE: study guide

Chapter 12

Use the following set of responses for the following questions. For each statement, decide which type of economic arrangement it best describes.
- a. low-technological tribal societies
- b. fortified households
- c. private households
- d. advanced market economies

63. Marriage between men and women from different families does little to increase a family's wealth or political power.

    ANS: A   PG: 351

64. Men assume the role of breadwinner.

    ANS: C   PG: 354

65. The honored male is one who can protect his property and conquer others' property.

    ANS: B   PG: 354

66. Women can enter relationships offering income and other personal achievements.

    ANS: D   PG: 355

67. There is no police force or militia; the household is an armed unit.

    ANS: B   PG: 354

68. The available technology does not permit the creation of surplus wealth.

    ANS: A   PG: 351

69. Women can offer men an income and other personal achievements.

    ANS: D   PG: 355

70. Women offer men sexual access in exchange for economic security.

   ANS: C   PG: 354

71. Sociologist Randall Collins argues that women must _____ if they are to be men's equals.
   a. be valued as mothers
   b. have access to combat roles in the military
   c. have access to agents of violence control
   d. become involved in athletics at an early age

   ANS: C   PG: 351   TYP: comprehension

72. _____ emerge with the establishment of a market economy, a centralized bureaucratic state, and agencies of social control.
   a. Low-technology tribal societies
   b. Fortified households
   c. Private households
   d. Advanced market economies

   ANS: C   PG: 354   TYP: knowledge

73. _____ offer widespread employment opportunities for women.
   a. Low-technology tribal societies
   b. Fortified households
   c. Private households
   d. Advanced market economies

   ANS: D   PG: 355   TYP: knowledge

74. _____ are characterized by the presence of a non-householder class consisting of propertyless laborers and servants.
   a. Low-technology tribal societies
   b. Fortified households
   c. Private households
   d. Advanced market economies

   ANS: B   PG: 351   TYP: comprehension   SOURCE: study guide

Chapter 12

75. The relatively permanent claim to exclusive rights over a particular person relates to the concept of
    a. sexual property.
    b. tribal property.
    c. reproductive property.
    d. rites of passages.

    ANS: A   PG: 351   TYP: comprehension

76. Which one of the following statements is most likely to be made by a person born and raised in Japan?
    a. I am thirty-five.
    b. I am cheerful.
    c. I am tall.
    d. I like the color orange.

    ANS: A   PG: 352   TYP: comprehension

77. Someone praises a Japanese mother whose son earned a grade of 100% on a math exam by saying, "He is very smart, isn't he?" Which one of the following represents her likely response?
    a. I know. He studied so hard.
    b. No. He is not so smart. He was just lucky.
    c. Yes. He is just naturally good at math.
    d. I don't know how he got to be so smart.

    ANS: B   PG: 353   TYP: comprehension   SOURCE: study guide

78. The Japanese job market is very "cold" to women over the age of
    a. 35.
    b. 45.
    c. 55.
    d. 65.

    ANS: B   PG: 352   TYP: knowledge

79. "Intimacy at a distance" is a term used to describe a situation in which norms specify that
    a. elders should not interfere in the lives of adult children.
    b. couples should practice celibacy until marriage.
    c. parents should not act as pals to their children.
    d. couples should lead separate lives.

    ANS: A   PG: 355   TYP: comprehension   SOURCE: study guide

80. Demographer S. Ryan Johnson argues that couples in industrialized economies have children for all but which one of the following reasons?
    a. for love and companionship
    b. economic investment
    c. an outlet for nurturing feelings
    d. enhancement of adult identity

    ANS: B   PG: 356   TYP: comprehension

81. _____ is the extent to which caregivers believe that their emotional balance, physical health, social life, and financial status suffer because of their caregiver role.
    a. Selective perception
    b. Self-fulfilling prophecy
    c. Life chances
    d. Caregiver burden

    ANS: D   PG: 360   TYP: comprehension   SOURCE: study guide

82. In which racial/ethnic category are men in the U.S. more likely to be caregivers to elderly family members?
    a. Asian and Pacific Islander
    b. Hispanic
    c. black
    d. white

    ANS: A   PG: 361   TYP: knowledge   SOURCE: study guide

Chapter 12

83. In most countries, including the United States, disabled and frail elderly persons are most likely to be cared for by
    a. daughters or daughters-in-law.
    b. sons or sons-in-law.
    c. nursing home attendants.
    d. private care nurses.

    ANS: A   PG: 362   TYP: knowledge   SOURCE: study guide

84. Which one of the following is a core concept sociologists use to think about the family?
    a. The family consists of a husband, wife, and children.
    b. Family life is harmonious.
    c. The structure of a family is timeless and unchanging.
    d. The aging of the population has no historical precedent.

    ANS: D   PG: 363   TYP: comprehension   SOURCE: new

Multiple-Choice Questions on the Web

1. In comparison to the United States, Japan has a
   a. higher total fertility rate.
   b. lower rate of reported domestic abuse cases.
   c. higher divorce rate.
   d. lower life expectancy.

   ANS: B   PG: 331   TYP: knowledge

2. People make decisions about which kin they will acknowledge as family and which kin they will "forget." This process is known as
   a. amnesia and recall.
   b. self-fulfilling prophecy.
   c. selective remembering and forgetting.
   d. differential association.

   ANS: C   PG: 332   TYP: comprehension

3. A conflict theorist would argue that families are structured to
   a. value reproductive work.
   b. confer social status that is unequal.
   c. provide care and emotional support.
   d. perpetuate social equality.

   ANS: B   PG: 337   TYP: comprehension

4. "Renewing life is a form of work, as fundamental to the perpetuation of society as the production of things." This statement relates to
   a. productive work.
   b. fertility.
   c. reproductive work.
   d. life chances.

   ANS: C   PG: 338   TYP: comprehension

5. Sociologist Kingsley Davis wrote about an economic arrangement in which the man's economic role was the link between the family and the wider market economy, and the woman's role was confined to running the household. Davis called that economic arrangement the
   a. fortified households.
   b. breadwinner system.
   c. advanced market household.
   d. traditional system.

   ANS: B   PG: 343   TYP: application

6. In Japan, men and women are reluctant to marry because of
   a. projected stresses associated with helping their children through the *juku* system.
   b. fear of commitment.
   c. tight bonds with parents.
   d. psychological insecurities.

   ANS: A   PG: 350   TYP: knowledge

Chapter 12

7. Sociologist Randall Collins argues that the extent to which women are subordinate to men depends on
   a. government policies.
   b. women's access to agents of violence control.
   c. employment options available to men.
   d. women's position relative to men in the domestic sphere.

   ANS: B   PG: 351   TYP: comprehension

8. The case of Chico Mendes was used to illustrate the
   a. status of wealthy children who happen to live in labor-intensive environments.
   b. role of children as consumers.
   c. plight of children in Brazil.
   d. economic role of children in labor-intensive poor countries.

   ANS: D   PG: 357   TYP: comprehension

9. Increases in life expectancy have altered family life in all but which one of the following ways?
   a. The chances that children will lose one or both parents before age 16 has decreased dramatically.
   b. The percentage of elderly people living in nursing homes has increased dramatically.
   c. The number of people surviving to old age has increased.
   d. People have time to choose and get to know a partner.

   ANS: B   PG: 358   TYP: comprehension

10. In Japan, approximately _____ percent of elderly individuals live with their adult children.
    a. 20
    b. 50
    c. 70
    d. 85

    ANS: B   PG: 362   TYP: knowledge

True-False Questions

1. The family is an unchanging, stable entity.

    ANS: False   PG: 331   SOURCE: new; study guide

2. Relative to the United States, Japan has a very small percentage of single-parent households.

    ANS: True   PG: 331

3. The size of any given person's family network is beyond calculation (i.e., comprehension).

    ANS: True   PG: 332

4. Sociologists argue that it is virtually impossible to keep track of everyone's living relatives.

    ANS: True   PG: 332

5. There is no concrete group that can be universally identified as a family.

    ANS: True   PG: 332   SOURCE: new; study guide

6. An aging population is one in which the percentage of the population 65 and over is increasing relative to other age groups.

    ANS: True   PG: 331

7. Endogamy means marriage within one's social group.

    ANS: True   PG: 331   SOURCE: new

8. Endogamy refers to norms requiring or encouraging people to choose partners that are of different religion, race, ethnicity, or social class.

    ANS: False   PG: 331   SOURCE: study guide

Chapter 12

9. Federal law defines a marriage as a legal union between two committed adults.

    ANS: False   PG: 333   SOURCE: new

10. By definition, family relationships are constructive and harmonious.

    ANS: False   PG: 336

11. Reproductive work is usually not rewarded on an economic level.

    ANS: True   PG: 338   SOURCE: new

12. The highest total fertility rates in the world are between four and five.

    ANS: False   PG: 338   SOURCE: new; study guide

13. The lowest total fertility rate in the world is between 1.1 and 1.2.

    ANS: True   PG: 338

14. It appears that American males do more housework than their counterparts in Japan.

    ANS: True   PG: 339   SOURCE: study guide

15. Men and women can decide to share in reproductive work but doing so involves costs to both parties.

    ANS: True   PG: 340

16. In the U.S., children classified as Asian are least likely to live in secure parental employment households.

    ANS: False   PG: 337

17. Viewed over a span of 100 years, the structure of the American family has changed quite dramatically.

    ANS: True   PG: 343   SOURCE: study guide

18. Viewed over the span of 100 years, the structure of the Japanese family has changed very little.

    ANS: False   PG: 347

19. Between 1955 and 1998, the percentage of arranged marriages in Japan fell from 63 percent to 7 percent.

    ANS: True   PG: 349

20. The Japanese government has set ambitious goals to relieve women of caregiving burdens but has failed to fund those programs.

    ANS: True   PG: 349   SOURCE: new

21. As human muscle and time became less important to the production process, children lost their economic value.

    ANS: True   PG: 356   SOURCE: study guide

22. Japan's labor laws forbid discrimination against women.

    ANS: True   PG: 350

23. For the most part, Japanese women are expected to quit working when they marry or have children.

    ANS: True   PG: 350   SOURCE: study guide

Chapter 12

24. The World Economic Forum ranks Japan higher than the United Sates in its ability to empower women.

    ANS: False   PG: 350   SOURCE: new

25. There is no historical precedent for the aging of the population.

    ANS: True   PG: 359

26. In Japan, approximately 50 percent of elderly persons reside in nursing homes.

    ANS: False   PG: 362   SOURCE: study guide

27. Advanced market economies offer widespread employment opportunities for women.

    ANS: True   PG: 355

28. Approximately 30 percent of American elderly live in nursing homes.

    ANS: False   PG: 360

29. Today, divorce dissolves marriages at the same rate that death did 100 years ago.

    ANS: True   PG: 358   SOURCE: new; study guide

30. Since 1955, in Japan, the proportion of people 65 and older living with adult children has declined

    ANS: True   PG: 362   SOURCE: new

Concept Application (also in study guide)

Consider the concepts listed below. Match one or more of the concepts with each scenario. Explain your choices.

   a. Aging populations
   b. Caregiver burden
   c. Exogamy
   d. Fertility rate
   e. Reproductive work

Scenario 1

Sam works hard at his job in the factory. His supervisor knows him as a diligent, focused employee. He barely missed a day of work during his first five years on the job. A year ago, however, Sam's mother was diagnosed with Alzheimer's disease, and he decided to have her cared for in his home. But costs mounted quickly, and after a few months, Sam could only afford to have the home health care worker visit three days a week. Now, Sam is struggling to balance his job responsibilities with caring for his mother. He's almost exhausted his supply of sick days, his lack of concentration at work has caused some costly mistakes, and his supervisor's patience is at an end. Something's got to give (Guttchen and Pettigrew 2000, p. 31).

   ANS: B

Scenario 2

Recently, the largest circulation Jewish newspaper in the country carried an opinion article pronouncing, with equanimity, that "the Jewish taboo on mixed marriage has clearly collapsed." Around the same time, and more startlingly, the *New York Times* published a photograph taken at the nuptials of a male rabbi and a female Protestant minister, a rite that was itself blessed by an assemblage of priests, ministers, and rabbis, all standing together under a Jewish wedding canopy. What this powerfully suggestive photograph tells us is not just that many American Jews, including at least some of the rabbis among them, have abandoned long-standing communal norms, but that they, again including at least some of the rabbis among them, seem to have replaced those norms with an entirely new set of beliefs about what constitutes an authentic expression of Judaism—and what, if anything, lies beyond the limits of such expression. Long in the building, the intermarriage crisis is now propelling a massive transformation of American Jewish life (Wertheimer 2001).

   ANS: C

Scenario 3

Next year, for the first time in history, people over 60 will outnumber kids 14 or younger in industrial countries. Even more startling, the population of the Third World, while still comparatively youthful, is aging faster than that of the rest of the world. In France, for example, it took 140 years for the proportion of the population age 65 or older to double from 9 percent to 18 percent. In China, the same feat will take just 34 years; in Venezuela, it will take 22 years (Longman 1999, p. 30).

ANS: A

Scenario 4

Italians have stopped making babies; the nation is aging fast; and, according to the country's chief statistical body, [Italian] women now bear 1.2 babies apiece. Only the Spaniards, in Western Europe, are as unproductive. At last count, in 1996, deaths had outpaced births for four years in a row. If Italy's population is slightly up, it is thanks to the 178,000 immigrants who took up legal residence two years ago (*The Economist* 1998, p. 51).

ANS: D

Scenario 5

[In China] sons and daughters play a crucial role in medical treatment and care for the elderly A scarcity of medical resources, which is characteristic of developing economies, forces hospitals to rely on the work of family members to provide food, purchase and administer medicine, deliver and pick up lab tests and x-rays, and monitor and bathe the patients. Relatives draw on their personal connections to doctors and nurses to obtain treatment and hospital beds (Otis 2001, p. 471).

ANS: E

Short Essay Questions

1. Why is Japan the focus of a chapter on family and aging? How does the U.S. compare to Japan on indicators related to family well-being and stability?

2. Why is "family" a difficult concept to define? What are some criteria that might be used to define family?

3. How does the family contribute to order and stability in society? What are some problems with defining family in terms of social functions?

4. What is the conflict view of family?

5. Distinguish between productive and reproductive work. Which type of work is more valued?

6. How is family related to social inequality in society?

7. How has family created racial divisions and boundaries?

8. Describe at least three major changes in American family life since 1900.

9. How did the Industrial Revolution destroy the household-based economy and lead to the breadwinner system?

10. According to Kingsley Davis, what strains and demographic factors led to the collapse of the breadwinner system?

11. Describe at least three major changes in Japanese family life since 1900.

12. What caused the *ie* family system to fall? What system replaced it?

13. Explain: "Japan does not have a couple's culture."

14. What is a "parasite single"? Explain the "new single concept."

15. How is Japan's employment system connected to the country's low fertility rate?

16. In general, how do economic arrangements shape the character of sexual stratification?

17. What is *intimacy at a distance*? What factors gave rise to this phenomenon?

Chapter 12

18. How has the status of children been affected by industrialization?

19. How do increases in life expectancy alter the composition of the family?

20. What is "caregiver burden"? Is care giving only a burden?

21. What are some of the major differences between the elderly-caregiver relationship in Japan and the United States?

Comprehensive Essay Questions

1. What are some of the major factors that can affect the structure of family life?

2. Does Japan or does the United Sates have the better family system? Explain.

3. Identify a family-related social issue that needs to be addressed in both Japan and the United States. Now, imagine you are a policy maker. What policy might you implement to encourage change? Explain.

Chapter 13

Education

Multiple-Choice Questions

1. When sociologist study _____, they focus on the formal and informal social interactions that train, discipline, or shape (or reshape) the mind and body in planned and unplanned ways.
    a. curriculum
    b. education
    c. schooling
    d. the adolescent subculture

    ANS: B   PG: 366   TYP: comprehension   SOURCE: new

2. _____ percent of American 15-year-olds expect to occupy a high-skilled white-collar job by age 30.
    a. Eighty
    b. Seventy
    c. Sixty
    d. Fifty

    ANS: A   PG: 367   TYP: knowledge

3. Early antidotal evidence from British observers suggests that the U.S. system of education seems to value
    a. dedicated study.
    b. income generation and wealth creation.
    c. experience with other ways of life.
    d. accumulated knowledge.

    ANS: B   PG: 367   TYP: comprehension   SOURCE: study guide

Chapter 13

4. In European Union countries, mandatory foreign language study begins as early as age
    a. five.
    b. ten.
    c. twelve.
    d. sixteen.

    ANS: A   PG: 367   TYP: knowledge

5. _____ was the first country in the world to embrace the concept of mass education.
    a. The United States
    b. South Korea
    c. Japan
    d. Canada

    ANS: A   PG: 367   TYP: knowledge

6. We focus on the European Union in the Education chapter for all but which one of the following reasons?
    a. The EU is investing heavily in education and research to boost its international competitiveness.
    b. The countries of the EU were the first to embrace mass education.
    c. The EU is working to limit opportunities for education beyond high school.
    d. EU openness to closing its borders to international students

    ANS: C   PG: 367   TYP: comprehension   SOURCE: new

7. Which one of the following characteristics applies to the process of informal education?
    a. purposeful
    b. systematic
    c. spontaneous
    d. planned

    ANS: C   PG: 368   TYP: comprehension   SOURCE: study guide

8. Which one of the following characteristics does not apply to the process of formal education?
    a. purposeful
    b. systematic
    c. spontaneous
    d. planned

    ANS: C   PG: 368   TYP: comprehension

9. A program of formal and systematic instruction that takes place primarily in classrooms is
    a. instruction.
    b. schooling.
    c. curriculum.
    d. skill-specific instruction.

    ANS: B   PG: 368   TYP: comprehension

10. _____ is a purposeful, planned effort intended to impart specific skills and modes of thought.
    a. Informal education
    b. Formal education
    c. Socialization
    d. Education

    ANS: B   PG: 368   TYP: comprehension

11. _____ occurs in a spontaneous, unplanned way.
    a. Informal education
    b. Formal education
    c. Tracking
    d. Education

    ANS: A   PG: 368   TYP: comprehension   SOURCE : new

12. Early school reformers in the United States viewed education as
    a. a setting promoting diversity and multiculturalism.
    b. a liberating force.
    c. a place where students could argue about the value of ideas.
    d. the vehicle for "Americanizing" a culturally and linguistically diverse population.

    ANS: D   PG: 369   TYP: knowledge   SOURCE: study guide

13. _____ argue that schools contribute to the smooth operation of society by facilitating change and progress, contributing basic and applied research, and integrating diverse populations.
    a. Conflict theorists
    b. Symbolic interactionists
    c. Functionalists
    d. Labeling theorists

    ANS: C   PG: 369   TYP: comprehension   SOURCE : new

14. Transmitting skills, contributing to personal reflection and change, and integrating diverse populations are considered _____ of education.
    a. functions
    b. informal aspects
    c. formal aspects
    d. the self-fulfulling prophecy

    ANS: A   PG: 369   TYP: comprehension   SOURCE : new

15. Which one of the following countries is not a current member of the European Union?
    a. Germany
    b. Ireland
    c. Turkey
    d. Poland

    ANS: C   PG: 370   TYP: knowledge

16. Although all countries in the world have education-based programs that address social problems, _____ is unique in that education is viewed as the primary solution to many of its problems.
    a. the United States
    b. Japan
    c. Canada
    d. Mexico

    ANS: A   PG: 370   TYP: knowledge   SOURCE: study guide

17. Some leading educators argue that the primary purpose of the university in the 21st century is to teach students to address the pressing problems of society. That purpose speaks to
    a. the informal curriculum.
    b. the hidden curriculum.
    c. service learning.
    d. self-fulfilling prophecy.

    ANS: C   PG: 370   TYP: comprehension   SOURCE : new

18. _____ argue that schools simply perpetuate the inequalities of the larger society.
    a. Structural strain theorists
    b. Conflict theorists
    c. Symbolic interactionists
    d. Functionalists

    ANS: B   PG: 372   TYP: comprehension   SOURCE : new

19. Philanthropist Bill Gates argues that in the United States, there is an "acceptance of a tiering approach, where over a third of students never graduate, and another third are trapped in a situation where they don't have the skills that are going to give them a good lifetime outcome." Gates' comment corresponds to which sociological perspective?
    a. Structural strain theorists
    b. Conflict theorists
    c. Symbolic interactionists
    d. Functionalists

    ANS: B   PG: 372   TYP: comprehension   SOURCE: new; study guide

20. Approximately _____ percent of funding for public education in the United States comes from the federal government.
    a. 7
    b. 15
    c. 20
    d. 40

    ANS: A   PG: 372   TYP: knowledge

21. In the most general and basic sense, illiteracy is the inability to
    a. read at the fourth-grade level.
    b. understand and use a symbol system.
    c. read enough to get through a typical day.
    d. understand principles of math and science.

    ANS: B   PG: 373   TYP: comprehension

22. People who cannot use a computer, read a map, make change for a customer, read traffic signs, follow instructions to assemble an appliance, *or* fill out a job application share one trait. They are
    a. uneducated.
    b. unschooled.
    c. illiterate.
    d. social misfits.

    ANS: C   PG: 373   TYP: application

23. The contextual nature of illiteracy suggests that it is
    a. like a disease.
    b. linked to a lack of desire to want to read and write.
    c. biologically rooted.
    d. a social phenomenon.

    ANS: D   PG: 373   TYP: application

24. The statement "Illiteracy is a product of one's social environment" means that people are considered illiterate when
    a. they cannot understand another culture's symbol system.
    b. they possess the literacy skills necessary to make it in society.
    c. they cannot understand or use the symbol system of the surrounding environment.
    d. they know little about the social issues affecting their lives.

    ANS: C   PG: 373   TYP: comprehension

Education

25. In the United States, the state of _____ spends the greatest amount of money per student; the state of _____ spends the least amount per student.
    a. New York; Mississippi
    b. Wisconsin; Iowa
    c. California; West Virginia
    d. Washington; Kentucky

    ANS: A   PG: 373   TYP: knowledge

26. Education critic Daniel Resnick argues that the U.S. focus on _____ "has cut students off from the pluralism of world culture and denied them a sense of powerlessness in approaching societies very different from their own."
    a. diverse curriculum
    b. textbooks modeled after catechism
    c. mass education
    d. a single language

    ANS: D   PG: 374   TYP: comprehension

27. The United States is probably the only country in the world that places so
    a. much emphasis on learning at least one other language.
    b. little emphasis on learning at least one other language.
    c. much emphasis on the connection between language and culture.
    d. much emphasis on language as a thinking tool.

    ANS: B   PG: 374   TYP: knowledge

28. _____ ranks number one among the top 20 countries sending students to the United States.
    a. France
    b. India
    c. Japan
    d. Great Britain

    ANS: B   PG: 375   TYP: knowledge

Chapter 13

29. Approximately _____ percent of U.S. students that study abroad attend schools in EU countries.
    a. 20
    b. 40
    c. 50
    d. 80

    ANS: C   PG: 375   TYP: knowledge   SOURCE: study guide

30. The most popular destination for U.S. students studying abroad is
    a. Japan.
    b. Great Britain.
    c. France.
    d. China.

    ANS: B   PG: 375   TYP: comprehension

31. _____ helps to explain why people living in countries other than the United States speak more than one language.
    a. Motivation
    b. The higher value placed on education
    c. Multiculturalism
    d. The legacy of colonialism

    ANS: D   PG: 376   TYP: comprehension

32. Approximately _____ percent of ninth graders enrolled in U.S. public schools graduate from high school four years later.
    a. 25
    b. 70
    c. 90
    d. 95

    ANS: B   PG: 377   TYP: knowledge

Education

33. Compared to its European Union counterparts, the United States ranks _____ in the percentage of postsecondary education costs paid by public (taxpayers) funds.
    a. 1st
    b. 5th
    c. 10th
    d. last

    ANS: D   PG: 378   TYP: comprehension   SOURCE: new

34. Which racial/ethnic category of high school graduates is most likely to drop out of high school?
    a. females
    b. males
    c. Hispanic
    d. Native Americans

    ANS: C   PG: 377   TYP: knowledge   SOURCE: study guide

35. In the 18 EU countries for which we have data, at least _____ percent of the cost of post-secondary education is paid for by public funds.
    a. 30
    b. 47
    c. 67
    d. 80

    ANS: C   PG: 377   TYP: knowledge

36. Which of the following statements about American curriculum is <u>false</u>?
    a. There is no uniform curriculum.
    b. Textbooks, assignments, and instructional methods vary across schools within each state.
    c. Curriculum requirements vary within a school.
    d. There are national guidelines in regard to appropriate curriculum.

    ANS: D   PG: 378   TYP: knowledge

Chapter 13

37. The _____ is the monthly student loan payment as a percentage of monthly income.
    a. annual interest rate
    b. debt burden
    c. college return
    d. income deficit

    ANS: B   PG: 378   TYP: knowledge

38. In _____ models, school districts and/or local authorities establish the curriculum.
    a. minimalist
    b. national
    c. decentralized
    d. centralized

    ANS: C   PG: 379   TYP: comprehension

39. Which one of the following countries does not have a national curriculum that applies to all types of schools, grades, and subjects?
    a. Austria
    b. Germany
    c. the United States
    d. Portugal

    ANS: C   PG: 379   TYP: comprehension   SOURCE: study guide

40. Sociologist Jeannie Oakes studied a wide range of school systems and came to the conclusion that _____ has/have the greatest effect on quality of education.
    a. tracking
    b. rural-urban environments
    c. type of school (public versus private)
    d. amount of cultural diversity

    ANS: A   PG: 379   TYP: comprehension

41. Research suggests that tracking has _____ effect on high-track students.
    a. no noticeable
    b. a positive
    c. a negative
    d. an invasive

    ANS: B	PG: 379	TYP: comprehension

42. _____ percent of U.S. college students borrow money to pay for college.
    a. 90
    b. 75
    c. 65
    d. 25

    ANS: C	PG: 379	TYP: knowledge

43. Which one of the following responses to the question, "What is the most important thing you learned or have done so far in class?" is the one mostly likely to be made by a student placed on the college preparatory track?
    a. "I think the most important thing I have learned so far is to come into math class and get out folders."
    b. "I have learned to be more imaginative."
    c. "I have learned nothing that I'd use in later life."
    d. "To be honest, I have learned nothing."

    ANS: B	PG: 380	TYP: application	SOURCE: study guide

44. Sociologist Jeannie Oakes wrote, "The schools themselves were different: some were large, some very small, some in the middle of cities…But the difference in what students experienced each day in these schools stemmed not so much from which school they happened to attend…but from differences within each school." Those differences within schools are connected to _____
    a. the type of school.
    b. rural-urban environments.
    c. hidden curriculum.
    d. tracking.

    ANS: D	PG: 380	TYP: comprehension

Chapter 13

45. _____ programs prepare students for direct entry into a specific occupation.
    a. College preparatory
    b. Transitional
    c. Vocational
    d. General studies

    ANS: C   PG: 381   TYP: comprehension

46. In Rosenthal and Jacobson's study of teachers' expectations of students identified as "academic bloomers," the authors found that the students identified as "bloomers" improved their test scores over the course of a school year. The researchers concluded that teachers communicated expectation of improvement to "bloomers"
    a. by paying more attention to bloomers than they had in the past.
    b. by giving them extra help before school.
    c. in subtle and complex ways that they could not identify.
    d. through the tone of their voice and extra attention.

    ANS: C   PG: 382   TYP: comprehension

47. A self-fulfilling prophecy begins with
    a. accurate assessment of a situation.
    b. a hidden curriculum.
    c. misguided parenting.
    d. a false definition of a situation.

    ANS: D   PG: 381   TYP: comprehension   SOURCE: study guide

48. The statement "If people define their situations as real, they are, in fact, real in their consequences" best describes the dynamics underlying
    a. informal education.
    b. the self-fulfilling prophecy.
    c. schooling.
    d. hidden curriculum.

    ANS: B   PG: 381   TYP: application

Education

49. Which European Union country has the largest percentage of students enrolled in vocational programs?
   a. Finland
   b. Denmark
   c. Czech Republic
   d. Greece

   ANS: C   PG: 381   TYP: knowledge

50. Most European vocational school programs are equivalent in rigor to U.S. _____ programs.
   a. vocational school
   b. general studies
   c. college prep
   d. charter school

   ANS: C   PG: 381   TYP: comprehension   SOURCE: study guide

51. The _____ curriculum is the things students learn along with the subject matter.
   a. formal
   b. unintended
   c. hidden
   d. planned

   ANS: C   PG: 382   TYP: comprehension

52. The various academic subjects make up the _____ curriculum.
   a. core
   b. hidden
   c. formal
   d. manifest

   ANS: C   PG: 382   TYP: comprehension

Chapter 13

53. Teaching method, tone of teacher's voice, and frequency of teacher's absences fall under the category of _____ curriculum.
    a. formal
    b. hidden
    c. unintended
    d. planned

    ANS: B   PG: 382   TYP: application

54. "Spelling baseball," and the various lessons other than spelling that students learn while playing that game, represents _____ curriculum.
    a. formal
    b. hidden
    c. unintended
    d. planned

    ANS: B   PG: 384   TYP: application   SOURCE: study guide

55. A student writes, "I remember in elementary school my class was divided into two teams. Classmates assigned to each team raced to the blackboard in pairs to see who could spell faster a word called out by the teacher. The winning team got candy." This memory represents an example of the _____ curriculum.
    a. intended
    b. planned
    c. formal
    d. hidden

    ANS: D   PG: 384   TYP: comprehension

56. Jules Henry believes that American schools teach three important values in addition to the subject matter. Which one of the following is not one that he named?
    a. to be critical thinkers
    b. to fear failure
    c. to envy success
    d. to be absurd

    ANS: A   PG: 384   TYP: comprehension

460

57. Jules Henry argues that classroom exercises, such as spelling baseball, teach children to be absurd or to make connections between unlike things. These lessons prepare children
    a. to question the reasons they do assignments.
    b. to care about social issues.
    c. to fit in with the group.
    d. to fit into a consumption-oriented culture.

    ANS: D   PG: 384   TYP: comprehension

58. To be absurd means
    a. to make connections between unlike things.
    b. to fear failure.
    c. to envy success.
    d. to fear achievement.

    ANS: A   PG: 384   TYP: comprehension   SOURCE: study guide

59. Compared to the math teachers in Japan and Germany, the American teachers
    a. spend less time teaching math and science.
    b. give out less homework.
    c. cover fewer topics.
    d. teach in a very dry way.

    ANS: D   PG: 385   TYP: knowledge

60. The first textbooks in the United States were modeled after
    a. encyclopedias.
    b. catechisms.
    c. novels.
    d. dictionaries.

    ANS: B   PG: 386   TYP: knowledge

61. Which one of the following groups earns the highest average weekly income?
    a. males with less than a high school diploma
    b. females with a bachelor's degree or higher
    c. males with some college
    d. females with a high school diploma

    ANS: B   PG: 382   TYP: application   SOURCE : new

62. The first textbooks in the United States were modeled after catechisms. Catechisms are
    a. novels that emphasize moral principles.
    b. rule books.
    c. volumes of books containing past and present knowledge arranged in alphabetical order.
    d. short books covering religious principles written in question-answer format.

    ANS: D   PG: 386   TYP: comprehension   SOURCE: study guide

63. Surveys of college graduates (sponsored by the U.S. government) show that approximately _____ responded that the degree was not required for the job they held.
    a. less than 10 percent
    b. 20 percent
    c. 40 percent
    d. two-thirds

    ANS: C   PG: 386   TYP: knowledge

64. Most Americans tend to equate education with
    a. increased job opportunities.
    b. personal empowerment.
    c. civic responsibility.
    d. national well-being.

    ANS: A   PG: 386   TYP: comprehension

65. Sociologist James Coleman defined _____ as a "small society—one that has most of its important interactions within itself, and maintains only a few threads of connection with the outside adult society."
    a. white flight
    b. schooling
    c. the adolescent subculture
    d. formal education

    ANS: C   PG: 389   TYP: comprehension   SOURCE: study guide

66. Sociologist James Coleman was interested in the adolescent _____, or those achievements resulting in popularity, respect, acceptance into the crowd, and disdain among them.
    a. status system
    b. self-fulfilling prophecy
    c. tracking
    d. academic achievement

    ANS: A   PG: 390   TYP: comprehension

67. Coleman maintained that the _____ contributes to students' lack of academic interest.
    a. fact that students work after school
    b. way the media portrays educators
    c. emphasis on athletes
    d. manner in which students are taught

    ANS: D   PG: 391   TYP: knowledge

68. The Coleman study of adolescent subcultures found that _____ is/are extremely important to boys and _____ is/are extremely important to girls.
    a. athletics; social success with boys
    b. social success with girls; social success with boys
    c. being good looking; good grades
    d. good grades; athletics

    ANS: A   PG: 391   TYP: comprehension

69. According to Coleman, students show their discontent with school by
    a. their high rate of absenteeism.
    b. getting involved with and acquiring things they can call their own.
    c. acting up in the classroom whenever teachers turn their backs.
    d. skipping out on detention.

    ANS: B   PG: 391   TYP: application

Chapter 13

70. Coleman believes that _____ is one of the major avenues open to adolescents in which they can act as a representative of the school and community.
    a. reading
    b. after-school employment
    c. academics
    d. athletics

    ANS: D   PG: 391   TYP: comprehension

71. According to Coleman's research, which one of the following is a characteristic of the adolescent status system?
    a. For the most part, peer groups are less influential in students' lives than are teachers.
    b. Under no conditions was the brightest male popular.
    c. The female student identified as the brightest has the most friends.
    d. The most admired girls are cheerleaders and those girls that are successful with the boys.

    ANS: D   PG: 391   TYP: comprehension   SOURCE: study guide

72. Coleman traces the strong influence of the adolescent subculture to
    a. the high rate of divorce.
    b. the passive, reactive roles into which adolescents are cast.
    c. dual career families.
    d. the amount of television students watch.

    ANS: B   PG: 391   TYP: knowledge

73. Students who perceive borders as insurmountable and immerse themselves in the world of their peers would be classified as
    a. congruent worlds/smooth transitions.
    b. different worlds/border crossings managed.
    c. different worlds/border crossings difficult.
    d. different worlds/border crossings resisted.

    ANS: D   PG: 392   TYP: comprehension

74. In *Equality of Educational Opportunity* (the Coleman Report), the single most important variable for explaining differences in test scores across various ethnic groups was
    a. ethnicity.
    b. funding.
    c. family background.
    d. personal motivation.

    ANS: C   PG: 392   TYP: knowledge   SOURCE: study guide

75. Brown v. Board of Education (1954) is a famous Supreme Court
    a. racial desegregation case.
    b. case dealing with the no pass-no play (sports) policy.
    c. school prayer case.
    d. school choice case.

    ANS: A   PG: 392   TYP: knowledge

76. Coleman's study of adolescent subcultures has this important implication for understanding why even the best students in the United States have difficulty in competing with top students in many other countries:
    a. The United States does not draw into competition everyone that has academic potential.
    b. The United States gives everyone access to education.
    c. Parents no longer "train" their children in the skills they know because those skills are outdated and obsolete.
    d. Parents exercise more influence than teachers over their children's lives.

    ANS: A   PG: 392   TYP: comprehension

77. Students who describe values, beliefs, expectations, and normative ways of behaving as similar across their worlds would be classified as
    a. congruent worlds/smooth transitions.
    b. different worlds/border crossing managed.
    c. different worlds/border crossings difficult.
    d. different worlds/border crossings resisted.

    ANS: A   PG: 392   TYP: comprehension

Chapter 13

78. Which of the following is <u>not</u> one of the major findings reported in "Equality of Educational Opportunity"?
    a. Variations in the quality of a school did not have much effect on student test scores.
    b. The social class of one's classmates had a significant effect on student test scores.
    c. School expenditures are an important predictor of educational attainment.
    d. Schools bring little to bear on a child's achievement independent of the child's immediate environment.

    ANS: C   PG: 393   TYP: knowledge

79. _____ is the term used in reference to the migration of middle-class white Americans from the cities to the suburbs.
    a. Outmigration
    b. White flight
    c. Gentrification
    d. Forced migration

    ANS: B   PG: 393   TYP: comprehension

80. Sociologist James Coleman wrote, "With families sorting themselves out residentially along economic and racial lines, and with schools tied to residence, the end result is the demise of the common school attended by children from all economic levels." Coleman was writing about the effects of
    a. busing and white flight.
    b. hidden curriculum.
    c. self-fulfilling prophecy.
    d. informal curriculum.

    ANS: A   PG: 394   TYP: comprehension   SOURCE: study guide

Multiple-Choice Questions on the Web

1. _____ percent of American high school students are enrolled in vocational education programs.
    a. Fifty
    b. Forty
    c. Twenty-five
    d. Less than 10

    ANS: D   PG: 367   TYP: knowledge

2. In the broadest sense, education is
   a. a purposeful, planned effort to impart specific skills.
   b. a program of formal and systematic instruction.
   c. those experiences that train, discipline, and develop mental and physical potentials.
   d. spontaneous, unplanned exposure to ideas.

   ANS: C	PG: 368	TYP: comprehension

3. Jenny does not possess the calculating skills to balance her checkbook or to file her tax return. From a sociological point of view, she is
   a. undereducated.
   b. unschooled.
   c. functionally illiterate.
   d. a social misfit.

   ANS: C	PG: 373	TYP: application	SOURCE: study guide

4. Which one of the following is a characteristic of the American system of public education?
   a. Americans tend to value education for education's sake.
   b. The United States seems to have one of the narrowest funding disparities in the world between the richest and poorest schools.
   c. Theoretically, anyone can attend college regardless of their academic history.
   d. Americans tend to stress the association between education and personal empowerment.

   ANS: C	PG: 376	TYP: comprehension

5. Sociologist Jeannie Oakes studied the effects of tracking and found that
   a. poor and minority students are not tracked.
   b. the different tracks are treated as equally valued instructional groups.
   c. low track students eventually catch up with those in the higher tracks.
   d. bright students' learning is not affected by the academic achievements of the students around them.

   ANS: D	PG: 379	TYP: comprehension

Chapter 13

6. Rosenthal and Jackson maintain that something in the way teachers talk, in their facial expressions and posture conveys their expectations to students. It seems that students respond by meeting these expectations. This process is known as
    a. formal curriculum.
    b. schooling.
    c. self-fulfilling prophecy.
    d. informal education.

    ANS: C   PG: 382   TYP: application

7. Jules Henry argues that students go along with teachers' requests and participate in activities, such as "spelling baseball" because these students
    a. do not care whether they learn or not.
    b. are terrified of failure and want so badly to succeed.
    c. find such academic "games" entertaining.
    d. find the competition enjoyable.

    ANS: B   PG: 384   TYP: comprehension

8. Sociologist James Coleman argues that _____ cut adolescents off from the rest of society and forced them to spend the majority of the day with their own age group.
    a. the historical shift in job training (from the family to the school)
    b. the emergence of a consumer-oriented society
    c. the breakdown of the family
    d. the widespread use of the automobile

    ANS: A   PG: 389   TYP: application

9. The Coleman report and other studies have found that _____ is the most powerful factor in determining students' level of school achievement.
    a. race
    b. social class
    c. home environment (e.g., family background)
    d. gender

    ANS: C   PG: 392   TYP: knowledge

10. Coleman's findings about test scores and their relationship to the characteristics of the student population were used to support
    a. racial segregation.
    b. white flight.
    c. busing as a means of achieving educational equality.
    d. a restructuring of the curriculum.

    ANS: C   PG: 393   TYP: knowledge

True-False Questions

1. Twenty-five percent of American 15-year-olds expect to occupy a high-skilled white collar job by age 30.

    ANS: False   PG: 367

2. The European Union is an economic and political alliance that includes 27 member countries.

    ANS: True   PG: 367

3. In some European Union countries, mandatory foreign language study begins as early as age five.

    ANS: True   PG: 367   SOURCE: study guide

4. Japan was the first country in the world to embrace the concept of mass education.

    ANS: False   PG: 367

5. Less than 10 percent of American high school students are enrolled in vocational programs.

    ANS: True   PG: 367   SOURCE: new

6. In the strict sense of the word, a person who cannot read a map is illiterate.

    ANS: True   PG: 373   SOURCE: study guide

Chapter 13

7. Everyone is illiterate in some symbol system.

    ANS: True   PG: 373

8. The first textbooks in the United States were modeled after catechisms.

    ANS: True   PG: 386

9. Every government in the world seems to think that its education system is failing in major ways.

    ANS: True   PG: 388   SOURCE: new; study guide

10. In some EU countries, more than 95 percent of the total cost of postsecondary education is publicly subsidized.

    ANS: True   PG: 377

11. Tracking persists because politically powerful parents of high-achieving students insist that it remain in place.

    ANS: True   PG: 380

12. Throughout the U.S., public education has always been in a state of crisis and under reform.

    ANS: True   PG: 388   SOURCE: new; study guide

13. No uniform curriculum exists in the United States.

    ANS: True   PG: 379

14. All evidence suggests that students learn better when they are grouped with those who learn at the same rate.

    ANS: False   PG: 379

15. A national or centralized curriculum sets achievement targets but allows schools to set their own curriculum.

    ANS: False   PG: 379   SOURCE: study guide

16. Decentralized curriculum models give individual teachers control over the curriculum.

    ANS: False   PG: 379

17. The size of the funding gap between the states in the U.S. with highest and lowest spending is $1,500 per pupil.

    ANS: False   PG: 372

18. Within the European Union, the spending gap between the wealthiest and poorest countries is greater than the spending gap between the wealthiest and poorest of the 50 states.

    ANS: True   PG: 372   SOURCE: study guide

19. Approximately 40 percent of college graduates in the United States regard themselves as under employed.

    ANS: True   PG: 386

20. Most people in the world have access to a college education today.

    ANS: False   PG: 396   SOURCE: new

21. Jules Henry uses the example of "spelling baseball" to illustrate how the hidden curriculum works.

    ANS: True   PG: 382   SOURCE: new; study guide

22. Research suggests that placing students in remedial courses contributes to their intellectual growth.

    ANS: False   PG: 379   SOURCE: new

Chapter 13

23. Less than 10 percent of European students are enrolled in vocational education programs.

    ANS: False   PG: 381

24. Self-fulfilling prophecies begin with a false definition of a situation.

    ANS: True   PG: 381   SOURCE: study guide

25. The amount of racial segregation in schools has changed little over the past four decades.

    ANS: True   PG : 393   SOURCE : new

26. The single most important factor in explaining academic success is family background.

    ANS: True   PG: 392

27. Sociologist James Coleman maintains that the adolescent society penalizes academic achievement.

    ANS: True   PG: 390   SOURCE: study guide

28. The most valued characteristic among male high school seniors is being a good athlete.

    ANS: True   PG: 391

29. About 65 percent of U.S. college students borrow money to pay for college.

    ANS: True   PG: 378

30. Relative to other systems of education, the U.S. system seems to promote a math curriculum that presents the subject in a less interesting and realistic way.

    ANS: True   PG: 385   SOURCE: study guide

Concept Application (also in study guide)

Consider the concepts listed below. Match one or more of the concepts with each scenario. Explain your choices.

   a. Ability grouping
   b. Formal education
   c. Functionally illiterate
   d. Hidden curriculum
   e. Informal education
   f. Schooling
   g. Self-fulfilling prophecy
   h. Status system
   i. Tracking

Scenario 1

"Many of the deaf are functional illiterates.... Hans Furth, a psychologist whose work is concerned with the cognition of the deaf ... argues that the congenitally deaf suffer from 'information deprivation.' There are a number of reasons for this. First, they are less exposed to the 'incidental' learning that takes place out of school—for example, to that buzz of conversation that is the background of ordinary life; to television, unless it is captioned, etc. Second, the content of deaf education is meager compared to that of hearing children; so much time is spent teaching deaf children speech—one must envisage between five and eight years of intensive tutoring—that there is little time for transmitting information, culture, complex skills, or anything else.

"Yet the desire to have the deaf speak, the insistence that they speak—and from the first, the odd superstitions that have always clustered around the use of sign language, to say nothing of the enormous investment in oral schools—allowed this deplorable situation to develop, practically unnoticed except by deaf people, who themselves being unnoticed had little to say in the matter." (Sacks 1989:28-29)

   ANS: G

Chapter 13

Scenario 2

"In 1897, Captain Richard Pratt arrived in Sioux country to enlist Sioux children for his Carlisle Indian Industrial School, the first and most famous of what would become a whole system of off-reservation boarding schools for Indian students. Eighty-four Sioux children from Pine Ridge and Rosebud, about two-thirds boys and mainly from prominent families, returned east with the stern captain. Neither parent nor pupil foresaw the short hair, the starched shirts and squeaky boots, the Christian names, or the other trappings…. Head shaving and even shackling with a ball and chain were common punishments for Indian pupils who ran away or spoke in their native tongue. Suppressing the Sioux language was high among both the Indian Bureau's educational priorities and the reasons Sioux parents kept children at home." (Lazarus 1991:101-03)

ANS: B, F

Scenario 3

"Given a paycheck and the stub that lists the usual deductions, 26 percent of adult Americans cannot determine if their paycheck is correct. Thirty-six percent, given a W-4 form, cannot enter the right numbers of exemptions in the proper places on the form. Forty-four percent, when given a series of 'help-wanted' ads, cannot match their qualifications to the job requirements. Twenty-two percent cannot address a letter well enough to guarantee that it will reach its destination. Twenty-four percent cannot add their own correct return address to the same envelope. Twenty percent cannot understand an 'equal opportunity' announcement. Over 60 percent, given a series of 'for sale' advertisements for products new and used, cannot calculate the difference between prices for a new rated and used appliance." (Kozol 1985:9)

ANS: C

Scenario 4

"The development of IQ tests lent an air of objectivity to the placement of procedures used to separate children for instruction....Test pioneer Lewis Terman wrote in 1916: 'At every step in the child's progress, the school should take account of his vocational possibilities. Preliminary investigations indicate that an IQ below 70 rarely permits anything better than unskilled labor; that range from 70 to 80 is pre-eminently that of semi-skilled labor, from 80 to 100 that of skilled or ordinary clerical labor, from 100 to 110 or 115 that of the semi-professional pursuits; and that above, these are the grades of intelligence which permit one to enter the professions or the larger fields of business....This information will be a great value in planning the education of a particular child and also in planning the differentiated curriculum here recommended.'" (Oakes 1985, p.36)

ANS: A, I

Short Essay Questions

1. Why was the education system of the European Union chosen as the emphasis for the Education chapter?

2. What impressions did Europeans have of early American education?

3. Distinguish between schooling, formal education, and informal education.

4. What are some of the functions schools perform to contribute to the smooth operation of society?

5. What kinds of factors do conflict theorists emphasize when they analyze systems of education?

6. What is functional illiteracy? Expand on the statement, "Illiteracy is a product of one's environment."

7. What is foreign language illiteracy? Why are Americans more likely to be illiterate in a foreign language?

8. Explain: "Only a handful of countries in the world give a significant share of their population the opportunity to go to college."

9. How does the United States compare with the European Union on providing its population opportunities to attend college?

10. What is tracking? What is the rationale for tracking? Is this rationale supported by research? Why does tracking persist?

11. How does Europe and the U.S. differ in regard to tracking?

12. Explain how the self-fulfilling prophecy can affect students' academic achievements.

13. Distinguish between formal and hidden curriculum. Give examples.

14. What is "spelling baseball"? What do children learn when they engage in such educational activities? Why?

15. Distinguish between the promise of education and the reality.

16. Explain: "Schools are the stage on which society's crises play out."

17. According to Coleman, how did the adolescent subculture emerge?

18. What are the major characteristics of the adolescent status system? How does it reflect values of the society? How does it affect education?

19. What did James Coleman uncover about American schools? What was the most controversial finding?

20. How were Coleman's findings "used"? What happened when his recommendation to bus students was implemented?

Comprehensive Essay Questions

1. Approximately 30 percent of ninth graders enrolled in public schools graduate from high school four years later. Use information in Chapter 13 to explain this phenomenon.

2. Think back to your primary and secondary school experiences. Relate these experiences to three ideas, concepts, and/or theories presented in Chapter 13. Your experiences do not have to support information in Chapter 13, but you do need to explain why you think your experiences do not correspond with the textbook.

3. What can we learn about the U.S. system of education by contrasting it with the systems in the European Union?

Chapter 14

Religion

Multiple-Choice Questions

1. The sociological study of religion is guided by
    a. the assumption that no religion is false.
    b. a conviction that there must be one true religion.
    c. the assumption that the supernatural can ultimately be observed.
    d. the belief that some religions are better for a society than others.

    ANS: A   PG: 402   TYP: comprehension

2. One of the most difficult tasks sociologists who study religion encounter is
    a. determining the ways people use religion.
    b. determining the purpose of religion.
    c. defining religion.
    d. getting people to talk about religion.

    ANS: C   PG: 402   TYP: comprehension

3. When sociologists study religion, they investigate
    a. whether God or some other supernatural force exists.
    b. the validity of certain religious beliefs.
    c. the social aspects of a religion.
    d. which religion is the one true vision.

    ANS: C   PG: 402   TYP: comprehension

Chapter 14

4. Almost all terrorist activity originates from _____ and is sustained by it as well.
   a. religious fundamentalism
   b. terrorist groups
   c. political antecedent
   d. crazed personality

   ANS: C   PG: 402   TYP: comprehension

5. _____ wrote "To define 'religion,' to say what it is, is not possible at the start of a presentation such as this. Definition can be attempted, if at all, only at the conclusion of the study."
   a. Karl Marx
   b. Max Weber
   c. Emile Durkheim
   d. George H. Mead

   ANS: B   PG: 402   TYP: knowledge   SOURCE: study guide

6. In *The Elementary Forms of the Religious Life*, Emile Durkheim cautioned that sociologists who study religion must assume that
   a. some religions are false.
   b. there are no religions which are false.
   c. a God does not exist.
   d. all religions include notions of higher beings and that humans are made in their likeness.

   ANS: B   PG: 402   TYP: comprehension

7. Which one of the following is not one of the three essential features of religion as identified by Durkheim?
   a. beliefs about the sacred and the profane
   b. "great" books such as the Bible, Koran, or Torah
   c. rituals
   d. a community of worshippers

   ANS: B   PG: 403   TYP: comprehension

8. Sacred things can include books, buildings, days, and places. From a sociological point of view sacredness stems from
    a. the item itself.
    b. an item's symbolic power.
    c. the meaning assigned to it by God.
    d. the bible.

    ANS: B   PG: 403   TYP: comprehension   SOURCE: study guide

9. The _____ includes everything that is regarded as extraordinary and that inspires in believers deep and absorbing sentiments of awe, respect, mystery, and reverence.
    a. sacred
    b. profane
    c. sacramental religions
    d. prophetic religions

    ANS: A   PG: 403   TYP: comprehension

10. "Our God is the sky and lives wherever the sky is. Our God is the sun and moon, too." This idea of sacred can be classified as a
    a. sacramental religion.
    b. prophetic religion.
    c. mystical religion.
    d. civil religion.

    ANS: A   PG: 404   TYP: application

11. In sacramental religions the sacred
    a. revolves around items that symbolize significant historical events.
    b. is sought in states of being.
    c. is sought in places, objects, and actions believed to house a god or spirit.
    d. revolves around the lives, teachings, and writings of great people.

    ANS: C   PG: 404   TYP: comprehension

Chapter 14

12. Which of the following statements does not apply to Native Spirituality?
    a. There are probably as many native religions as there are Indian tribes.
    b. The basic tenets of Native Spirituality can be found in the "Great Book".
    c. None of the native religions have man-made churches in the Judeo-Christian sense.
    d. Religious beliefs are tied to nature.

    ANS: B   PG: 405   TYP: knowledge   SOURCE: study guide

13. Some of the most well-known _____ religions include Judaism, Confucianism, Christianity, and Islam.
    a. sacramental
    b. prophetic
    c. mystical
    d. profane

    ANS: B   PG: 405   TYP: application   SOURCE: study guide

14. In mystical religions, the sacred
    a. revolves around items that symbolize historical events.
    b. is sought in states of being.
    c. revolves around the lives, teachings, and writings of great people.
    d. is sought in places, objects, and actions believed to house a god or spirit.

    ANS: B   PG: 406   TYP: comprehension

15. A religion that revolves around the lives, teachings, and writings of great people can be classified as
    a. prophetic.
    b. mystical.
    c. sacramental.
    d. secular.

    ANS: A   PG: 405   TYP: comprehension

16. Buddhism and philosophical Hinduism are two examples of religions in which the sacred is sought in
    a. historical events.
    b. sacred books.
    c. states of being.
    d. places, objects, and actions.

    ANS: C   PG: 406   TYP: application

17. Confucianism, Christianity, Islam, and Judaism can be classified as _____ religions.
    a. prophetic
    b. mystical
    c. sacramental
    d. secular

    ANS: A   PG: 406   TYP: application

18. Native spirituality that locates the sacred in the spiritual forces of nature can be classified as a _____ religion.
    a. prophetic
    b. mystical
    c. sacramental
    d. secular

    ANS: C   PG: 404   TYP: application

19. Confession, immersion, and fasting are examples of
    a. mystical acts.
    b. ecclesiae.
    c. rituals.
    d. sacraments.

    ANS: C   PG: 407   TYP: comprehension   SOURCE: study guide

Chapter 14

20. Codes of religious conduct aimed at governing the performance of everyday activities are
    a. prophetic acts.
    b. ecclesiae.
    c. rituals.
    d. sacraments.

    ANS: C   PG: 407   TYP: comprehension

21. An _____ is a professionally trained religious organization governed by a hierarchy of leaders which claims everyone in a society as its member.
    a. ecclesiae
    b. denomination
    c. sect
    d. established sect

    ANS: A   PG: 408   TYP: comprehension

22. _____ include(s) everything that is not sacred.
    a. Powerful symbols
    b. Evil
    c. The profane
    d. Exorcism

    ANS: C   PG: 406   TYP: comprehension   SOURCE: study guide

23. _____ are rules that govern how people must behave in the presence of the sacred to achieve an acceptable state of being.
    a. Religious laws
    b. The Ten Commandments
    c. Rituals
    d. Beliefs

    ANS: C   PG: 407   TYP: comprehension

24. Durkheim maintained that rituals are
    a. elaborate sequences of activities that must be followed closely.
    b. enacted only in sacred places.
    c. not applicable to everyday activities.
    d. behaviors coordinated to an inner intention to achieve a desired state.

    ANS: D   PG: 407   TYP: comprehension

25. Durkheim used the word "church" to designate a group whose members do all but which one of the following?
    a. hold the same beliefs with regard to the sacred and the profane
    b. behave in the same way in the presence of the sacred
    c. gather together to affirm commitment to beliefs and practices
    d. adhere to the belief that the religion members follow is one of many true religions

    ANS: D   PG: 408   TYP: application   SOURCE: study guide

26. Durkheim wrote: "Sometimes it embraces an entire people…sometimes it embraces only a part of them…sometimes it is directed by a core of priests, sometimes it is almost devoid of any official body." Durkheim was describing a
    a. church.
    b. ecclesiae.
    c. cult.
    d. denomination.

    ANS: A   PG: 408   TYP: comprehension

27. The 2004 Afghanistan constitution declares the country an Islamic Republic, makes Islam the official religion, and announces that "no law can be contrary to the sacred religion of Islam." Based on this information, Islam in Afghanistan can be classified as a(n)
    a. ecclesiae.
    b. denominations.
    c. sect.
    d. cult.

    ANS: A   PG: 408   TYP: application

28. In Islam the most pronounced split occurred after the death of Prophet Muhammad over the issue of Muhammed's successor. That split is between
    a. Sunni and Shia.
    b. Hezbollah and Druze.
    c. Iranian Sunni and Iraqi Shia.
    d. Muslims and Jews.

    ANS: A   PG: 410   TYP: knowledge   SOURCE: study guide

Chapter 14

For the following questions, decide which type of religious organization best fits the description.
      a. Ecclesiae
      b. Denomination
      c. Sect
      d. Cult

29. Members accept the religion as the official religion of the state/country.

    ANS: A   PG: 408

30. Membership is not voluntary; it is the law.

    ANS: A   PG: 408

31. Membership is composed of people who broke away from a denomination.

    ANS: C   PG: 409

32. A charismatic leader plays a central role in attracting members.

    ANS: D   PG: 410

33. Buddhism, Christianity, and Judaism are among the religions classified as such.

    ANS: B   PG: 409

34. This kind of religious organization claims to be the one true faith and does not recognize other religions as valid.

    ANS: A   PG: 408

35. Leaders may require members to break all ties with the outside world.

    ANS: D   PG: 410

36. The Afghanistan constitution defines _____ as the official religion of the country.
    a. Islam
    b. Christianity
    c. Hinduism
    d. Shintoism

    ANS: A   PG: 408   TYP: knowledge

37. _____ is a hierarchical organization led by a professionally-trained clergy in which church and state remain separate.
    a. Ecclesiae
    b. Denominations
    c. Sect
    d. Cult

    ANS: B   PG: 408   TYP: comprehension

38. _____ are very small, loosely organized groups, usually founded by a charismatic leader who attracts people by virtue of his or her personal qualities.
    a. Ecclesiae
    b. Sects
    c. Cults
    d. Churches

    ANS: C   PG: 410   TYP: comprehension

39. Renegades from denominations or ecclesiae that have existed long enough to acquire a large following and widespread respectability are known as
    a. ecclesiae.
    b. denominations.
    c. sects.
    d. established sects.

    ANS: D   PG: 410   TYP: comprehension

40. Sunni and Shia branches of Islam are known as
    a. denominations.
    b. established sects.
    c. sects.
    d. cults.

    ANS: B   PG: 409   TYP: application

Chapter 14

41. In his State of the Union Address on January 7, 1991, President George Bush said, "We know why the hopes of humanity turn to us. We are Americans; we have a unique responsibility to do the hard work of freedom. And when we do freedom works." His statement appeals to sentiments associated with
    a. civil religion.
    b. cults.
    c. secularization.
    d. mystical religion.

    ANS: A   PG: 411   TYP: application

42. Critics of Durkheim's definition of religion argue that
    a. he was an atheist and not qualified to study religion.
    b. his underlying assumptions about how to approach the study of religion are wrong.
    c. the combination of characteristics Durkheim attributed to religious activity can be found in many "nonreligious" activities.
    d. he failed to make a clear distinction between the sacred and the profane.

    ANS: C   PG: 411   TYP: application

43. In light of Durkheim's definition of religion, which one of the following does not qualify as a religious phenomenon?
    a. displays of patriotism
    b. 21-gun salutes
    c. national holidays
    d. traffic jams in which everyone gets out of their cars to interact

    ANS: D   PG: 411   TYP: application   SOURCE: study guide

44. When the Soviet Union invaded Afghanistan in 1979, the U.S.
    a. let the Soviets control the country.
    b. dropped an atomic bomb.
    c. sent 250,000 troops to the region.
    d. supported the Afghan freedom fighters, known as the *mujahidin*.

    ANS: D   PG: 412   TYP: knowledge   SOURCE: study guide

45. The Soviets justified their involvement in the Cold War as their "internationalist duty" and with the belief "that workers around the world are linked by a bond that transcends nationalism." This rationalization appeals to sentiments associated with
    a. civil religion.
    b. cults.
    c. secularization.
    d. mystical religion.

    ANS: A   PG: 412   TYP: application

46. _____ reflects a long-standing ideology that the United States, by virtue of its moral superiority, was destined to expand across the North American continent to the Pacific Ocean and beyond.
    a. Manifest destiny
    b. Secularism
    c. Fundamentalism
    d. Civil religion

    ANS: A   PG: 411   TYP: comprehension

47. The Cold War is the name given to the political tension and military rivalry that existed between the United States and former Soviet Union from
    a. 1900-1945
    b. 1945-1989
    c. 1966-1976
    d. 2001-2003

    ANS: B   PG: 412   TYP: knowledge

48. The phrase "under God" was added to the Pledge of Allegiance during
    a. WWI.
    b. WWII.
    c. the Vietnam War.
    d. the Cold War.

    ANS: D   PG: 414   TYP: knowledge

Chapter 14

49. During the Cold War, the economic and political beliefs central to U.S. and Soviet life assumed a sacred quality that unified and motivated each side to sacrifice millions of human lives at home and abroad in the name of those principles. Sociologists would argue that these economic and political beliefs qualify as a
    a. church.
    b. civil religion.
    c. sect.
    d. ecclesiae.

    ANS: B   PG: 411   TYP: application

50. Which one of the following is not one of the countries bordering Afghanistan?
    a. China
    b. Iran
    c. Pakistan
    d. Israel

    ANS: D   PG: 413   TYP: knowledge

51. The Soviet Union invaded Afghanistan in
    a. 1979.
    b. 1994.
    c. 1945.
    d. 1890.

    ANS: A   PG: 412   TYP: knowledge   SOURCE: study guide

52. Which historical event made Afghanistan a geographic region of intense national interest to the U.S. and the Soviet Union in the late 1970s?
    a. the Gulf War
    b. World War I
    c. the rise of Islam
    d. the Cold War

    ANS: D   PG: 412   TYP: knowledge

53. After the Soviet Union invaded Afghanistan, the United States supported the Afghan freedom fighters known as the
    a. Hamas.
    b. Tajiks.
    c. mujahidin.
    d. madrassas.

    ANS: C   PG: 412   TYP: knowledge

54. The United States worked with _____ to recruit 35,000 Muslims from 43 countries to fight with their Afghan brothers against the Soviet Union.
    a. Iran
    b. Pakistan
    c. Tajikistan
    d. India

    ANS: B   PG: 412   TYP: knowledge   SOURCE: study guide

55. *Madrassas* are Islamic
    a. churches.
    b. mujahidin.
    c. freedom fighters.
    d. religious schools.

    ANS: D   PG: 412   TYP: knowledge

56. _____ definition of religion is one of the best and most widely used definitions of religion.
    a. Robert C. Coles'
    b. Robert K. Merton's
    c. Emile Durkheim's
    d. Rodney Stark's

    ANS: C   PG: 416   TYP: knowledge

Chapter 14

57. At the time "under God" was added to the Pledge of Allegiance, supporters argued that the word "God" was
    a. a reference to the God of Christianity.
    b. inclusive of all "Supreme Beings."
    c. equivalent to the Trinity (God, Son, Holy Spirit).
    d. inclusive of Jesus Christ.

    ANS: B   PG: 414   TYP: comprehension

58. The term al-Qaida was first used in
    a. 1949.
    b. 1969.
    c. 1979.
    d. 1989.

    ANS: D   PG: 412   TYP: knowledge

59. A historian writes…when the Soviets pulled out of Afghanistan, "it left behind a legacy of expert and experienced fighters, training camps, and logistical centers, elaborate trans-Islam networks of personal and organizational relationships, a substantial amount of military equipments…and most importantly a sense of power and self-confidence." The legacy became the foundation of
    a. Hamas.
    b. Tajiks.
    c. al-Qaida.
    d. Tajiks.

    ANS: C   PG: 413   TYP: comprehension

60. In 1990 at the request of the _____ government, the United States sent 540,000 troops to the Persian Gulf Region after Iraqi troops invaded Kuwait.
    a. Kuwaiti
    b. Afghanistan
    c. Saudi Arabia
    d. Tajikistan

    ANS: C   PG: 413   TYP: knowledge

61. Functionalists maintain that religion must serve some vital social function because
    a. there are very few atheists in the world.
    b. all people turn to religion in times of deep distress.
    c. some form of religion has existed as long as humans have been around.
    d. people who communicate with their god find extraordinary strength.

    ANS: C   PG: 417   TYP: application   SOURCE: study guide

62. Durkheim maintained that society transcends individual life because
    a. it frees us from the bondage of nature.
    b. people have no free will.
    c. people turn to it in times of crisis.
    d. it frees us from the blinders of nurture.

    ANS: A   PG: 418   TYP: comprehension

63. Durkheim maintained that for the individual, society is the reality from which everything that matters to us flows. He used this argument to support his belief that
    a. people embrace religion in the face of uncertainty.
    b. it is impossible to define religion.
    c. the something out there that people worship is actually society.
    d. there are no religions that are false.

    ANS: C   PG: 418   TYP: comprehension

64. Durkheim argued that _____ is a reality from which everything that matters to us flows.
    a. religion
    b. the sacred
    c. society
    d. the profane

    ANS: C   PG: 418   TYP: application

Chapter 14

65. Which one of the following sociologists observed that whenever a group of people have a strong conviction, that conviction almost always takes on a religious character?
    a. Robert Coles
    b. Robert K. Merton
    c. Emile Durkheim
    d. Max Weber

    ANS: C   PG: 418   TYP: knowledge   SOURCE: study guide

66. Marx focused on the _____ of religion.
    a. humane qualities
    b. comforting qualities
    c. functional qualities
    d. exploitive qualities

    ANS: D   PG: 420   TYP: application

67. Durkheim concluded that
    a. religion is a disruptive force.
    b. the "something out there" that people worship is society.
    c. the "something out there" must be God.
    d. religion is the "opiate of the people."

    ANS: B   PG: 418   TYP: comprehension

68. Critics of the functionalist perspective on religion maintain that it
    a. overemphasizes religion's unifying, bonding, and comforting functions.
    b. overemphasizes religion's repressive, constraining, and exploitative qualities.
    c. defines religion as ultimately problematic.
    d. overlooks the order and stability functions.

    ANS: A   PG: 418   TYP: comprehension

69. If religion were truly an integrative force
    a. there would be no conflict or tensions among religious groups within the same society.
    b. everyone would have the same religion.
    c. there would be fewer struggles between the political and the religious.
    d. everyone would be a member of a religion.

    ANS: A   PG: 418   TYP: comprehension   SOURCE: study guide

70. Marx maintained that religion is
    a. a positive force.
    b. not necessary.
    c. analogous to a sedative.
    d. a liberating force.

    ANS: C   PG: 420   TYP: comprehension

71. A _____ is a propertyless society with equal access to the means of production.
    a. caste system
    b. communist society
    c. socialist society
    d. classless society

    ANS: D   PG: 420   TYP: comprehension

72. Durkheim observed that whenever a group of people has a strong conviction
    a. religious values are secondary to the conviction.
    b. that conviction always takes on a religious character.
    c. they fight among themselves.
    d. they work to make the world a better place.

    ANS: B   PG: 418   TYP: comprehension   SOURCE: study guide

73. Critics of conflict theory point to _____ as an example of religion taking an active role to bring about political and economic justice.
    a. civil religion
    b. secularization
    c. Liberation theology
    d. Calvinism

    ANS: C   PG: 421   TYP: comprehension

Chapter 14

74. The major criticism of the conflict perspective is that religion should not be viewed as an opium if only because of
    a. liberation theology.
    b. civil religion.
    c. secularization.
    d. modern capitalism.

    ANS: A   PG: 420   TYP: comprehension

75. Critics of the conflict perspective on religion argue that religion
    a. is the sigh of an oppressed creature.
    b. in an opiate.
    c. has been used as a vehicle to protest inequalities.
    d. can be twisted to serve the interest of the dominant group.

    ANS: C   PG: 421   TYP: application

76. _____ is/are an example of a religion that emerged in the United States in the 1930s as a vehicle of protest or change.
    a. Liberation theology
    b. The Quakers
    c. Black Shia
    d. Nation of Islam

    ANS: D   PG: 422   TYP: application   SOURCE: study guide

77. The "X" in the name Malcom X signifies
    a. danger.
    b. the rejection of a slave name.
    c. resistance to white power.
    d. the tenth person.

    ANS: B   PG: 422   TYP: knowledge

78. Max Weber was interested in understanding the role of religious beliefs in the origins and development of
    a. the Protestant ethic.
    b. Liberation theology.
    c. modern capitalism.
    d. socialism.

    ANS: C   PG: 422   TYP: comprehension

79. Danielle believes that God has foreordained all things including the salvation or damnation of individual souls. This belief is known as
    a. liberation theology.
    b. secularization.
    c. predestination.
    d. fundamentalism.

    ANS: C   PG: 423   TYP: application   SOURCE: study guide

80. _____ is a belief in the timeless nature of sacred writings and the belief that such writings apply to all kinds of environments.
    a. Fundamentalism
    b. Predestination
    c. Secularization
    d. Subjective secularization

    ANS: A   PG: 425   TYP: comprehension

81. In his book *The Protestant Ethnic and the Spirit of Capitalism*, Weber asked
    a. what are the function of religion for human existence?
    b. why did modern capitalism emerge and flourish in Europe rather than China or India?
    c. why did Islam, Christianity, and Judaism originate in the Middle East?
    d. why were India and China dominant civilizations at the end of the sixteenth century?

    ANS: B   PG: 422   TYP: comprehension

Chapter 14

82. _____ is the belief that God has preordained all things.
    a. This-worldly asceticism
    b. Religion
    c. Fatalism
    d. Predestination

    ANS: D   PG: 423   TYP: comprehension

83. According to *The Protestant Ethic and the Spirit of Capitalism*, the calculating orientation among Calvinists grew out of
    a. ideas about the sacred and profane.
    b. doctrines of this-worldly asceticism and predestination.
    c. modern capitalism and specialization.
    d. alienation and false consciousness.

    ANS: B   PG: 423   TYP: application

84. Weber regarded _____ as the Eastern parallel and opposite of Calvinism.
    a. Islam
    b. Confucianism
    c. Buddhism
    d. Judaism

    ANS: C   PG: 423   TYP: knowledge

85. _____ emphasized the basic illusory character of worldly life and regards the highest religious aspirations to be released from the material demands of the everyday world.
    a. Islam
    b. Confucianism
    c. Buddhism
    d. Judaism

    ANS: C   PG: 423   TYP: knowledge

86. Weber maintained that the Protestant ethic
    a. caused capitalism to come into being.
    b. led to the rise of fundamentalism.
    c. was a significant force in the emergence of capitalism.
    d. must be present in a society if it is to achieve economic success.

    ANS: C   PG: 423   TYP: comprehension   SOURCE: study guide

87. Weber maintained that once capitalism became established, religion would become a/an _____ factor in maintaining the system.
    a. necessary, but not sufficient
    b. increasingly insignificant
    c. sufficient
    d. increasingly important

    ANS: B   PG: 548   TYP: comprehension

88. For the most part, Muslims in the Middle East associate secularization with
    a. an increase in scientific understanding.
    b. modernization.
    c. exposure to the most negative of Western values.
    d. fundamentalism.

    ANS: C   PG: 424   TYP: knowledge

89. _____ is a process by which religious influences on thought and behavior are reduced.
    a. Secularization
    b. Fundamentalism
    c. Predestination
    d. This-worldly asceticism

    ANS: A   PG: 424   TYP: comprehension

90. Religious studies professor John L. Esposito prefers the term Islamic _____ to Islamic fundamentalism.
    a. terrorism
    b. militants
    c. revitalism
    d. majority

    ANS: C   PG: 425   TYP: comprehension

Chapter 14

91. Which one of the following is not a characteristic of fundamentalist thought?
    a. A belief in the timeless truth of sacred writing.
    b. History is a process of decline from an original ideal state.
    c. Religious behavior and beliefs should not interfere with the secular aspects of society.
    d. Sacred writings provide a blueprint for how to live life.

    ANS: C   PG: 425   TYP: comprehension

92. The Taliban and other Muslim groups in Afghanistan reject Western capitalism and Marxist socialism as foundations on which to build a society because
    a. Islamic laws prohibit the economic behaviors each encourages.
    b. the disintegration of Afghanistan is a product of the Cold War which pitted capitalism against socialism.
    c. both are ideals which can never be achieved.
    d. capitalism is associated with Christianity and socialism with atheism.

    ANS: B   PG: 426   TYP: comprehension

93. Daniel Pipes estimates that there are _____ million persons "who do not accept the particulars" of militant Islam but are sympathetic and supportive of the anti-American stance.
    a. 1
    b. 10
    c. 100
    d. 500

    ANS: D   PG: 427   TYP: knowledge   SOURCE: study guide

94. From a political or militant viewpoint *jihad* is the
    a. constant struggle of Muslims to conquer their inner base instincts.
    b. struggle to follow the path to God.
    c. struggle to do good in society.
    d. armed struggle against non-Muslims and Muslims who stand or get in the way.

    ANS: D   PG: 427   TYP: comprehension

Religion

For the following questions, choose the name of the person from the list below that best fits the statement made.
    a. Karl Marx
    b. Emile Durkheim
    c. Max Weber

95. The true object of religious worship is society.

    ANS: B   PG: 418

96. A belief in the doctrine of predestination created a crisis of meaning among Calvinist adherents.

    ANS: C   PG: 422

97. For the individual, society is the reality from which everything important flows.

    ANS: B   PG: 418

98. Religion is the sigh of the oppressed creature, the sentiment of a heartless world, and the soul of soulless conditions.

    ANS: A   PG: 420

99. Religion is a source of false consciousness.

    ANS: A   PG: 420

100. The Protestant ethic was a significant ideological force in the rise of a capitalist economy.

    ANS: C   PG: 423

101. Whenever a group of people has a strong conviction, that conviction almost always takes on a religious character.

    ANS: A   PG: 418

Chapter 14

Multiple Choice Questions on the Web

1. The sociological perspective on religion is one that is guided by
    a. emotional involvement.
    b. subjectivity and personal beliefs.
    c. scientific method.
    d. personal conviction.

    ANS: C   PG: 402   TYP: comprehension

2. _____ wrote *The Elementary Forms of the Religious Life*.
    a. Max Weber
    b. Emile Durkheim
    c. Karl Marx
    d. Robert Coles

    ANS: B   PG: 402   TYP: knowledge

3. In prophetic religions the sacred revolves around
    a. the lives, teachings, and writings of great people.
    b. states of being.
    c. holy places.
    d. the profane.

    ANS: A   PG: 405   TYP: comprehension

4. Speaking the name of God in vain, a women refusing to cover her hair or face during worship, and a male keeping his baseball cap on during religious services are all actions that Durkheim would classify as falling under the category of
    a. the profane.
    b. the sacred.
    c. rituals.
    d. sacraments.

    ANS: A   PG: 406   TYP: application

5. _____ is a small community of believers who broke away from a denomination and are led by a lay ministry, with no formal governing body.
    a. Ecclesiae
    b. Sect
    c. Cult
    d. Church

    ANS: B   PG: 409   TYP: comprehension

6. The U.S. started to print the phrase "In God We Trust" on its coins in the
    a. 1750s.
    b. 1880s.
    c. 1930s.
    d. 1950s.

    ANS: D   PG: 414   TYP: knowledge

7. Osama bin Laden was opposed to the U.S. military intervening in the region after Iraq invaded Kuwait. He had hoped
    a. the UN would intervene.
    b. the Saudi Royal family could use their own army.
    c. to raise a force composed of Afghan war veterans.
    d. Pakistan would intervene.

    ANS: C   PG: 414   TYP: knowledge

8. Which one of the following sociologists described religion as "the sigh of the oppressed creature, the sentiment of a heartless world, and the soul of a soulless condition. It is the opium the people"?
    a. Max Weber
    b. Emile Durkheim
    c. Karl Marx
    d. J. Milton Yinger

    ANS: C   PG: 420   TYP: comprehension

Chapter 14

9. The belief that _____ placed the greatest pressure on Calvinists to find some sign of salvation.
   a. people have free will
   b. people could change their fate if they worked hard enough
   c. God foreordained all things
   d. not everyone could be saved

   ANS: C   PG: 423   TYP: comprehension

10. In thinking about the meaning of *jihad* it is important to distinguish between
    a. long-term and short-term.
    b. fundamentalist and secular *jihad*.
    c. religious and political *jihad*.
    d. *jihad* against Jews and Christians.

    ANS: C   PG: 427   TYP: comprehension

True-False Questions

1. When sociologists study religion, they take on the task of proving "God" exists.

   ANS: False   PG: 402

2. The belief in an "ever-living God" seems to be the most widely used sociological definition of religion.

   ANS: False   PG: 402

3. In studying religions, sociologists must assume that there are no religions that are false.

   ANS: True   PG: 402   SOURCE: study guide

4. Definitions of what is sacred vary according to time and place.

   ANS: True   PG: 403

5. There are probably as many native religions as there are Indian tribes.

   ANS: True   PG: 405

6. Judaism, Confucianism, Christianity, and Islam are prophetic religions.

    ANS: True   PG: 405

7. Rituals can be codes of conduct aimed at governing the performance of everyday activities such as eating.

    ANS: True   PG: 407   SOURCE: study guide

8. In an ecclesiae, membership is voluntary.

    ANS: False   PG: 408

9. An ecclesia is a small community of believers led by a lay ministry.

    ANS: False   PG: 408

10. All the major religions encompass splinter groups that have sought to preserve the integrity of their religion.

    ANS: True   PG: 410   SOURCE: study guide

11. Shiaism represents the dominant religion of the Islamic Republic of Iran.

    ANS: True   PG: 410   SOURCE: new

12. Cults often dissolve after their leader dies.

    ANS: True   PG: 410   SOURCE: study guide

13. One can argue that the Cold War between the United States and the former Soviet Union elevated each country's economic and political systems to the level of a religion.

    ANS: True   PG: 412

Chapter 14

14. Afghanistan is a land-locked country with mountainous terrain.

    ANS: True   PG: 413

15. The words "under God" were added to the Pledge of Allegiance in the 1950s during the Cold War.

    ANS: True   PG: 414

16. Sporting events, graduation ceremonies, and political rallies possess some characteristics that make them indistinguishable from religion.

    ANS: True   PG: 418

17. Durkheim maintained that whenever a group of people has a strong conviction, it almost always takes on a religious character.

    ANS: True   PG: 418   SOURCE: study guide

18. Archeological evidence suggests that Jesus was at least 6 feet 2 inches tall.

    ANS: False   PG: 419   SOURCE: study guide

19. Karl Marx maintained that people need the comfort of religion in order to make the world bearable and justify their existence in it.

    ANS: True   PG: 420   SOURCE: study guide

20. Karl Marx believed that religion was the most humane feature of an inhuman world.

    ANS: True   PG: 420

21. In the United States, faith-based organizations cannot receive federal funds

    ANS: False   PG: 421   SOURCE: new

22. The Protestant Ethic <u>caused</u> capitalism to emerge.

    ANS: False   PG: 423   SOURCE: study guide

23. Fundamentalism is a process by which religious influences on thought and behavior are reduced.

    ANS: False   PG: 425   SOURCE: study guide

24. Data collection by the Gallup Poll organization shows that most Americans have no religious preference.

    ANS: False   PG: 425

25. In the religious sense of the word, *jihad* is the constant struggle of Muslims to conquer their inner basic instincts.

    ANS: True   PG: 427   SOURCE: new

26. There are no features common to all religions

    ANS: False   PG: 428   SOURCE: study guide

27. The functionalist perspective tends to underestimate the negative ways in which people use religion.

    ANS: True   PG: 429   SOURCE: new

28. People play a fundamental role in determining what is sacred and how they should act in its presence.

    ANS: True   PG: 429   SOURCE: new

29. Modern capitalism first emerged and flourished in China

    ANS: False   PG: 430   SOURCE: new

Chapter 14

30. Secularization and fundamentalism fuel each other's growth.

    ANS: True   PG: 431   SOURCE: new

Concept Application (also in study guide)

Consider the concepts listed below. Match one or more of the concepts with each scenario. Explain your choices.

    a. Church
    b. Civil religion
    c. Liberation theology
    d. Mystical religions
    e. Rituals
    f. Sect

Scenario 1

"As for my own religious practice, I try to live my life pursuing what I call the Bodhisattva ideal…. The Bodhisattva idea is thus the aspiration to practice infinite compassion with infinite wisdom. As a means of helping myself in the quest, I choose to be a Buddhist monk. There are 253 rules of Tibetan monasticism (364 for nuns) and by observing them as closely as I can, I free myself from many of the distractions and worries of life. Some of these rules mainly deal with etiquette, such as the physical distance a monk should walk behind the abbot of his monastery; others are concerned with behavior. The four root vows concern simple prohibitions: namely that a monk must not kill, steal, or lie about his spiritual attainment. He must also be celibate. If he breaks any one of these, he is no longer a monk." (Gyatso 1990:204-05)

ANS: D, E

Scenario 2

"There were usually three services each day: morning, mid-afternoon, and evening. A ram's horn summoned everyone to the nine-o'clock morning service, at which time people would leave their camps and congregate in the shed. Sunday was the biggest day of the week, and for many years it was also the day of the Lovefeast. Bread and water were passed around and people would make their testimonials. During the evening service there would inevitably be an altar call, often accompanied by a lot of shouting." (Jenkins 1996:562)

ANS: A, E

Scenario 3

"The 'miracle' was Brazil's accelerated economic growth between 1968 and 1975; Brazil moved from twenty-first to fourteenth in rank among developing countries, based upon per capita GNP. The 'miracle' did not help most Brazilians, however. The imbalances in the distribution of wealth were made yet worse. The Brazilian bishops have openly denounced the 'Brazilian miracle' for the poverty it has engendered. They have attacked the economic policies that have pushed thousands of peasant farmers off the lands their families have farmed for generations, and they have questioned development projects (such as the exploitation of the Amazon) which displaced the native Indians and poor farmers but brought them no benefit. Indeed, one observer has concluded that 'the church has become the primary institutional focus of dissidence in the country.'" (McGuire 1987:215)

ANS: C

Scenario 4

"Mennonites trace their roots to a small group of Christians after 1530 who sought a reformation even more radical than those advocated by Lutherans and Calvinists. They were called Mennonites after Menno Simons, one of their early leaders. Their most distinctive practice is adult baptism offered only to those who have made a decision to follow Christ's teachings." (Lorimer 1989:212)

ANS: F

Scenario 5

"The old fascist marching songs were sung, a moment of silence was observed for all who died defending the fatherland, and the gathering was reminded that today was the 57th anniversary of the founding of Croatia's Nazi-allied wartime government. Then came the most chilling words of the afternoon.

'For Home!' shouted Anto Dapic, surrounded by bodyguards in black suits and crew cuts.

'Ready!' responded the crowd of 500 supporters, their arms rising in a stiff Nazi salute.

The call and response—the Croatian equivalent of 'Sieg!' 'Heil!'—was the wartime greeting used by supporters of the fascist Independent Sate of Croatia that governed the country for most the Second World War and murdered hundreds of thousands of Jews, Serbs and Croatian resistance fighters." (Hedges 1997:3Y)

ANS: B

Chapter 14

Short Essay Questions

1. Why was Afghanistan chosen as the country to emphasize with regard to religion?

2. When sociologists study religion, what do they study?

3. According to Durkheim, how should sociologists approach the study of religion?

4. According to Durkheim, what are three fundamental and indispensable features of religion? How do these features figure into a definition of religion?

5. Distinguish between the sacred and the profane. What are the three major types of religion, as categorized in terms of sacred phenomena?

6. According to Durkheim, what are rituals? What are the most important outcomes of rituals?

7. Distinguish between ecclesiae, denominations, sects, established sects, and cults.

8. What are some problems with Durkheim's definition of religion? Give examples. Are there better definitions?

9. What is civil religion? What role did civil religion play in the Cold War?

10. How did Muslims come to be partners to the U.S. during the Cold War?

11. Is the question "What is religion" only of interest to sociologists? Explain.

12. What function does religion serve for the individual and the group?

13. Explain what Durkheim means by the statement, "The something out there that people worship is actually society." How is it that society is worthy of such worship?

14. Is religion strictly an integrative force? Why or why not?

15. How did Karl Marx conceptualize religion?

16. What are some criticisms of Marx's views of religion?

17. According to Weber, what role did the Protestant ethic play in the origins and development of modern capitalism? In what ways has Weber been misinterpreted?

18. What is secularization? Distinguish between Muslim views and American-European views about the causes of secularization.

19. What is fundamentalism? How are fundamentalism and secularization related?

20. What are the factors behind the surge of fundamentalism in Muslim countries?

21. Distinguish between religious and political *jihad* (including militant Islam).

22. How many militant Islamic political *jihadists* exist in the world today?

Comprehensive Essay Questions

1. Does knowing the religious affiliation of the Taliban and al-Qaida help us understand the events of September 11 or any other terrorist action? Why or why not?

2. In what ways did Max Weber, Karl Marx and Emile Durkheim each contribute to our understanding of the sociological significance of religion?

Chapter 15

Population and Urbanization

Multiple-Choice Questions

1. India's population reached 1 billion in May of 2000. The country might have reached this milestone in 1989 had it not been
    a. for the devastating natural disasters of the prior 20 years.
    b. the first country in the world to adopt a national family planning program.
    c. the first country in the world to close its doors to immigrants.
    d. for a history of emigration.

    ANS: B   PG: 433   TYP: knowledge   SOURCE: study guide

2. _____ has the second largest population in the world.
    a. Brazil
    b. India
    c. The People's Republic of China
    d. The United States

    ANS: B   PG: 433   TYP: knowledge

3. India accounts for _____ percent of the world's population.
    a. 11
    b. 17
    c. 27
    d. 37

    ANS: B   PG: 433   TYP: knowledge

Population and Urbanization

4. _____ accounts for 20 percent of the world's total population.
   a. China
   b. India
   c. The United States
   d. Japan

   ANS: A   PG: 433   TYP: knowledge   SOURCE: new

5. Together, China and India account for _____ percent of the world's total population.
   a. 10
   b. 20
   c. 30
   d. 40

   ANS: D   PG: 433   TYP: knowledge   SOURCE: new

6. Almost _____ of India's current population is classified as hungry.
   a. 1/3
   b. 1/2
   c. 2/3
   d. 4/5

   ANS: A   PG: 433   TYP: knowledge

7. The United States has the _____ largest population in the world.
   a. second
   b. third
   c. fifth
   d. tenth

   ANS: B   PG: 434   TYP: comprehension

8. The country with the largest population in the world is
   a. India.
   b. the People's Republic of China.
   c. the United States.
   d. Brazil.

   ANS: B   PG: 433   TYP: knowledge

Chapter 15

9. The United States accounts for _____ percent of the world's population.
   a. 30
   b. 10.5
   c. 4.6
   d. 1.9

   ANS: C   PG: 434   TYP: knowledge   SOURCE: study guide

10. Which one of the following countries is <u>not</u> among the ten most populous countries in the world?
    a. the United States
    b. Mexico
    c. Pakistan
    d. China

    ANS: B   PG: 434   TYP: knowledge

11. In July, the population of the United States was 301,139,947. Over the next 12 months, 4,218,971 babies were born. The birth rate is calculated by which one of the following?
    a. (301,139,947÷4,218,971) * 1000
    b. (4,218,971 ÷ 301,139,947) * 1000
    c. (4,218,971 * 1000) + 301,139,947
    d. (4,218,971 +301,139,947) * 1000

    ANS: B   PG: 435   TYP: application   SOURCE: new

12. The _____ is the average number of children that women in a specific population bear over their lifetimes.
    a. total fertility rate
    b. crude birth rate
    c. age-specific birth rate
    d. infant mortality rate

    ANS: A   PG: 435   TYP: knowledge

Population and Urbanization

13. Use the following information to calculate the age-specific birth rate for India; total births in year—27,116,788; number of women ages 15-54—300,527,000. The age-specific birth rate is _____ per 1,000.
    a. 51.99
    b. 5199
    c. 76.5
    d. 90.2

    ANS: C   PG: 435   TYP: application   SOURCE: study guide

14. A subspecialty within sociology that focuses on the study of human population is
    a. epidemiology.
    b. ethnomethodology.
    c. demography.
    d. conflict theory.

    ANS: C   PG: 434   TYP: knowledge   SOURCE: study guide

15. Every _____ years, the U.S. Bureau of the Census surveys the entire U.S. population.
    a. 5
    b. 10
    c. 15
    d. 20

    ANS: B   PG: 435   TYP: knowledge   SOURCE: new

16. With regard to crude death rate, the United States has _____ India.
    a. a higher rate than
    b. a lower rate than
    c. a dramatically lower rate than
    d. the same rate as

    ANS: A   PG: 436   TYP: knowledge

17. Use the following information to calculate the crude death rate for India: total population (January)—1,129,866,154; number of deaths—7,909,063; total population (December 31)—1,046,230,697. The crude death rate is
    a. 488.
    b. 105.
    c. 21.
    d. 9.

    ANS: D PG: 436 TYP: application SOURCE: new

18. Typically, the infant mortality rate is calculated for the age group that is
    a. less than one day old.
    b. less than one week old.
    c. one year old or younger.
    d. three years old or younger.

    ANS: C PG: 436 TYP: comprehension

19. Which one of the following countries attracts the greatest number of Americans living abroad?
    a. Israel
    b. Germany
    c. South Africa
    d. Mexico

    ANS: D PG: 439 TYP: knowledge SOURCE: new

20. A population's age and sex composition is commonly depicted as a
    a. three-dimensional graph.
    b. cohort.
    c. population pyramid.
    d. demographic transition.

    ANS: C PG: 441 TYP: comprehension SOURCE: study guide

21. Country Y has a population of 149.3 million people. Life expectancy is 73 years for men and 79 years for women. The total fertility is below replacement level. The population pyramid for this country would be
    a. expansive.
    b. constrictive.
    c. stationary.
    d. triangular.

    ANS: B PG: 441 TYP: application SOURCE: study guide

22. India's population pyramid is classified as _____ because it is broadest at the base, and each successive bar is smaller than the one below it. The relative sizes of the cohorts indicate that India's population is increasing and that it consists disproportionately of young people.
    a. expansive
    b. constrictive
    c. stationary
    d. triangular

    ANS: A PG: 443 TYP: application SOURCE: new

23. The United States age-sex distribution yields a nearly _____ pyramid because, except for the older categories, each cohort is roughly the same size.
    a. expansive
    b. constrictive
    c. stationary
    d. triangular

    ANS: C PG: 443 TYP: application SOURCE: new

24. The age-sex distribution for Italy can be labeled as _____ because it is narrower at the base than in the middle, which illustrates that the population consists disproportionately of middle-aged and older people.
    a. expansive
    b. constrictive
    c. stationary
    d. triangular

    ANS: B PG: 443 TYP: application SOURCE: new

Chapter 15

25. A population pyramid allows us to view all <u>but</u> which one of the following?
    a. relative size of age cohorts
    b. relative size of males in each age cohort
    c. relative size of females in each age cohort
    d. relative size of in and out migration for each cohort

    ANS: D PG: 441 TYP: comprehension

26. A _____ is a group of people who share a common characteristic or life event.
    a. population pyramid
    b. population base
    c. cohort
    d. lifestyle

    ANS: C PG: 441 TYP: comprehension

27. Stewart is moving out of his hometown because there are no jobs. The reason he is moving is called a
    a. push factor.
    b. pull factor.
    c. demographic.
    d. self-motivating factor.

    ANS: A PG: 436 TYP: application SOURCE: study guide

28. Which one of the following factors represents an example of a <u>pull</u> factor?
    a. discrimination
    b. unemployment
    c. favorable climate
    d. political persecution

    ANS: C PG: 436 TYP: comprehension

29. Which one of the following factors represents an example of a <u>push</u> factor?
    a. favorable climate
    b. employment opportunities
    c. equal opportunity
    d. natural disaster

    ANS: D PG: 436 TYP: comprehension SOURCE: study guide

30. Movement within the boundaries of a single country is known as
    a. emigration.
    b. immigration.
    c. internal migration.
    d. intercontinental migration.

    ANS: C   PG: 438   TYP: comprehension

31. Within the United States, the greatest amount of internal migration is movement
    a. within the same county.
    b. from one county to another.
    c. from one state to another.
    d. into adjacent counties.

    ANS: A   PG: 439   TYP: knowledge   SOURCE: study guide

32. _____ is the number of births minus the number of deaths that occur in a given year.
    a. Crude birth rate
    b. Immigration
    c. Natural increase
    d. Age-specific death rate

    ANS: C   PG: 440   TYP: comprehension   SOURCE: new

33. Almost 30 percent of India's total population changed residences in the past 10 years. This movement is dominated by short-distance, rural-to-rural movements within India. Sociologists classify this kind of migration as
    a. immigration.
    b. emigration.
    c. internal migration.
    d. international.

    ANS: C   PG: 440   TYP: application   SOURCE: study guide

Chapter 15

34. Within India, the greatest amount of internal migration involves
    a. single people moving to the city.
    b. urban-to-rural migration.
    c. the elderly moving to children's homes.
    d. women moving from their village to their husband's village upon marriage.

    ANS: D   PG: 440   TYP: knowledge

35. How is the natural increase calculated?
    a. number of births - number of deaths
    b. immigration - outmigration
    c. emigration - immigration
    d. (births - deaths) + (immigration - outmigration)

    ANS: A   PG: 440   TYP: comprehension

36. In 1850, the world's population reached 1 billion. It took _____ years to double to 2 billion.
    a. 5
    b. 15
    c. 40
    d. 80

    ANS: D   PG: 441   TYP: knowledge

37. Doubling time is the estimated number of years it will take to double
    a. the size of the population.
    b. the gross national product.
    c. per capita income.
    d. life expectancy.

    ANS: A   PG: 441   TYP: comprehension

38. The number of people in the world today is approximately _____ billion.
    a. 11
    b. 6.6
    c. 3.1
    d. 2.7

    ANS: B   PG: 441   TYP: knowledge

Population and Urbanization

39. The demographic transition
    a. is a two-stage model of population growth.
    b. depicts the history of birth and death rates in labor-intensive poor countries.
    c. depicts the history of disease in core economies.
    d. depicts the history of population growth in Western Europe and North America.

    ANS: D   PG: 442   TYP: comprehension   SOURCE: study guide

40. The world population remained less than 1 billion before _____, at which point it began to grow explosively.
    a. 1600
    b. 1492
    c. 1850
    d. 1960

    ANS: C   PG: 441   TYP: comprehension

41. Stage 1 of the demographic transition is often referred to as the stage of high potential growth because
    a. the fertility rate is so high.
    b. the mortality rate is so low.
    c. if something happened to cause the death rate to decline, population would increase dramatically.
    d. the potential crude death rate is 50 per 1,000.

    ANS: C   PG: 442   TYP: application

42. 50/1000 is believed to be the highest _____ rate possible for any society.
    a. death
    b. fertility
    c. marriage
    d. birth

    ANS: D   PG: 444   TYP: knowledge   SOURCE: study guide

Chapter 15

43. A large proportion of the native populations in North, Central, and South America died after the Europeans arrived in the fifteenth century. The people of these native populations died because they
    a. had no resistance to diseases, such as smallpox and measles, that the colonists brought with them.
    b. refused to use the medicines the Europeans brought with them.
    c. lost their will to live.
    d. were denied access to medical care.

    ANS: A   PG: 444   TYP: knowledge

44. In demographic terms, the Black Death is an example of
    a. a mortality crisis.
    b. a life expectancy crisis.
    c. a tragedy.
    d. a degenerative disease.

    ANS: A   PG: 444   TYP: application   SOURCE: study guide

45. The birth rate in the United States is 14/1000. The death rate is 8.4/1000. The difference between the two rates is known as the
    a. demographic gap.
    b. total fertility rate.
    c. crude birth rate.
    d. demographic trap.

    ANS: A   PG: 446   TYP: comprehension

46. According to Thomas Malthus, epidemics, war, and famine are examples of
    a. positive checks.
    b. demographic traps.
    c. demographic gaps.
    d. catastrophic events.

    ANS: A   PG: 445   TYP: application   SOURCE: study guide

47. From the perspective of Thomas Malthus, a famine is
    a. a mortality crisis.
    b. a preventive check.
    c. a plague.
    d. a positive check.

    ANS: D   PG: 445   TYP: comprehension

48. _____ are frequent and violent fluctuations in the death rate caused by war, famine, and epidemics.
    a. Mortality crises
    b. Life expectancy crises
    c. Crude death rates
    d. Tragedies

    ANS: A   PG: 442   TYP: comprehension

49. Which one of the following factors is least responsible for the decline in mortality crises associated with Stage II of the demographic transition?
    a. the development of winter fodder for cattle
    b. the discovery of canning as a method for food preservation
    c. the manufacture of cheap cotton cloth
    d. the discovery of antibiotics

    ANS: D   PG: 445   TYP: knowledge

50. Which one of the following characteristics best applies to Stage II of the demographic transition?
    a. Advances in medical technology caused the death rate to drop.
    b. The fertility rate declines followed by a decline in death rate.
    c. Infants, children, and young women account for the largest share of deaths.
    d. Mortality crises become less frequent, and the death rate begins to decline.

    ANS: D   PG: 445   TYP: comprehension

Chapter 15

51. The <u>least</u> important reason for the decline in death rates in Western societies is
    a. improvement in agricultural technology.
    b. improvement in sanitation.
    c. medical advances.
    d. proper disposal of sewage.

    ANS: C   PG: 446   TYP: comprehension   SOURCE: study guide

52. Which one of the following is the <u>least</u> likely explanation for the decline in fertility that took place in Western countries during Stage II of the demographic transition?
    a. a change in the status of women
    b. a decline in infant and childhood mortality
    c. a decline in the economic value of children
    d. innovation in contraceptive technology

    ANS: D   PG: 446   TYP: comprehension

53. Which one of the following countries is least likely to be in Stage III of the demographic transition?
    a. The United States
    b. Germany
    c. India
    d. Japan

    ANS: C   PG: 447   TYP: comprehension   SOURCE: study guide

54. The difference between birth and death rates is knows as the demographic
    a. division.
    b. trap.
    c. gap.
    d. transition.

    ANS: C   PG: 446   TYP: comprehension

55. In which stage of the demographic transition is the demographic gap widest?
    a. Stage I
    b. Stage II
    c. Stage III
    d. Stage IV

    ANS: B   PG: 446   TYP: comprehension

56. Urbanization includes all but which one of the following characteristics?
    a. increase in the number of cities
    b. growth of the population living in cities
    c. rural-to-urban migration
    d. urban-to-rural migration

    ANS: D   PG: 446   TYP: comprehension   SOURCE: study guide

57. The textbook uses the broad categories _____ and _____, rather than industrialized and developing, to divide the countries of the world.
    a. core and labor-intensive economies
    b. First World and Third World
    c. developed and developing
    d. industrialized and industrializing

    ANS: A   PG: 448   TYP: comprehension

58. If the doubling time of a country's population is 20 years, that country's economy would be classified as
    a. mechanized-rich.
    b. labor-intensive poor.
    c. industrial.
    d. post-industrial.

    ANS: B   PG: 450   TYP: comprehension

59. Afghanistan has an infant mortality rate of 160 per 1,000 births and a per capita income of $800. Its population is projected to double in 20 years. Based on this information, Afghanistan is a _____ country.
    a. core economy
    b. Fourth World
    c. middle-income
    d. labor-intensive poor

    ANS: D   PG: 450   TYP: application   SOURCE: new

Chapter 15

60. Germany has an infant mortality rate of 6.3, and its per capita income is $16,580. Based on this information, Germany is classified as
    a. a core economy.
    b. Fourth World.
    c. middle income.
    d. labor-intensive poor.

    ANS: A   PG: 450   TYP: comprehension

61. The U.S. has an infant mortality rate of 6/1000 and a per capita income of $43,800. Based on this information, the United States is a
    a. core economy.
    b. labor-intensive poor economy.
    c. developing country.
    d. Fourth World country.

    ANS: A   PG: 450   TYP: application

62. Perhaps the most important historical reason that the demographic transition cannot apply to labor-intensive poor countries is that
    a. most of these countries have not yet made it out of Stage I.
    b. the people in these countries have never admired Western ways.
    c. most of these countries were once colonies of core economies.
    d. the best and brightest people in these countries emigrate to the Western economies.

    ANS: C   PG: 449   TYP: knowledge

63. _____ was considered the "crown jewel" of the British Empire.
    a. The United States
    b. South Africa
    c. Canada
    d. India

    ANS: D   PG: 448   TYP: knowledge

64. The _____ is considered "the most illustrious and most flourishing commercial association that ever existed in any age or country."
    a. Bank of India
    b. General Electric Company
    c. East India Company
    d. Domino Sugar Company

    ANS: C   PG: 448   TYP: knowledge   SOURCE: study guide

65. The British Empire lasted approximately _____ years.
    a. 75
    b. 150
    c. 200
    d. 350

    ANS: D   PG: 447   TYP: knowledge

66. A British historian writes, "She has been for her masters, the richest and most valuable of their colonies of exploitation." The historian is writing about which one of the following countries?
    a. China
    b. India
    c. South Africa
    d. Mexico

    ANS: B   PG: 448   TYP: comprehension

67. India was once a colony of
    a. the United States.
    b. Portugal.
    c. Spain.
    d. Britain.

    ANS: D   PG: 448   TYP: knowledge   SOURCE: study guide

Chapter 15

68. The Japanese government managed to ban low dose oral contraceptives until
    a. 1955
    b. 1970
    c. 1999
    d. 2004

    ANS: C   PG: 449   TYP: knowledge

69. Which city in India was the site of one of the worst industrial accidents in human history?
    a. Bombay
    b. Calcutta
    c. Delhi
    d. Bhopal

    ANS: D   PG: 453   TYP: knowledge

70. One of the worst industrial accidents in human history—the Bhopal crisis—involved which one of the following the chemical companies?
    a. DuPont
    b. Union Carbide
    c. Eli Lilly, Inc
    d. Monsanto

    ANS: B   PG: 453   TYP: knowledge

71. The high death toll associated with the Bhopal incident is explained, in part, by the fact that
    a. two squatter settlements were located directly across from the Union Carbide plant.
    b. India is a backward country.
    c. the Indian population is largely undereducated.
    d. the medical system in India lacks Western-trained physicians.

    ANS: A   PG: 453   TYP: knowledge

72. Which one of the following U.S. cities is not among the world's top 30 economies?
    a. San Francisco
    b. Boston
    c. Houston
    d. Philadelphia

    ANS: A   PG: 454   TYP: knowledge   SOURCE: study guide

73. A central city is
    a. the largest one or two cities within a metropolitan statistical area.
    b. a mega city.
    c. at least one million in population.
    d. the largest city within a state.

    ANS: A   PG: 453   TYP: comprehension

74. MSAs include one or more cities with at least _____ residents.
    a. 10,000
    b. 50,000
    c. 100,000
    d. 1 million

    ANS: B   PG: 453   TYP: comprehension

75. Agglomerations are urban areas with populations of
    a. 10 million or more.
    b. 5 million or more.
    c. at least one million.
    d. 500,000 or more.

    ANS: C   PG: 451   TYP: knowledge

Multiple-Choice Questions on the Web

1. There are two countries in the world with a population of at least one billion. Those two countries are
    a. the United States and India.
    b. Brazil and India.
    c. the United States and China.
    d. China and India.

    ANS: D   PG: 433   TYP: knowledge

Chapter 15

2. Constrictive pyramids indicate that
   a. all age cohorts in a population are roughly the same size.
   b. a population is composed disproportionately of middle-aged and older people.
   c. a population is composed disproportionately of young people.
   d. each age cohort is progressively smaller than the preceding cohort.

   ANS: B   PG: 441   TYP: comprehension

3. Selma is departing from Croatia to live in the United States. In demographic terms, she is _____ out of Croatia.
   a. immigrating
   b. emigrating
   c. moving
   d. traveling

   ANS: B   PG: 437   TYP: application

4. In sociological terms, the forced migration by slave traders of more than 11 million Africans to the Americas is an example of _____ migration.
   a. massive
   b. internal
   c. international
   d. external

   ANS: C   PG: 437   TYP: application

5. Each year, 21.7 million Americans move from one residence to another within the same county. This type of migration is known as
   a. immigration.
   b. emigration.
   c. internal migration.
   d. international.

   ANS: C   PG: 438   TYP: application

6. Which of the following is not represented on the graph of the demographic transition?
   a. birth rates
   b. death rates
   c. time
   d. life expectancy

   ANS: D   PG: 444   TYP: comprehension

7. The 2004 earthquake and tsunamis tragedy, which killed 123,000 people in Asia and Africa and left millions homeless, represents a
   a. mortality crisis.
   b. life expectancy crisis.
   c. tragedy.
   d. degenerative disease.

   ANS: A   PG: 444   TYP: application

8. In Stage III of the demographic transition,
   a. life expectancy at birth remains under 70.
   b. the risk of dying from infectious diseases increases.
   c. persons 50 years and over account for the largest share of deaths.
   d. the goal is to live a long life at all costs.

   ANS: C   PG: 447   TYP: comprehension

9. When comparing the historical decline of birth rates and death rates in the United States and India, one notices that the demographic gap was
   a. much wider and more persistent in India than in the U.S.
   b. much wider and more persistent in the U.S. than in India.
   c. almost nonexistent in the United States.
   d. about the same in each country.

   ANS: A   PG: 450   TYP: concept

10. Accidents, homicides, and suicides become the leading causes of death among young people during which stage of the demographic transition?
    a. Stage I
    b. Stage II
    c. Stage III
    d. the transition stage

    ANS: C   PG: 447   TYP: comprehension

Chapter 15

True-False Questions

1. It is likely the U.S. population will reach 1 billion by 2025.

    ANS: False   PG: 433

2. China is the country with the largest population in the world.

    ANS: True   PG: 433   SOURCE: study guide

3. India is expected to have the largest population in the world by the year 2050.

    ANS: True   PG: 433

4. Japan is among the 10 most populous countries in the world.

    ANS: True   PG: 434   SOURCE: study guide

5. A woman has the potential to bear 20 to 25 children over her lifetime.

    ANS: True   PG: 436

6. The death rate in India and the United States is about the same.

    ANS: True   PG: 436   SOURCE: study guide

7. To alleviate a nursing shortage, the United States recruits nurses from India and other places.

    ANS: True   PG: 437

8. Historically, emigration rates for India were especially low during times of major famine and epidemics.

    ANS: False   PG: 437   SOURCE: study guide

Population and Urbanization

9. Demographers use the term *emigration* to denote the entrance of individuals into a new country.

   ANS: False   PG: 437

10. Non-citizens of the United States serve in that country's military.

    ANS: True   PG: 438   SOURCE: new

11. Mexico is the country that attracts the greatest number of Americans living abroad.

    ANS: True   PG: 439   SOURCE: study guide; new

12. If the United States continues at its current rate of growth, its population will double in 76 years.

    ANS: True   PG: 441   SOURCE: new

13. The total population in the world reached one billion in 1492.

    ANS: False   PG: 441

14. Within the next 70 years, the U.S. population will increase to 1 billion.

    ANS: False   PG: 441

15. India's sex ratio is skewed in favor of males.

    ANS: True   PG: 442   SOURCE: study guide

16. The United States possesses an expansive population pyramid.

    ANS: False   PG: 443   SOURCE: new

17. Positive checks are factors that work to increase population size.

    ANS: False   PG: 445

Chapter 15

18. The Industrial Revolution was an event confined to the world's core economies.

    ANS: False   PG: 447   SOURCE: study guide

19. The East India Company possessed a private army larger in size than the British army.

    ANS: True   PG: 448

20. In India, female sterilization appears to be a major form of contraception.

    ANS: True   PG: 449   SOURCE: study guide

21. In India, almost all women are married by age 19.

    ANS: True   PG: 449

22. In India, total fertility has increased over the past four decades.

    ANS: False   PG: 449   SOURCE: study guide

23. The difference between birth and death rates is known as the demographic trap.

    ANS: False   PG: 450

24. Humans produce enough food each year to feed the world's population.

    ANS: True   PG: 451   SOURCE: study guide

25. New York, Los Angeles, and Chicago are considered mega cities.

    ANS: True   PG: 452   SOURCE: new

26. Bhopal, India, was the site of one of the worst industrial accidents in human history.

    ANS: True   PG: 453

27. MSA stands for Metropolitan Statistical Area.

    ANS: True   PG: 453

28. The New York metropolitan area is among the 30 largest economies in the world.

    ANS: True   PG: 454

29. India's equivalent of a nonmetropolitan area is the village, a settlement consisting of fewer than 5,000 people.

    ANS: True   PG: 454   SOURCE: new

30. The age-sex composition of a population helps demographer's predict birth, death, and migration rates.

    ANS: True   PG: 452   SOURCE: new

Concept Application (also in study guide)

Consider the concepts listed below. Match one or more of the concepts with each scenario. Explain your choices.

   a. Cohort
   b. Demographic trap
   c. Internal migration
   d. Migration
   e. Positive checks
   f. Pull factors
   g. Push factors
   h. Stationary pyramids
   i. Urbanization

Chapter 15

Scenario 1
"By 2025, over 1 billion people in Africa and southern Asia will live under conditions of water scarcity. Many North African and Middle Eastern countries are already faced with absolute water scarcity. In Jordan and Israel, over 3,000 people compete for every flow unit of renewable water. By 2025, virtually all North African countries will be faced with high levels of population pressure on their scarce water resources. And, except for Turkey, all of Western Asia will also experience the highest levels of water scarcity." (Falkenmark and Widstrand 1992:20)

ANS: B

Scenario 2
"The reality is of course that, since World War II, tens of millions of people have opted to leave the quiet of the countryside, either 'expelled' by drought, disease, or political strife or drawn by dreams broadcast over transistor radios. Some, like the half-million Guatemalan Indians who travel each winter with their wives and families to the Pacific lowlands to pick coffee and cotton or to cut sugarcane, do so in order to survive in their villages during the rest of the year. But for most, migration is a one-way experience because those who break with their families and communities, their traditional language, clothes, and food change too much to be able to return." (Riding 1986:8)

ANS: C, F,G, I

Scenario 3
The population pyramid for Denmark looks more like a rectangle than a pyramid. "Each cohort is about the same size as every other one because the birth rate and the death rate have been low and relatively constant for a long time. This means that each age group is about the same size at birth, and since relatively few people die before old age, the cohorts remain close in size until late in life when mortality rates must rise and eat away at the top of the rectangle." (McFalls 1991:22-23)

ANS: H

Scenario 4
"The villages were as quiet as death.... In one village, I remember we had as our guide a tall, middle-aged peasant who had blue eyes and a straw-colored beard.. . . He led us into timbered houses where Russian families were hibernating and waiting for death. In some of them, they had no food of any kind. There was one family I saw who left an indelible mark on my mind. The father and mother were lying on the floor when we entered and were almost too weak to rise. Some young children were on a bed above the stove, dying of hunger. " (Gibbs 1987:494)

ANS: E

Scenario 5

"The theme of this book is the lives and reactions of certain patients in a unique situation—and the implications which these hold out for medicine and science. These patients are among the few survivors of the great sleeping-sickness epidemic fifty years ago, and their reactions are those brought about by a remarkable new 'awakening' drug (L-Dopa). The lives and responses of these patients, which have no real precedent in the entire history of medicine, are presented in the form of extended case histories or biographies." (Sacks 1989:1)

ANS: A

Short Essay Questions

1. Why is India the focus of a chapter on population? How do China and the U.S. compare to India in terms of population size?

2. Distinguish between crude birth rate, age-sex specific birth rate, and total fertility rate.

3. How is population size determined? Explain.

4. Define crude death rate and infant mortality rate.

5. Why is India's mortality rate lower than the rate of the United States?

6. What are the various types of migration and immigration? What are push and pull factors?

7. What is doubling time? At what point in history did the world's population reach 1 billion? How long did it take to reach 2 billion? 3 billion? 6 billion?

8. How are labor intensive economies different from core economies?

9. Why is Stage I of the demographic transition called the stage of "high potential growth"?

10. According to the model of the demographic transition, which factors contributed to a decline in the death rate? To a rise and then an eventual decline in fertility?

11. Why does the demographic transition model not apply to India and other labor intensive countries?

12. What factors contribute to declines in total fertility? To what extent has India realized these factors?

13. What is a population pyramid? What shapes can it take?

14. When referring to countries, how is the dichotomy "industrialized—industrializing" misleading? What are more appropriate terms?

15. What is a demographic trap?

16. What is urbanization?

17. What is a mega city?

18. How does urbanization in labor-intensive poor countries differ from urbanization in core economies?

19. Distinguish among a central city, a suburb, and a nonmetropolitan area.

Comprehensive Essay Questions

1. Think about the composition of your extended family. How is its composition affected by birth (number and spacing of children), death (how and when someone dies), life expectancy, migration, and employment?

2. Compare and contrast the United States and India on the key demographic traits of births, deaths, migration, and population size.

Chapter 16

Social Change

Multiple-Choice Questions

1. _____ possesses the largest reservoir of freshwater on the planet.
   a. Greenland
   b. Antarctica
   c. Canada
   d. the United States

   ANS: B   PG: 459   TYP: knowledge   SOURCE: new

2. When studying a social change, sociologists ask
   a. Is social change good for society?
   b. How can we stop social change?
   c. Is social change necessary?
   d. What are consequences of change for social life?

   ANS: D   PG: 459   TYP: comprehension   SOURCE: study guide

3. The United States accounts for 4.6 percent of the world's population and contributes about _____ percent of Greenhouse gas emissions.
   a. 5
   b. 15
   c. 25
   d. 40

   ANS: C   PG: 459   TYP: knowledge   SOURCE: new

Chapter 16

4. A 2007 UN report announced that climate change can no longer be denied or doubted and that human activity since _____ has very likely caused the rise in the planet's temperatures.
    a. 1500
    b. 1750
    c. 1850
    d. 1950

    ANS: B   PG: 459   TYP: knowledge   SOURCE: new; study guide

5. _____ is any significant alteration, modification, or transformation in the organization and operation of social life.
    a. Globalization
    b. Scientific revolution
    c. Social change
    d. Global interdependence

    ANS: C   PG: 460   TYP: comprehension   SOURCE: study guide

6. The tipping point is
    a. sudden at first and then people adjust.
    b. a process by which people ignore change.
    c. gradual at first, but then reaches a critical point such that change becomes dramatic.
    d. something that cannot be observed.

    ANS: C   PG: 460   TYP: comprehension   SOURCE: new

7. The year 1971 was the first time in history that the U.S. turned to foreign sources of oil to meet it domestic consumption needs. That year is considered a
    a. a cultural lag
    b. a tipping point
    c. a social movement
    d. an anomaly

    ANS: B   PG: 460   TYP: application   SOURCE: new

8. Currently the U.S. produces about _____ of its domestic oil needs.
   a. 10
   b. 30
   c. 40
   d. 60

   ANS: C   PG: 461   TYP: knowledge   SOURCE: new

9. The most critical factor driving the industrial revolution was
   a. mechanization.
   b. the information explosion
   c. planned obsolescence.
   d. human muscle.

   ANS: A   PG: 461   TYP: comprehension   SOURCE: new; study guide

10. Approximately _____ percent of global oil production is needed to produce plastics and plastic-encased products?
    a. 1
    b. 8
    c. 15
    d. 25

    ANS: B   PG: 462   TYP: knowledge   SOURCE: new

11. _____ is a state in which the social, political, financial, and cultural lives of people are intertwined.
    a. Globalization
    b. Global interdependence
    c. Social change
    d. Diffusion

    ANS: B   PG: 462   TYP: comprehension

Chapter 16

12. _____ is a situation in which social activity, including social problems, transcends national borders
    a. Mechanization
    b. Globalization
    c. Urbanization
    d. Global interdependence

    ANS: D   PG: 462   TYP: comprehension   SOURCE: new

13. _____ is the ever increasing flow of goods, services, money, people, information, and culture across political borders.
    a. Mechanization
    b. Globalization
    c. Urbanization
    d. Global interdependence

    ANS: B   PG: 462   TYP: comprehension   SOURCE: new

14. _____ involves producing goods that are disposable after a single use, have a shorter life cycle than the industry is capable of producing, or go out of style quickly even though the goods can still serve their purpose.
    a. Mechanization
    b. Rationalization
    c. Planned obsolescence
    d. A tipping point

    ANS: C   PG: 464   TYP: comprehension   SOURCE: new; study guide

15. Sociologists Max Weber used the term _____ to refer to the way in which daily life is organized socially to accommodate large numbers of people.
    a. mechanization
    b. rationalization
    c. planned obsolescence
    d. tipping point

    ANS: B   PG: 463   TYP: comprehension   SOURCE: new

16. Most UPS employees are based in
    a. Europe.
    b. Japan.
    c. the United States.
    d. the Middle East.

    ANS: C   PG: 463   TYP: knowledge

17. To stay in "fashion" many people buy a new car even though their old car is still in excellent-to-good condition. Similarly, people tend to buy new clothes before they wear out the clothes they already have. Such actions speak to
    a. mechanization
    b. rationalization
    c. planned obsolescence
    d. a tipping point

    ANS: C   PG: 464   TYP: application   SOURCE: new

18. The principles efficiency, quantification/calculation, predictability, and control govern the organizational trend known as
    a. McDonaldization.
    b. planned obsolescence.
    c. tipping points.
    d. innovation.

    ANS: A   PG: 464   TYP: comprehension   SOURCE: new

19. A company maintains "We deliver within 30 minutes!" That company is applying which of the following McDonalization principles?
    a. efficiency
    b. quantification/calculation
    c. predictability
    d. control

    ANS: B   PG: 464   TYP: application   SOURCE: new; study guide

20. A company installs a soft drink dispenser that automatically shuts off after specified amount is delivered into a glass. That company is applying which one of the following McDonalization principles?
    a. efficiency
    b. quantification/calculation
    c. predictability
    d. control

    ANS: D   PG: 464   TYP: application   SOURCE: new

21. _____ is a transformative process in which people migrate from rural to urban areas and change the way they use land, interact, and make a living.
    a. McDonalization
    b. Urbanization
    c. Global interdependence
    d. Planned obsolescence

    ANS: B   PG: 464   TYP: comprehension   SOURCE: new

22. About 40 percent of the world's population lives in _____ environment.
    a. an urban
    b. a rural
    c. a suburban
    d. city

    ANS: A   PG: 465   TYP: comprehension   SOURCE: new

23. Highways and automobiles have created _____ and making it difficult to distinguish between city, suburbs, and nonurban environments
    a. urban sprawl
    b. planned obsolescence
    c. globalization
    d. an anomaly

    ANS: A   PG: 465   TYP: comprehension   SOURCE: new

24. Which analogy did sociologist Orrin Klapp use to describe the dilemma of sorting through and keeping up with the massive amount of information being generated?
    a. A sociologist drowning in quicksand.
    b. A student trying to take notes while 10 professors talk at one time.
    c. A researcher working on a gigantic jigsaw puzzle while additional pieces are flowing onto the table from a funnel overhead.
    d. A person entering a crowded six-lane highway with thousands of signs.

    ANS: C   PG: 466   TYP: comprehension   SOURCE: study guide

25. Sociologists Orrin Klapp used the jigsaw puzzle analogy to show that
    a. most people cannot possibly register all the messages they encounter during the day.
    b. the speed by which information is produced and distributed overwhelms the brain's capacity to organize and evaluate it.
    c. there are thousands of important newspapers, magazines, and journals that people will never have the time to read.
    d. people do not have the reading and writing skills to comprehend information.

    ANS: B   PG: 466   TYP: comprehension

26. Sociologists Orrin Klapp maintains that in the context of the information explosion, poor-quality information exists because
    a. no one pays attention.
    b. there is a dearth of feedback.
    c. the creators of this information lack basic research skills.
    d. few people are computer literate.

    ANS: B   PG: 467   TYP: comprehension

27. According to sociologist Orrin Klapp, the use of exaggerated headlines
    a. contributes to quick understanding of a topic.
    b. lures people into reading and listening.
    c. scares people away from investigating a problem.
    d. discourages our interest in a topic.

    ANS: B   PG: 466   TYP: knowledge

Chapter 16

28. Sociologist Orrin Klapp cites dearth of feedback as one factor in creating poor quality data. Dearth of feedback means
    a. readers are free to pick and choose the stories they wish to read.
    b. an unprecedented increase in the volume of data.
    c. publishers use eye-catching headlines, misleading titles, and shocking stories to attract potential readers' attention.
    d. not enough critical readers and listeners evaluate material before it is used by the popular media.

    ANS: D   PG: 467   TYP: comprehension

29. Which one of the following is an example of an improving innovation?
    a. cotton gin
    b. an upgrade to the personal computer's CPU
    c. steam engine
    d. a first generation PC

    ANS: B   PG: 467   TYP: comprehension

30. Revolutionary, unprecedented, or ground-breaking inventions that are the cornerstones for a wide range of applications are termed
    a. basic innovations.
    b. improving innovation.
    c. science.
    d. cultural inventions.

    ANS: A   PG: 467   TYP: comprehension

31. Improving innovations are _____ inventions.
    a. modifying
    b. revolutionary
    c. unprecedented
    d. ground-breaking

    ANS: A   PG: 467   TYP: comprehension

32. Each upgrade of a personal computer's CPU (central processing unit) represents a
    a. an invention
    b. a basic innovation
    c. an improving innovation
    d. a paradigm shift

    ANS: C   PG: 467   TYP: comprehension

33. Each "upgrade" of the 1903 Wright Flyer (the first successful airplane) increased the airplane's capacity to fly farther, higher, faster, and with more passengers. Upgrades are equivalent to
    a. an invention
    b. a basic innovation
    c. an improving innovation
    d. a paradigm shift

    ANS: C   PG: 467   TYP: application   SOURCE: new

34. Leslie White suggested that the number of inventions in the cultural base increased geometrically. A geometric increase is represented by the following:
    a. 2, 4, 6, 8, 10…
    b. 1, 2, 4, 8, 16, 32…
    c. 1, 2, 3, 4, 5…
    d. 10, 20, 30, 40, 50…

    ANS: B   PG: 468   TYP: comprehension

35. Anthropologist Leslie White maintained that inventions control people. He supported this conclusion with the argument that
    a. necessity is the mother of invention.
    b. when the cultural base is capable of supporting an invention that invention will come into being whether we want it or not.
    c. human beings have no free will.
    d. the best things in science are found because they are useful at the time.

    ANS: B   PG: 468   TYP: comprehension

Chapter 16

36. "We invent the automobile to get us between two points faster, and suddenly we find we have to build new roads. And that means we have to invent traffic regulations... and then we have to invent a whole new organization called the highway patrol." This assessment supports the idea that
    a. necessity is the mother of invention.
    b. if a new invention is to come into being, the cultural base must be large enough to support it.
    c. invention is the mother of necessity.
    d. if people have the power to create material innovations they also have the power to destroy them.

    ANS: C   PG: 469   TYP: comprehension   SOURCE: study guide

37. Leslie White maintains that if an invention is to come into being, the inventor must
    a. be a genius.
    b. invent something that people view as a necessity.
    c. have the ability to market the product.
    d. be born at the right place and time.

    ANS: D   PG: 469   TYP: comprehension

38. Inventors may be geniuses, but they also must be born in the right place and at the right time; this means that
    a. they must be born in a capitalist country free of government control.
    b. the society into which they are born must allow the masses access to education.
    c. they must live in a society with a cultural base sufficiently developed to support their invention.
    d. people must perceive their inventions as useful.

    ANS: C   PG: 469   TYP: comprehension

39. White argued that an invention will come into being when the cultural base is capable of supporting an invention. White supported this conclusion by pointing to the existence of
    a. simultaneous-independent inventions.
    b. collaborative research.
    c. the scientific method.
    d. patents.

    ANS: A   PG: 469   TYP: comprehension

40. _____ is a situation in which the same invention is created by two or more people working independently of one another at about the same time.
    a. Cultural diffusion
    b. A scientific revolution
    c. An improving invention
    d. A simultaneous-independent invention

    ANS: D   PG: 469   TYP: comprehension   SOURCE: study guide

41. The problem of managing nuclear waste is analogous to getting on a plane, and in mid-air asking the pilot: How are we going to land? This scenario speaks to the problem of
    a. paradigms.
    b. anomalies.
    c. cultural lag.
    d. improving innovations.

    ANS: C   PG: 469   TYP: application

42. Simultaneous-independent inventions are
    a. inventions created by two or more persons working independently of one another at about the same time.
    b. syntheses of existing inventions.
    c. modifications on existing inventions.
    d. revolutionary, unprecedented, ground-breaking inventions.

    ANS: A   PG: 469   TYP: comprehension

43. A technological determinist believes that human beings
    a. have free will.
    b. are controlled entirely by their material innovations.
    c. decide how to use their material innovations.
    d. adjust to new material innovations in predictable ways.

    ANS: B   PG: 469   TYP: comprehension

Chapter 16

44. Thomas Kuhn defines a paradigm as
    a. equivalent to a hypothesis.
    b. a trial and highly tentative idea.
    c. the dominant and widely accepted theories and concepts in a particular field of study.
    d. the most controversial theories and concepts within a discipline.

    ANS: C   PG: 470   TYP: comprehension

45. On the positive side, dominant paradigms
    a. are the glue that binds a group of people with common interests into a scientific community.
    b. are expansive thinking tools that broaden the kind of questions people ask.
    c. are threatened by anomalies.
    d. challenge theories most basis to a discipline.

    ANS: A   PG: 470   TYP: comprehension

46. The explanatory value and hence the status of a paradigm is threatened by the existence of an anomaly. An anomaly is
    a. a dominant and widely accepted theory.
    b. an observation that the paradigm cannot explain.
    c. a modification of a basic invention.
    d. a transformation of the social structure.

    ANS: B   PG: 470   TYP: comprehension

47. _____ is a term for that portion of nonmaterial culture that adjusts to material innovations.
    a. Cultural lag
    b. Improving innovation
    c. Technological determinant
    d. Adaptive culture

    ANS: D   PG:469   TYP: comprehension

48. _____ is the author of *The Structure of Scientific Revolution*.
   a. Thomas Kuhn
   b. Karl Marx
   c. Leslie White
   d. William F. Ogburn

   ANS: A   PG: 470   TYP: knowledge

49. When a new paradigm causes converts to see the world in an entirely new light and wonder how they could possibly have taken the old paradigm seriously, _____ has occurred.
   a. a scientific revolution
   b. innovation
   c. cultural lag
   d. adaptive reasoning

   ANS: A   PG: 470   TYP: comprehension   SOURCE: study guide

50. A scientific revolution occurs when
   a. the cultural base increases geometrically.
   b. an improving innovation emerges.
   c. the cultural base is sufficiently developed to support an invention.
   d. a new paradigm changes a discipline's elementary theoretical generalizations.

   ANS: D   PG: 470   TYP: comprehension

51. Copernicus upset the prevailing views at the time that humankind or the earth was the center of the universe, causing converts to see the world in an entirely new light and to wonder how they could possibly have taken the old paradigm seriously. This mind-altering experience is known as
   a. a scientific revolution.
   b. an anomaly.
   c. a reformist movement.
   d. a paradigm.

   ANS: A   PG: 470   TYP: application   SOURCE: new

52. "Of all discoveries and opinions, none may have exerted a greater effect on the human spirit than the doctrine of Copernicus. The world had scarcely become known as round and complete in itself when it was asked to waive the tremendous privilege of being the center of the universe. Never, perhaps, was a greater demand made on mankind—for by this admission so many things vanished in mist and smoke!" (Goethe 2004). This description describes
    a. a scientific revolution.
    b. an anomaly.
    c. a reformist movement.
    d. a paradigm.

    ANS: A   PG: 471   TYP: application   SOURCE: new

53. The internet began in the late 1960s linking four _____ together.
    a. military bases
    b. universities
    c. defense contractors
    d. generals

    ANS: B   PG: 471   TYP: knowledge

54. Perhaps the most outstanding feature of the internet is that it was designed to operate
    a. from a central command station in Washington.
    b. on solar power.
    c. automatically.
    d. absent a central control.

    ANS: D   PG: 471   TYP: knowledge   SOURCE: study guide

55. The invention of the internet is directly connected with which one of the following historical events?
    a. the Industrial Revolution
    b. the Cold War
    c. the information explosion
    d. World War I

    ANS: B   PG: 471   TYP: knowledge

56. During World War II hundred of thousands of soldiers were injured by machine gun shrapnel. The need to restore lost blood resulting from these injuries motivated doctors to create a system of collecting and preserving blood plasma. This dynamic supports the idea that
    a. power resides in the position of physician.
    b. conflict can lead to change.
    c. paradigm shifts help people to see the world in new ways.
    d. the actions of leaders influence who is in charge of a situation.

    ANS: B   PG: 571   TYP: application

57. World system theorists argue that the world-economy is essentially
    a. dominated by trade barriers.
    b. a myth.
    c. market socialism.
    d. capitalist driven.

    ANS: D   PG: 472   TYP: comprehension

58. Marx believed that _____ was the first economic system capable of maximizing the immense productive potential of human labor and ingenuity.
    a. the capitalist system
    b. socialism
    c. communism
    d. a centrally planned economy

    ANS: A   PG: 472   TYP: comprehension   SOURCE: study guide

59. A U.S. corporation contracts with computer programmers in India who work for *lower wages* than U.S.-based programmers to write software. The strategy represents
    a. creating a new product consumers' "need."
    b. lowering production costs by hiring employees who will work for lower wages.
    c. improving on an existing product.
    d. expanding the outer boundaries of the world economy.

    ANS: B   PG: 472   TYP: application

Chapter 16

60. Which one of the following theories influenced world system theorists to write about capitalism as the agent of change underlying global interdependence?
    a. Emile Durkheim
    b. Max Weber
    c. Karl Marx
    d. Immanuel Wallerstein

    ANS: C   PG: 472   TYP: comprehension

61. By the _____, the capitalist world-economy included virtually the whole inhabited earth.
    a. late 1600s
    b. early 17th century
    c. late 19th century
    d. mid-20th century

    ANS: C   PG: 472   TYP: knowledge

62. Karl Marx argued that _____ is a "boundless thirst...a werewolf-like hunger that takes no account of the health and length of life of the worker unless society forces it to do so."
    a. change
    b. globalization-from-below
    c. globalization-from-above
    d. the drive for profit

    ANS: D   PG: 472   TYP: comprehension

63. Immanuel Wallerstein is the sociologist associated with
    a. the development of hypertext.
    b. the Functionalist perspective.
    c. World Systems Theory.
    d. Resource Mobilization Theory.

    ANS: C   PG: 472   TYP: knowledge

64. _____ is formed when a substantial number of people organize to change, to resist change, or undo change in some area of society.
    a. A scientific revolution
    b. A social movement
    c. A basic innovation
    d. Resource mobilization

    ANS: B   PG: 472   TYP: comprehension

65. A social movement depends on three conditions. Which one of the following is not one of those conditions?
    a. an actual or imagined condition that enough people find objectionable
    b. a shared belief that something needs to be done about this condition
    c. some organized effort aimed at attracting supporters, articulating the problem, and defining a strategy
    d. enough financial support to get the movement off the ground

    ANS: D   PG: 474   TYP: comprehension   SOURCE: study guide

66. A _____ social movement seeks broad, sweeping and radical structural changes to a society's basic social institutions.
    a. reformist
    b. revolutionary
    c. counter revolutionary
    d. regressive

    ANS: B   PG: 473   TYP: comprehension

67. _____ targets some specific feature of society as needing change.
    a. Regressive
    b. Reformist
    c. Revolutionary
    d. Counter-revolutionary

    ANS: B   PG: 581   TYP: comprehension

Chapter 16

68. Objective deprivation is a term that applies to those who are
    a. the worst off or most disadvantaged.
    b. in the middle class.
    c. underemployed.
    d. the most advantaged.

    ANS: A   PG: 474   TYP: comprehension

69. Tyrone earns an annual income of $100,000. His friends earn between $300,000 and $500,000 a year. Tyrone feels left out because he cannot afford the kind of cars his friends drive. Tyrone is experiencing
    a. objective deprivation.
    b. relative deprivation.
    c. regressive thoughts.
    d. a feeling of being an anomaly.

    ANS: B   PG: 474   TYP: comprehension

70. Relative deprivation is a condition that is measured by
    a. the scientific method.
    b. objective standards.
    c. comparing one group's situation to another more advantaged group.
    d. impartial analysis of one's situation compared to the worst off.

    ANS: C   PG: 474   TYP: comprehension

71. Every authority structure contains at least two groups:
    a. the power elite and the masses.
    b. the bourgeoisie and the proletariat.
    c. those with charismatic authority, who lead by virtue of their personality, and those with legal-rational authority, who lead according to the rules.
    d. those with power who have an interest in preserving the system; those without power who have an intent in changing it.

    ANS: D   PG: 474   TYP: comprehension

72. According to sociologist Ralf Dahrendorf, the structural origins of conflict can be traced to
    a. the nature of authority relations.
    b. decision-making powers of the power elite.
    c. invention and innovation.
    d. workers' demands for higher wages.

    ANS: A   PG: 474   TYP: comprehension

73. Vaclav Havel, the president of the Czech Republic, believes that _____ may have played an important role in causing the revolutions in central Europe.
    a. Chernobyl
    b. the fall of the Berlin Wall
    c. the WIPP project
    d. the collapse of the Soviet Union

    ANS: A   PG: 475   TYP: knowledge

74. Which one of the following groups is most likely to join a social movement to address their situation?
    a. the objectively deprived
    b. the relatively deprived
    c. the world's poorest peoples
    d. oil executives

    ANS: B   PG: 474   TYP: comprehension

75. Ralf Dahrendorf wrote "It is immeasurably difficult to trace the path on which a person…encounters other people just like himself, and at a certain point says 'Let us join hands, friends, so that no-one will push us off one by one.'" Dahrendorf was writing about
    a. globalization-from-above.
    b. social movements.
    c. globalization-from-below.
    d. the Chernobyl meltdown.

    ANS: B   PG: 474   TYP: application   SOURCE: study guide

76. _____ theorists maintain that a core group of sophisticated strategists is key to getting a social movement off the ground.
    a. Social change
    b. Cultural diffusion
    c. World system
    d. Resource mobilization

    ANS: D   PG: 475   TYP: comprehension

77. The anticipated economic boom associated with a lengthened shipping season (once four months long and now eight months long due to climate change) allowing goods to move into and out of Greenland is a
    a. manifest function
    b. latent function
    c. manifest dysfunction
    d. latent dysfunction

    ANS: A   PG: 476   TYP: application   SOURCE: new

78. The unexpected emergence of a working alliance between Inuit Greenlanders and tropical island peoples, both of whom face cultural extinction from rising sea levels associated with climate change is a
    a. manifest function
    b. latent function
    c. manifest dysfunction
    d. latent dysfunction

    ANS: B   PG: 476   TYP: application   SOURCE: new

79. The anticipated consequences of a growing tourism industry associated with climate change such that the number of tourists visiting Greenland each year overwhelms the resident population of towns visited is a
    a. manifest function
    b. latent function
    c. manifest dysfunction
    d. latent dysfunction

    ANS: C   PG: 476   TYP: application   SOURCE: new

80. A _____ of climate change is a growing interest in Greenland, the Arctic, and Antarctica such that popular films are set in or give prominent attention to these locations
    a. manifest function
    b. latent function
    c. manifest dysfunction
    d. latent dysfunction

    ANS: B   PG: 476   TYP: application   SOURCE: new; study guide

81. A _____ connected to climate change in Greenland is the loss of status among Inuit elders who can no longer predict the weather.
    a. manifest function
    b. latent function
    c. manifest dysfunction
    d. latent dysfunction

    ANS: D   PG: 476   TYP: application   SOURCE: new

82. Which one of the following theorists would ask "Who benefits from climate change, and at whose expense?
    a. functionalists
    b. conflict theorists
    c. symbolic interactionists
    d. structural strain theorists

    ANS: B   PG: 476   TYP: comprehension   SOURCE : new

83. In study the effects of climate change on Greenland, _____ key in on the many industries that have moved operations to Greenland to exploit the territory for commercial interests.
    a. functionalists
    b. conflict theorists
    c. symbolic interactionists
    d. structural strain theorists

    ANS: B   PG: 476   TYP: application   SOURCE: new

Chapter 16

84. _____ are particularly interested in ways climate change is affecting interaction among Greenlanders.
   a. Functionalists
   b. Conflict theorists
   c. Symbolic interactionists
   d. Structural strain theorists

   ANS: C   PG: 476   TYP: comprehension   SOURCE: new

85. One effect of climate change in Greenland is gradual extinction of marine species which disrupts or destroys the Inuit hunting—and, by extension, their eating—habits. This change directly affects the Inuit's way of life or
   a. paradigm.
   b. culture.
   c. innovation.
   d. cultural lag.

   ANS: B   PG: 477   TYP: comprehension   SOURCE: new

86. Sociologists use the term _____ to describe a group with which people identify and to which they feel closely attached—particularly when that attachment is founded on opposition to another group
   a. primary group
   b. ingroup
   c. outgroup
   d. secondary group

   ANS: B   PG: 477   TYP: comprehension   SOURCE: new; study guide

87. An _____ is a group toward which people feel a sense of separateness, opposition, or even hatred.
   a. primary group
   b. ingroup
   c. outgroup
   d. secondary group

   ANS: C   PG: 477   TYP: comprehension   SOURCE: new

88. Climate change is fueling the emergence of two opposing groups (an ingroup and an outgroup). Those groups are
    a. Arctic peoples/tropical islanders versus people who live in highest greenhouse gas producing societies.
    b. capitalists versus ecotourists.
    c. cold weather versus warm weather peoples.
    d. wind versus solar power users.

    ANS: A   PG: 477   TYP: comprehension   SOURCE: new

89. Sociologists look to identify the scarce resources that pulled Greenlanders into the global division of labor. From the 16th through the late 19th centuries that resource was
    a. oil, extracted from the ground.
    b. oil, extracted from whales.
    c. rubber.
    d. ivory.

    ANS: B   PG: 478   TYP: knowledge   SOURCE: new; study guide

90. _____ are viewed as coordinating mechanisms, because they bring together people, resources, and technology and then channel social activity toward achieving a specific outcome.
    a. Ingroups
    b. Outgroups
    c. Formal organizations
    d. Paradigms

    ANS: C   PG: 479   TYP: comprehension   SOURCE: new

91. The government of Greenland joined with four large corporations—Air Greenland, KNI, Royal Greenland, and Greenland Tourism and Business—to create an export promotion strategy and an international branding strategy for the country. Sociologists classify such corporations as
    a. formal organizations.
    b. voluntary associations.
    c. paradigms.
    d. Informal organizations.

    ANS: A   PG: 479   TYP: application   SOURCE: new

Chapter 16

92. During the 17th, 18th, and 19th centuries, European and American whalers killed tens of thousands of whales in Arctic waters for commercial purposes, with little effective resistance from environmental or animal rights groups. Today whaling is a highly monitored activity subject to quotas. This change in reaction to whaling suggests that
    a. behavior considered deviant at one time and place may not be considered deviant at another.
    b. people have consistent ideas about what is considered deviant.
    c. something is deviant only if it considered deviant across time and place.
    d. Native people who still whale should be punished.

    ANS: A   PG: 479   TYP: comprehesion   SOURCE: new

93. From a global perspective people who live in _____ have the lowest access to sustainable water, with the equivalent of 2,640 gallons available to each person each year.
    a. Kuwait
    b. United States
    c. Canada
    d. Greenland

    ANS: A   PG: 480   TYP: knowledge   SOURCE: new; study guide

94. Sociologists define _____ as a critical set of potential social advantages, including everything from the chances that a person will survive through the first year of life to the chances that a person will live a long life.
    a. social status
    b. life chances
    c. rationalization
    d. an anomaly

    ANS: B   PG: 480   TYP: comprehension   SOURCE: new

95. The 500-600 Danish civilians who work at the U.S. Thule Air Base in Greenland are most likely to work as
    a. computer analysts.
    b. truck drivers
    c. cooks
    d. d   snow plow operators

    ANS: A   PG: 481   TYP: comprehension   SOURCE: new

96. The Inuit Greenlander civilians who work at the U.S. Thule Base in Greenland are most likely to work
    a. computer analysts
    b. weather specialists
    c. truck drivers
    d. therapists

    ANS: C   PG: 480   TYP: comprehension   SOURCE: new

97. The sex ratio imbalance in Greenland favoring males is likely caused by
    a. immigration patterns
    b. lack of employment opportunities.
    c. the extreme cold weather environment.
    d. the higher cultural value placed on women.

    ANS: A   PG: 482   TYP: comprehension   SOURCE: new

98. Sociologists expect that climate change will affect the Greenland's sex ratio in which one of the following ways?
    a. an increasing imbalance favoring females.
    b. an increasing imbalance favoring males.
    c. a sex ratio with men equal in numbers to women.
    d. an increasing imbalance favoring females in most age categories.

    ANS: B   PG: 482   TYP: comprehension   SOURCE: new

99. The few people who occupy such lofty positions in the social structure of leading institutions that their decisions affect millions, even billions, of people worldwide are known as
    a. the bourgeoise.
    b. proletariat.
    c. power elite.
    d. bureaucrats.

    ANS: C   PG: 482   TYP: comprehension   SOURCE: new

Chapter 16

100. The origins of U.S. military presence in Greenland can be traced to which one of the following conflicts/wars?
    a. September 11
    b. War on Terrorism
    c. World War I
    d. World War II

    ANS: D   PG: 482   TYP: knowledge   SOURCE: new

101. The Distance Early Warning line, a radar and satellite system in place to warn of an impending ballistic missile attack against North America,
    a. stretches from Alaska through northern Canada to Greenland.
    b. stretches through Russia and into Greenland.
    c. is located exclusively in Greenland.
    d. is located along the U.S. Canada border.

    ANS: A   PG: 482   TYP: knowledge   SOURCE: new; study guide

102. Sociologists would predict that as Greenland opens its borders to various foreign corporations total fertility will
    a. continue to decline further.
    b. start to decline.
    c. increase.
    d. remain the same

    ANS: A   PG: 483   TYP: comprehension   SOURCE: new

103. _____ is the average number of live children women bear in their lifetime.
    a. The crude birth rate
    b. The age-specific birth rate
    c. Total fertility
    d. Family size

    ANS: C   PG: 482   TYP: comprehension   SOURCE: new

104. _____ about Greenland occurs when audiences who do not consciously seek out stories on Greenland are exposed to related news stories.
    a. Informal education
    b. Formal education
    c. Schooling
    d. Hidden curriculum

    ANS: A   PG: 482   TYP: application   SOURCE: new

105. When audiences hear on the nightly news that Santa Claus has left his North Pole home and is crossing Greenland and heading to the United States to deliver presents, they come to associate Greenland with the North Pole. This kind of learning process is known as
    a. informal education
    b. formal education
    c. schooling
    d. hidden curriculum

    ANS: A   PG: 483   TYP: application   SOURCE: new

106. The major religions of Greenland are
    a. Islam and Catholic.
    b. Lutheran Christianity and shamanism.
    c. Protestant and Catholic.
    d. Buddhism and Catholic.

    ANS: B   PG: 483   TYP: knowledge   SOURCE: new

107. Greenland is a former colony of the
    a. the United States.
    b. Russia.
    c. Denmark.
    d. Canada.

    ANS: C   PG: 484   TYP: knowledge   SOURCE: new

Chapter 16

108. The Inuit do not build sacred buildings known as churches. They consider nature sacred and themselves as children of nature. For the Inuit everything has a soul and is spiritually connected. The universe is in harmony, and the powers of nature are neutral toward humans. When evil (which can take such forms as bad hunting, bad weather, or illness) occurs, the source is almost always people's bad behavior. This description corresponds to which one of the following religions?
    a. Buddhism
    b. Islam
    c. Lutheran Christianity
    d. Shamanism

    ANS: D   PG: 484   TYP: application   SOURCE: new

109. Entering the term "global warming" into the search engine Google yields 7.6 million sites, with Wikipedia listed first. It would take a reader about ____ years to review just the titles (assuming the reader could process a title every second).
    a. 10 days
    b. 6 months
    c. 2 years
    d. 10 years

    ANS: C   PG: 484   TYP: knowledge   SOURCE: new

110. Which one of the following statements best describes the plight of polar bears in connection to global warming?
    a. Polar bears are stranded on ice floes with nowhere to go.
    b. The number of polar bears have increased due to warming climate.
    c. The polar bears of Greenland are migrating to Canada.
    d. Polar bears must make riskier and longer swims to reach a solid platform.

    ANS: D   PG: 484   TYP: knowledge   SOURCE: new

111. With regard to climate change, there appear to be two opposing camps both of which agree
    a. that the planet is warming, that ice sheets are melting, and that greenhouse gas emissions have risen.
    b. that the climate change is man-made.
    c. that the climate change is part of a natural cycle.
    d. that Greenhouse gases are dangerous.

    ANS: A   PG: 485   TYP: knowledge   SOURCE: new

112. With which one of the following are the 1,250 authors and 2,500 scientists involved with the UN report Climate Change report likely to be affiliated?
    a. Conoco Phillips
    b. the airlines, hotels, rental cars, and cruise line industries.
    c. a city attorney.
    d. National Center for Atmospheric Research

    ANS: D   PG: 485   TYP: comprehension   SOURCE: new

113. Signers of the Petition Web project, a group that believes climate change is part of natural weather patterns rather than increased fossil fuel use, would likely be associated with which on of the following?
    a. Conoco Phillips
    b. Netherlands Environmental Assessment Agency
    c. Canadian Centre for Climate Modeling and Analysis.
    d. National Center for Atmospheric Research

    ANS: A   PG: 485   TYP: comprehension   SOURCE : new; study guide

Multiple-Choice Questions on the Web

1. _____ is a situation in which a previously rare or seemingly rare event, response, or opinion becomes dramatically more common.
    a. Cultural lag
    b. A tipping point
    c. A social movement
    d. An anomaly

    ANS: B   PG: 460   TYP: comprehension   SOURCE: new

2. A hydrocarbon society is one in which the use of _____ shapes virtually every aspect of human personal and social life.
    a. mechanization
    b. metals
    c. minerals
    d. fossil fuels

    ANS: D   PG: 461   TYP: comprehension   SOURCE: new

3. Refrigerators, ovens, washers, and dryers built since 2000 are expected to last 8–12 years, while those built in the 1970s and 1980s lasted 20 years or more. This shift in product life is an example of
   a. Mechanization
   b. Rationalization
   c. Planned obsolescence
   d. A tipping point

   ANS: C   PG: 464   TYP: application   SOURCE: new

4. Pharmacies, banks, and car wash have adopted "drive-thru" services to facilitate their goal of moving customers from one state of being to another quickly. This strategy speaks to which one of the following McDonaldization principles
   a. efficiency
   b. quantification/calculation
   c. predictability
   d. control

   ANS: A   PG: 464   TYP: application   SOURCE: new

5. Leslie White maintains that _____ is tied to the size of the cultural base.
   a. the rate of cultural diffusion
   b. scientific progress
   c. the rate of change
   d. a population's openness to new ideas

   ANS: C   PG: 468   TYP: comprehension

6. "The internet presents a whole new way of thinking about information." This statement reflects the dynamics of
   a. an anomaly.
   b. a scientific revolution.
   c. a paradigm.
   d. a cultural lag.

   ANS: B   PG:470   TYP: application

Social Change

7. A _____ social movement seeks to turn back the hands of time to an earlier condition or state of being.
   a. reformist
   b. revolutionary
   c. counter revolutionary
   d. regressive

   ANS: D   PG: 472   TYP: comprehension

8. A _____ would ask "What are the anticipated and unintended consequences of climate change on Greenland?"
   a. functionalist
   b. conflict theorist
   c. symbolic interactionist
   d. structural strain theorist

   ANS: A   PG: 476   TYP: comprehension   SOURCE: new

9. From a global perspective, people who live in _____ have the greatest access to sustainable water— the equivalent of 2.8 billion gallons available to each person each year.
   a. Kuwait
   b. United States
   c. Canada
   d. Greenland

   ANS: D   PG: 480   TYP: knowledge   SOURCE: new

10. In Greenland the only age category in which females outnumber males is
    a. 0-6 years
    b. 15-17 years
    c. 25-59 years
    d. 67 and older.

    ANS: D   PG: 482   TYP: comprehension   SOURCE: new

True/False Questions

1. Greenland is the region of the world known as the Arctic.

   ANS: True   PG: 459   SOURCE: new

Chapter 16

2. Since 1900 humans have burned fossil fuels to transport people and goods (among other things)

   ANS: False   PG: 459   SOURCE: study guide; new

3. The sociological concept tipping point is borrowed from physics.

   ANS: True   PG: 460   SOURCE: new

4. There has never been a time in U.S. history where the country produced more oil domestically than it consumed

   ANS: False   PG: 460   SOURCE: new

5. Sociologists are in agreement that globalization was triggered by the invention of the printing press.

   ANS: False   PG: 462   SOURCE: new

6. "Earn a college degree in 24 months" falls under the McDonaldization principle of quantification.

   ANS: True   PG: 464   SOURCE: new

7. The definition of what is "urban" is consistent across countries.

   ANS: False   PG: 465   SOURCE: new

8. The internet has the potential to give users access to every word, image, and sound that has ever been recorded.

   ANS: True   PG: 466   SOURCE: new

9. Each upgrade of a personal computer's CPU represents a basic innovation.

   ANS: False   PG: 467

10. Conflict is a key trigger of social change.

    ANS: True   PG: 467   SOURCE: study guide; new

11. Geometric expansion can be represented by the following sequence: 1, 2, 4, 8, 16, 32...

    ANS: True   PG: 468   SOURCE: study guide

12. The size of the cultural base determines the rate of change.

    ANS: True   PG: 468

13. The concept of simultaneous independent inventions proves that an invention or creation depends on a single inventor to come into being.

    ANS: False   PG: 469

14. From a sociological point of view, invention is the mother of necessity.

    ANS: True   PG: 469   SOURCE: study guide

15. A technological determinist believes that humans have control over their material innovations.

    ANS: False   PG: 469

16. An anomaly supports an existing paradigm.

    ANS: False   PG: 470

17. From a sociological point of view, the most significant scientific advances are made when someone breaks away from a prevailing paradigm.

    ANS: True   PG: 470

18. Some inventions, such as the bicycle, generate no conflict in society.

    ANS: False   PG: 471   SOURCE: study guide

19. Conflict is both a cause and consequence of social change.

    ANS: True   PG: 471

20. It seems that any kind of social change has the potential to trigger conflict.

    ANS: True   PG: 471

21. In a capitalist system profit is the most important measure of success…

    ANS: True   PG: 472   SOURCE: study guide

22. Capitalist responses to economic stagnation and downturn helped to create a global network of economic relationships.

    ANS: True   PG: 472   SOURCE: study guide

23. Revolutionary movements seek to turn back the hands of time to an earlier condition or "golden era."

    ANS: False   PG: 473

24. Objective deprivation is a condition that applies to those who are the worst off or most disadvantaged.

    ANS: True   PG: 474

25. Research on social movements shows that the most objectively disadvantaged people join social movements to change their condition.

    ANS: False   PG: 474   SOURCE: study guide

Social Change

26. The relatively deprived are less likely than the objectively deprived to form or join social movements to address their conditions.

   ANS: False   PG: 474

27. For a conflict perspective, corporations and their customers will benefit from the effects of climate change on Greenland at the expense of Greenland's native peoples.

   ANS: True   PG: 476   SOURCE: study guide; new

28. One person's ingroup in another person's outgroup

   ANS: True   PG: 477   SOURCE: new

29. Greenland was once a colony of Denmark.

   ANS: True   PG: 480   SOURCE: study guide

30. The climate change debates centers around whether global warming is man-made or part of the natural changes in climate.

   ANS: True   PG 485   SOURCE: study guide

Concept Application (also in study guide)

Consider the concepts listed below. Match one of more of the concepts with each scenario. Explain your choices.

   a. Globalization
   b. Paradigms
   c. Planned obsolescence
   d. Scientific revolution
   e. Technological determinism

Chapter 16

Scenario 1

"It is difficult to recapture the medical world of 1800; it was a world of thought structured around assumptions so fundamental that they were only occasionally articulated as such, yet assumptions alien to a twentieth-century medical understanding.... The body was seen as a system of intake and outgo, a system that had to remain in balance if the individual were to remain healthy.... Equilibrium was synonymous with health, disequilibrium with illness.... The physician's most effective weapon was his ability to 'regulate the secretions' to extract blood, to promote the perspiration, the urination, or defecation that attested to his having helped the body regain is customary equilibrium." (Rosenberg 1987:71-72)

ANS: B

Scenario 2

Of course, Federal Express is our largest business unit by far. It is quite simply, the largest global express transportation network ever assembled. On our first night of operations - back in April of 1973 - we delivered just 186 packages to 25 U.S. cities, using a fleet of 14 small Falcon jets. Twenty-five years later, FedEx delivers about 3 million shipments every business day to 211 countries that generate better than 90 percent of the world's GDP. The Federal Express workforce has grown to about 142,000 employees.... FedEx has the largest commercial cargo fleet in the world, with 615 aircraft, and about 100 more on order. That ranks us as the fourth largest airline worldwide - not just in the cargo industry, but among passenger airlines as well. In addition, the FedEx ground network includes about 42,000 trucks and vans, which are linked back into our data network to provide real-time information, from pick-up to delivery. And by utilizing one of the largest interactive computer networks in the world, better than 60 percent of all FedEx transactions are now handled electronically. (Smith 1998)

ANS: A

Scenario 3

"In public discussions of biotechnology today, the idea of improving the human race by artificial means is widely condemned. The idea is repugnant because it conjures up visions of Nazi doctors sterilizing Jews and killing defective children. There are many good reasons for condemning enforced sterilization and euthanasia. But the artificial improvement of human beings will come, one way or another, whether we like it or not, as soon as the progress of biological understanding makes it possible. When people are offered technical means to improve themselves and their children, no matter what they conceive improvement to mean, the offer will be accepted. Improvement may mean better health, longer life, a more cheerful disposition, a stronger heart, a smarter brain, the ability to earn more money as a rock star or baseball player or business executive. The technology of improvement may be hindered or delayed by regulation, but it cannot be permanently suppressed. Human improvement, like abortion today, will be officially disapproved, legally discouraged, or forbidden, but widely practiced. It will be seen by millions of citizens as a liberation from past constraints and injustices. Their freedom to choose cannot be permanently denied." (Dyson 1997:49)

ANS: E

Scenario 4

"Thomas Kuhn's seminal work, *The Structure of Scientific Revolutions*, affected working scientists as deeply as it moved those scholars who scrutinize what we do. Before Kuhn, most scientists followed the place-a-stone-in-the-bright-temple-of-knowledge tradition, and would have told you that they hoped, above all, to lay many of the bricks, perhaps even the keystone, of truth's temple, the addictive or meliorists model of scientific progress. Now most scientists of vision hope to forment revolution." (Gould 1987: 27)

ANS: B, D

Scenario 5

"In the 1930s an enterprising engineer working for General Electric proposed increasing sales of flashlight lamps by increasing their efficiency and shortening their life. Instead of lasting through three batteries he suggested that each lamp last only as long as one battery. In 1934 speakers at the Society of Automotive Engineers meetings proposed limiting the life of automobiles. These examples and others are cited in Vance Packard's classic book The Waste Makers." (Beder 1998)

ANS: C

Short Essay Questions

1. Why is Greenland the focus on the chapter on social change?

2. What is social change? Why are sociologists interested in tipping points?

3. What questions do sociologists ask when they study social change?

4. What has changed since 1750? Why is 1750 and important date?

5. What about industrialization and mechanization has contributed to fossil fuel dependence?

6. Distinguish between global interdependence and globalization. How are they connected to fossil fuel dependence?

7. What is rationalization and value-rational thought? How have the two contributed to fossil fuel dependence?

8. What is McDonalization? How has it contributed to fossil fuel dependence?

9. What is urbanization? How has it contributed to fossil fuel dependence?

10. What is the information explosion? What technological innovations are responsible for this phenomenon?

11. What factors does Orrin Klapp identify as the causes underlying distorted, exaggerated presentation of information?

12. When thinking about social change, why is it difficult to pinpoint a single cause of change?

13. What is an innovation? Distinguish between basic and improving innovations. What makes an innovation sociologically significant?

14. What is the cultural base? How is the rate of change tied to the size of the cultural base?

15. What is cultural lag? Why did Ogburn emphasize the material component of culture in this theory of cultural lag?

16. Is Ogburn a technological determinist? Why or why not?

17. Ogburn maintains that one of the most urgent challenges facing people today is adapting to material innovations. Does the work of Leslie White lend support to Ogburn's thesis? Why or why not?

18. How does Kuhn define a paradigm?

19. According to Thomas Kuhn, is science simply an evolutionary process? Why or why not? Under what conditions are paradigms threatened? When does a scientific revolution occur?

20. How is conflict both a cause and an effect of social change?

21. Describe the essential dynamics of the Cold War and how those dynamics are connected with the development of the internet.

22. From a world system perspective, how has capitalism come to dominate the global network of economic relationships?

23. What is a social movement? What conditions are necessary for social movements to occur?

24. What are the types of social movements? Give a brief description of each.

25. Distinguish between objective and relative deprivation. How are these concepts related to social movements?

26. What are the three stages in the life of a social movement?

Chapter 16

27. What kinds of social interactions give insights into climate change's effect on Greenland?

28. How do sociologists use the three theoretical perspectives to frame a discussion about Greenland and climate change

29. How is the culture of Greenland's Inuit and of other Artic peoples changing because of climate change?

30. How do ingroup and outgroup memberships related to climate change shape identity?

31. What social forces bring Greelanders into interaction with outsiders and shape the relationship between the two groups?

32. Because of climate change, what new formal organizations have emerged in Greenland?

33. How do ideas about what constitutes deviance relate to outsiders' interest or lack of interest in Greenland?

34. How is climate change shaping life chances in Greenland and elsewhere?

35. What is the sex composition of Greenland? How might it be affected by climate change?

36. How did the U.S. military-industrial complex pull Greenland into the international arena?

37. How might climate change affect Greenland's fertility rate?

38. What are formal and informal ways outsiders are coming to learn about Greenland, other Arctic cultures, and climate change?

39. What religions did outsiders bring to Greenland?

40. What is the population size of Greenland, and is the population increasing or decreasing because of climate change?

41. In light of the information explosion, how does one identify credible sources about climate change?

Comprehensive Essay Questions

1. What are the major factors that cause something in society to change?

2. Identify a social change that has occurred in your lifetime. What sociological concepts can you draw upon to help you explain that change and its consequences?

Scenario References

Chapter 1

Bearak, Barry. 2002. "Children as Barter in a Famished Land." *The New York Times* (March 8):A1.

Brune, Adrian. 2004. "Baltimore Judge's Suicide Leaves Friends Puzzled." *Washington Blade* www.washingtonblade.com.

Harrison, Paul. 1988. *Inside the Third World: The Anatomy of Poverty*, 2nd ed. New York. Viking Penguin.

Moore, Brenda L. 1996. Review of *Black Soldiers in Jim Crow Texas 1899-1917*, by Garna L. Christian. *Contemporary Sociology* 25(4):478-79.

Rayburn, Kelly and Angela Hill. 2007. "Suicide Note Pins Blame on Family's Failing Finances." *Inside Bay Area* (June 21). www.insidebayarea.com.

Rupp, Allison. 2007. "Shortage grows in Casper." *Jackson Hole Star-Tribune* (June 21). http://www.jacksonholestartrib.com/articles/2007/06/21/

Shields, David. 2002. "Foreign Guys Can Shoot." *The New York Times Magazine* (March 3): 56-57.

Chapter 2

Haub, Carl and Machiko Yanagishita. 1994. *1994 World Population Data Sheet*. Washington, DC: Population Reference Bureau.

Herzog, Sergio. 2003. "Does the Ethnicity of Offenders in Crime Scenarios Affect Public Perceptions of Crime Seriousness? A Randomized Survey Experiment in Israel." *Social Forces* 82:2(757).

Light, Ivan and Edna Bonacich. 1988. *Immigrant Entrepreneurs: Koreans in Los Angeles 1965-1982*. Los Angeles: University of California Press.

Murray, Thomas H. 1990. "The Poisoned Gift: AIDS and Blood." *The Milbank Quarterly* 68(2):205-25.

Samora, Julian, Lyle Saunders, and Richard F. Larson. 1965. "Medical Vocabulary Knowledge Among Hospital Patients." Pp. 278-91 in *Social Interaction and Patient Care* edited by J. K. Skipper, Jr. and R. C. Leonard. Philadelphia: Lippincott.

U.S. Department of State. 2004. "Background Notes: Mexico" www.state.gov.

Chapter 3

Fulbright, Leslie. 2004. "East Bay Black Biker Clubs Rev in a New Era. Not All Members Ride Harleys, Some Even Wear Heels." *The Chronicle* (December 19).

Haub, Carl and Machiko Yanagishita. 1994. *1994 World Population Data Sheet*. Washington, DC: Population Reference Bureau.

Hogan, Mary Ann. 1994. "The Joy of Crying." *Los Angeles Times* (February 1):E1+.

Japan Information Center. 1988. *What I Want to Know about Japan*. New York: Consulate General of Japan.

Koehler, Nancy. 1986. "Re-Entry Shock." Pp. 89-94 in *Cross-Cultural Reentry: A Book of Readings* Abilene, TX: Abilene Christian University.

U.S. Department of State. 2004. "Background Note" www.state.gov

Chapter 4

Hafezi, Parisa. 2005. "Iranian Hardliners Register as Suicide Bombers." Reuters Foundation. http://www.alertnet.org/thenews.

Haub, Carl and Machiko Yanagishita. 1994. *1994 World Population Data Sheet*. Washington, DC: Population Reference Bureau.

Lidz, Theodore. 1976. *The Person: His and Her Development Throughout the Life Cycle*. New York: Basic Books.

Mura, David. 1996. *Where Body Meets Memory*. New York: Anchor.

Rabin, Yitzhak. 1993. "Making a New Middle East. 'Shalom, Salaam, Peace.' Views of Three Leaders." *Los Angeles Times* (September 14):A7.

Vaughn, Diane. 1996. *The Challenger Launch*. Chicago: University of Chicago.

Zajonc, Arthur. 1993. "Seeing the Light." *Los Angeles Times Magazine* (July 25):22-25.

Chapter 5

Gallagher, Hugh. 1992. *NPR* "Morning Edition." (July 3).

Marcus, Amy. 2002. "When Janie Came Marchin Home." *The New York Times* (March 23):A17.

Nelson, James Lindemann and Hilde Lindemann. 1996. *Alzheimer's: Answers to Hard Questions for Families*. New York: Doubleday.

Stolberg, Sheryl. 1994. "Doctors' Dilemma." *Los Angeles Times* (April 5):E1+.

Chapter 6

Anderson, Patricia. 1991. *Affairs in Order: A Complete Resource Guide to Death and Dying*. New York: Macmillan.

Dyer, Gwynne. 1985. *War*. New York: Crown.

Ohmae, Kenichi. 1990. *The Borderless World: Power and Strategy in the Interlinked Economy*. New York: Harper Business.

Tucker, James. 1993. "Everyday Forms of Employee Resistance." *Sociological Forum* 8(1):25-45.

UFCW Action. 1993. "The Boss Is Watching." *Utne Reader* (May/June):134-35.

Wright, Lesley and Marti Smye. 1996. *Corporate Abuse*. New York: Macmillan.

Chapter 7

Chayet, Neil. 1983. "Law and Morality." Pp. 418-19 in *Life Studies: A Thematic Reader*, edited by D. Cavitch. New York: St. Martin's.

Dunne, John Gregory. 1991. "Law and Disorder in Los Angeles." *The New York Review of Books* (October 10): 23-29.

Dunne, John Gregory. 1991b. "Law and Disorder in Los Angeles." *The New York Review of Books* (October 24):62-70.

Janofsky, Michael. 1994. "Antismoking Forces at the Barricades? Bring 'em On!" *The New York Times* (April 24):8.

Levine, Dennis B. and William Hoffer. 1991. *Inside Out: An Insider's Account of Wall Street*. New York: Putnam.

Tomashoff, Craig. 1993. "America's Least Wanted Criminals." *Los Angeles Times* (May 10):E1+.

The New Yorker. 1993. "Wrongful Death." (August 16):4-6.

Chapter 8

Coles, Robert. 1978. *Privileged Ones: The Well-Off and the Rich in America*. Boston: Little, Brown.

Davis, Robert Murray. 1996. *A Lower-Middle Class Education*. Norman, OK: University of Oklahoma Press.

Halberstam, David. 1987. *The Best and the Brightest*. New York Penguin.

Mouer, Ross E. and Yoshio Sugimoto. 1990. *Images of Japanese Society: A Study in the Social Construction of Reality*. New York: Routledge, Chapman & Hall.

Passell, Peter. 1994. "Economic Scene." *The New York Times* (January 27):C2.

Chapter 9

Fleras, Augi and Jean Leonard Elliott. 1992. *Multiculturalism in Canada*. Scarborough, Ontario: Nelson Canada.

Hess, Demian. 1997. "But You Don't Look Chinese" Interracial Voice. http://www.webcom.com/~intvoice/hess1.html.

Hogue, W. Lawrence. 1996. *Race Modernity, Postmodernity*. Albany, NY: State University of New York.

Stryker, Jeff. 1997. "Tuskegee's Long Arm Still Touches a Nerve." *The New York Times* (April 13):4E.

Wang, George. 1994. "A Few Good Images." *Interrace* (June/July):20-21.

Chapter 10

Greenhouse, Linda. 1994. "High Court Bars Sex As Standard in Picking Jurors." *The New York Times* (April 20):A1+.

Lemann, Nicholas. 1996. "High in the Lower Depth." *The New York Review* (December 19):19-21.

Lewin, Tamar. 1994. "As the Boss Goes, So Goes the Secretary: Is It Bias?" *The New York Times* (March 17):A1+.

O'Hara, Patricia. 2001. "Divisions of Labour on Irish Family Farms." Pp. 270-279 in *Gender in Cross-Cultural Perspective* edited by C.B. Brettell and C.F. Sarent. Uper Saddle River, NJ: Prentice-Hall.

Scarboro, Allen. 1991. "Sexual Ambiguity" Pp. 339-340 in *Women's Studies Encyclopedia* edited by H. Tierney. New York: Peter Bedrick Books.

Visser, Margaret. 1994. *The Way We Are*. Boston: Faber and Faber.

Chapter 11

DiSilvestro, Roger. 1996. "Investigating the Last Great American Gold Heist." *National Wildlife*. (Dec-Jan v35 n1 p70(1)

Faucheux, Ron. 1998. "The Indirect Approach." *Campaigns & Elections*. (June):v19 n6 p18(6)

Goldstein, Steven M. 1991. *Minidragons: Fragile Economic Miracles in the Pacific*. New York: Ambrose Video.

Herman, Edward S. 1996. "The Media Mega-Mergers." *Dollars & Sense*. (May-June):n205 p8(6)

Rohter, Larry. 1997. "Trade Storm Imperils Caribbean Banana Crops." *The New York Times* (May 9):A6.

Chapter 12

The Economist. 1998. "Why Italians don't make babies." 347(8067):53.

Guttchen, David, and Mary L. Pettigrew. 2000. "Easing the Caregiver Burden." *Risk & Insurance* 11(11):31.

Longman, Phillip J. 1999. "The World Turns Gray." *U.S. News & World Report* 126(8):30.

Otis, Eileen M. 2001. Review of *Giving Care, Writing Self: A "New" Ethnography* by J. Schneider and W. Laihua. New York: Peter Lang.

Wertheimer, Jack. 2001. "Surrendering to Intermarriage." Commentary 111(3):25.

Chapter 13

Brenson, Michael. 1991. "Images of People Who Live Outside Power." *The New York Times* (April 5):B1.

Falkenmark, Malin and Carl Widstrand. 1992. "Population and Water Resources: a Delicate Balance." *Population Bulletin* 47(3):1-35.

Gibb, Philip. 1987. "Famine in Russia, October 1921." Pp. 493-95 in *Eyewitness to History*, edited by J. Carey. Cambridge: Harvard University Press.

Haub, Carl and Machiko Yanagishita. 1994. *1994 World Population Data Sheet*. Washington, DC: Population Reference Bureau.

McFalls, Joseph A., Jr. 1991. "Population: A Lively Introduction." Washington, DC: *Population Bulletin* 46(2): 1-40.

Riding, Alan. 1986. "Introduction." Pp. 7-9 in *Other Americas*, by Sebastiao Salgado. New York: Pantheon.

Sacks, Oliver. 1983. *Awakenings*. New York: Dutton.

U.S. Department of State. 1990. "Brazil." *Background Notes* (#7756). Washington, DC: U.S. Government Printing Office.

Chapter 14

Barzun, Jacques. 1991. *Begin Here: The Forgotten Conditions of Teaching and Learning*, edited by M. Philipson. Chicago: University of Chicago Press.

Kozol, Jonathan. 1985. *Illiterate America*. Garden City, NY: Anchor.

Lazarus, Edward. 1991. *Black Hills, White Justice: The Sioux Nation versus the United States, 1775 to the Present*. New York: HarperCollins.

Oakes, Jennie. 1985. *Keeping Track: How Schools Structure Inequality*. New Haven: Yale University Press.

Sacks, Oliver. 1989. *Seeing Voices: A Journey into the World of the Deaf*. Los Angeles: University of California Press.

References

Chapter 15

Gyatso, Tenzin. 1990. *Freedom in Exile: The Autobiography of the Dalai Lama*. New York: HarperCollins.

Hedges, Chris. 1997. Fascists Reborn as Croatia's Founding Fathers." *The New York Times* (April 12): Y3.

Jenkins, Emyl. 1996. *The Book of American Traditions*. New York: Crown Publishers

Lorimer, Lawrence. 1989. "Mennonite Churches." P. 213 in *The Universal Almanac 1990*, edited by J. W. Wright. Kansas City, MO: Universal Press Syndicate.

McGuire, Merridith B. 1987. *Religion: The Social Context*, 2nd ed. Belmont, CA: Wadsworth.

Steinfels, Peter. 1993. "Papal Birth-Control Letter Retains Its Grip." *The New York Times* (August 1):Y1+.

Yoachum, Susan and David Tuller. 1993. "Think Tank Tries to Prove Bible is Literal Truth." *San Francisco Chronicle* (September 14):A7.

Chapter 16

Dyson, Freeman. 1997. "Can Science Be Ethical?" *The New York Review* (April 10):46.

Goldstein, Steven M. 1991. *Minidragons: Fragile Economic Miracles in the Pacific*. New York: Ambrose Video.

Gould, Stephen J. 1987. *An Urchin in the Storm: Essays about Books and Ideas*. New York: Norton.

Rohter, Larry. 1997. "Trade Storm Imperils Caribbean Banana Crops." *The New York Times* (May 9):A6.

Rosenberg, Charles E. 1987. *The Care of Strangers: The Rise of America's Hospital System*. New York: Basic Books.

Smith, Frederick W. 1998. "Defining the global economy." *Vital Speeches*. (Dec 1):v65 i4 p125(4).